STUDIES IN CHRISTIAN HISTORY AND THOUGHT

Prophecy, Miracles, Angels
and Heavenly Light?

**The Eschatology, Pneumatology, and Missiology
of Adomnán's *Life of Columba***

STUDIES IN CHRISTIAN HISTORY AND THOUGHT

A full listing of all titles in this series
appears at the close of this book

STUDIES IN CHRISTIAN HISTORY AND THOUGHT

Prophecy, Miracles, Angels, *and* Heavenly Light?

The Eschatology, Pneumatology, and Missiology of Adomnán's *Life of Columba*

James Bruce

Foreword by Thomas Owen Clancy

PATERNOSTER

First published 2004 by Paternoster Press

Paternoster Press is an imprint of Authentic Media
P.O. Box 300, Carlisle, Cumbria, CA3 0QS, UK
and
P.O. Box 1047, Waynesboro, GA 30830–2047, USA

10 09 08 07 06 05 04   7 6 5 4 3 2 1

British Library Cataloguing in Publication Data
A catalogue record for this book is available from the British Library

ISBN 1–84227–227–6

Typeset by James Bruce
Printed and bound in Great Britain
for Paternoster Publishing
by Nottingham Alpha Graphics

STUDIES IN CHRISTIAN HISTORY AND THOUGHT

Series Preface

This series complements the specialist series of *Studies in Evangelical History and Thought* and *Studies in Baptist History and Thought* for which Paternoster is becoming increasingly well known by offering works that cover the wider field of Christian history and thought. It encompasses accounts of Christian witness at various periods, studies of individual Christians and movements, and works which concern the relations of church and society through history, and the history of Christian thought.

The series includes monographs, revised dissertations and theses, and collections of papers by individuals and groups. As well as 'free standing' volumes, works on particular running themes are being commissioned; authors will be engaged for these from around the world and from a variety of Christian traditions.

A high academic standard combined with lively writing will commend the volumes in this series both to scholars and to a wider readership.

Series Editors

Alan P.F. Sell, Visiting Professor at Acadia University Divinity College, Nova Scotia, Canada

David Bebbington, Professor of History, University of Stirling, Stirling, Scotland, UK

Clyde Binfield, Professor Associate in History, University of Sheffield, UK

Gerald Bray, Anglican Professor of Divinity, Beeson Divinity School, Samford University, Birmingham, Alabama, USA

Grayson Carter, Associate Professor of Church History, Fuller Theological Seminary SW, Phoenix, Arizona, USA

I ngwraig a mhlant i,
Valerie,
Madeleine,
Baby Sam,
Alexander,
William Finlay,
ag Eléa,
ac i'r gogoniant Dduw,
efo niolchgarwch wybodus.

(To my wife and children…
And to the glory of God,
With grateful thanks.)

Contents

Foreword

Since Adomnán's *Vita Sancti Columbae* first began to come to the critical attention of the modern British public, the fact that the text focuses on miracles has been a problem. Nineteenth-century authors, especially from certain doctrinal backgrounds, were brusquely annoyed, and twentieth-century historians have been perplexed to find that a writer like Adomnán, who seems in so many ways a man of a similar mind-set to themselves, bothers himself with such credulous stories. If the past is 'a foreign country', then historians who deal with early medieval hagiography find the miraculous a strange type of fare which they cannot quite stomach.

What miracles need is a sensitive, scholarly and serious treatment, and that is just what we get in James Bruce's book. Unlike those who have tried to examine the miracles merely as foils for political, contextual or allegorical meaning, Dr Bruce attempts here to understand Adomnán's treatment of the miraculous on the writer's own terms, which are fundamentally the terms of a Christian. For Dr Bruce also succeeds here in the tricky balancing act of writing as a scholar and as a Christian of conviction. This is similar to the balancing act which Adomnán himself was trying to achieve—though one suspects that for Adomnán, the difference between recounting history, telling a story, and believing that God's work is to be found in the wonderful and strange, would have been meaningless.

Understanding how Adomnán understood the miraculous must in many ways be the key to understanding Adomnán himself. His is the Saint's Life most closely defined and organised by its categories of thaumaturgy; no other life from the insular world is so shot through with visions and angels. These cannot be left to one side as mere wallpaper—they are the furniture and fabric of Adomnán's mental construct. Dr Bruce here teaches us to listen with respect to the miraculous in the *Vita Columbae* as the product of a theologian, and a product that can thus be read theologically.

What is exciting about this book, however, is that it weds scholarly concerns to real belief. In so doing, we are presented with Adomnán, the convinced and spiritual man, a Christian in whose writings we are able to find ways to grapple with God in the world, and who can inspire us to grapple likewise. It makes living words out of what can sometimes appear to be a historian's plaything, and for that I can only imagine, Adomnán himself would be pleased indeed.

Thomas Owen Clancy
Department of Celtic
University of Glasgow
July 2004

Preface and Acknowledgements

Supernatural marvellous phenomena were dominant among the spiritual aspects of the mediaeval world, as their filling so much of the popular literature of the day shows. They continue to engender fascination in both scholarly and popular circles, with reactions ranging from outright denial, through demythologizing rationalizations, common scepticism, tentative acceptance, and vigorous desire for their renaissance, to naïve credulity. The most recent translator of Adomnán's *Life of St. Columba*, Richard Sharpe, concludes the introduction to his *Mediaeval Irish Saint's Lives* with a comment on Charles Plummer's earlier work on the same corpus

> His recognition that the *vitae* illuminate aspects of how the authors of the *vitae* and their audience perceived the spiritual aspects of their world has still to be followed up.[1]

This book is an attempt to take on Sharpe's challenge. One of these early mediaeval authors, Adomnán, ninth abbot of Iona, peers into the world of first abbot the Holy Columba, and presents to us a world filled with the marvellous. Through Adomnán's perception, we will be seeking to understand these marvellous spiritual aspects of their world.

Students of hagiography have become familiar with the identification of the function of this literary genre as a tool for its authors to use at the time of writing. Political and didactic aims are built upon the foundation of proving the sanctity of the saint whose repute is to be employed in making the author's case. Sanctity is demonstrated using the device of attributing to the saint various supernatural virtues. However, the underlying nature and function of the phenomena that provide these devices, as understood by their hagiographical employers, remain poorly understood, whatever the way in which they are employed to meet the author's aim. I hope to probe the perception of Adomnán to investigate what he understood the phenomena *were*, their ontological nature, and what he thought they *were for*, their teleological function, in the context in which he depicts them, as he employed them to his purposes in writing the

---

1   Sharpe (1991, 388) citing Plummer (1910).

Life. This detailed investigation, through, as we will see, the purple-tinted lens Adomnán himself provides, and through which he perceives the spiritual aspects of his day, is, I hope, a significant advance in our understanding of him and his work, and tangentially of his world too.

Marvellous phenomena provide a particularly problematic challenge to modern historical analysis. They are a category inadmissible as possible to modern rationalism.[2] However, these phenomena have been integral to Christian tradition from before its foundation, and many claim that they have remained so stubbornly even in the late modern world, despite the enlightenment. Eastern Orthodoxy has maintained a pneumatology that includes such phenomena. They continue to form the essential qualification for beatification and canonization in the Roman Catholic Church. They are claimed as continuing by the various pentecostal movements. This book aims to explore the view of marvellous phenomena Adomnán held in seventh-century 'Scotland' and 'Ireland', as the Christian faith became established there, as we seek understanding of how and why this Christianization took place. In so doing, it may suggest to the church in Scotland, Ireland, and England today both a lost aspect of their heritage, and an aspect perhaps to be reconsidered as the late-modern task of re-evangelization, following in Columba's wake, is engaged.

The incidences of the various types of marvellous phenomena in the *VC* are collated and displayed in exhaustive tabular, summary and graphical form in the appendix. Perhaps the most interesting feature to note is the incidence of the manifestation of prophetic marvels throughout. Adomnán's presentation is not what we might expect for one deliberately created to display various phenomena in clearly delineated categories. Rather, they reflect the interrelatedness of the marvellous phenomena that we observe in biblical accounts of their use in the mission to establish the kingdom of God.

The book contains perhaps over many footnotes, and the bibliography extends beyond works cited, and includes some very recent publications with which it has not, unfortunately, been possible to interact. This is an attempt to let you, the reader, engage as I have with the source materials and secondary literature underlying what I am saying, and so to engage critically with my conclusions. I hope that any mistakes, for which I take full responsibility, will be uncovered. For this I will be grateful.

---

2   See Heffernan (1988) for a comprehensive critique of the weakness of this
     approach in bringing understanding to the study of hagiography.

The book is substantially the doctoral thesis I presented for examination in 1999 following a happy three years of research at St Mary's College in the University of St Andrews. I had only meant to spend a year studying what I now think is a modern invention, 'Celtic Christianity', in an attempt to understand the movement of interest in things 'Celtic' sweeping both church and popular culture. My supervisor, Dr James Alexander, to whose patient guidance and wise counsel the thesis owes its existence, handed me a copy of the *Life of Columba* as background reading. Some years before, I had been intrigued by a series of presentations and popular publications by among others John Wimber and Dr Jack Deere, concerning the ongoing history of marvellous phenomena in the Christian tradition. Columba had not been mentioned, and yet here was a systematized, albeit hagiographical account of these phenomena accompanying the one who is credited with bringing the Christian faith into sixth century northern Scotland, the land now of a theologically reformed, miracle-sceptic church, the home of common sense rationalism. I had to find out more, and here is the report of progress so far.

Again, it is to Dr Alexander that I owe the study on Plummer's work, over a very small hedge but in a different field to my own. He rightly persisted against my hesitation to tackle the Irish sagas, for though I have some Welsh, I have no Irish. I have had to rely on translations, but I hope the study, important as it is to the overall task of understanding these phenomena here, will prove adequate and enlightening. I am also most grateful for encouragement to present papers from the thesis at the Scottish Universities Ecclesiastical History Reading Parties. Constructive criticism and advice during these was most beneficial. I would particularly mention Prof. Donald Meek of Aberdeen, who gave an early affirmation of the validity of my study, and Dr Alan MacQuarrie of Strathclyde who kept asking the question, 'why is the *Life of Columba* different?' Two others in St Mary's College, in complimentary disciplines, were more help than they can imagine: Revd Professor Trevor Hart, now Principal, and Professor Richard Bauckham. I wish to record my gratitude to the college for the grants of the Tulloch Scholarship, the Cook and MacFarlan Scholarship, and a St Mary's College Bursary, and for giving me opportunities to tutor undergraduates. I am in debt to the Doctor Kenneth Charles Briand Trust for its kind support. My former postgraduate colleagues, now Dr Darrel Cosden, Lecturer in Theology at the International Christian College, Glasgow, and Dr Steve Guthrie, Lecturer in Theology in St Andrews, spent many a lunchtime grappling with mediaeval miracles. Their insight and support has been invaluable.

Across the street in the Department of Medieval History, Dr. Barbara Crawford, Dr. Simon Taylor, and the St Andrews University Committee for Dark Age Studies, on which I was privileged to sit, provided further critical stimulus and enlightenment. Mrs Marjorie Anderson was not only most generous with loans from her and her late husband's library (which resembled my bibliography in shelved form), but was also kind enough to discuss numerous questions on the text so central to my study. Christine Gasgoine, Keeper of the University Library Special Collections, Colin Bovaird, Librarian of St Mary's College, and Linda Innocent, Assistant Librarian, also provided never failing help.

I am most grateful to my examiners, Dr Thomas Owen Clancy, Head of Department and Reader in Celtic at the University of Glasgow, editor of the *Innes Review*, and Dr Ian Bradley, Reader in Practical Theology at the University of St Andrews, for their constructive criticisms of the work, which have been incorporated in this revision, and for their encouragement to seek publication. I am also grateful to the *Senatus Academicus* of the University for accepting the thesis, and for awarding it the Samuel Rutherford Prize, which I count an especial honour named as it is after a former Principal of St Mary's, one of Scotland's greatest theologians. Dr Tony Sargent, Principal of ICC Glasgow, where I lectured Early Christian History, also kindly read the thesis. His enthusiastic reaction and warm encouragement towards publication, with that of Trevor Hart, led me to Paternoster, Jeremy Mudditt, Dr Anthony Cross, and their processes of scrutiny and help. Finally, Dr Clancy has added a forword to make an author sing. And so here we are, with my deep gratitude.

Valerie, my wife, tolerated magnificently my spending three years sitting in a chair reading then, and another six months at the computer now, and has sustained us, in many forms, through the present sabbatical. At the same time she has nurtured our children, Madeleine, Alexander, Finlay-William, and Eléa, who have shown immense patience and interest even when 'Papa's book' prevented them playing the latest game. In this, our fourteenth year of marriage, I honour her, and dedicate to her this work, insignificant though it is in comparison with her achievement.

James Bruce
The Feast of Columba
9 June 2004

Abbreviations

A&A   A.O. and M.O. Anderson (1961 or 1991 editions indicated by date).

A   The English translation of the *Vita Columbae* by A&A.

B   The English translation of the *Vita Columbae* by A.P. Forbes, Bishop of Brechin.

CC   *Corpus Christianorum* (Brepols: Turnholti).

C&M   Clancy and Márkus (1995).

CMCS *Cambrian Medieval Celtic Studies* (formerly Cambridge).

Conf. *The Confession of St Patrick,* quoted from Howlett (1994), but retaining the traditional chapter numbering.

Coll.   The *Conferences* of John Cassian, English tr. from Luibheid (1985), based on the edition of Pichery (1955).

DIAS Dublin Institute for Advanced Studies.

F   The English translation of the *Vita Columbae* by Fowler (1895).

H   The English translation of the *Vita Columbae* by Huyshe (1905).

HE   Bede, *Historia Ecclesiastica Gentis Anglorum,* ed. and tr. Colgrave and Mynors (1969).

ITS   Irish Texts Society.

JRSAI Journal of the Royal Society of Antiquaries of Ireland.

Lap&S Lapidge and Sharpe (1985), *Bibliography of Celtic-Latin Literature.*

L&S   Lewis and Short, *Dictionary of Latin* (Oxford 1879).

NBD   *New Bible Dictionary,* ed. Douglas (1982).

NIDNTT New International Dictionary of New Testament Theology, ed. Colin Brown (1980).

NPNCF Nicene and Post-Nicene Christian Fathers.

NT   New Testament, quotations from the *RSV.*

ODCC The Oxford Dictionary of the Christian Church, 3rd edn, 1997.

OT   Old Testament, quotations from the *RSV.*

PG   *Patrologia Graecae*, ed. J.P. Migne (Paris, 1857-66).

PL   *Patrologia Latina*, ed. J.P. Migne (Paris, 1844-64).

RIA   Royal Irish Academy.

S   The English translation of the *Vita Columbae* by Sharpe (1995).

SC   *Sources Chrétiennes* (Paris: Editions du Cerf).

SLH   *Scriptores Latini Hiberniae.*

SHR   *Scottish Historical Review.*

TBC   *Táin Bó Cúalnge (Cattle Raid of Cooley).*

VA   *Vita Antonii.* English quotations from Gregg (1980), based on *PG* 26, 835-978, (now see Bartelink (1994), *SC* 400), corrected against Evagrius' Latin tr. (*PL* 73.125-170) (now see Bartelink, *Vita de Santi*, I, Milan 1974).

VC   Adomnán's *Vita Columbae (Life of Columba).* Unless otherwise attributed, all English and Latin quotations of *VC* are from A&A (1991).

VSH   *Vitae Sanctorum Hiberniae*, Plummer (1910).

VSM   *Vita Sancti Martini,* the *Life of St Martin* of Tours by Sulpicius Severus, ed. Fontaine (1967), tr. Hoare (1954).

Following Picard (1987), and McNamara (1987), Latin Biblical quotations are Vulgate, with Psalms from *Psalmi Iuxta LXX,* ed. Weber (1969). English quotations are RSV (Swindon: British and Foreign Bible Society, 2nd edition, 1971). Where Vulgate and RSV diverge, I have suggested an English transliteration.

Chapter references to the *VC* are those established by Fowler, now standard. They differ in places from those of Reeves. Where reference is made to longer chapters, I have suggested subdivisions where obvious, e.g. (i.37a, b, c), and/or the MS folio references from A&A.

CHAPTER 1

De Virtutibus:
Approaches to the Study of the Marvellous

Why Use Adomnán's *Life of Columba?*

Adomnán's *Life of St. Columba* (*Adomnani Vita Sancti Columbae,* hereafter *VC*), was written, as is well known, a century after the death of Columba, first abbot of Iona (d. 597), by the ninth abbot, Adomnán (d. 704) about a hundred and thirty years into the development of Columba's *familia.*[1] This *Life* is relatively close to its subject compared with those of Brigit and Patrick, and has an established provenance in linguistic, literary, and historical terms,[2] and thus provides a firm text for the study of Irish/Scottish[3]

---

1 For a recent discussion of the evidence and terminology with regard to sixth / seventh century ecclesiastical organization in the region, and the nature of Columba's ecclesiastical legacy, see Etchingham (1999). I was persuaded by Sharpe's challenge to 'Hughesian' orthodoxy, now developed by Etchingham, to see a mixed, not essentially monastic, ecclesiastical economy in the Celtic realms.

2 Adomnán's *Vita Columbae* was first edited in modern times by Bollandist Stephen White SJ, in 1621. He was followed by John Colgan (1647), William Ussher (1656), and William Reeves (1857). In 1874, Reeve's notes were edited and rearranged by W.F. Skene, and a free translation supervised by A.P Forbes added to augment a work still highly regarded. Fowler further edited Reeve's text, including additional notes (1894, new edition 1920) and added a more literal translation (1895). In this century Wentworth Huyshe rendered a further translation in 1905 (corrected 1937), then came the Anderson's standard edition and translation (1961, revised 1991, hereafter A&A), and Sharpe's translation (1995). For extensive bibliographies of secondary studies, see Herbert (1988a), Sharpe (1995), Clancy and Márkus (1995, hereafter C&M), and Broun and Clancy (1999). Columba died 'Sunday, 9 June 597' (Sharpe, 1995, 1; C&M 96). All *VC* chapter references are to those found in A&A (1991).

3 It needs hardly be said that the geo-political terminology for Ireland, Scotland and England we use today does not apply to Adomnán's time. Translators do not aid accuracy in this, so reading the *VC* in translation can introduce terminological anachronisms. Briefly, Adomnán's *scotii, scotia* and *scoticae linguae* (e.g. i.1:9a-b) are translated 'Irish', 'Ireland' and 'Irish language'. *Scot-* can refer generally to that island, but also more precisely to the people, language, and territory, of Columba's kinsmen. *Scot-* can thus also refer to the

ecclesiastical history.[4] As one of the four earliest Latin *Lives* of Irish saints, written before the explosion of hagiographical interest in that region, it gives us an early text with which to investigate the nature and purpose of the marvellous. *VC* was written at a time close to the earliest evangelization of the Pictish Provinces, so this study may also help to illuminate Christian origins in Scotland north of the Forth. The definitive edition and translation published by Alan Orr and Marjorie Ogilvie Anderson in 1961, revised by Marjorie Anderson in 1991, provides our foundation.

Conventionally, the Andersons accept Adomnán's reliability for historical features of his own time, and not for the time of Columba, though they are not consistent.[5] In her history of the Irish church, Kathleen Hughes describes the *VC* as

---

people and area to which they brought their name and language, now Argyll etc. (e.g. i.1:9a). *Hibernia* (or its cognates, (e.g. i.2:11a; see A&A, 1990, 18 note i), also translated 'Ireland', may refer more precisely to mid-'Ireland' (i.3), but is usually interchangeable with the general meaning of *scotia* (e.g. i.22; i.48; ii.38, 40) to refer to the whole island. *Hibernia* is thus the island on which the *scotii* originally lived, *scotia* the land(s) of the *scotii*. Columba, as one of these migrants, sailed from *Scotia* to *Brittania* (sp:4a), translated 'Britain' (e.g. i.34), which included Iona (i.36; ii.39:91a). Adomnán refers to a *proselytus brito homo sanctus, quidam* and *de suis monacus Brito* translated 'British stranger, a holy man', and, 'one of his monks, a Briton' (sp:3a; iii.6). These Britons would have come from that (western) part of the island of 'Britain' under the rule of the Britons, and spoken 'p' Celtic, an ancestor of what we call Welsh. Adomnán refers to the king of the Strathclyde Britons, Rhydderch ap Tydwal, based at *Petra Cloithe* (Dumbarton, i.15), and to the Saxon ruler Oswald defeating a later ruler of the Britons, Cadwallon (i.1:8a). Adomnán's *Saxo-* is translated 'English', or 'Englishman' (i.1:8a,9a; iii.10), and *Saxonia*, 'the land of the English' (iii.22), referring only to the area of Britain under Saxon rule. Adomnán's majestic term for the British Isles, *insularum ociani prouincias* 'The Provinces of the Isles of Ocean' (sp:3a; cf. ii.46) has never, in my view, been bettered. See O'Loughlin (1997, 20f.) for the eschatological significance of the designation. For an introduction to geographical questions, see Smyth (1992), and Sharpe (1995).

4   I am relying on the now standard account by Herbert (1988a), which sees *VC* as based on an earlier account by seventh abbot Cumméne (d. 669), probably written AD 640-50. Herbert believes Cumméne based his account on an even earlier record compiled by his uncle, abbot Ségéne (623-652), thus the written authority may stretch back to within 27 years of Columba's death. The Schaffhausen codex identifies the scribe as Dorbbéne, Bishop of Iona (d. 713) [or abbot, there is some dispute (cf. Anderson, 1991, xliv-xlv)]; it is thus closer in date to its original than any other Latin Irish *Life.*

5   '...[Adomnán] implies that all the land to the west of the spine, or watershed, was the territory of the Scots of Britain; not only in his own time, for which his evidence about this must be accepted, but in the time of Columba, for which he is not evidence' A&A (1961, 76), but their comment on Columba conversing with Broichan without an interpreter is taken as an historical indication of the Druid's facility in 'Irish' in Columba's day (84).

...the work of a learned man with conscientious scholarly standards. We should therefore be able to rely on its incidental information.[6]

Building on Hughes' sympathy, and following the Andersons, Picard argues for the reliability of Adomnán's historical style which he compares favourably with that of Bede: 'Adomnán uses some of the methods and techniques which have been attributed only to the best historians.' He argues against too dismissive an attitude on the basis of the hundred-year gap: '...in mediaeval historiography one hundred years is a relatively short period...'[7] Like Bede, Adomnán provides witnesses for many of the events he records. In her seminal study of Ionan historiography, Máiri Herbert records

> [Adomnán] is often concerned to provide authentication for the miracle stories he tells, and it has been suggested that some effort was made at Iona to collect formal *testimonia* during the early seventh century.[8]

While being generally supportive of Adomnán as a reliable author, Sharpe re-introduces an important caution in referring to the hagiographical *VC*.

> Adomnán sometimes cites informants by name even when he is borrowing from a literary source such as Gregory. We cannot be confident of the exact fidelity of Adomnán's account, nor even whether he was concerned to write what he thought to be factually correct. Historical truth has always been alien to the aims of hagiography.[9]

However, Sharpe takes Adomnán's lack of references to written materials and preference for testimonial from named witnesses to underline the credibility of what he writes as being in accord with current Irish legal preference for eyewitness over documentary testimony. Adomnán was not writing history in the modern sense of being concerned with time, but in being concerned with the veracity

---

6 Hughes (1966, 224). Hughes' own conscientious scholarly standards in her hitherto standard two-phase model of Irish ecclesiology is itself now challenged as mentioned above, principally by Sharpe (1984, 1992) and Etchingham (1999).
7 Picard (1984, 51f). Citing A&A (1961), he also says: 'Adomnán inclines to use battles as dating points' (67), referring to events which are independently supported in Annular records, and often preferred by modern commentators even over-against Bede. Picard names the quotation of sources (53), the use of the Iona chronicle (54), and his formal historical style after the Classical and Latin historians (55-6). Picard agrees with Duncan (1981) on *VC* being a better historical source than *HE* for the careers of Columba and Adomnán (69). He concludes in a comment on Hughes' contrast of 'Celtic' and Bede's history '[Bede's more modern] approach does not necessarily make his history more reliable' (70).
8 Herbert (1988a, 7-9).
9 Sharpe (1991, 11).

of his sources in attesting to the miraculous events described.[10] In his studies of Adomnán's earlier *Of Holy Places* (*De Locis Sanctis*), O'Loughlin affirms his opinion of Adomnán as

> ...a most careful and accurate scholar...[whose work] can stand alongside Augustine, equalling it in exegetical skill and augmenting it in content.[11]

In all, the acceptance of Adomnán as *verax historicus*[12] appears to be gaining ground. However, the material for which he is respected only embraces historical data not including the marvellous. While Adomnán may borrow a sentence occasionally, and have adopted the idea of writing the *Life*, he does not simply assume the emphases and priorities of his models.[13] Sharpe takes the account as the writer intends

> While borrowing the basic shape of the *Life of St Martin*, Adomnán has set out his own argument, organising his book around the three proofs that St Columba was a man of God.[14]

This leads us to the central feature of Adomnán's *Life of Columba* that marks it out as especially pertinent as a work upon which to perform this study. Many commentators have noted the careful and deliberate division of the *VC* into its three *libelli:* collections of prophecies, miracles of power, and visions of angels and heavenly light.[15] Picard points to what he sees as a progression in importance of phenomenon, reaching the ultimate accolade of the glory of

---

10   Sharpe (1995, 56-7; 60). However, Sharpe sees his sixth-century politics is dubious as he is more interested in divine ordination (60-1).

11   O'Loughlin (1997b, 110-111). O'Loughlin builds on his earlier studies (1992, 1994a/b, 1995, 1997a) to form this high opinion of Adomnán's merit as a writer.

12   Picard (1984, 56).

13   See Picard (1985) and Stancliffe (1992) for comparative treatments.

14   Sharpe (1995, 58). The *Lives* of SS. Antony, Martin, and Benedict are generally accepted as the primary influences.

15   E.g. Stancliffe (1983, 86-102), McCone (1984, 30), Picard (1985, 74-6), and Herbert (1988a, 138) make similar points, dependent upon Fontaine (1967-9, 92-5), regarding a possible influence from *VSM*. Herbert confirms the uniqueness of the threefold division of subject matter in Latin hagiography. Irish Augustine's *Treatise* (for which see McGinty (1971), Esposito (1919) and Ó Cróinín (1989)) has a three-part structure, but it is based on the distribution of the marvellous in the Bible, not the categories of marvellous phenomena themselves. Sulpicius Severus' three-part division of the short account of miracles in *VSM* (miracles vs. rural pagans (12-15); miracles vs. urban garrisons (16-19); diabolic illusions (20-24), is wholly unlike Adomnán's both in length and more especially, subject matter.

heavenly light.[16] Whatever the rationale for his division, the fact identifies Adomnán as a seventh-century Christian leader, about whom we have collateral evidence in his *On Holy Places* and *Law of Innocents*,[17] who demonstrates a particular, somewhat systematic understanding of the varied nature of the marvellous he employs to make his case.

That the church in the Provinces in which Adomnán depicts Columba as ministering were in direct interaction with Continental and Mediterranean Christianity is now affirmed, for example, by Leslie Alcock

> Despite the clear literary evidence of contacts in the religious field between Britain and Ireland on the one hand, and Gaul, North Africa, and even Egypt on the other, it was generally held that the Anglo-Saxon invasions had cut the Celtic west off from Mediterranean civilisation: hence the peculiarities of the Celtic church. We now see that in archaeological as well as in religious terms the concept of the isolation of the Celtic west is a myth, or at best only a very partial truth...[18]

The *VC* is written with a clear sense of this connection in Adomnán's thought (e.g. ii.32; ii.46; iii.23:135b), and we will observe this connection with the mainstream tradition of the faith from the perspective of his accounts of the marvellous.

One of the underlying questions to the investigation concerns the influence of the foundational text of the Bible on Adomnán's thought. Students of early Irish literature, in Latin and the vernacular, are increasingly confident of the profound influence of the Latin Bible upon these writers' thoughts, structures, themes, and descriptions.[19] I wish to analyse the marvellous phenomena in *VC*

---

16 Picard (1985, 76). Being depicted as surrounded by heavenly light of glory remains the sixth of seven honours authorised to a canonized saint in the Roman Constitution (ODCC (1997, 280b).

17 *De Locis Sanctis* also incorporates mention of marvellous phenomena, though they occur in the eastern Mediterranean context of the work. They are chronologically removed from Columba's time, and the marvels are posthumous. As such, though it would provide an important comparative study to this present, they fall outside our immediate area of inquiry. I have made the decision to concentrate on the *VC* and its context so as to give its marvels the fullest possible attention. *De Locis* shows Adomnán to have a wider than hagiographical interest as well as belief in the marvellous, confirming the importance of a study of the *VC*'s record. For *Law of Innocents*, see Meyer's edition, Márkus' translation, and Smyth (1984, 133-40).

18 Alcock (1971, 206), and see pp.134-5. It may be worth noting in passing the doubt cast over the existence of a medieval pan-Celtic, monolithic church, ecclesiology, culture or spirituality by other scholars, e.g. Hughes (1970); Meek (1991; 1992; 1997; 2000); Davies (1992); Clancy and Márkus (1999).

19 For instance, most recently: O'Reilly (1997; 1999), McCone (1984), Hardinge (1972), O'Loughlin (1992; 1994a,b; 1995; 1997a,b), Clancy (1995; 1997).

taking full account of biblical archetypes, rather than modern
functional categories such as those used by Derouet, followed by
Picard and Stancliffe. As the discussion will show, dividing the
marvellous into 'vertical' and 'horizontal or practical' takes account
neither of the described effect of all categories, nor of the functional
nature which Adomnán describes for them. Healing, discernment,
demonic expulsion, miracles of power all depend in the *VC* on God's
direct 'vertical' intervention, though they are applied in the
'horizontal' plane. Prophecy and angelic manifestations directly
affect others in the 'horizontal' plane, though they derive from a
'vertical' relationship. All can be termed 'miracles', though Paul,
with Adomnán following, discerns a particular category of 'miracle'
as one of the whole collection. I thus adopt their taxonomy, but will
refer to the whole collection as 'the marvellous'.[20]

The Study of the Marvellous Within the Study of Hagiography

The phenomena we are studying include nature miracles of various
sorts, such as power over the elements, transmutation, cures, and
displays of what is often termed vengeful power. There are also
manifestations of supernatural insight and foresight, visions of
earthly and heavenly scenes, and encounters both in vision and in
'real life' with angelic and demonic spiritual beings. These marvellous
attributes are what identify the sanctity, the closeness to God, of an
individual, and thus provide the authority for the literary purposes of
the hagiographer. The nature and function of the phenomena are
thus understood at the level of literary employment. The literary
forms of the descriptions of the marvellous as we have them in the
extant texts are also understood as literary devices adopted and
adapted from the genre. That the hagiographers believed in the
possibility and historical occurrence of these phenomena is becoming
clearer.[21] However the question of what it was they believed the
phenomena to be, and what it was they believed the phenomena to
be for, in the theatre in which they are described as operating, is
poorly understood. This book aims to elucidate the understanding of
one of these early authors in regard to examples of one group of
those phenomena less investigated even than the rest. These are the
marvellous phenomena recorded as operating through the ministry of
an earthly, as distinct from an heavenly, saint. In other words
marvels *reported as* accompanying the ministry of a saint during his

---

20   For the essential background of biblical descriptions of these phenomena, see
      e.g: 1 Kgs. 17- 2 Kgs. 13; the Gospels and Acts, Rom. 12; 1 Cor. 12 and 14;
      and Eph. 4.
21   See, for instance, Peterson (1984, 90-121), and McCready (1989 and 1994).

life on earth, not after his burial as his cult was being established.[22] We will do this through the lens of arguably the most important example of the genre for the purpose, Adomnán's *Life of St. Columba*.

Before commencing a study of Adomnán's descriptions of the marvellous, we must survey extant approaches to these phenomena. The question is made particularly complicated with the epistemological and hermeneutic problems of how marvellous phenomena should be treated. The world-view of the reader has been shown in recent years deeply to influence what they will allow the author to have meant when he wrote.[23] Modern interest in hagiography has coincided historically with the philosophical dominance of liberal rationalism, and its positivist approach to history. This world-view may inhibit the enlightened modern reader from understanding the world-view of the authors of these so called Dark-Age documents, especially in regard to elucidating the place of the marvellous in their thought and claimed experience.

In 1945, Felim Ó Briain noted four classes of scholarly approach in a regrettably brief statement, which has not been pursued. The first and largest group were those who, '...have adopted an attitude of credulous reverence for miracle and wonder narratives,' whose research has '...been rendered almost valueless for want of sane critical attitude towards the marvellous'.

The second, smaller group of

> ...agnostic historians...denied *a priori* the possibility of divine intervention in human affairs, and, prior to and independently of all evidence, they vitiated their historical vision by excluding the miraculous on philosophical or supposedly scientific principles of problematic and unverifiable validity.[24]

The third group neither accept nor reject the miracles in their narrative form and position. They seek rather to rationalize them, finding naturalistic explanations in a de-mythologizing approach familiar to biblical scholars after Bultmann.

Ó Briain places himself in a fourth group. These appeal to 'sane historical principles that permit a more objective approach'; they are thereby saved 'from the naïve credulity of the hagiographical novice, and the philosophical, and entirely unhistorical, prejudice of

---

22 For a preliminary but detailed discussion of Columba's posthumous miracles, see Clancy (1997).

23 Again, this monograph is not able to enter the debate, except in the sense that it acknowledges its existence, and that it is involved at a practical level in applying the findings to its own subject of study. For an introduction, see Hart (1994).

24 All three quotes Ó Briain (1945, 339f.).

the sceptic.' He appears however to limit the work of this fourth group to the verification of the historical occurrence of the miracle. To proceed, they must demand 'unassailable evidence' (as in investigations leading to canonization). They must be cautious in studying commonplace thematic miracles: Ó Briain rejects the possibility of verifying cures, food, nature, and animal miracles on the basis of their nature as common themes. They must also become conscious of the motives inspiring the writing.

Ó Briain was perceptive in his assessment of the approach of students of hagiography, and his taxonomy remains recognizable, though may require some reorganization. The first group while still active is not tolerated within liberal academic circles, and leaves little to be discussed. The second, rejectionist school remains influential, and drives much positivist historiography, merging almost seamlessly with the third de-mythologizing approach in seeking explanation for the marvellous purely as literary devices. For the fourth, the possibility of finding unassailable evidence for the period we are investigating is so remote that the demand is unanswerable. However, the sleuth-like pursuit of the (secret) motives of the authors has proved engaging, and has become a mainstay of hagiographical research. Thus the investigation of the use of literary devices employed to service the author's motives has grown in importance.

My approach grows out of this last. While not attempting the impossible task of verification, I seek to discern the nature and function of the marvellous with a mind open cautiously towards the possibility that the world-view of the writer in this case, Adomnán, might be shown to have intellectual integrity despite it leading to him having filled his account of Columba with marvellous phenomena. In order to set the study in context, I aim now to give examples of various recent approaches.

Attitudes to the Marvellous: Rejecting Historical Reality

Hippolyte Delehaye set the foundation in 1905 for twentieth century methodology in regard to the study of hagiography.[25] His underlying attitude is encapsulated in the following passage

> We have surely said enough to show how, among the people, the senses predominate over the intelligence, and how owing to the lethargy of their brains they are unable to rise to an ideal conception, but stop short at the

---

25   See Smith (1992, 69); Aigrain (1953). Grégoire (1987) insists that the ultimate meaning of a hagiographic document lies 'below its surface, anterior to its particular historical details,' and highlights 'the need to go beyond narrow textual criticism and positivistic historical reconstruction' (20-1, 182, 208-9, 251).

matter, the image, the sound. It is furthermore by this spiritual feebleness that one must account for the blind attraction of the populace for the miraculous and the sensibly supernatural... the mysterious colloquies of the soul with God must be translated into palpable results in order to produce any impression on the popular mind. The supernatural is only impressive when combined with the marvellous. Hence it is that popular legends overflow with marvels.[26]

In other words, hagiographers act as the mouthpiece in stating the vulgar imagination's version of the legends of the saints. Platonic devaluation of the material over the spiritual sounds out clearly here. Intellectual scepticism concerning the miraculous became the orthodoxy of hagiographic study. Delehaye's condemnation is not indiscriminate in that he does allow that some writers of saint's *Lives* have been more faithful guardians of historical tradition. He distinguishes, 'a class of writers, possessing both literary power and the necessary information' whose narratives constitute authentic historical memoirs no less than works of edification, e.g. Sulpicius Severus, one of Adomnán's models. He says 'their writings must not be confused with the artificial productions of later periods, which affect at times to be inspired by them...'[27]

The profound influence of post-enlightenment epistemology in the methodology of historical-criticism has thus tended to predispose modern historians to treat the stories of the marvellous with a wide degree of circumspection. Kenney makes the *VC* something of an exception in its record of contemporary monastic, ecclesiastical and social practice, but does not differentiate its record of the marvellous from the generic form.[28] Ó Briain says, 'the Irish...loved to fill their annals with naive narrations...imagined by the *credulous* and *simple* medieval mind.'[29] Anderson comments on the *VC* specifically

> About the supernatural powers of Columba, as described by Adomnán, there will be different opinions. But before forming any opinion, it is necessary to consider whether Adomnán's statements are evidence for the facts involved. The historian is entitled to require at least as good evidence for less credible phenomena as he would for matters of everyday experience.[30]

Their conclusion is that Adomnán had too little genuine tradition to keep him from falling back on other sources such as his 'own experience and training in the doctrine and practice of the Irish church.' This caution, taken with their presentation of Adomnán's

---

26   Delehaye (1905, 49-50).
27   Delehaye (1905, 60).
28   Kenney (1968, 301).
29   Ó Briain (1947, 38), my emphasis.
30   A&A (1961, 19).

methodology, suggests scepticism on their part regarding the
possibility of the marvellous having any foundation in historical
reality. McCone repeats the same formula: the thaumaturgical
section of the *VSM* 'contains episodes scarcely credible by modern
standards', and, 'no scholar of the present or fairly recent past would
be likely to be fooled into accepting the more bizarre features of
even the oldest extant *Lives* at face value.'[31] Hillgarth identifies this
same ambivalence with regard to one of Adomnán's major influences

> Many historians would agree with Gustavo Vinay that no discussion of
> early medieval culture can begin without considering Pope Gregory I...
> but... he continues to perplex historians... one can sense the
> embarrassment caused by a whole side of Gregory (which cannot be
> confined to the *Dialogues*) that it has seemed kindest to dismiss as
> 'naïve'.[32]

Thus the supernatural and eschatological features of even Gregory's
thought are regarded as irrational in the modern age, and have been
dealt with by dismissing them as not genuinely Gregorian.

Such devices have applied equally to our otherwise respectable
Adomnán. Sharpe writes: 'Many modern readers find such stories of
miracles difficult to accept or believe.' He illustrates by citing the
eighth Duke of Argyll who, at the turn of the century questioned
whether *Adomnán* believed in the miracles he wrote about or
whether he resorted to 'deliberate invention'. The Duke rejects 'the
substance of the book, the argument for Columba's sanctity... as
"childish and utterly incredible"'.[33] The approach does not admit the
possibility of miracle in the sense of an event that does not follow
the normal laws of 'nature'. This value-laden response has been the
one operative in 'orthodox' historiography of the last century in
relation to hagiographic documents. While nothing less than
scrupulously orthodox by the modern canon in requirement,
scepticism, and conclusion, the statements do not address the
question of credibility within-the-tradition being studied, and may
make unhistorical assumptions about what is 'everyday' in the
seventh century by the standards of the twentieth century. A major
question they leave untouched is whether Adomnán's training 'in the
doctrine and practice of the Irish church' did in fact include an
understanding, acceptance and practice of prophecy, miracles and
visions?

Thus a (usually undeclared) presupposition is identified. It rejects *a
priori* the objective possibility of the actual occurrence of these

---

31   McCone (1984, 26; 46).
32   Hillgarth (1992, 214).
33   Sharpe (1995, 3-4).

marvellous phenomena, and of their having done so as a result of the mechanisms described. Thus the marvellous aspects of this genre of extraordinarily popular literature are the product of human imagination. The genre is built upon a tissue of insubstantial commonplace folk-tales that themselves ultimately derive from the fertile imaginations of superstitious, naïve, credulous, childish, primitive, mentally lethargic folk. The presupposition renders any putative belief of the author in the phenomena manifestly false, and thus requires the modern interpreter to seek alternative explanations for them. Otherwise respected early writers are rescued from charges of naïve credulity by identifying political and other motives for which they employ the marvels, as we will see. The approach thus opens the interpreter to the possibility of missing an important key both to understanding the spiritual understanding of the writer, of his audience, of the evidence to hand, and in a wider application, to understanding how things actually may be.

Attitudes to the Marvellous: Historical-Critical and Allegorical Interpretations

The rejection of miracles as actual or potential historic events bequeaths an approach that accepts marvellous phenomena only as literary devices, employed, in the present case by Adomnán, for particular purposes. Once the approach is adopted, the rejection of their historical reality becomes implicit and usually unquestioned. Hillgarth records the prevailing tradition of the dismissal of hagiographies as sources for historical knowledge in the Merovingian context, as espoused by Wallace-Hadrill and his predecessors, in a challenge to it. His statement could be seen as equally applicable in the present study. While acknowledging the drawbacks, he states

> My own view is that these works should not, in general, be dismissed as artificial in nature and utilitarian in aim. They appear to express interests and feelings not limited to professional 'cult-builders' (if one may coin the phrase) but shared by the local community as a whole. A more basic objection to these lives – one often raised in the past – that, because of the miracles which fill most of them, they are valueless (in Bruno Krusch's succinct phrase, '*kirchliche Schwindelliteratur*'), is not so liable to be heard today. The use of modern anthropological studies has helped us... we are just beginning to glimpse how, through these lives, we can hope to enter into the 'mental universe' of the time, how they can introduce us, as no other source can do, to the religion (that is the interpretation of the world and of the place of God and man in it) which was available to seventh-century man.[34]

---

34 Hillgarth (1987, 315-6).

The rehabilitation of the *VC* has identified three inter-related purposes or motives that Adomnán may have had in his 'mental universe,' which may have led to his presenting Columba accompanied by the marvellous in the way that he does.

PROVING SANCTITY: MARVELS MAKETH THE HOLY MAN

As we have noted, the significance of an individual could be asserted by proof of their sanctity. This sanctity then acts as a foundation upon which various purposes of an author might rest. In relation to the *VC*, Anderson stands firmly in the tradition of Delehaye

> [The biographer of a saint's] special function was to prove the sanctity of the person whose life he wrote. Sanctity meant the merit that God rewarded with miracles, and therefore it was necessary for Adomnán to devote his book to miraculous occurrences.[35]

Smyth takes up the theme

> His task was to tell good miracle stories which would reinforce the belief already established in men's minds that Columba was a saint... Columba's sanctity was the central point at issue in Adomnán's work.[36]

Herbert sees Adomnán's fundamental attitude being a 'conviction that his subject was a man of God', based on his own experience of the saint's posthumous intervention. She sees Adomnán's experiences and his reports of them as extending the tradition into a new era.[37]

Smyth is bothered by the lack of miracles for the 42 years of Columba's life spent in Ireland, a remarkable point, he says, which 'cannot be explained away' in view of Adomnán's central aim. He suggests the absence is simply due to there being little such information in circulation that Cumméne and Adomnán could relate.[38] The model may, as Picard observes, owe something to classical biography.[39] Sharpe also notes the gap: 'with the exception of the passages in which Adomnán mentions these teachers [i.e. his fosterer Cruithnechán (iii.2), and his masters Gemmán (ii.25) and (British) bishop Uinniau/ Finnbarr (ii.1)], no authority exists for any statement relating to the first forty or so years of Columba's life.'[40] Sharpe sees Adomnán's implicit belief in the call of Columba into the church from birth as surprising, the lack of a 'conversion' tradition being 'odd to the modern mind'. He explains it as indicative of

---

35   A&A (1961, 18).
36   Smyth (1984, 85; 89).
37   Herbert (1988a, 138).
38   Smyth (1984, 89).
39   Picard (1985, 78).
40   Sharpe (1995, 11-12).

Adomnán's lack of interest in a chronological account of Columba's life, and by reference to its parallel in Cogitosus where Brigit is presented as holy from birth. It is later sources that present their heroes rejecting their pagan origins for the baptism into Christ.[41]

The pre-figuring was perhaps added later, in a similar way to which the apocryphal gospels pre-figure the ministry of Christ in his boyhood miracles. The gospel record is itself sparing with regard to annunciatory and natal mirabilia.[42] If the gospel account of Christ is Adomnán's primary model of sanctity, the 'surprise' is reduced further. Adomnán was presenting the view that Columba was holy throughout his life just as their mutual master, Christ, was himself holy throughout his life. With this as his conscious model, we should not expect Adomnán to see the need to furnish a conversion story, especially if the historical circumstance, and the received tradition did not provide such. That later hagiographers found the need to include such a regular feature of their *Lives* is no reason to suspect Adomnán, in his earlier location, of fabrication in not including such. On the contrary, this gap in Adomnán's record is perhaps a significant factor in our interpreting Adomnán's purpose in writing *VC*, and far from needing to be 'explained away', actually furnishes a major clue towards understanding. What we may observe with some confidence here is that either the traditional concept of Columba's supernatural ministry, or Adomnán's selective record of the tradition, or indeed both accounts, see the miraculous as properly beginning with his peregrination by water to Iona, and not before. Adomnán's focus was on Columba's marvellously accredited apostleship, and he built his account of Columba as a modern type of Jesus who began his own marvellously accompanied public ministry after his baptism in the Jordan, and what we might term his 'peregrination' in the Judean desert. A lesser, but nevertheless important model is Moses, whose miracles begin after he leaves his earthly inheritance as Pharaoh's adopted grandson to follow the call of God passing through the waters of the Red Sea (Ex. 2) and into the Sinai wilderness.

As for Adomnán's audience, Picard notes that he may have had a continental audience in mind, wanting to place Columba 'on the record' as it were, alongside Columbanus and the many other

41 Sharpe (1995, 10).
42 In only two of the four canonical gospels: Matthew records only the conception (1:18); Joseph's dreams (1:20f, 2:13f,19f,22); and the natal star (1:2ff). Luke records the angelic annunciation (1:26ff); the foetal Baptist's greeting (1:41f); angelic birth-announcement (2:9ff); and the prophetic revelations of Simeon and Anna (2:26ff;36ff).

Merovingian saints.[43] Herbert believes he has 'internalized the portrayal of sanctity' of his exemplars to the extent of both interpreting Ionan tradition by their models, and also possibly fashioning his own action by the same. From this Herbert, taking a step further, infers a thesis important not only to our understanding of Adomnán's notion of sanctity, but also, significantly, to the debate over 'Celtic' autonomy and 'Celtic' distinctiveness

> Adomnán intended that his work should link Columban monastic tradition with the mainstream of Western hagiography, so that it should affirm that *Colum Cille*, venerated as a saint by his own community, merited acknowledgement also as a member of the communion of saints of Christendom.[44]

Sharpe agrees, but steps still further. He 'was concerned to present St Columba to his readers as the equal of those continental saints whose Lives were widely read.' He observes that in comparison to Patrick's biographers

> He is without question more spiritual in his biblical and his monastic understanding of the saint, and he is more international in his approach to depicting Columba as a saint in the mould of St Martin, St Antony and St Benedict.[45]

He suggests that Adomnán sought to present Columba in three proofs as a man of God 'in a mould that was both biblical and universal.'[46] He mentions Adomnán's homiletic appeal in ii.32 to equality with none less than the prophets and apostles.[47] Far from propagating an indigenous 'Celtic' sainthood, this early recorder of a 'Celtic' saint wants his presentation to show him as one with universal Christianity.

Sharpe sees Adomnán's major purpose as to attest Columba's miracles rather than seeking to make 'historical' sense.[48] A part of this process is perhaps an intention to record the continuation of God's dealings with men through chosen servants, as in the past. Adomnán presents Columba as sharing in the society of angels, showing his place in the heavenly kingdom.[49] This itself is a vital component of the Judao-Christian tradition of which Adomnán was

---

43   Picard (1984, 172-5).
44   Herbert (1988a, 138).
45   Sharpe (1995, 57; 63).
46   Sharpe (1995, 59).
47   Sharpe (1995, 57-58).
48   Sharpe (1995, 60), though of course this is the standard means of affirming sanctity in the genre.
49   Sharpe (1995, 57-58). This reference to kingdom is important to note as we progress; see chapter 3.

consciously an heir. Julia Smith has called for the discovery of a 'new alembic' in which to distil a deeper understanding of what these writers perceived as sanctity. Gregory of Tours' posed a rhetorical question, 'should we say the life or the lives of the saints?' Smith's still would seek a common essence shared by its varied manifestations; its timeless standards; and a separation of the distinguishing factors forming putative degrees of sanctity.

> What should it be? ...We might start by giving greater thought to the reasoning which informed Gregory's answer to his own question, that, 'there is a diversity of virtues and merits among [the saints], but the one life of the body sustains them all in this world'. If saints are those who reflect a Christ-like holiness in their life or the manner of their death, what notion of holiness could produce manifestations as variegated as did the early Middle Ages? ...Early medieval hagiography has benefited enormously from the recent spate of work on hagiographers as authors... That, however, does not obviate the need to move beyond text and context in search of a meaning, authority and relevance which plumbs the depth of Gregory's question.[50]

It is this search in which we here engage.

POLITICAL EXPEDIENCY

A major function commonly now identified for establishing the sanctity of a significant person is its place in giving authority to political activity and propaganda. Smyth believes Adomnán seeks to establish his own credentials as leader of the Ionan ecclesia, linking himself strongly with the famous Columba who is favoured in God's eyes. Thus opposition is unwise. He shows Columba's and therefore his own impartiality as to kings and earthly kingdoms. He thus writes to prepare the ground for his *Law of Innocents*.[51] Herbert concurs, highlighting the royal connections of Adomnán, as a son of the ruling Uí Néill Cenél Connaill family of Sétna, son of Fergus. Adomnán's fourth cousin Loingsech mac Oengusso acceded to the Uí Néill overkingship of Tara in 696. 'It is understandable, then, that he should exploit the close links between the country's leading secular ruler and the successor of Colum Cille, in order to advance the position of the saint's *familia*'.[52]

---

50 Smith (1992, 76), which also contains Smith's description of the optative still.

51 Smyth (1984, 92). Again, the reference to kingdom is important to note, see chapter 3. For Adomnán's *Law*, see bibliography.

52 Herbert (1988a, 51; 55) shows the support Adomnán was able to gather from the secular rulers of Uí Néill, Northumbria, Dál Riata and Pictland, as well as ecclesiastical support from his competitors at Armagh. Though his establishing the law was undoubtedly a coup for himself and Iona's prestige, the material and moderating benefits were not only to his own *familia*.

Hibernia and the Lands of the *Scotii*

Cogitosus champions Kildare.[53] Muirchú and Tirechán assert
Patrick's supremacy (i.e. that of Armagh and Uí Néill supporters) in
Ireland, and claim jurisdiction over Columban foundations. Picard
follows Binchy in accusing the Patrician biographers of buying
protection from the then Uí Néill leaders by writing documents of
historical fabrication to prove the historical validity of their claims,
and believes Adomnán does the same with Dál Riata.[54]

Herbert finds no evidence to support the view that it was the
Columban *familia*, Armagh, or Kildare that Adomnán had in mind.[55]
She calls the most important aspect of the achievement of Columba
that 'his career may be seen to have shown the potential for mutual
benefit arising out of co-operation between church and dynasty.'[56]
We can interpret from this that she sees Adomnán's purpose in
writing as he did as being to present this achievement on both sides
of the North Channel, and to further its development in his own
time.[57] She shows, citing the guarantor list and Ionan source of *Law
of Innocents* that Iona was in the dominant position in Ireland at the
end of the seventh century, and that the seventh-century
hagiographers of Patrick and Brigit directed their competing
propaganda towards gaining their own influence. Abbot Ségéne
presided over an expansion into the Southern Uí Néill territory of
Brega, where Rechra was established in 635. It was thus in his, and
Iona's interest to promote the repute of their patron in writing, and
it was from his hagiographical activity with his nephew Cumméne
that Adomnán derived his major source.[58] The brief quotation of this
source in Dorbbéne's manuscript shows its author's interest in
continuing the propagation of Cenél Conaill interests.[59] Herbert
notes that Adomnán used his connection with Aldfrith to secure the
release of Uí Néill prisoners from Northumbria, and asserted through
VC the divine approval of Uí Néill high kingship. Armagh apparently

---

53   McCone (1984, 30) regards the aggrandising tendency in *VC*, shown in 128a
      and 135a/b is 'far less prominent' than in Cogitosus.
54   Picard (1982, 171f.).
55   'It is difficult to concur with the opinion that the Columban familia in
      Adomnán's day felt its position threatened... and urged the composition of
      the *Vita Columbae* as "the master-work which would raise morale."' Herbert
      (1988, 146), referring to Picard (1982a, 172). This is based on Iona's evident
      strength as indicated by Cáin Adomnán, the lack of claim to status or property
      in the *VC*, and clear evidence of the promotion of Columba in Ireland in
      seventh century eulogies (Herbert, 1988, 147).
56   Herbert (1988a, 35).
57   Herbert (1988a, 13-25 and 13).
58   Herbert (1988a, 18, 24-5).
59   Herbert (1988a, 43), referring to the passage ascribed to Cumméne in iii.3.

felt this success keenly, as the claims of Patrick's propagandists show.[60]

Sharpe suggests that Adomnán has arranged his material to give precedence to the Cenél nGabráin succession in Dál Riata over that of the Uí Néill, and thus supporting a shift in allegiance for Iona from the latter, who supplied the first nine abbots, to the former. He suggests that Adomnán is directing his citations of Áedán mac Gabráin, king of Scottish Dál Riata, to an audience who already perceived Áedán's importance.[61] Adomnán is either stressing Iona's role in the history of the kingdom, or reminding the incumbents of Iona's present authority and claim of influence, growing out of this history, in framing his descriptions of Columba's dealing with the famous ancestor of the kingdom in the way he does. Sharpe rejects any basis for the suggestion that Iona was loosing the support of Uí Néill to Armagh, and that in consequence, Adomnán was writing to seek the special favour of Dál Riata. He cites Adomnán's own co-operation with the Uí Néill High King over the *Law of Innocents*, in which the first guarantor was the bishop of Armagh, with Muirchú far down the list.

Sharpe concludes, nevertheless, that Adomnán wrote principally for other monasteries in the Ionan *familia,* possibly even Lindisfarne, to inform them about their founder, about monastic devotion, and about the dependence of kings on the church, but that his writing for a continental audience is debatable.[62] However, he concedes, 'It is certainly probable that he meant to present a portrait of St Columba that could stand alongside that of Patrick.'[63] He thus agrees with Herbert, Adomnán is not expansionist, but defensive in asserting Columba's sanctity, though one of his statements borders on the equivocal, and is not illustrated

> The seventh-century Lives of St Patrick made extravagant claims for his power, his property and his jurisdiction, which Adomnán did not confront or challenge. His approach is less arrogant, more subtle.[64]

Did he, or did he not confront and challenge Patrick's propagandists, however subtly or humbly? It is hardly disputable that

---

60 Herbert (1988a, 54), cites Bieler, *The Patrician Texts*, SS18(1), 22(1), pp.138, 140. This should read SS18(2-4), 22(4).
61 Sharpe (1995, 27-8, and note 84).
62 Sharpe (1995, 64), see section ii below. We might add Wearmouth and Jarrow, founded ca. 674 and 682 by St Benedict Biscop, who was born in Northumberland ca. 628, spent his youth in the Northumbrian court, became a monk of Lérins and died at Wearmouth ca. 689, and who we might find was under the influence of Iona in his early life after Aidan's arrival in 635.
63 Sharpe (1995, 62-3).
64 Sharpe (1995, 63).

competition from the other cults barely raises Adomnán's explicit interest. Etchingham acknowledges the lack of any attempt to catalogue or claim churches in their style.[65] Indeed in Adomnán's only mention of Patrick, he seems rather to suggest peaceful coexistence of the two *familiae*: 'The fields of our two monasteries, mine and his, will be separated by the width of one small hedge'.[66] However, this reference to the 'fields' and 'hedge' may find a conceptual foundation in 2 Corinthians 10:12-18, Paul's ironic defence of his ministry against competing forces, and may show us this subtlety that Sharpe intuits, but in another light.

> *We* do not dare to classify or compare ourselves with some who commend themselves...neither do *we* go beyond *our* limits by boasting of work done by others...for *we* do not want to boast about work already done in another man's territory...it is not the man who commends himself who is approved, but the man whom the Lord commends.[67]

It is difficult to resist suggesting that these notions of Paul regarding territories and boundaries might be in Adomnán's mind as he writes of the two fields and the little hedge. If so, the reference could be a subtle rebuke to the ambitions of Armagh as published by Tirechán, busy claiming churches not founded by Patrick. For the biblically knowledgeable, the subtlety might, contra Sharpe, have been a razor sharp confrontation, all the more challenging for all its subtlety. However, Adomnán was otherwise content for Columba to be commended by the divinely empowered signs of sanctity: prophecy, miracles and visions.

Northumbria

Picard sees restoring the reputation of Iona after the Synod of Whitby as the first purpose of the *VC*. He supports this view with reference to the many seventh-century Irish ecclesiastical canons being promulgated at the time in an attempt to re-establish Irish authority; the introduction of the *Law of Innocents* of Adomnán; and the proliferation of Saints' *Lives* from the period.[68] He sees Adomnán writing in response to pressure from the establishment of Cuthbert's cult, and from the taunting of Wilfrid of York, against

---

65 Etchingham (1999, 127).

66 *VC* (2nd pref:3a): *Mei et ipsius duorum monasteriolorum agelluli unius sepisculae interuallo disterminabuntur.* The monasteries referred to are not identified; Sharpe surmises the reference is to adjacent holdings known to Adomnán (1995, note 12). The reference to 'field' may be significant in another way, see chapter 3 below.

67 2 Cor. 10:12,15,16b,18. For a discussion of the geographical references, see Barrett (1973, 263-269).

68 Picard (1982, 166f.).

which he asserted Columba's likeness to the apostles Peter, John and Paul in virtue, both of power and holy life.[69] Herbert suggests that Ségéne, Abbot of Iona 623-652, and Cumméne, Abbot 657-669, the first [known] Ionan hagiographers, were strongly motivated by this factor. It was during Ségéne's rule that Iona established Lindisfarne, invited soon after the Northumbrian victory of the once fugitive Oswald in 634. The non-Roman Easter that Iona celebrated had been defended strongly by Ségéne against the (Irish) synod of Mag Léne (ca. 630), and even, according to Bede, against Pope John IV.[70] Adomnán's monks needed reassurance that in adopting the computus of the universal Easter, which he brought from Northumbria, Adomnán was not thereby abandoning Ségéne's legacy, or veneration of Iona's founder.[71] In 664, after three pioneering decades, Iona had ceded her control of her once flourishing Northumbrian daughter church, which led to the adoption of 'a defiant and somewhat embattled position in regard to the customs of its beloved founder.'[72] This left a perception on Iona of Northumbrian doubt as to their patron's repute and orthodoxy, and of the strength of his link with universal sainthood. Herbert believes Adomnán to have detected Northumbrian ambivalence on his visits to the east coast in 685-7.[73] He wished to make clear his continued devotion to Columba despite his adoption of universal observance. Thus he produced his defence of the saint whom he believed ranked with the greatest of Christendom, and employed the conventions of contemporary hagiography, i.e. the sanctity accrediting power of the marvellous.

Herbert confirms Picard's view that Adomnán reminded Northumbria of their debt to Colum Cille's church for their faith, but does not respond to the suggestion of competition with Cuthbert. *VC* not only affirmed existing Columban hagiography, but added to it both Adomnán's own testimony of continued patronal influence, and, in Herbert's opinion, a collection of more acceptable sanctity-

---

69 Picard (1984, 172-5).

70 Herbert (1988a, 40-41).

71 It is perhaps one of the most remarkable features of this *Life* that Adomnán did not use the opportunity openly to claim direct succession from Columba to himself. This would assert his own authority in the face of his monks' disobedience over the question of dating Easter then in contention. Neither does he use the opportunity to complain of this disobedience.

72 Herbert (1988a, 45). I use the term daughter-church here carefully, recognising the lack of resolution over the question of the status of episcopally governed Lindisfarne, but extending Sharpe's idea of the 'Mother/Minster-church' (see Sharpe (1984 and 1992, passim).

73 Though his ambassadorial success in releasing the Bregan hostages in AU686 suggests a not insubstantial reputation, aided though he was by his friendship with Aldfrith.

affirming tales from outwith Iona itself, thus enhancing the existing repute.[74] In showing Columba as one with the universal church, he emphasised that his sanctity and ongoing intervention depended not on ritual observance,[75] but on universal qualities and qualifications. Thus in changing observance, the monks would not be denying their patron's holiness, or status, but would be uniting with the church of which Columba was a clear first ranking companion. Thus the *VC* is designed to 'restore perspective'.[76] Similarly Sharpe draws attention to Adomnán's point that although Columba's popular reputation had spread widely, the details of his life were not similarly known, and that it was Adomnán's intent to correct this lack.[77]

However, Adomnán refers to Northumbria only twice: i.1, probably written after the main body of the *Life*, almost in afterthought; and in ii.46, mentioning his own two visits to Northumbria in the context of his discussion of posthumous protection. He makes nothing of the exile of Oswald and his twelve men, except to say it was 'among the Irish'. He fails to make an opportunity to mention Columba's vicarious mission to Northumbria through Aidan. He writes three decades after Colman's retiral from Lindisfarne, and two decades into his own abbacy, a long delay. This series of missed opportunities must leave a question mark hanging over this proposition.

---

74 Herbert (1988a, 145). She believes the 'Cumméne' stratum of tales have been shown to be only 'invested with the hue of the supernatural' rather than 'overtly miraculous' (139). This view is dependant on numerous assumptions, i.e. that the Cumméne stratum is identified by tales containing contemporary historical 'fulfilments' to which a fabricated prophecy is posthumously attached (135); that the concern of the earlier hagiographer was as much to make the tales comment on contemporary events, as with recording the deeds of the founder (136); that none of the 'overtly miraculous' tales which Adomnán does record were derived from Cumméne; that none of the tales from outwith Iona were derived from Cumméne. Many of this last group could properly have been communicated to the *seniores* of Iona by members of the travelling companions of Columba, or by members of monasteries/communities from the place of occurrence. For example his prophetic knowledge at Trevet is observed by 'fellow-soldiers' (i.40).

75 She says, 'He describes his own personal experiences of Colum Cille's intervention, linking them with accounts of similar manifestations to the monks of the saint's own day, and indicating that in all cases the mediation of the saint did not depend on adherence to particular customs, but on prayer and devotion' (143). She does not say what these accounts were, nor what the customs were.

76 Herbert (1988a, 144 and 147-8), 'guiding both sides to a more constructive view of the situation, one focuses on the central figure of Colum Cille, whose sanctity is confirmed by supernatural signs.'

77 Sharpe (1995, note 5), on the first preface.

Pictland

Eleven of the tales (including the summary i.1, and i.37c) contain material relating to Pictland, and of these there is a single reference, ii.46, relating to the continuity of the church in Pictland in the intervening century. Again, Adomnán's does not seem to take the opportunity to emphasise the historical importance of Columba and Iona in the foundation of the (northern) Pictish church. Given the attention Adomnán does give to Pictland, especially compared with that given to Northumbria, we might discern Adomnán being motivated by foresight of problems ahead. Adomnán may be posited as asserting the position of Iona as the progenitor of Pictish Christianity in relation to Northumbrian oversight of the church there in his day. The case is weak for lack of Adomnán's clarity over the conversion process (see chapter five below). If it was Adomnán's project to reassert Columban history, however tentative, and to bolster Ionan authority in Pictland, it fails in 717 as Nechtan expels the Ionan clergy beyond the *Dorsum Brittaniae*.

Adomnán's Geopolitical Mental Map

Gilbert Márkus has recently suggested a further political function of the marvellous in the *VC,* though not connected with establishing Columba's sanctity as such. He identifies patterns of circumstantial detail in nature miracle stories associated with animals which suggest that he differentiated between geopolitical areas in his reporting.[78] Noticing after Meek the political significance of the crane story as a link with the dynasty of Columba/Adomnán, Márkus identifies three 'Scottish' geographical spaces in Adomnán's mental map. Pictland saw confrontation with a boar, and the water beast, in a hostile environment.[79] In Dál Riata, where we are among Columba's protégés who gave him land (according to AU) and where Columba became patron, animals are treated differently. The hungry are fed with salmon; two herds are multiplied following hospitality; a stake provides food and a surplus for sale; and a bull is revealed as bewitched. Márkus notes that all of these occur in the north, in Cenél Loairn, and may have political significance in reinforcing claims of Adomnán as abbot. Thirdly, on Iona incidents show an unnatural harmony between Columba and animals. Snakes are prevented from

---

78 Márkus (1999, 115-138).
79 Márkus sees this as a cultic reference, as had Picard (1981, 99). Ross (1986, 130) suggests the boar was an important cultic animal, and a dangerous, fearsome hunting quarry. Perhaps this is a symbol of evil strength representing Pictish paganism?

harming other creatures;[80] a knife is blunted; we meet a weeping horse. Thus the benefit of rule under godly authority is demonstrated. The unmistakable eschatological reference to the medieval concept of the monastery as a 'heaven on earth,'[81] may also be showing the benign paternal care of the abbot demonstrating the presence of God.

This entertaining and perceptive exposition of Adomnán's political view of 'Scotland' has a sharp focus, but might miss information available from outside its field of view. For the Christian saint, the spiritual environment of Pictland was hostile because of its paganism, thus we should expect signs of spiritual warfare here, and it comes most notably from a higher group of biped mammals, the *Magi*.[82] However, as well as hostility, Pictland also saw rescue (of Luigne from the monster, and the Irish slave-girl from Broichan, ii.27,33), healings (via a well, of Fintán, and of Broichan himself, ii.11,31,33), and resuscitation (ii.32).[83] The animal miracles in Dál Riata are joined by examples of serious human sinfulness (persecutors, a thief, raiders i.41,46, ii.22,24,25), though are themselves used as examples of eschatologically significant signs of the blessings of the kingdom, for which, see chapter three. ii.23 refers to pigs fattened for the table, and concerns a Pictish noble in exile under Columba's protection. He is murdered by the warden, who had been appointed by Columba, on the refuge of Islay. Thus we have a Dál Riata-based Iona appointee rebelling against Columba's authority whilst on Ionan business, and the victim is a Pictish noble. *VC* shows that rams were castrated, and confirmed by archaeological evidence, that Ionan monks ate various animals, used leather, and even close-tethered a goat, jarring Márkus' 'unnatural harmony' on the island. We see that taking the animal miracles in isolation from others to determine Adomnán's mental map of 'Scottish space' may produce an incomplete picture. Though not encoded within animal miracles, we must add Strathclyde and Northumbria as fourth and fifth mental spaces, also, depending on the definition, 'Scottish'

---

80   *VC* ii.28, iii.23. This implies that he prevents snakes from catching prey (see chapter 3 below).

81   See Macdonald (1997, 33), 'Adomnán seems sure, indeed, that a monk's heavenly life also is lived with his community: monastic profession has explicitly an eternal dimension.' This statement is made without supporting evidence from the *VC*. Markus suggests this harmony is an eschatological reference to swords beaten into ploughshares (see chapter 3 below).

82   As Paul warns in Ephesians 6, and see e.g. *VC* i.37, ii.11,32-34, and as Márkus shows (1999, 133).

83   MacDonald (1997, 56-60). The story of the knife remains a conundrum in the light of the references to Iona's livestock, unless we assume Columba and his community became vegetarians at that point, for which there is no other evidence.

territories.[84] Thus Adomnán's mental spaces may not be so clearly delimited by these creaturely indicators.

Having summarised the main scholarly opinion regarding political motive in the *VC*, the comments of Julia M.H. Smith are worth bearing in mind

> These comments might be taken to suggest that in the hands of early medieval writers, the *vita* became a form of political literature. It would be fairer to say that recent scholarly preoccupation with the hagiographer as an author working in a specific context can easily generate such an impression.[85]

TEACHING THE FAITH

Bede describes Columba as the first teacher of the Northern Picts.[86] Anderson makes the point

> It seems that next to the object of extolling his predecessor, Adomnán is in this work inspired by a desire to instruct his readers in what they should believe, and what they ought to do. He was an abbot, and did not forget his obligations to his community. In every contestable matter that he touches upon his words pronounce his own opinion, expressed by him as a teacher. Apparently-casual remarks were intended to influence his monks, and we must take them seriously.[87]

They go on to cite the place of bishops; the Sabbath; and consequences of sinful behaviour such as dissension, as teaching elements. Thus the writer's focus is on the monastic community in contradistinction to the description of journeys or missionary enterprise.[88] Smyth agrees. Sharpe and Etchingham describe aspects of this life.[89] The list could be added to almost indefinitely: the authority of the abbot, and of the presbyter; ascetic lifestyle; the place of work, prayer, reading etc.

Hillgarth reminds us that Gregory of Tours saw the Christian hold over Gaul remaining fragile.[90] Could something similar be detected in Adomnán's writing for Ireland/Dál Riata, and therefore be part of the reason for writing as he does? In an important epilogue to his paper on the pagan origin of *VC* i.47, Picard suggests this more subtle

---

84   *VC* i.15; i.1:8a-b.
85   Smith (1992, 71). Although Smith is reviewing a much wider period and geographical setting than our own, her comment returns relevance here.
86   Bede *HE* v.9, and see MacDonald (1997, 34) for a brief description of Irish teacher-student activity.
87   A&A (1961, 24).
88   A&A (1961, 86 cf. 24b).
89   Smyth (1984, 85), Sharpe (1995, 65ff.), Etchingham (1999, 332-4), and see MacDonald (1984 and 1997).
90   Hillgarth (1992, 228).

didactic intent and approach. Overturning Ó Briain's rejection of
Christian censorship of pagan saga, and adopting Mac Cana's view,
he suggests that missionary Christians were engaged in a process of
replacing pagan religious belief and practice, particularly in the
critical areas of cosmology and eschatology. The beliefs and
symbolic rituals that manifested these beliefs were 'a prime target'.
Those associated with death, as 'the core of christian eschatology',
'had to be replaced'. [91] In i.47, Adomnán reduces a commonplace
kingly death myth to a minor historical tale and transfers the supernatural element to the Christian saint who prophesies the death. The
emphasis is on the prophecy fulfilled. Picard makes a persuasive case
for the 'juxtaposition' and 'intermingling' of pagan and Christian
motifs here, and his identification of Adomnán's purpose being to
replace pagan death ritual symbolism, and pagan 'para-nature', as he
calls it, with Christian eschatological categories and Christian super-
nature is attractive. He grants to Adomnán a great subtlety:
infiltrating, insinuating, subversively weaving Christian theology into
a well-known pagan folk motif, and thereby eclipsing and eventually
replacing the original meaning. The tale has been de-mythologized
(and some would say then re-mythologized again) and used as a
didactic tool to aid the conversion of the pagans.

This attractive scheme is not, however, without its problems. The
tale openly acknowledges the ambient tenaciousness of pagan
magic, [92] and makes no attempt, subtle or otherwise, to demonstrate
its deceit (as in ii.17), nor its eclipse by more powerful magic, nor to
place the practitioner under judgement. No Christian eschatology,
with the possible exception of prophetic activity, nor cosmology, is
introduced. Picard does not demonstrate what pagan eschatology was
replaced. Nor is it clear what pagan supernatural element is
transferred; we only observe the Christian element in place. In
imputing subtle craft to Adomnán, the theory makes him a cunning
fabricator, not simply a skilful, theologically aware author making
the best of a garbled legend. Nevertheless, Picard's suggestion that a
purpose of the hagiographer was to acquaint his readers with
Christian eschatology and super-natural belief and practice as part of
a mission to convert the pagans is worth pursuing. [93]

O'Reilly takes the eschatological theme further, showing
Adomnán's considerable learning brought to bear upon the task of

---

91　　Picard (1989, 368f; esp. 373) referring to Mac Cana (1986, 57f.). See chapter 2
　　　　below.

92　　*Maleficium*: sorcery, or poison used by sorcerers (Souter). Whether this makes
　　　　Gúaire's wife a sorceress, or a regular user of sorcery is not told. Sorcery is,
　　　　however, not portrayed as having been superseded.

93　　See chapter 3 below.

teaching his readers 'the fear of the Lord', and, 'the revelation of the continuing meaning of God's word for the believer.' Through spiritual exegesis in the tradition of *lectio divina*, Adomnán expounds scripture in his account of the very life of Columba himself.

> Adomnán, like Báithíne had succeeded to Columba's role as teacher...Instead of quoting Columba's exegesis on particular passages, he shows how the saint exemplified their precepts.[94]

In so describing this function of the *VC*, O'Reilly infers that it has the nature of a carefully and learnedly composed didactic treatise of biblical exegesis – we might call it hagiographical variations on a theme of biblical eschatology. She might also hint that the actual life of Columba was itself seen as a living interpretation, a living out, of biblical revelation. The *VC* would thus be Adomnán's attempt to record this praxis as a didactic example of its possibility.[95] O'Reilly's acute observations thus form a significant stimulus and background to the present investigation.

Adomnán was certainly writing to help his readers to be better monks, to follow the rule more faithfully, to develop their ascetic self-discipline. This is a strong element in *VC*, but we are still left with the question of how the marvels which make up so much of the *Life* fit.[96] Adomnán deliberately records marvellous manifestations that were believed to be accompaniments to the proclamation of the gospel.[97] Are they being used here mainly in accreditation of ethical holiness, as encouragement towards coenobitic asceticism? Is it possible that the teacher might also be communicating, albeit implicitly, his views on the functional place of the marvellous in the life of any holy Christian? If so, what are we able to learn of contemporary attitudes to the marvellous, and its place in the ordinary Christian life, as it could be received by Adomnán's monks. At the close of his account of the political function of *VC*, Picard mentions the possibility that 'it is likely that Adomnán's primary aim was to write what he saw as a faithful account of the life of Columba, which could serve as a model for the Christians of his time.'[98] He then O'Reilly thus suggest this as a possible function of the *Life*, again a strand we shall be pursuing.

---

94 O'Reilly (1997, 106).
95 As Patrick would have it from scripture, 'we who are the "epistle of Christ"...' *Conf.* 1.4.
96 MacDonald (1997, 24).
97 See Herbert (1988a, 140), 'From his hagiographical reading, Adomnán no doubt was familiar with the convention that miraculous signs assisted the process of conversion of a heathen people.' She notes the final sentence of *VC* ii.34.
98 Picard (1982, 177).

Attitudes to the Marvellous: Cautious Openness

Having summarised interpretations of the marvellous in *VC* as literary devices, we go on to examine the beliefs of seventh-century Christians regarding the nature and function of these marvels in practice.

RECOGNISING THE VALIDITY OF EARLY BELIEFS

The demythologizing 'orthodoxy' described above has not held the field unchallenged. An approach that recognises the subjectivity of adopting a purely rational approach to historical analysis, of uniform incredulity, has been emerging. Henry Chadwick implies recognition of this point, as well as a caution in applying it, in a comment regarding the more general approach to historical research

> Probably it is only partly fair to say that disagreements principally spring
> from the adoption of divergent value-systems, any of which can assert
> equal claims to hold the field.[99]

The translator of Sulpicius Severus, another of Adomnán's major influences, stands with feet on both sides of the debate, on the one hand desirous of accepting Martin's status as a wonder-worker, but troubled by extravagant excesses. In his introduction to the translation, Hoare reviews the debate over the question of Sulpicius' reliability as a recorder and transmitter of factual information, as of contemporary popular impressions and devotion pertaining to Martin, saying

> No biographer of his period was better qualified to write a truthful life of
> a contemporary saint, and no biographer of his period – we may almost
> say, of any period – has written a life more full of astounding
> prodigies.[100]

He speculates that God may have raised Martin as a pre-eminent miracle worker for the special purpose of establishing the faith in what was pagan Gaul, which was under the Franks to act as 'the corner-stone of Catholic Christendom during its formative period'.[101] However Hoare is troubled by the extravagance of the later works, suggesting

> ...the result was to create for St Martin a second and a very vulnerable
> reputation by superimposing upon popular devotion a literary vogue.
> *Worse still,* Sulpicius fixed for centuries a hagiographic tradition that
> rates the anecdotes of wonder-working above spiritual portraiture, to the
> great detriment of our understanding of both the natural psychology and

---

99 H. Chadwick (1981, 3).
100 Hoare (1954, 4).
101 Hoare (1954, 6).

the supernatural spirituality of the saints... here and there we get delightful glimpses of a real person and occasionally, *surely*, of a real wonder-worker; but all the time we have to be making allowances for literary requirements and poses, which is not restful.[102]

Hoare raises acutely the question of the function of the marvellous in early Christian hagiography, in common cause with Hilary of Arles, Gregory I, and John Cassian who saw much earlier the danger of concentrating on the marvellous. However, with them, Hoare does not reject the possibility of 'supernatural spirituality' that means more than profound contemplative asceticism, as his wistful glimpsing of a 'real wonder-worker' shows. Meyvaert identifies the modern desire to separate hagiography from history on account of its miraculous content, criticising it in the case of *HE* as 'trying to fit Bede into our own standard of scholarship.' Bede embraced the Fathers' acceptance of biblical miracles, but was restrained in accepting contemporary phenomena, and thus treats the elements of his own time 'with discretion and good judgement.'[103] Sr Benedicta Ward, in her *Miracles and the Mediaeval Mind,* sees the possibility that the ancients were in some ways more sophisticated than the moderns, and saw things which the modern may not

[a] number and diversity of events were regarded as in some way miraculous not out of naïvety but from a more subtle and complex view of reality than we possess.[104]

Picard notes the problems associated with using hagiographical material for historical purposes,[105] but questions the legitimacy of the marvellous simply being dismissed. Again the perspicacity of modern epistemology is under question. He encapsulates the point

While recognising the importance of the *Vita* as a major historical source for sixth and seventh century Ireland and Scotland, many historians hesitate to accept Adomnán's testimony when it contradicts Bede. The origin of this reticence seems to be a question of literary genres.[106]... The importance given to supernatural phenomena is bound to put off a modern rationalistic mind. However... I shall remind the reader of the

---

102 Hoare (1954, 7), my emphasis.
103 Meyvaert (1977b, IX, 51-55).
104 Ward (1982, 2).
105 Picard (1984, 51 note 8). Now conventional. He notes firstly the time lapse to writing and the lateness of many manuscripts, and the consequent need to treat the *Life* as a source for the period of writing rather than its object; secondly the object of the writer to prove the saint's holiness by appeal to miracle, rather than to produce biography.
106 Picard (1984, 51).

complexity and scope of the range of possible realities for facts of subjective experience, an area which should also be studied.[107]

Sharpe takes the argument further referring to the dismissive attitude of the eighth Duke of Argyll, noted above.

> This attitude springs from his distaste for Adomnán's cast of mind, which reverenced holiness displayed in miracles. In his own day and with the life of a saint as his object, Adomnán could hardly have written a book that was not full of miracle stories, *for prophecy and miraculous powers were among the gifts of the Spirit* (1 Cor. 12:10). These were the proofs that Columba was a saint, so this was the heart of the *Life*. Whether or not one wishes to believe that the events happened as told, they are true to the image of saint that was familiar throughout the seventh century.

However, he goes on to retain an unresolved caution: 'None the less, in the nature of the case, there is a major problem of historical credibility.'[108] Part of this problem is the identification in sixth/seventh century of the operation of 'gifts of the Spirit'.[109]

Berger warns that commentators should hesitate to venture opinions on the justification of particular beliefs. He concludes saying he has tried to show that

> ...secularized consciousness is not the absolute it presents itself as... If the signals of transcendence have become rumours in our time, then we can set out to explore these rumours - and perhaps to follow them up to their source. A rediscovery of the supernatural will be, above all, a regaining of openness in our perception of reality.[110]

He calls for 'an "infinite care" in the affairs of men to observe reactions to these phenomena.' This same care should be adopted in dealing with the account of a seventh-century monk who claims to observe, albeit mostly at a distance, phenomena which modern scholarship has made itself unwilling to admit as sensible to awareness. I hope to 'explore these rumours' which Adomnán has deposited, seeking to test their congruence with his tradition, and to further improve our knowledge of the development of belief in such phenomena up to his seventh-century insular context.

---

107 Picard (1984, 51 note 8).
108 Sharpe (1995, 4), my emphasis. Sharpe's statement here regarding the gifts belies numerous unresolved questions. Why, given the importance of Cassian to monasticism in general, Iona included, and his strictures on the use of miracle to signify holiness, is Adomnán so at home with the practice. What is the connection between miracles and gifts of the Spirit? Did Adomnán have any such concept in mind? Did not these phenomena end with the death of the Apostles as John Chrysostom asserted (Kydd 1984). See chapter 5 below.
109 For which, again, see chapter 5 below.
110 Berger (1969, 19).

ANTIQUE AWARENESS OF DOUBTFUL VERACITY

An important observation, missed in applying modern criteria to the analysis of the marvellous, is that the ancients themselves, despite their 'naïvety', commonly doubt the veracity of reports of the marvellous. A few examples will illustrate the point.

In Bede's account of Wilfrid's casuistic debate with Colmán over the date of Easter, Colmán makes the typical claim that the holiness and virtue of Columba and his successors is confirmed by heavenly signs and miracles, and that they can thus be emulated. It suits Wilfrid's argument to pour heavy ironic doubt upon the marvellous basis of this authority, citing the classic gospel put-down to workers of marvels. For Wilfrid, authority derived from law, not dubious miracle.[111]

The *Amra* tells us that Columba read Basil, whose younger brother, Gregory of Nyssa (c.330-c.395), tells a story of a military officer who came to him soon after his sister Macrina's death and related a story of a miracle through her. The officer's daughter had a severe eye infection. Macrina prayed for her healing, and she was healed. The officer relates how in this healing he comprehended the miracles in the gospel, which he had not believed before. Gregory comments

> most men judge the credibility of what they hear according to the measure of their own experience, and what is beyond the power of the hearer they insult with the suspicion of falsehood as outside of the truth ... the healing of disease, the casting out of devils, true prophecies of future events, all of which are believed to be true by those who knew the details accurately, amazing although they are. But for the material-minded, they are beyond what can be accepted.[112]

Gregory thus writes arguing for the occurrence of miracle, in the awareness that his readers will doubt the veracity unless they have personal experience, as Greek rational scepticism was an important strand of thought in the early Christian world.

Other witnesses to early scepticism include Patrick, who refuses to deny signs and wonders granted to him just because of incredulity of his detractors.[113] Gregory I appears to differentiate, accepting

---

111 Especially miracles claimed as confirming the authority of an opponent. *HE* iii.25, citing Mt. 7:21-3//Lk. 13:25-7. Wilfrid does go on diplomatically to say he does not apply this to Columba etc., but the damage is done, and the irony is re-introduced a few lines later in the account, '...even if your Columba... was a saint potent in miracles...' tr. Sherley-Price (1968, 192).

112 Gregory of Nyssa, (*Life of St. Macrina*, tr. Woods Callahan, 1967, 190-191). Modern scholars have assessed Gregory of Nyssa as surpassing Basil and Gregory Nazianzus as philosopher and theologian, being more learned and profound, possibly the most versatile theologian of his century (Woods Callahan, 1967, ix).

113 *Conf.* 45.

miracles in missionary situations, but only accepting them in a spiritual sense in established situations.[114] However, McCready has shown that Gregory I maintained belief in and expectation of the presence and practice of miracles.[115] Adomnán himself is well aware of this doubting tendency

> The credibility of miracles of this kind, that happened in past times and that we have not seen, is confirmed for us beyond doubt by those of the present day, that we ourselves have observed.[116]

Thus the practice of dismissing early writers as uniformly naïve and credulous must be questioned. Historians, as we have seen, are increasingly recognising their need to 'get into the minds' of their subjects who lived with very different world-views. This coincides with a growth amongst theologians and within the church of interest in, and claimed experience of, just the sort of phenomena of which Adomnán wrote. Adomnán may well have been perfectly at ease with idea of divine intervention. We reject this possible seventh-century opinion in anachronistic imputation of modern epistemology, and thereby risk missing the opportunity to observe the phenomena as Adomnán did.

RECOGNISING A DIFFERENT REALITY

During the latter part of this century, this more open approach has begun to affect scholarship in the field. Gilbert Márkus has said that the *VC's* description may be firstly a real revelation of sixth century life; secondly how Adomnán thinks things were then; thirdly a revelation of how things were at the close of the seventh century; and fourthly prescriptive of how Adomnán would have liked things to be in his own time.[117] A combination of the four is, of course, a fifth possibility. Meek recognises that the Christians of Adomnán's day shared a 'scriptural mind', and as such, the use of scriptural imagery, including the marvellous, surrounding Columba was to afford him the ultimate accolade.[118] A similar approach is today being established in the canonical school of biblical studies: some scholars now accept miracle as a valid category.[119] Heffernan demonstrates persuasively the ways in which modernist assumptions have confused and defeated attempts to understand hagiographical writings, arguing that we must interpret the *Lives* as far as possible from the

---

114   Turner (1996, 289); O'Reilly (1997, 95).
115   McCready (1994, passim).
116   *VC* ii.45:99b.
117   Márkus (1999, 121-2).
118   Prof. Donald Meek in papers presented at the Sixth Annual SCHA Conference, Spes Scotorum, 7th June 1997, Edinburgh.
119   E.g. K. Barth, J. Moltmann, C.S. Lewis, Colin Brown, N.T. Wright.

perspective of their contemporary readers.[120] 'Popular' opinion, and certainly opinion in the Pentecostal / Charismatic Christian tradition, might be perceived to be more accepting of these phenomena.[121] For the sixth/seventh centuries we might not be incorrect to say that such supernatural phenomena *were* part of everyday experience, as Smyth suggests

> Adomnán was writing for a monastic community and for pious Christians who accepted direct intervention in human affairs as normal.[122]

Studying the Marvellous in the Life of Columba

In each of the above cases, we have seen that it is not so much the function of the marvellous phenomena themselves that have been studied, as the function of the literature within which they form so central a part in providing authority for the writer. Fewer studies have focussed on the phenomena *qua* phenomena.

Picard collects citations of similar types of the marvellous from the seventh-century *Lives* of Irish saints Patrick, Brigit and Columba, and 40 or 50 *Lives* of continental saints of Merovingian Gaul.[123] He seeks to show both their common themes, and the differences in treatment of the various motifs in the two geographical groupings. He sees differences in the Irish *Lives* chiefly in their relatively minor interest in 'evangelical' miracles of healing, resuscitation and exorcism,[124] and in their comparatively rare treatment of the demonic. In *VC* however, Adomnán devotes the whole of one of the three books to what he terms '*uirtutum miraculis*' and the number of angelic references are less than double the number of demonic references, viz. 20:11 (see appendix 1). Picard also sees the Irish as extending the common motif of light as a metaphor for the gift of 'clairvoyance';[125] that visions of heaven do not occur in the seventh

---

120 Heffernan (1988).

121 At the 8th Lambeth Conference 1998, Stephen Sykes, Bishop of Ely, reported '480 million people who belong to Pentecostal churches or are associated with charismatic churches in the world.' He said that for the first time Anglicans from all parts of their Communion wanted 'to evaluate this vast phenomenon . . . and what [it] signifies for world Christianity' (Cobbey, 1998).

122 Smyth (1984, 85).

123 Picard (1981). He gives both: 'Some forty continental lives survive [the Merovingian period]'(91); 'The motifs found in fifty continental lives, scattered over two centuries...'(99). Hillgarth (1987, 314-5 note 14) records a total of 38 pre-AD750 Merovingian *Vitae*, not including Gregory of Tours and Venantius Fortunatus, plus a few dubious cases.

124 A term he derives from Fontaine (1967-9).

125 Sharpe also uses this term to describe Columba's prophetic gifts. McCone (1989, 136) gives a perspicacious warning about such mixing of terminology:

century Irish *Lives*; and that monsters are more fantastic in continental examples. Of folk tales, especially of natural marvels, he says

> ...it would be difficult to identify the general tendencies, but one could say that there is a greater concentration of these stories in insular *Lives*. This last remark is the dominant impression that results from comparing Irish and continental *Lives*.[126]

Davies attempts a more statistical approach still.[127] She notes the relative paucity of healing miracles in seventh century Irish *Lives* compared with contemporary continental *Vitae*. She explains the difference as due to the lack in Ireland of both the academic study and practice of medicine as a high art; the tradition of care until cured; and the pre-Christian influence of physicians operating by blood-letting and bone-setting, and of charm-wielding women who heal by magic. Davies correctly identifies a problem at a statistical level. On my own figures for the *VC* (see appendix 1), the problem is exacerbated. Healing makes up only 2.3 per cent of particular marvellous incidence (cf. Davies' 9 per cent). Davies does not include statistics from the New Testament or the *Lives* of Antony, Benedict or Germanus, all known influences on Adomnán. However, to say, 'obviously clerical Irish writers did not initially see healing as an appropriate manifestation of saintly power nor local magic as translatable into christian modes of explanation', while using the *VC* as evidence for this state of affairs leaves numerous questions. Davies notes *VC* healings. Thus Adomnán, as an early writer, does see healing as a very appropriate manifestation of saintly power, as his general appeal in ii.6 shows. Tirechán, on the other hand, is not interested in this sort of evidence.

Davies' use of evidence from secular tales is problematic. In assuming that the use for example of spoken charms, recorded even from the seventh century, witnesses genuine pre-Christian tradition in Ireland, she ignores the central Christian practice of prayer for

---

'Nativists prone on etymological and other grounds to stress the 'pagan' mantic attributes of the *fili* as 'seer' would do well to reflect on the following Old Testament passage..." for he that is now called a prophet was beforetime called a seer" (1 Sam 9:9).' The main thrust of this comment warns of the danger of making all seers pagan. We should note this explicit change of terminology in the Judaeo-Christian tradition regarding the prophet: a similar convention should perhaps be observed regarding prophetic gifting, or a pagan origin and character to Christian prophecy might, as it were, be imposed.

126 Picard (1981, 99). Picard's remarks are of an impressionistic nature.
127 Wendy Davies (1989). She does not show how her figures are derived, making checking and comparison difficult. Nevertheless, her observation has general validity.

healing, introduced there at the latest by the mid-fifth century. In the Judao-Christian tradition, 'local magic' was to be replaced, not translated, as her quote from *Penitentialis Vinniani* shows.[128] These last problems will be addressed in chapter two.

Stancliffe uses Derouet's functional categorisation of the miracles in continental *Lives*, and compares his analyses with her own applied to the five earliest (seventh century) Irish *Lives*. Her results draw similar conclusions to Picard's observation of the differences in proportions of miraculous function. She shows that Irish interest in 'Vertical' and nature miracles (with what she calls a folkloric magical function),[129] overtook interest in miracles with what Derouet calls 'practical' or 'horizontal', and what Picard might term 'evangelical' functions.[130] She notices the relative unimportance of the demonic in 'Irish' *Lives*, positing the influence of eastern, pre-Augustinian anthropology as the reason. This reasoning does not apply to the *VC*, however, in which as she recognises, demonic stories are 'more common,' as a result, she suggests, of Adomnán's continental reading. This is despite his recording Columba's 'predestination to sanctity', a principle she sees as removing the need for a satanic role.[131] Earlier in the paper, Stancliffe makes a curious statement

> I begin with the observation that the devil, and demons, do not play a prominent role in the Judaeo-Christian revelation contained in the Bible. The reason why they loom so large in patristic writing and early saint's *Lives* is because they were part of the shared thought world of late antiquity.[132]

It is too simplistic to treat the biblical revelation as a whole for this purpose, as the relative part played by the demonic changes markedly with time. In the (Christian) New Testament, her claim is insupportable. Demons play a crucial role in the demonstration of the coming of the kingdom in the ministry of Christ and the apostles. By 'late antiquity', we assume she means the time of writing of the *Lives* of Antony and Martin, (i.e. 357/379). Their 'shared thought-world' was pre-eminently influenced by the Bible, and the New Testament is a product of a not dissimilar 'thought world' itself. To separate a 'biblical' world-view from this late

---

128 Davies (1989, 49).
129 For example: prophesy, angels, visions, regaining paradisiacal state, i.e. miracles which brought the saint into direct contact with the divine (Stancliffe, 1992, 94).
130 '...*miracles de salut*', i.e. healings, exorcisms, calming storms, stopping fires, routing monsters and thieves; and 'punishment' miracles (Stancliffe, 1992, 95).
131 Stancliffe (1992, 106).
132 Stancliffe (1992, 102).

antique world-view on the basis of their divergent treatment of the demonic, and to employ this as explaining the lack of demonic in (some) Irish hagiography is thus inadequate.

A second statement of Stancliffe bears further investigation here. Her section on folkloric influence is predicated on an extraordinary thought. She concedes the acceptance of the place of the marvellous in the Christian tradition by the Irish hagiographers, but says

> They were all the more likely to [accept its place], in that they were not heirs to the Greek tradition of rational philosophical thought. On the contrary, their culture recognized magic, *druidecht*, and its practitioners, the druids...

Stancliffe infers here that the non-Irish world was heir to Greek rationalism, and thus was less accepting of the idea of 'magic'. We may wonder if any culture of the period we are considering could be described as heir to a Greek rationalistic tradition which did not recognise magic, the supernatural, or metaphysical dimension of reality. The Christian tradition which Stancliffe concedes influenced the Irish was itself born and propagated in a world heavily influenced by Greek thought, yet the tradition was founded on miracle, and propagation of the tradition in every geographical milieu was surrounded in claims of the continuation of marvellous phenomena. While there were Greek sceptics who questioned the notion of non-material existence, and Christian sceptics followed them, it is difficult to imagine what Stancliffe understands by 'the' tradition of 'Greek rational philosophical thought' which was inherited by the non-Hibernian world, but was absent in Ireland. Various cultures represented in the Bible, Greek included, had their magi, and magical supernaturalism, as did the (extra-biblical) Asian, Gaulish and Greek worlds.[133] Her thesis rests on the insecure idea of Irish isolation (see above). Many of the differences noted may simply be due the small available sample of very disparate Irish hagiographies that hardly form a coherent genre against which to make comparisons. In addition, we have noted Adomnán's acknowledgment of local scepticism, and should note the rationalistic de-mythologizing explanation of scriptural marvels in Irish Augustine's seventh century *De Mirabilibus Sacrae Scripturae*.

The Question of Functioning Nature

The preceding discussion aims to summarise existing approaches to the study of the marvellous in hagiography in general, and in the *Life*

---

133 See, for example, Dodds (1951) for an account of non-rational Greek thought systems and/or practices.

of Columba in particular. The accounts of the marvellous are literary devices designed to encode Adomnán's purpose in writing. Heavenly signs confirm sanctity; miracles confirm virtue.[134] They demonstrate authority; differ according to geography; and furnish the narrative vehicles for 'apparently-casual remarks'. The studies of Picard, Davies, and Stancliffe on the varying incidences recorded for the phenomena illuminate some questions of source and influence on the way Adomnán composes the *Life*.

However, while these approaches illuminate our understanding of these texts and of the historical period in which they are written, the question of the nature of the phenomena themselves, so important as the vehicle upon which the writer is conveying his intended message, is left open. Each of the hypothetical functions depends for its force on the account Adomnán gives of the marvellous phenomena around which each story is built. The systems of categorization adopted for comparative studies do not help us to relate the manifestations in the *Lives* to their most obvious archetypes in the Bible, nor to other descriptions in the Fathers. These do not record classes of 'vertical', 'horizontal' or 'evangelical' miracles. As we shall see, Adomnán himself would be unlikely to recognise such a functional distinction. For him, all the marvellous phenomena surrounding Columba depend for their direction and empowerment on the sovereign work of God. They all come from God, and all affect God's creation. All demonstrate intimate connection with their divine source.

I am not here wishing to make a foray into the impossible world of verifying the actual occurrence of an historical miracle. Miracles as phenomena are fraught with difficulty in terms of verification even at close range with multiple attestations. However, no attempt has hitherto been made to elucidate what it is that Adomnán understands by the phenomena whose description he employs to make his case. The question of correspondence of the descriptions he records to archetypes from which the descriptions may be derived is left unaddressed. These may be literary archetypes; or they may be historical. Adomnán may be reporting actions which consciously follow, even emulate or seek to duplicate biblical models. However the account is derived, it is the nature of the marvellous phenomena as marvels which underlies the effectiveness of any putative sanctificatory, political, or didactic function. They witness to his understanding of the interaction between the natural and supernatural worlds; of the operation of the Spirit of God in the natural world; and of the expectations he might hold of how this interaction might be

---

134 Cf. Colmán, *HE* iii.25.

manifested. How did Adomnán perceive their nature, source, pedigree, and purpose in the ministry of these holy ones whose *Lives* they are reported to have punctuated? This I wish to call the question of the functioning nature of the phenomena, a nature that once clarified, in view of the important place held in the narratives, may affect our understanding of how they are being used, and what they signify.

The Way Forward

Sixth and Seventh-Century Understanding

It was to the common monks of his day that Adomnán says he addressed his work.[135] The work may thus be better understood by acknowledging its probable reception by its intended biblically literate audience, and in its seventh-century milieu, with a cautious suspension of judgement as to its reality in absolute terms. As we have noted, what is accepted as reality depends much on the perspective of the observer. It is part of this book's intention to illuminate our understanding of what in the realm of the marvellous sixth-seventh century Christians included in their understanding of reality. Herbert says of her own work

> The Lives are assessed as literary works, marked, moreover, by the circumstances of their background and time. They are products of a learned milieu in which native and ecclesiastical areas of interest had merged, and they emerge from monastic institutions which were part of the political and social fabric of their society. A text-centred approach to the Columban works seeks to take account of all these considerations, as it sets out to discover the agenda of the hagiographers and the manner in which they presented their design and purposes to their public.[136]

While taking account of these considerations, we are seeking to pay particular attention not to political, sociological or even ecclesiastical considerations, but to what the author may be shown to understand as the underlying spiritual aspects of the work that contains all these various strands. The monastic institutions, such as they were, were also, perhaps primarily to Adomnán, expressions of the spiritual fabric of their society. Explicit references to the spiritual pervade his work, indeed they make up its very fabric. It is to seek a deeper understanding of some of the spiritual aspects of this remarkable witness to seventh century Irish/Scottish Christianity that this book is directed. As Sharpe has pointed out, early Irish

---

135 Sharpe (1995, 63-5).
136 Herbert (1988a, 133).

euhemerized version of the oral myths with the purpose of eradicating paganism. The incipit of saga writing (i.e. recording the myths) closely followed the genesis of the Irish hagiographical venture, four early survivals of which are the two Latin *Lives* of Patrick; Cogitosus' *Life of Brigit*; and Adomnán's *Life of Columba*. The saint's *Lives* may thus retain features of pre-Christian religion derived from the 'fixed' oral tradition, or its early literary forms. Thus *Lives* may too yield information regarding pagan religious belief and practice as their writers allow this to influence their writing.

The principal challenge to nativist theories came from James Carney, now carried forward principally by Kim McCone.[8] The critics noted that sagas might suffer from faulty transmission, political distortion, historical overlays, and possibly church censorship. They are insecure as sources due to their late preservation, and our inability to check the late manuscripts against oral stories putatively formed before the arrival of Christianity. McCone insists that the existence of the oral avatars essential to this theory has never been substantiated,[9] and challenges the Indo-Celtic hypothesis, which claims retention of archaic cultural and institutional features on grounds of dialect geography. The challenge questions the assumed isolation of Celtic as it developed, arguing for its separation while still in central Europe. It became peripheral, but as a separate language. It has developed significantly, and though it retains archaisms, it has so much influence from ecclesiastical Latin that the meaning of linguistic archaism cannot be certainly linked to Indo-Iranian meanings.

Rudolph Thurneysen had posited a formative influence on the structure and content of the sagas of the Greek hero tales, notably the *Iliad*, imported via Latin translation through the agency of the Christian missionaries.[10] Carney proposed a theory of active literary composition by Christian monastic scribes, or rather authors.[11] They took the remnant survivals of oral myths, and wove them into an historical framework formed from a biblical / ecclesiastical understanding of history. They sought to equate pre-Christian Irish society with pre-Christian Israel, complete with pre-Christian heroes. Thus the new literature presents the history of Ireland according to biblical structures and patterns. It fashions the religion of pre-

---

by instances of explicit disapproval of the content of the tales, and reinstated by T.F. O'Rahilly (1946 and 1952) and P. Mac Cana (1986).

8   Carney (1955 and 1983) and McCone (1990): called 'emerging orthodoxy' by Harvey, as cited by Ó Cathasaigh (1996, 61).

9   McCone (1990, 5, 13, 17); Gantz (1981, intro.).

10   Thurneysen (1921, 188).

11   Carney (1955), preceded unnoticed by Ó Briain (1947, 34).

Christian Ireland in the biblical image of those who worshipped other gods than Yahweh. The writers were 'unenthusiastic' towards paganism,[12] but nevertheless used its imagery to represent the old order, as the Jewish priesthood does in the NT. The same scribes had earlier begun the composition of saint's *Lives* following continental models, set in the same historical frame, but representing the biblical hero.[13] Carney shows that Adomnán's *Life of Columba* and other ecclesiastical writings came, with the Bible, to influence the sagas, and the entire early Irish literary corpus.[14] Thus the sagas are not reliable or comprehensive guides to pre-Christian religion in Ireland, though they may serve to evince some of its features. Similarly, pagan features of the *Lives* which may have been derived from the sagas, may themselves turn out to be features gained from the Christian interpretation of Irish pagan religion in this Greek and/or biblical/ecclesiastical conformation.[15]

The 'nativist' theory, however, remains influential. In the 1986 revision of her earlier work on pagan Celts, Anne Ross records

> ...such was the longevity and strength of the oral tradition in Celtic society, where information was handed on by a professional class of tradition-bearers trained in the art, that when the native tradition was finally committed to writing under the aegis of the Christian church, it contained memories of a more archaic world which can be seen to be valid and reliable.[16]

Heathen Mythology in Plummer's *Vitae Sanctorum Hiberniae*

As I note above, more recent scholars caution against treating the whole corpus as uniform in both the processes involved in delivering the received text to us, and what it portrays or betrays. I wish to examine Plummer's substantial contribution in this light.

The assertion of Plummer, that comparison of marvellous motifs in the sagas with similar marvellous motifs in the *Lives* suggests a common source in pagan religious belief and practice, is unchallenged. In his introduction to *Vitae Sanctorum Hiberniae,*

---

12   McCone's intentional understatement (1990, 7).
13   Thurneysen (1921, 188).
14   Carney (1955, 35f.).
15   Thus the interplay between secular saga and Christian tale remains a current field of investigation. See e.g. Binchy (1982); Carney (1983); McCone (1984) and (1990); Mac Cana (1986ab); Picard (1989). McCone confirms and develops Carney's hypothesis in relation to Christian influence on the sagas. That there are common themes in the two genres is established; the question of the major vector of influence remains in debate. The specific question of the nature and function of the marvellous in these tales is my interest here.
16   Ross (1986, 26).

published in 1910, Plummer attempts to lay down the foundation of documentary evidence for the suggestion of MacCulloch and others that the source and explanation of the marvellous in the Irish *Lives* is to be found in the mythology of the secular Irish saga materials.[17] He collects an extensive set of references to illustrate and undergird this hypothesis, which has retained currency since its publication. Part five of Plummer's introduction is entitled 'Heathen Folk-Lore and Mythology in the Lives of Celtic Saints'. He asserts the impossibility of understanding the *Lives* without knowledge of the secular literature. The section is a collection of categories of miracles and stories from Irish *Lives*, including Adomnán's *Life of Columba*, hence his relevance here.[18] He cites parallels in secular literature where found. These parallels are not as common as one might be led to expect, and in fact he criticizes others for excessive finding of pagan motifs in Christian literature.[19] However, they form a useful and unique body of evidence with which we can engage in this exploration.

Plummer gives the references from the *Lives* in his collection as examples of both the uniform occurrence of marvellous motifs in pagan and Christian sources, and of the way in which pagan influence has affected the recording of the saints' *Lives*. He identifies the effects partly as un-Christian morality, with which we are not primarily concerned here, but mainly as the uncritical adoption of pagan mythological supernaturalism. The concept evinced by Plummer continues to be read into Adomnán's account of Columba. Many of the *Lives* do have what might look like saga-based stories. Ó Briain, Binchy and Picard have demonstrated this clearly. Watson bases his analysis of the relationship between the 'Celtic' Church and paganism on Plummer.[20] Drawing analogies between *VC* reports of Scottish druidism with the (Christian) *Vita Tripartita*, and the (secular) *Táin Bó Cúalnge,* and *Death of the Sons of Uisneach*, he presents the occupation of the Druid's position as key to the success of the Christian mission. This conflict, Watson says, influenced and coloured the account of the miracles ascribed to Columba, 'most' of which are 'decidedly not' inspired by scripture.[21] MacInnes mentions

---

17   *VSH*, cxxix-cxcii.
18   Now see D.A. Bray (1992).
19   *VSH*, clxxxviii and note 7.
20   Ó Briain (1947), Binchy (1982), Picard (1985), Watson (1915).
21   Watson (1915, 273-4). He cites five examples: the stake [ii.37], sailing against contrary wind [ii.34], abating of storm [ii.13], unwetable book [ii.8,9], salt unaffected by fire [ii.7], and Watson says, 'He is also a prophet and a clairvoyant' (274), mentioning the Gregorian influence, and the Oswald prophesy (see chapter 4 below). Watson calls fasting 'pure paganism' (277), an astonishing assertion in the light of Christian scripture and tradition. He cites

the blend of pagan and Christian religion. He cites two 'breastplate poems', one 'of St Patrick', and another which he calls a pagan invocation. He cites their translator as saying: 'one is a Christian breastplate with druid ornamentation, while the other is a druid breastplate with Christian ornamentation'. MacInnes notices a growth in sceptical ambivalence towards what he calls preternatural phenomena in the Gaeltacht from the eighteenth century onwards. He specifically mentions *precognition* as sanctified foreknowledge, which had been accepted as a Christian miracle, and *clairvoyance*, distinguished by its connection with the powers of darkness.[22] John McQueen names Columba a 'Celtic Seer'.[23] Plummer presents the marvellous in the *Lives* as substantially pagan, i.e. pagan marvels with Christian ornamentation. I wish to pursue the possibility that rather they were substantially Christian, i.e. they contain survivals of a genuine (to Adomnán) spiritual 'power encounter' with pagan religion.

In the first major re-visitation of Plummer's work, Sharpe comments on the then contemporary criticism of the study of heathen folkloric and mythological aspects of the saints' *Lives*. He believes their criticism may have been partly motivated by the prevailing attitudes to holiness and the holy life amongst early twentieth-century critics, an attitude which Sharpe suggests would have been quite alien to seventh-ninth century authors of the *Lives*.[24] It could be, however, that he himself comes under the influence of the interpretation Plummer suggests. In his recent translation of Adomnán's *Life of Columba*, Sharpe occasionally adopts the English term 'clairvoyantly' to translate Adomnán's various terms for prophecy.[25] In this he diverges from all of his predecessors and his

---

an example of what he calls Adomnán's rejection of a tale of pagan 'wave knowledge' which is recorded in the Irish *Life*, 'which supplied Adomnán with much of his material' (278). He calls Adomnán's rejection of the tale 'instructive.' While we now know the Irish *Life* was not Adomnán's source, the tradition from which he did select eventually produced it, and Watson's observation of Adomnán's selectivity is worth noting.

22 MacInnes (1982, 225f.).

23 John McQueen (1989). Given the historic note by the writer of 1 Sam 9:9 ('for he that is now called a Prophet was beforetime called a Seer'), this title may be seen to be particularly anachronistic for a Christian presbyter, unless, again, the author is suggesting Columba's prophecy was pagan clairvoyance (see note 125, chap. 1 above).

24 Sharpe (1991, 388).

25 'said clairvoyantly' for *prophetice profatur* (i.17); 'clairvoyantly described' for *praedicta* (i.28), and 'clairvoyantly said' for *profetizans ait* (i.35). He also describes Columba's prophecy as clairvoyance on p.16, and notes 133 and 265. In this he emulates Picard (1981, 95), who derived the term from Mac Cana, a 'Nativist'.

own practice elsewhere in the translation, but with no obvious contextual requirement. I wish to suggest that although the choice might simply be to add variety, the term brings with it a field of interpretive meaning to the translation and commentary which is more associated with pagan religious categories. It is thus perhaps a little uncomfortable in the context of a Christian 'biography', unless perhaps the biography is, indeed, using pagan marvellous phenomena to establish the saint's repute.[26]

My aim here is to explore the literary evidence supporting the theory that pagan supernaturalism influenced Adomnán. The particular usefulness of *VC* in this context is its reliability as an early witness, as I have outlined in my introduction; it thus provides a firm seventh-century 'snapshot' of the development of the tradition.

Plummer attempts to determine 'what elements in these lives are derived from the mythology and folk-lore of Celtic heathenism which preceded the introduction of Christianity.'[27] He claims that the advantage of examining the whole group of *Lives* and comparing similar elements is that whole groups of miracles and legends find a common explanation as derivations from pre-Christian pagan mythology, and thus we can explain away some of the 'offensive' elements such as excessive thaumaturgy in some of the *Lives*.

> Moreover, by means of this comparison many things in these lives, which at first sight naturally cause offence, find an explanation, if not an excuse of which those who are jealous for the honour of the Celtic saints may be glad to avail themselves.[28]

In other words he wished to defend the reputation of the saints. He also wants to use these abstracted elements to throw light on the

---

26 In ii.11; ii.32; ii.33 and 34, Sharpe chooses the term 'wizard' to translate Adomnán's *magus*. Here he is in mixed company, with APF and F choosing 'druid', and AA choosing the near equivalent 'magician.' (MacCulloch records that the modern Irish term *drui* means 'sorcerer'). Here he introduces a magical element to the naming of the pagan holy men, where it no doubt fits the context, but differentiates the Pictish *magi* from those in Ireland, where the term may signify wise or knowing ones. That part of their knowledge may be called magic does not mean that the performance of magic is their whole function; they were also teachers and advisors. Ross speculates the loss of their political advisory and teaching function as the Christian mission developed (1986, 115).

27 *VSH*, iv. He later notes the stress laid by Thomas Wright (1844) on the close connexion of saint's legends and fairy tales (clxxxi note 8).

28 *VSH*, iv. Binchy was likewise troubled by the inheritance by Patrick of 'disagreeable characteristics of the very druids who were overthrown by him' (1962, 58). McCone notes this, but observes 'the fact is, however, that there was a ready supply of biblical models...' citing Moses, Elijah and Elisha (1990, 195).

mythology that putatively spawned them. Plummer adopts Harnack's opinion of the growth of the church in Asia Minor for Ireland, 'without the alteration of one word.'

> Heathenism was absorbed without any violent conflict. It disappears, in order to reappear, proportionately strong, in the Church. Nowhere else did the conquest and 'uprooting' of heathenism cause so little difficulty. It was, in fact, not uprooted, only modified.[29]

He says that there are few records of conflict,[30] and no martyrs in Ireland, suggesting this to be due to the clan system where the chief adopted the new faith, carrying the masses who retained their old faith under a veneer of politically necessary Christianity. He observes that conversion takes time fully to transform even individuals and that the early Irish clergy as a group were tolerant of heathen literature and its mythology. This led to a retention of heathen elements within the new faith. Plummer appears to be saying here that the distinction normally drawn between the popular Christianity of the masses who follow their chief in nominal conversion, and the Christianity presented by its leaders and recorders is not seen in Ireland.[31] The Christian leaders and authors are as unconscious of their continued heathenism as are the illiterate masses.

Here we reach the central tenet of Plummer's understanding. It is the familiarity of the Christian scribes with the sagas (Plummer does not distinguish the oral from the written form) that leads them to incorporate pagan tales into their Christian writings. The sagas often incorporated saints and other Christian motifs, 'with a fine disregard for chronology and morality.'[32] He goes on to state, articulating the belief we are here probing

> Much greater was the influence of secular story on ecclesiastical legends.[33]

He remains in some doubt as to whether whole classes of miracles (resuscitation, transmutation, multiplication, tongues, walking on

---

29   Harnack (1902, 42), as quoted and cited in *VSH*, cxxx note 3. I quote it again in full here because of its importance in my later discussion of Plummer's preconceptions as he approaches this work.

30   Though later in part five he says: 'In all the legends which have anything to do with the beginnings of Christianity in Ireland the druids meet us at every turn as the chief, if not the only, opponents of the new faith.' This appears to be at variance with his point here concerning the lack of opposition.

31   See Cameron (1991), for a critique of this distinction.

32   *VSH*, cxxxi-ii.

33   *VSH*, cxxxii. I have displayed this small, absolutely key quote to give it the emphasis I believe it has in Plummer's thought.

water) are secular, or Christian. 'Often we can feel pretty sure that in spite of ecclesiastical assimilation, the substratum comes from popular tradition.'[34] This influence came by direct importation, conscious imitation, and unconscious permeation. His debt to Delehaye is made explicit: the sameness of the miracles in the *Lives* of saints is largely due to the sameness of the folk-tales to which they are related.[35]

Plummer summarized his view of pagan Celtic religion

> Celtic heathenism seems to have consisted of two main elements: a system of nature worship with departmental gods, of whom the sun and fire god was the chief; and a system of magic, or Druidism.

He traces the former to the Celtic in-comers, and the latter to the pre-Aryan inhabitants.[36] He focuses his description of Celtic nature-worship on what he calls the influence of the *solar* cult. Plummer identifies certain 'solar saints', who manifest features of this 'solar cult' of the Celts. These often have a name including 'Lug' the sun deity, and include in their stories: fiery manifestations, heavenly light, face of blazing flame, extinguishing or kindling fire.[37] Plummer suggests animal stories may be associated with the solar cult, including relationships, savings, and wolves. He says (without justification)

> It is clear that the ideas underlying these stories go back to a time when no hard and fast line was drawn between men and animals...[38]

He also identifies influences of a Celtic water deity, predominantly among southern Irish saints. They walk on water, produce animals from it, record a submarine city, and produce fountains.[39] The cult of sacred trees is also represented, as is the 'pre-Aryan' cult of stones.[40]

Magicians and druids from the sagas and *Lives,* Plummer claims, are part of an older tradition.[41] He draws a close comparison between the activities of the druids and what he calls the derivative Christian

---

34   *VSH*, cxxxiii.
35   *VSH*, cxxxiii, note 1, citing Delehaye (1905, 29-30). Given the discrete range of marvellous phenomena in both secular and Christian record, it is difficult to conceive of how this could be otherwise.
36   *VSH*, cxxxiii. It is worth noting Plummer's acceptance here of the prevailing view of Irish pre-history which was based on a reading of the sagas as records of pre-Christian history.
37   *VSH*, cxxxvi ff. McCone (1990, 57) notes from Thompson (1946) that Andrew Lang debunked the theory, but that it remained an influence on O'Rahilly (1946). See McCone's chapter 7, 'Fire and the Arts'.
38   *VSH*, cxli ff.
39   *VSH*, cxlvii f.
40   *VSH*, clii-clvii.
41   Plummer here follows Bertrand (1897).

sancti.[42] Both held court positions: he cites numerous examples where druids and clergy are together serving in the courts of rulers as advisors and confessors. He denies the victory of the spiritual over the magical; people saw only the triumph of a more powerful sort of magic.[43] Intellectual knowledge was wisdom and power.[44] Both druids and clerics acted as prophets, foretelling the future, and often communicating in poetry.[45] The druid was a 'clairvoyant' with second sight, the Christian saw absent events 'in the spirit',[46] and both remotely detect and punish crime.[47] They both have extended hearing and voice and both are recorded as being involved in 'sight shifting' or 'ocular illusion' e.g. bull's milk and recovery.[48] Miracles, which he calls fairy tales,[49] include the iron knife of *VC* ii.29, and the stake of *VC* ii.37; vermin expulsion, e.g. of snakes, is compared with druidic delousing.[50] Plummer believes angels replace the fairies, 'the most favoured of all [in receiving visitations of angels] being saint Columba'.[51] Stones are printed, holed by a finger, used in healing; cursing stones occur in only one life.[52] Plummer believes the maledictory character of some saints probably derives from druids, though he acknowledges Bede mentioning it of the saints specifically.[53]

A Question of Origins

I want to investigate whether Plummer's explanation has adequately considered the possibility that the marvels in the *Lives* might have a more demonstrable origin, function and nature than pagan religion. Indicating the line we will pursue, Meek stated recently

---

42   *VSH*, clix.
43   *VSH*, clxvii. Binchy sees a similar progression; Patrick 'beats them at their own game, for he wins by "bigger and better magic" '(1962, 58). This is no more than the apostles do (Acts 8:9f; 16:16). Whether Patrick or Adomnán would accept this description of God's power as magic is questionable.
44   *VSH*, clxvi.
45   *VSH*, clxii ff, see note 6 on foretelling the future of individuals; clxx note 7 recording the *Amra* claim that no company ever reached Columba without his foreknowing (*RC*, xx.140).
46   *VSH*, clxx. Here, in drawing the parallel, Plummer makes the distinction.
47   *VSH*, clxvii, cf. *VC* i.22,41,46.
48   *VSH*, clix and clxix; *VC* ii.17.
49   *VSH*, clxxxiv.
50   *VSH*, clxx; *VC* ii.28, iii.23.
51   *VSH*, clxxxi-ii.
52   *VSH*, clv ff. Plummer gives no secular parallel for the stone in *VC* ii.33.
53   *VSH*, cxxxv and clxxiii f. citing *HE* ii.260. Again, see McCone (1990, 195f.), note 16 above. Other parallels include: sleep (clxxii f.); soul travel; Bachall (clxxiv); pastoral staff used variously cf. bell; taboos (clxxxiii).

> It is... evident that writers are now rather less inclined to find parallels
> for the visions and miracles of the saints in the alleged paganism of the
> Celtic past, and are turning more effectively, and in my view more fairly,
> to the Bible.[54]

A more subtle question still regards the line which the investigator
draws between what may be described as acceptably 'Christian' and
what, in contradistinction, must be regarded as essentially pagan. The
lines are often difficult to draw, and may change with time and
locality, and especially with the view of the observer. Due to the
richness of the collection, an exhaustive analysis would be beyond
the scope of this project, and beyond its direct interest. However,
Plummer does refer to the *VC* specifically at various points, drawing
comparisons and giving parallels to the pagan mythological
phenomena he distinguishes. I wish to proceed to review this
collection of cross-references to assess the validity of his hypothesis
of the pagan origin and nature of marvellous phenomena as it applies
to *VC* specifically.

A second delimiter is to disregard Plummer's very many cross-
references to other *Lives* of saints and Christian writings. He makes
the point that his broad approach is more 'scientific' in tracing
common themes and motifs in the whole genre, thus dispensing with
the laborious need to explain individual phenomena as in Baring-
Gould's work, and giving a macro-explanation to each class of
phenomenon. However, citation of a supernatural phenomenon in
other Christian *Lives* cannot be accepted as exemplifying pagan
influence in *VC*, no matter how close the parallelism, unless there is
both convincing evidence proving a pagan source for the other
Christian text, and the influence of this text on the *VC*.[55] Often, the
natures of Plummer's parallels are not clear without detailed
knowledge of his sources.

An example of Plummer's citation of parallels which turn out to
be Christian comes in his description of the druids. In reference to
the 'druidic hedge', he cites *AU* 560; *RC* xvii.144; *LS* xxviiif; and

---

54   Meek (1997, 54-55).
55   Dating of the composition of the *Vitae* edited in Plummer's collection has yet
    to be established, with the exception of the *Vitae Brigidae* in Sharpe's edition
    (1991), and *VSS Ailbe, Ciarán and Déclán*, Sharpe (1989, 396). However, the
    documentary witnesses of the remainder appear to be late, thus at this stage it
    would appear unlikely to be able to place their composition with any
    confidence as being before *VC*. What *is* readily apparent in examining
    Plummer's collected references is that various motifs do recur in the *Lives*, and
    that some of these same motifs appear in some of the secular sagas, as we shall
    see.

Silva Gadelica i.79.[56] All four are in fact Christian sources. *RC* xvii.144 refers to Columba's prayer for the mist to lift at the battle of Cúl Drebene in the *Annals of Tigernach* (*AU* 560). There seems little need for the mist here to be anything other than natural. Columba's reference to his 'druid' is his often noticed metaphorical designation for Christ, and not a reference to an actual pagan priest. The texts cited from *Silva Gadelica* and *LS* are both of the twelfth century Irish homiletic *Life of Columba*. As such, they demonstrate only the commonplace nature of this motif in Christian writing. There is a clear parallel from here with the druidic mist of *VC* ii.34, not noted by Plummer. The saga record of a similar phenomenon leads Plummer to reason that the Christian sources have been influenced by the (earlier) pagan sources, thus corroborating his theory.

The ethical dimension provides a form of the correlative evidence I mention, in that its character is taken to show pagan influence on the writers. But unless it is demonstrably present at each point of the particular reference, and is in direct relationship to a particular supernatural manifestation, affecting its character by, for instance, giving it a pagan source of power, or an ethical outcome which was indefensible for a Christian miracle, it is perhaps difficult to identify other supernatural phenomena albeit in the same literary source, as pagan in origin.

Some of Plummer's sources are suspect in other ways, e.g. Kuno Meyer says of *Silva Gadelica*, 'It is impossible to use the book with any degree of confidence either for linguistic or for other purposes...'[57] Thus while the references are in themselves interesting, and show the presence of such stories in the later literary traditions, they cannot be adduced as evidence for the pagan origin of stories in the *VC*. It is, conversely, in so far as it is reliable, evidence for later Christian belief regarding a contest with pagan religion which took place as the faith was introduced into the Provinces.

Late Oral Secular Sources Cited by Plummer with a Parallel in the VC

Plummer's evidence may be divided into two broad categories. The first is that collected mainly from oral sources in more recent times, especially during the surge of popularity of folk-tale collection in the nineteenth century. One example of such comes in Plummer's

---

56   *VSH,* clxi, note 1. This example serves to illustrate both the need to be able to interpret Plummer's code, and why the numbers of references to secular sources are fewer than at first one might suppose.

57   Meyer (1894, 122).

section on 'second sight'.[58] He cites an example from Rhys' *Celtic Folklore* of the transfer by physical contact of 'the faculty of vision...magically or miraculously extended.'[59] This fairy story tells of a farmer of Deinant, near Aberdaron in North Wales, who was visited by a member of the *Tylwyth Teg* while relieving himself outside his front door. Touched by the visitor, the farmer is shown his fairy mansion beneath the location, never before seen, and asked to stop the nightly flood. The farmer is so ready to oblige that he bricks up the door, and from then on, uses the back door as his main entrance. This is evidently a clear secular example of the phenomenon of 'second sight', and of the mode of transmission of the gift (see discussion below). The phenomenon of such visionary revelations, though differing in actual content, form a significant section of Adomnán's account of the prophetic ministry of Columba. Plummer mentions from *VC* only i.1 and i.43.[60]

Rhys collected his tale from Evan Williams, a smith of Yr Ardd Las, Rhos Hirwaen, in the late nineteenth century. It is thus chronologically remote, and is from another, albeit 'Celtic', land. The question of precedence is unequivocal: *VC* is the earlier witness. The question of a demonstrable provenance for the tale anterior to the farmer is in all probability unanswerable, and remains firmly within the realm of speculation. That Adomnán could have derived his category of what he calls 'declaring absent things to those present'[61] from this tale is so improbable that the evidence cannot be taken seriously. Plummer cites numerous such sources in connection

---

58 *VSH*, clxx-clxxi.
59 Rhys (1901, i.230); *VSH*, clxxi note 9.
60 In the note following (clxxi note 10), Plummer refers to the phenomenon extended to the envisioning of the whole world. He cites *VC* i.1 and i.43, the two accounts of Columba's Gregorian explanation of this gift, with a parallel from Grimm (1883, i.136). Grimm traces the record from Paul the Deacon and others of the characteristic of the supreme Teutonic deity Wuotan looking down from his throne and seeing the whole earth (135). This prospect is only afforded from the seat, and may be enjoyed by others there seated. Grimm makes it clear that this is a commonplace in folk literature, is a 'god-like' attribute, and has links but not precise parallels in the Bible (136). The throne is clearly not significant to this ability in *VC*; Columba is depicted as exercising the gift in various places. God-like attribute it may be, but, as we shall see in chapter 4 below, the Christian system had a sophisticated explanation of its nature and function. Grimm is cited variously by Plummer. The citations refer to parallel manifestations in the pagan Teutonic traditions, and as Plummer's critics made clear, show only the commonplace nature of the motifs in folk mythology. In the attempt to limit the scope of this inquiry to pagan Irish sources, I will not further consider them.
61 *VC* i.1:10a.

with the *VC*.[62] The accumulated evidence does build a clear picture of the presence of the categories of phenomena he illustrates with it in (nineteenth-century) folklore. The similarity between these accounts and many in the *Lives* of saints, including Columba, is accepted. The longevity of the tales of the phenomena into modern folklore may also be accepted. However, none of these tales can be adduced to demonstrate anything of the influence on sixth-seventh century writers, nor of the origins or nature of the tales of the phenomena. For this, we must pass on to assess the second category of Plummer's evidence.

Late Literary Secular Sources Cited by Plummer with Parallels in the VC

LATE TEXTS

Parallels from sources whose codification is reckoned to be late, and whose extant documentary evidence is more or less secure, are fewer. For some types of phenomena in tales from each group, Plummer draws a direct parallel with the *VC*. Others have parallels, but Plummer does not note them. I have examined and quoted the editions cited by Plummer. That there are parallels to be observed with *VC* will be shown in the following examples.

Keating

(a) Plummer cites Keating's *History* in a short section regarding the expulsion of vermin. He cites *VC* ii.28 and iii.23 as parallels. In Keating's account of the journeying of Niul to Egypt from Scythia, a serpent bit Gaedheal son of Niul, ancestor of the Irish nation. Niul takes his son to Moses, who heals him by applying the rod he held in his hand. *VC* parallels are evident.

---

62 *VSH*, clxxxix-cxcii. I record here for the sake of completeness the modern publications with which Plummer associates tales from the *VC* to which I do not refer elsewhere: M. Martin (1716), *A Description of the Western Isles*, 2nd ed.; Andrew Lang (1887/1906), *Myth, Ritual and Religion*, 2 vols; W.G. Wood-Martin (1895), *Pagan Ireland, an Archaeological Sketch*; (1902), *Traces of the Elder Faiths of Ireland*; P.D. Hardy (1836), *Holy Wells of Ireland*. Hardy published various works opposing the restoration of Roman Catholicism in Ireland, e.g. *Ireland in 1846-7: A Consideration of the recent rapid growth of Popery; with suggestions for remedying the evil and for promoting the moral and spiritual improvement of the people, (1847)*. A possible motive of Plummer the Anglican in resisting the acceptance of the marvels in relation to the Irish saints could be to undermine the restoration; this publication of Hardy would appear to confirm the existence of this resistance in one of the authors we know Plummer to have used sympathetically, though we can only conjecture that he might have read this particular tract.

Moses said that in what place soever the stock of that youth would settle, there no serpent would ever have venom, and this is verified in Crete... in which some of his posterity are; it is without serpents as Ireland is. And although there were serpents in Ireland up to the coming of Patrick, I do not think they had venom; or I imagine it is the demons that are called serpents in the Life of Patrick.[63]

[Columba] tried to comfort them as far as might be, and raising both his holy hands he blessed all this island of ours, and said, 'From this moment of this hour, all poisons of snakes shall be powerless to harm men or cattle in the lands of this island, so long as the inhabitants of that dwelling-place shall observe the commandments of Christ' (*VC* ii.28).

After which, still sitting in the wagon, he turned his face to the east, and blessed the island, with the islanders its inhabitants. And from then to the present day, as has been written in the above-mentioned book, the poison of three-forked tongues of vipers has not been able to do any injury to either man or beast (*VC* iii.23:125a).

(b) In his section referring to the cult of fountains, Plummer cites a tale from Keating of the magical production of a fountain from a rock.[64] He includes *VC* ii.10 as an example of a similar phenomenon by a different means. Cormac, King of the Ulaid had

...druids from Alba with him there, who practiced magic against the King of Munster... the King of Munster was obliged to send for Moga Ruith, a druid...[he] threw up into the air a magic spear which he had, and in the place in which the spear fell there burst forth a well of spring water.[65]

...because water was not to be found anywhere near, (Columba) turned aside to a rock close by, bowed his knees, and prayed for a little while. And rising after his prayer, he blessed the face of the rock, from which thereupon water flowed in an abundant cascade (*VC* ii.10).

O'Flaherty

Plummer cites *VC* ii.17 as an example of what he terms 'sight shifting' and gives a tale in *Iar-Connaught* as a parallel.[66] Plummer's reference here is to the notes appended to O'Flaherty by James Hardiman on 'The Craft of Evil Spirits'. In the text, O'Flaherty is referring to the enchanted isle of O'Brazil (*Beg-Ara* or Lesser Aran). He says

---

63   Keating (1908, I:XV = *ITS* VIII:19), from *VSH,* clxx note 3.
64   *VSH,* cxlix-clii, cl note 3.
65   Keating (1908, II:321); *VSH,* cl note 9.
66   *VSH,* clxix notes 1 and 9 referring to O'Flaherty (1846, 261 note u) by James Hardiman. Plummer misses Reeves' (1857, 126-7) reference to a reminiscent story in St Fechin's *Life* (Colgan, *Acta SS.,* 131a).

> Whether it be reall and firm land, kept hidden by speciall ordinances of
> God as the terrestiall paradise, or else some illusion of airy clouds
> appearing on the surface of the sea, or the craft of evil spirits, is more
> than our judgments can sound out.

In elucidation, Hardiman notices the 'art magic' of Mannanán Mac
Lir, first ruler of Man, from what he calls 'The Old Statute Book of
Man'

> He kept the land under mists by his necromancy. If he dreaded an enemy,
> he would of one man cause to seem one hundred.

He notes that William Sacheverall, Governor of Man, states that the
Manx nation place Mac Lir about the beginning of the fifth century,
thus he predates Columba.[67] Plummer's parallel from *VC,* ii.17, tells
of a sorcerer (*maleficus)* who is commanded to draw milk from a bull
by his diabolic art. Columba then reveals the true nature of the milk
as blood 'bleached by the imposture of demons to deceive mankind'
and heals the bull which has been bled near to death.

COMMENTARY ON LATE TEXTS

Keating

While we can readily accept the parallelism Plummer observes in
Keating for *VC,* the problem of chronology is acute. The edition of
Keating cited by Plummer was based on a manuscript written
ca.1645.[68] Keating finished his work around 1634, having gathered
his material from manuscripts then in circulation. Many are now
lost, so critical comment on the work is difficult. Thus nearly 1000
years separates his collection from that of Adomnán. The origin
legend is here clearly being linked to the Judao-Christian tradition,
and so in this form is heavily Christianized, and thus must post-date
the introduction of the faith to Ireland. Plummer says

> The classical instance is, of course, Patrick expelling serpents and other
> reptiles from Ireland, c.f. Tr.Th. p.102. But Columba did the like for
> Iona, Adamn. ii.28, iii.23...[69]

The writer of Keating's story refers to a *Life of Patrick.* The
earliest extant reference to this tale of snakes is that of Jocelyn,
compiled after 1185.[70] Thus the writer of this section of the Niul
myth is likely to have been writing later than these traditions, and
arguably after Jocelyn. Plummer does not notice the chronological

---

67   O'Flaherty (1846, 261 note u), referring to Sacheverall (1702, 20).
68   Keating (1908, II:xiii).
69   *VSH,* clxx note 3.
70   Fowler (1894, xxxii), referring to *Tr.Th.,* 102. *Vitae* II and IV are eleventh, and
       III ante-twelfth century (Lapidge and Sharpe, 1985, 107)), and do not have it.

disparity between *VC* of the seventh, and Keating of the twelfth century. The chronology makes it difficult for Adomnán to have been influenced by this version of the myth. All we are left with is evidence of a motif from an early Christian *Life* turning up in a late secular myth.

Now, if the tradition records an oral myth which had been extant in the seventh century, it is of course possible that Adomnán could have known it.[71] Is there circumstantial evidence of influence? The stories differ in important detail. For protection to be maintained on Iona, the commandments of Christ as distinct from those of Moses will need to be followed. (Here is a further sign of monastic composition placing pre-Christian Ireland in parallel with Old Testament history.) The protection appears to have been limited to Iona, and not to extend across a whole territory of influence, as with Gaedheal or Patrick.

Moses' prophecy over Gaedheal in the Irish origin myth is that serpents in Ireland would not have venom, and eventually results in the total absence of serpents from Ireland from Patrick's time onward.[72] Adomnán by contrast, and more subtly in line with the habit of venomous serpents, records the inability of the venom of serpents to harm man or beast on Iona after Columba's blessing. His story accepts the presence of venomous serpents on Iona, and their retention of venom which is necessary for their own habit. (Naturally-venomous serpents deprived of their venom could not survive naturally.) Divine protection against the harmful effect of this venom on man or cattle, the latter being important to the insular economy, is prophesied. This has a completely different point from both Keating's author and Jocelyn. The habit of the Ionan venomous serpent is not interrupted; his presence is not terminated; only the effect of a strike on an animal not normally prey to the serpent is affected. We thus have not only a more subtle tale, but one with a clear precedent in a tradition which certainly preceded Adomnán, and which we can be virtually certain he would have known

> And these signs will accompany those who believe: in my name they will cast out demons; they will speak in new tongues; they will pick up serpents, and if they drink any deadly thing, it will not hurt them (Mk. 16:17-18//). Behold, I have given you authority to tread upon serpents

---

71 I am not aware of any earlier record of this redaction of this story of Niul than Keating, but it is this redaction to which Plummer refers, and thus this which I address.

72 See my further discussion below, chapter 3. Sharpe (1995, note 276) notes Gregory's equivalent of this motif for Florentius (*Dial* 3:15), and see Hilary, *Life of Honoratus* (Hoare, 1954, §15:260).

and scorpions, and over all the power of the enemy; and nothing shall hurt you (Lk. 10:19).

Paul had gathered a bundle of sticks and put them on the fire, when a viper came out because of the heat and fastened on his hand. When the natives saw the creature hanging from his hand, they said to one another, 'No doubt this man is a murderer. Though he has escaped from the sea, justice has not allowed him to live.' He, however, shook off the creature into the fire and suffered no harm (Acts 28:3-5).

These NT eschatological features are in turn pre-figured by OT prophecy.

The wolf and the lamb shall feed together, the lion shall eat straw like the ox; and dust shall be the serpent's food. They shall not hurt or destroy in all my holy mountain, says the LORD (Isa. 65:25).

Though here the exact fate of the serpent does not anticipate *VC*, the general eschatological prophecy with the reference to its geographical situation 'on my holy mountain' may have had a certain resonance for those staying on the flanks of *Dùn Í*. The island itself may, in common with monastic islands elsewhere (e.g. Lérins) and the monasteries themselves, have been regarded as an expression of the new Zion.[73]

Keating's second reference regarding the spear and the spring likewise suggest a strong biblical precedent, as Plummer himself concedes. He observes in reference to a similar phenomenon in the *Life of Ailbe* that 'the biblical parallel of Moses smiting the rock has clearly been at work.'[74] If for the writer of Ailbe's *Life*, perhaps also for Keating's source? All that can safely be accepted here is that traditions concerning snakes and water occur in both Christian and secular/pagan traditions. Keating cannot be accepted as authority for pagan borrowings or influence in *VC*. That the Christian biblical tradition acts as source for Adomnán is both chronologically and circumstantially suggested, and there is a possibility that the Christian tradition as represented in Jocelyn might *on the contrary* have influenced Keating's author.

O'Flaherty

In Plummer's reference to O'Flaherty, Hardiman notes a reference to Manannán in Cormac's *Glossary*, which reads

---

73   This conjecture will be followed up as we proceed.
74   *VSH* cl note 2. Again I am not aware of an earlier redaction of this tale in alternative sources which would help with the chronological question.

He used to know by studying the heavens (i.e. using the sky) the period which would be fine weather and the bad weather, and when each of the two times would change.[75]

The Annals of the Four Masters records Cormac's death in 903 (AU 908). His entry can be interpreted as giving the impression that Manannán used omens to foretell the weather, but this is not necessary. It could be his skill as an early weather forecaster that is being noted. While the parallel tale of the bull in *VC* has no direct biblical antecedent, there is no lack of biblical background by which the account could be inspired. Moses' encounter with the Pharaoh's magicians (*malefici* in Vulgate) sees a river turned to blood both by Moses and by the incantations of the magicians (Ex. 7:19ff). This is not described as illusion, but it is an example of the phenomenon. The prophet Ezekiel delivered a promise of freedom from the snare of magic charms (Ezek. 13:20); it is thus possible that Adomnán had Ezekiel's freedom from the snares of magic charms in mind as he wrote of the exposure of demonic deceit in the blood of the bull. Acts 8:11 records the ending of the bewitching influence of the Samaritan *magus* Simon,[76] though notably here it is described as having been ended by the agency of preaching the kingdom of God, and Simon only saw the *signa et virtutes maximas* after he began to follow Philip, whereas in *VC*, it is the prophetic insight and the truth-revealing blessing of Columba which confounds the sorceries. Conversely, Cormac had adequate scriptural background in, for instance, Elijah's reading the clouds (1 Kgs. 18:43-46), and precedent in Columba reading the pestiferous clouds in *VC* ii.4.

Earlier Secular Sources

EARLIER TEXTS

We now proceed to assess Plummer's references to nine textual references with *VC* parallels, and additional sources to which he makes no direct link, all of which have earlier textual authority. I have grouped them where possible as they deal with three sets of manifestations of the marvellous.

Healing Wells

In his section on fountains, Plummer refers to *VC* ii.11 as an example of making wholesome a noxious 'fountain'. He does not say if 'wholesome' includes healing, though Adomnán does. He goes on to

---

75   *Sanas Cormaic* ed. Stokes, tr. O'Donovan (1868).
76   Simon also appears extensively in the NT Apocrypha, well known to the early 'Celtic' writers.

refer further to the healing properties of fountains, with three secular parallels:[77]

The Battle of Mag Tuired (Cath Maige Tuired)

In a mythical contest between the Tuath Dé Danaan and the Fomorians, the narrative describes a well over which Diari-cecht, his two sons, and his daughter sang spells.

> Their mortally wounded men were cast into it... they were alive (when) they would come out. Their mortally wounded became whole through the might of the chant of the four leeches who were about the well.[78]

Dindsenchas

In the opinion of the author of the quoted section of the prose *Dindsenchas*, 'Loch Dergdeirc' received its name when Ferchertre of the Ulaid took the eyes of Eochaid, King of Munster. Eochaid went to wash in the well

> ...and as he dipt his head thrice under the water all the well became red. Then because of the miracle of generosity...both his eyes came to the king, and as he looked on the well he said: 'A red hollow *[derg derc]* is this hollow, and this will be every one's name for it.' Whence Loch Dergdeirc is said.[79]

The Battle of Ventry (Cath Finntrágha)

This tale from the Finn cycle refers to the three daughters of Terg mic Dolair from Tiberias in the east. They say they have come to help Finn and his army against the king of Spain.

> 'Our help to thee will be good,' said they, 'for we shall form a druidical host around thee from the stalks of... and from the top of the watercress, and though armies and multitudes be killed around thee, they will cry to the foreigners, and beat their weapons out of their hands, and take away their strength and their sight. And the King of Spain and 400 of his people will be killed by thee, and the battle of Ventry will be fought a day and a year, and there will be fresh fighting in it every day during that time. And be thou of good cheer, for if even thou art killed every day, thou wilt be whole again in the morning, for we shall have the well of healing for thee, and the warrior that thou lovest best of all the Fianns of Erinn shall obtain the same as thou.'[80]

---

77   *VSH*, cl notes 9 and 14, noting. *VC* ii.11.
78   *VSH*, cl note 14, citing *RC* xii.94 = *Cath Maige Turedh* (Stokes, 1891, 94).
79   *VSH*, cl note 14, citing *RC* xv.462 = *Dindsenchas*, (Stokes, 1894/5, 462).
80   *VSH*, cl note 14, citing *Cath Finntrága* [= Meyer (1885)] 7: *tr.* O'Rahilly (1962, 7).

To Plummer's cross-references, there are further examples. After the battle, in various episodes involving the druidic host taking their strength and their sight of the 'foreigners,' Concrithir, Finn's watchman at the harbour of Ventry, goes wounded to the three women

> And he went to seek them, and they put him under the healing spring, and he came out whole.[81]

We can confirm a clear parallel between *VC* ii.11 and these secular works

> after the saint's blessing... many infirmities among the people were in fact cured by the same well.

Second Sight / Prophecy.

Next is a selection which deal with the parallel Plummer draws between druidic second-sight and saintly prophecy for which Plummer cites as parallel *VC* i.44.

The Voyage of Mael Dúin's Boat (Immram Curaig Maíle Dúin)[82]

The section of the tale relates how a woman welcomes the voyagers by name as they arrive, and tells them their coming has been foreknown. In *VC* i.44, Crónán, a bishop of Munster, comes incognito to Iona. However Columba recognises his episcopal status as he goes to assist him at the Lord's table.

The Training of Cúchulainn (Do Fogluim Chonculainn)

Plummer cites this work in his section on 'second sight' regarding the foreknowledge of guests.[83] This knowledge of unknown arrivals occurs five times in the *VC* (i.2, 4, 26, 27, 33.) Plummer does not note these, though he does note a reference in the *Amra* to Columba's unfailing foreknowledge of guests.[84] In the secular tale, Scáthach, daughter of the King of Scythia, said:

> look well at that youth for it was shewn to me a short time ago that a young, childlike unold youth was coming to me from the West... that he would be the prophesied son.[85]

81   *Cath Finntrága,* O'Rahilly (1962, 10).
82   *VSH,* clxxi note 5 citing *Immram Curaig Maíle Dúin,* (Stokes 1888, XVII: 490).
83   *VSH,* clxx note 7.
84   The reference Plummer cites is to the extended preface to the *Amra* proper in Stokes' edition of the 12th century Bodleian *Amra.* Its antiquity is uncertain, but in common with glosses and scholia would be later than the poem.
85   *Do Fogluim Chonculainn,* (Stokes 1908, 120).

The similarity of this prophecy to that regarding the young man Fintán mac Tulcháin (*VC* i.2) is striking.

The Battle of Mag Lena (Cath Maighe Léna)

[(a) Charms for protection: In a motif related to second-sight / prophecy, Plummer draws the parallel with Adomnán's record of the posthumous power of hymns commemorating Columba to protect their singers from attack, and *Mag Lena's* record of a 'path protection'.[86] Eadoin the druid declares that he will send a 'Path Protection' charm with Eoghan on his expedition to Spain. It will bring him back safely to Erinn.]

(b) Druidic prophecy: though Plummer does not draw further parallels with vc and this tale, he does cite it with reference to druidic prophecy. He says, "'*mórfis*', '*morfastina*' and '*druidecht*' (great knowledge, great prophecy, and druidism) are coupled together."[87] As part of the same discourse, Eadoin declares that Eoghan will be nine years deprived of Erinn (i.e. in exile) during which time he will make the expedition to Spain, because he had spent nine nights recovering from the battle.[88] We may compare this to the tale of the seven-year penitential exile of Librán declared by Columba (*VC* ii.39).

(c) Later the King of Spain ordered Dadrona the druid to his presence; he requested him to procure knowledge for him of the man who his daughter should espouse.

> 'I know that right well,' said the druid, 'for it was out of Spain itself that the race of the man whose spouse she shall be, went; and he shall arrive this night in Spain.'

He instructs the king's daughter to take the lustrous coat of a salmon she finds and make it into a coat for the husband to be. The druid hears the arrival, and proclaims the sound of a wave an omen, a harbinger of the visiting king of Erinn.[89]

Plummer cites two further references to druidic prophecy as being contained in 'Magh Lena', actually occurring in:

The Courtship of Monera (Tocmarc Monera)

Plummer cites this work twice (as 'Magh Lena') in this section on druidic prophecy. I have included the references as further archetypal examples of Plummer's secular sources which he accumulates to describe the druids as models upon which the saints were designed, and

---

86   *VSH*, clxxix note 1, citing *VC* i.1 [9b] and *Cath Mhuige Léana* (Curry, 1855, 36-7).

87   *VSH*, clxii note 6.

88   *VSH*, clxii note 6, citing *Cath Mhuige Léana* (Curry, 1855, 36-7).

89   *VSH*, clxii note 6, citing *Cath Mhuige Léana* (Curry, 1855, 38-9).

druidic clairvoyance as the inspiration for descriptions of the saintly prophecy. They are not given parallels with the *VC*.
(a) The divination of Antipater, the druid out of Spain, was delivered to Eoghan by three youths, his sons. The storyteller went to order the druid to make a prophecy for the king for the fortunes of his daughter

> And the druid consulted his highest knowledge; and it was revealed to him that it was out of Caesar's island, viz, out of Erinn, the spouse of his daughters should be.

And he sends his sons as messengers to fulfil the calling and the prophecy.[90]
(b) The king of Spain asks his druid to discover the history of the youths. The druid predicts their imminent return.[91]

The Cattle Raid of Cooley (Táin bó Cúalnge)[92]
Still in Plummer's section on druidic prophecy he notes the following examples from this famous epic tale:
(a) During the preparations for the raid

> When Medb came to where her druid was, she asked her foreknowledge and prophecy of him... 'and find out for us whether we shall come back or not.'

> And the druid said: 'Whoever comes or comes not back, you yourself will come.'[93]

(b) Later we meet a group of 'prophets'

> Then came the harpers of Caínbile...they were men of great knowledge and prophecy and magic.[94]

(c) In addition to Plummer's references, we could also note the following. Medb is questioning a wonderful young woman, whose skin shone through her garments.

> 'Who of my people are you?' said Medb.
> 'That is not hard to tell. I am Feidelm the prophetess from Síd Chrúachna.'
> 'Well then Fiedelm Prophetess, how do you see our army?'
> 'I see red on them. I see crimson.'

---

90   *VSH*, clxii note 6, citing *Cath Maige Léna* (Curry, 1855, 154-5).
91   *VSH*, clxii note 6, citing *Cath Maige Léna* (Curry, 1855, 158-9).
92   Plummer referred to the 1905 edition of Windisch, which collates *LL, Stowe, LU* and other manuscript versions of the *TBC*. I quote the equivalent passages in translation from O'Rahilly (1970).
93   *VSH*, clxii note 6, citing *TBC* (Windisch, 1905, 27): tr. O'Rahilly (1970, 142-3).
94   *VSH*, clxii note 6, citing *TBC* (Windisch, 1905, 181): tr. O'Rahilly (1970, 173).

The question and answer is repeated five times

> And Fiedelm began to prophesy and foretell Cú Chulainn to the men of Ireland, and she chanted a lay…[95]

(d) Medb sought knowledge of who should accompany her.

> Medb was the last of the hosts that day for she had been seeking foreknowledge and prophecy and tidings, that she might learn who was loath and who was eager to go on the expedition.[96]

(e) Later, Fergus, Cú Chulainn's foster father, has a 'sharp premonition' of Cú Chulainn's arrival.

> A sharp premonition of the arrival of Cú Chulainn came to Fergus and he told the men of Ireland to be on their guard… and Fergus was thus prophesying the coming of Cú Chulainn, and he made the lay and Medb answered him…[97]

(f) Cathbad the druid pronounces that a boy taking up arms that day would be famous, but short lived. Cú Chulainn takes up arms, so achieves fame.[98]

(g) In the tale proper, after the battle with Fer Diad, Cú Chulainn asks Fíngin Fáthlíaig the seer-physician to come and examine the wounds of Cethern mac Fintain. He examines nine wounds in all, identifying the attacker each time. He's asked for advice, and Fíngin gives Cethern the choice of either long illness and then help and succour, or temporary healing for vengeance. The latter chosen, Fíngin prescribes a marrow mash in which Cethern is placed for three days and three nights to cure and heal him.[99]

The Cloak of Invulnerability

(h) The final selection from the *TBC*, with the following citation from *The Combat*, concerns the *congancness,* the 'horn skin'. Plummer describes this as making its wearer invincible. In order to counterbalance Cú Chulainn's use of the *ga bulga,* Fer Diad wore a 'horn-skin' (*congancness*) to the battle on the ford. However, it does not prevent his being wounded and eventually being slain horribly with a thirty-barbed weapon.[100]

---

95   O'Rahilly (1970, 143).
96   O'Rahilly (1970, 146).
97   O'Rahilly (1970, 148).
98   O'Rahilly (1970, 163).
99   O'Rahilly (1970, 236-240).
100 Plummer (clxxx, note 2) cites Windisch (1905, 439; 563). For the *ga bulga* and the *congancness,* see O'Rahilly (1970, 222; 228-9). Plummer also cites Windisch (317 note), which refers to the *LU* version, and Windisch (553), which refers to the Stowe version. For discussion of the *congancness,* see *The Combat of Cú Chulainn with Senbecc* next.

The Combat of Cú Chulainn with Senbecc

In the same note, Plummer refers to a meeting of Cú Chulainn and Senbecc whose cloak and shirt will fit anyone, and will prevent him from drowning or from being burnt. He also has a shield which will protect the bearer in battle or in combat.[101]

The parallel for both these secular tales is drawn with Adomnán's tale of a spear attack by Lám Dess (Right Hand), one of a company of excommunicate persecutors of churches on Hinba who intended to kill Columba

> In order to prevent this, one of the monks, by name Findlugán, wearing the holy man's cowl, came between, ready to die for him. But miraculously that garment of the blessed man, like a coat of well-fortified and impenetrable armour [*lurica*], could not be pierced even by the strong man's powerful thrust of a very sharp spear, but remained uninjured; and the man who was clad in it was shielded by that covering from hurt or harm. But the miscreant...withdrew, believing that the spear had transfixed the holy man *(VC* ii.24).

The thrust of these passages appear to confirm Plummer's view that it is an example of the pagan motif of a magical 'cloak of invulnerability'.

COMMENTARY ON THE EARLIER SOURCES

There is much to stimulate discussion here, but there is perhaps an unidentified subjectivity in addition to the now identified problems of chronology and vector of influence. As we have seen, Plummer posits the adoption by Irish Christianity, after its arrival in Ireland, of prevailing pagan religious mythology and motifs, evinced by the inclusion of such motifs in the Christian *Lives.* The pagan origin of these motifs may be determined by comparison with the secular sagas, which are taken to record pre-Christian (or unconverted contemporary) pagan mythology and religious practice. The inclusion of the pagan motifs from the sagas in the *Lives* thus shows that the Christians have adopted the practices, recording them as their own, as they enter the Irish milieu.

Now, as I have suggested, Sharpe's variant translations of *VC* may indicate that he has been influenced by Plummer's thesis. In his 1991 revisiting of the three collections, however, Sharpe has this to say

> Plummer's interests had... strayed into mythology, an area fashionable at the time... Plummer's speculations on this front incurred immediate censure from reviewers when his book was published in 1910.[102]

---

101 *Combat,* Meyer (1883, 184).
102 Sharpe (1995, 79).

Because at this remove these reviews may not be familiar, I will summarize them as they relate to our question, working from Sharpe's list. This will confirm that Sharpe represents accurately the response to Plummer's thesis.

E.C. Butler does not fault the editorial work, but says of part V

> the mythologising method, so fashionable a generation ago, but now discredited in other subjects, is just now running riot in Hagiology (see the last chapter of Père Delehaye's *Légendes Hagiographiques*). Mr Plummer's mythological method is of a sober kind... but... many of them [i.e. the parallels] could be paralleled from documents where there is no reason for suspecting this influence.[103]

E.J. Gwynn compares the 'comparatively modest and sober' infusion of supernatural marvels in Adomnán's *Life of Columba* and the Armagh *Lives* of Patrick, with [the]

> gross and palpable fictions which abound in the later compilations... [in which] ...as time went on... the miraculous element tended to predominate.

Gwynn goes along with much of Plummer's opinion. However, he points out (influenced by the fashionable Indo-European theory) that stories associating holy ascetics with animals, of prestige derived from mortification, and of claims upon the celestial powers are also told of Indian Fakirs. Gwynn disagrees with Plummer over his assumption that the personalities of saints have been identified with pre-Christian pagan deities. He agrees that the solar may be one element in 'Celtic' religious belief, but dissents from the view that it was established generally in Ireland at the time Christianity was introduced, and challenges Plummer's apparent preconception that solar attributes were transferred wholesale to the saints. He observes that the so-called 'solar miracles' all have perfectly orthodox biblical parallels, and indeed the whole of Irish literature of 'post-Christian origin' is full of such imitations. (Again we have the question of which belief influenced which record, and an early expression of Carney's theory.)

However, Gwynn accepts wholeheartedly Plummer's posited influence of the old magic, fairies and druidism. The superstition of the former is simply transferred to new figures; saints replace sorcerers / druids; angels and demons replace fairies and evil spirits. He points out though that this is not uniquely Irish. Here he betrays his own 'nativism' clearly. What is curious is that Gwynn does not apply the same criticism to these features as he did for the solar miracles; all the examples he gives have perfectly conventional

---

103 Butler (1910, 490-2).

biblical parallels, with no need to appeal to the adoption of old-faith mythologies. (The major exception to this are the stories which exhibit a counter-Christian morality, but then the members of the church have it seems never been immune from such activity; the curiosity here is that it should be recorded of saints in contexts designed to show their sanctity.) Gwynn perhaps catches the right spirit in his closing remarks

> Evidently these stories are not all meant to be taken too seriously. They are intended for entertainment as well as instruction. Even a monk must relax a little occasionally, especially if he is also an Irishman.[104]

Van der Essen sees Plummer's rapprochements as forced, and the conclusions too sweeping, especially with respect to the solar myths. These elements are found, he says, in all ages and countries, where the substratum is, as in Ireland, the mentality of the crowd. He questions whether the mythological traits Plummer identifies as Irish do originate expressly in Ireland, asserting that they are found ubiquitously.[105] This comment is anticipated by J.A. MacCulloch, who sounds a cautionary note: we must discriminate between what in the folk-tales is Celtic and what is universal.[106] Vendryes asserts the impossibility of establishing a firm theory, wondering if Plummer has applied too rigorous an interpretation of the pagan elements. The solar elements are not demonstrable, and may be a bit *out of date*. There are abundant comparisons from Hindu, Greek and Germanic mythologies.[107] In a quote we have seen part of before, Sharpe summarizes the reviews, and points to the way forward.

> [Plummer's] approach to the Lives ... included a good deal of rather primitive study of what he called 'heathen folk-lore and mythology'... In 1910 he was criticised for naïve speculations on the divine attributes of saints. That criticism may have been in some measure motivated by a desire to perceive the saints of the *uitae* in the light of an attitude to holiness and the holy life which would have been quite alien to their authors. Plummer was seen as trying to make pagan gods out of minor heroes of modern Christianity. His methods were misguided, but his recognition that the *uitae* illuminate aspects of how the authors of the *uitae* and their audience perceived the spiritual aspects of their world has still to be followed up.[108]

Our present study can only claim also to be primitive, though it has the benefit of the attempts of its predecessors from which to

---

104 Gwynn (1912, 62-81).
105 Van der Essen (1911, 526-8).
106 MacCulloch (1911).
107 Vendryes (1911, 104-6).
108 Sharpe (1991, 388).

learn. While shedding a flickering light on some of the more bizarre incidents in these lives, however, Plummer's thesis is challenged heavily upon the question of the Irish, and the pagan, identity of the traits he so identifies. He is challenged over the questions we have identified of chronology and the vector of influence. Which came first: the Christian miracles or those in the sagas? Which influenced which? Is it possible that the earliest miracles of the earliest Irish Christian saints (or the biblical and other literary accounts of such) might have been incorporated into the oral sagas, where they could grow and develop, then be re-exported into the later *Lives*? Plummer's reviewers are somewhat unfair in accusing him of imputing the traditions only to the Irish milieu, as he himself makes numerous references to continental and Indian traditions. He must be correct in his assertion that the many commonplace motifs to be found in the *Lives* he publishes have been drawn from common tradition, or traditions. The question is, which tradition? His particular thesis, shared by his contemporary and subsequent hagiologists, folklorists, historians and others, (e.g. MacCulloch, Stokes, Hyde, Delehaye, Curry, the Andersons, Hughes etc.), is that the marvellous therein was largely derived from the marvellous in the secular myths, sagas and folk-traditions of Ireland, which were themselves part of the wider folk tradition of Indo-European language users. As an example, the master folklorist Sean O'Sullivan says of Hyde's *Legends of Saints and Sinners*

> It focussed on a pattern that had already intrigued Irish collectors, the blending of pagan with Christian lore. St Patrick and St Peter performed wonders not unlike those credited to the ancient Tuatha de Danaan but with a moral purpose and Christian motive.[109]

The extent to which this thesis is supported by Plummer's evidence, a representative selection of which I present above, is dependent upon two factors. Firstly, Plummer must face the question of chronology. Do the sources he cites as evidence of pagan influence on, for our purpose, Adomnán, present a chronological relationship with the *VC* which supports such influence as having occurred? Secondly there is the question of similarity of description and vector of influence. Do the narratives in the two media present a picture of the same phenomena at work? Is the similarity decisive in leading us to conclude that the phenomena so described are of the same nature and purpose, or are there differences which might suggest that while similar on a surface level, the underlying nature and purpose of the phenomena in the two media are fundamentally distinct. Even if we should conclude that the descriptions are

---

109 O'Sullivan (1966, xxvi), commenting on Hyde (1900).

substantially identical, does this necessarily mean that we are observing a single set of phenomena common to both genres. We have here the oft-voiced question of the similarities and/or differences between the supernatural phenomena of the Judao-Christian tradition and those of other traditions, including the pagan Celtic religious tradition of the early to mid first millennium AD.[110] We are seeking to determine the extent to which Adomnán could be seen to have been influenced by his particular context of pagan Irish religion, and more particularly still, by the pagan Irish folktales represented by the survivals in the literary record as cited by Plummer in evidence of such an influence. Adomnán writes self consciously from within a Christian tradition, but was this tradition in his case polluted/enriched by pagan ideas and legends, as Plummer claims, or does the tradition include such phenomena as part of its corpus of belief? The last contains a further element: is there any evidence of a preceding Christian tradition, in addition to biblical and hagiographical sources, on which Adomnán could have drawn for his images as an alternative influence. Is Plummer sufficiently discerning in his identification of pagan with Christian marvellous phenomena?

Thus we will proceed to investigate in detail these two areas: (i) chronology, and (ii) similarity and vector of influence.

Chronology

I will record the dating information available to Plummer for each of these early textual sources, plus more recent work in this regard. I have also included two sources which Plummer cites in reference to second sight / prophecy, but which he does not cross-reference to *VC* (*Death of the Sons* and *Da Choca*). Here the sources are arranged in order of their putative date.

---

110 Colin Brown (1984), *Miracles and the Critical Mind*, is a survey of the discussion of miracles (both in philosophy and in biblical criticism) since the seventeenth century. Theissen (1983) part 3 Chapter 2, argues for the relative distinctiveness of the Gospel miracle stories in the ancient context; Kingsbury argues that the era of drawing analogies between Hellenistic miracles and gospel miracles is itself drawing to a close (1986, 449). See also Hull (1974), *Hellenistic Magic and the Synoptic Tradition*; Jones (1936), 'Primitive Magic in the Lives of the Celtic Saints'; Kolenkow (1976), 'A problem of Power: How Miracle Doers Counter Charges of Magic in the Hellenistic World'; Latourelle (1988), *The Miracles of Jesus and the Theology of Miracles*; Moule (1965), *Miracles*; Remus (1982), 'Does Terminology Distinguish Early Christian from Pagan Miracles?'; Remus (1983), *Pagan-Christian Conflict over Miracle in the Second Century*; Twelftree (1993), *Jesus the Exorcist*.

Cattle Raid of Cooley (Táin Bó Cúalnge)[111]

The earliest manuscript is contained in *The Book of the Dun Cow*, compiled by the second half of the eleventh century.[112] That in the *Book of Leinster* is thought to have been written originally around 1100, and compiled by 1160.[113] Windisch argues that parallels drawn between the Táin's presentation of the early Irish milieu and that of Gaul and Britain during the Roman invasion produce a date of second-first century BC for their setting. If the composition was contemporary, this suggests a consequent oral transmission of some 1000 years. Ridgeway placed it in the first century AD. Jackson makes the tale pure fiction, noting that any documentation cannot go back earlier than the fifth century AD (the advent of Christian writing in Ireland), but that the tales reached the form in which they were preserved by the fourth century. He sees them written first in the mid-seventh century, and thus having been transmitted orally for around 300 years in their settled form.[114] Chadwick sees the period of the tales being the fifth-century end of Ulaid dominance with the destruction of their stronghold close by Armagh, Emain Macha, by the Uí Néill of Tara, and their codification 'probably not before the seventh century'.[115] O'Rahilly re-asserts ultimate oral inspiration, though she does not date this, leaving open the question of its chronological relationship to the Christian mission.[116] Carney sees the earliest compilation of *TBC (Recension I)* as 'based to a large extent on eighth- or ninth-century material,'[117] though archaisms may be traced which can be dated around AD 600 or earlier.[118] He takes an intermediate view, proposing the saga as partly traditional, with the balance being imaginative reconstruction of the remote pagan past in the form of the mixed culture of early Christian Ireland. He thus sees the saga as historical fiction, with an oral tradition to the seventh century, and a skeletal historicity.[119]

---

111 Recent surveys may be found in *TBC*, O'Rahilly (1970); Carney (1983, 114-117); Mallory (1992) and (1995).

112 Ó Concheannain (1996, 65) argues for this date, earlier than previous opinion.

113 Chadwick (1971, 263; 270).

114 Jackson (1964, 44f).

115 Chadwick (1971, 87, 267). He sees no reason to suspect any writing in Ireland before Patrick's fifth-century autographs (87).

116 O'Rahilly (1970, xiii).

117 Carney (1983, 113).

118 Carney (1983, 117-122). Carney notes *Conailla Medb Míchuru*, one of these [indirect] sources, 'unquestionably the oldest source' of *TBC*. He suggests its author's claimed 'ancient knowledge' is at least a century older than the writer's own day (earlier than AD 600), thus bringing the tradition of *TBC* 'almost to the brink of the pagan period' (122).

119 Carney (1983, 116-7). It may be worth noting here that prior to reading Thurneysen, Carney, and McCone, my own reading of the sources had

The Voyage of Mael Dúin's Boat (Immram Curaig Maíle Dúin)

The earliest surviving manuscript is in *The Book of the Dun Cow*, written as we've seen by the second half of the eleventh century. Kenney follows Zimmer in dating the origin of the tale before the ninth-century *Voyage of Brendan*, but believes the extant text has 're-borrowed' from Brendan.[120] Chadwick dates the story from the tenth century, based probably on an eighth-century original, and the inspiration for Brendan.[121] Oskamp believes it was not in its present form before the ninth century, though it has roots in the pre-Viking survivals in *Immram Bran*. The setting is Christian, though of uncertain date.[122]

Death of the Sons of Uisneach (Oidheadh Chloinne hUisneach), 'Deirdre'

The text Plummer refers to is from the Glenn Masáin MS, probably written in the fifteenth century.[123] Mac Giolla Léith believes there are two separate traditions, the earliest version of which, *Longes mac nUislenn*, is in the mid-twelfth century *Book of Leinster*.[124] Under this title it is listed among the chief tales (*primscéla*), which a poet is bound to know. Thus, we have firm evidence of the tale's importance by the twelfth century, and firm indications that, in view of its inclusion in the *primscéla*, it has a more ancient origin. Composition is dated to the late eighth-early ninth centuries, making it the earliest love-story in Irish literature.

The Battle of Ventry (Cath Finntrága)

Plummer used Meyer's 1885 edition. The oldest extant version of the tale is preserved in Bodleian MS *Rawl.* B487ff 1-11, dated fifteenth century. Meyer states

> No mention of it is found in older Irish literature, and thus it is likely that... the origin of the story itself must *not* be referred back to a much earlier date than that of its oldest MS. Indeed the language of the text

---

suggested that Christian writers of the tales might themselves have imported features of Greek/Teutonic heroic culture to enrich the history of their nation, and to emphasize the contrast of the old pagan with the new Christianized culture. In other words, they were writing a creative 'history' against which to view the new civilization. This jejune impression, formed from an independent consideration of the evidence, is thus confirmed by the masters.

120 Kenney (1968, 411 note 144).
121 Chadwick (1971, 281).
122 Oskamp (1970, 4), Chadwick (1971, 280).
123 Nat. Mus. Scot., Advocates Lib. Mss. 56, 63, Edinb., ed. and tr. Whitley Stokes (1887). Hull (1949) and Mac Giolla Léith (1993) are the latest editions with a full history of the collection of tales gathered around the Deirdre story. We will refer to this saga below.
124 *LL* 259b-261b, see Mac Giolla Léith (1993, 19); Hull (1949, 29-32).

plainly shows that it cannot have been copied from a much older MS (viii-ix, my emphasis).

O'Rahilly, in contrast, suggests that though B487 contains no archaisms itself, the tale must have existed in some form by the twelfth century from evidence in *Accallam na Senorach*. She believes it to be 'a deliberate literary composition...later taken into folk tradition.' Stokes suggests the origin of many of these stories is in the classics *Togail Troy* (*sic*) and *Merugud Uiliux* (*sic*), as they were translated into Irish in the twelfth century, and thus the stories came into Irish literature. [125]

The Battle of Mag Tuired (Cath Maige Tuired)

Plummer cited Stokes' 1891 edition. This chief saga of the Mythological Cycle[126] is taken from Brit. Lib *Harleian* MS 5280, 63a-70b, and is described by the editor as being fifteenth-century. Stokes argues from linguistic evidence that its composition must be later than ninth century, possibly fourteenth century, but certainly during or following Scandinavian occupation. Chadwick believes the language is probably as early as the ninth century, but Gray followed by McCone concur that there is no reason to suppose it was composed before the ninth century. [127]

Dindsenchas (History of Places)

Plummer used the Stokes edition of 1894-5. Stokes believed the manuscript was probably written in the fourteenth or fifteenth centuries, but the collection may have been started in the eleventh or twelfth century. An earlier copy exists in the mid-twelfth century *Book of Leinster*.[128]

The Courtship of Monera (Tocmarc Monera)

Plummer cites this saga as 'Magh Lena'. The references in fact refer to the second piece published in the volume of that name, which, although it is part of the same cycle as Mag Lena, and shares characters and activity, is a distinct work, with different chronology. The text of the *Courtship of Monera* here cited is taken from the manuscript preserved in the *Yellow Book of Lecan (Leabhar Buide Lecan)*,) which was compiled in 1391. Curry states 'The composition

---

125 *Cath Finntrágha* (O'Rahilly, 1962, x, xviii).
126 Chadwick (1971, 265).
127 Chadwick (1971, 171); Gray (1982); McCone (1989, 136).
128 *Dindsenchas* (Stokes, 1894, 272). Other copies listed are in *Book of Ballymote* (end fourteenth century); YBL; *Rawl* B406.

of this tract is certainly much older than the date of the book in which it is preserved.' I have no other dating information.[129]

The Combat of Cú Chulainn with Senbecc

Plummer refers to the edition by Meyer, from Stowe MS 992 fo. 50b. Meyer believes it was written around the end of the fourteenth century.[130]

Da Choca's Hostel (Bruiden Da Choca)

Plummer used Stokes' edition, made from two manuscripts: *TCD* H.3.18 (sixteenth century) and H.1.17 (seventeenth century).[131]

The Battle of Mag Lena (Cath Maighe Léna)

The text cited by Plummer is taken from a seventeenth century paper manuscript (Hodges and Smith, *RIA*, No.104), edited in 1855 by O'Curry. Jackson produced the modern edition. He notes that the earliest manuscripts belong to the long recension, MS 'F', dated 1554-1558. Though there are some survivals from Middle Irish, its early modern Irish makes it 'not easy to date the tale more nearly' than late thirteenth-early fourteenth century.[132]

The Training of Cú Chulainn (Do Fogluim Chonculainn)

Plummer uses the 1908 edition of Whitley Stokes, taken from the oldest extant manuscript, Egerton 106, written in 1715.

The available data is collected in the following table:

---

129 The *YBL* MS of *Tocmarc* is ref. 4.2.16 - Col.3(c), TCD. Curry notes a reference in the '*Cath Mhuighe Léana*' (1855, 72/3 note) of a precise reference to 'Cross days', prohibited days in the calendar: 'For it is certain that the calculations of the moon and of nature said that it was a lucky conjuncture with a seventh...' It refers to druids choosing a particular day for advance, and continues: 'But one thing is certain now: knowledge was concealed from their prophets, on this occasion, and delusive omens were presented to their diviners; and fortune hardened their senses; and pride deceived their understandings; and anger and inordinate ambition intoxicated their chiefs' (1855, 74/5). Eoghan's action ended in disaster. The point of interest here is that the origin of Cross days is thought to be given, according to Curry, in TCD vellum MS H.2.16, where they are recorded as relating to various biblical events. Curry cites for example Dec. 13th as the day 'Judas was born that betrayed Christ.' This is an example of the Christian composition of the saga materials: the oral saga may have been codified by Christian scribes who interpolated a Christian chronological concept to explain the druids' failure; or the saga could have been composed *de novo*, using the motif anachronistically.
130 *The Combat*, Meyer (1883-5, 184).
131 *Da Choca*, Stokes (1900, 154-5). We will refer to the saga below.
132 *Cath Maighe Léna*, Jackson (1938, ix).

Source	Earliest MS	Earliest written composition
Cattle Raid of Cooley	AD 1100	7th century
Voyage of Mael Dúin	AD 1100	8th century
Death of the Sons	AD 1160	8/9th century
Battle of Ventry	15th century	12th century
Battle of Mag Tuired	15th century	9-14th century
Dindsenchas	12th century	12th century
Courtship of Monera	AD 1391	'older'
Combat of Cú Chulainn	14th century	14th century
Da Choca's Hostel	16th century	16th century
Battle of Mag Lena	17th century	13th century
Training of Cú Chulainn	AD 1715	AD 1715

What is clear is that none of the saga materials Plummer cites has a manuscript source earlier than the twelfth century. None has a firm suggested codification earlier than the seventh century.[133] This is not to say that the tales did not exist before Adomnán wrote his *Life of Columba*, but (with the exception of *TBC*) we have no evidence on which to base any putative use he might be thought to have made of any such source. The *Táin* furnishes intriguing possibilities, depending so much upon its date of composition. If, as Jackson asserts, its final form was achieved in the fourth century, and it was written in the mid-seventh century, there is reason to argue that Adomnán could have know it, and that he could have been influenced by it. However, Carney has demonstrated that it was the *VC* which influenced at least the written version of *TBC*, the reverse vector from that suggested by Plummer. The *Voyage of Mael Dúine's Boat*, a Christian tale, though

---

133 See Carney (1983, 127). He says some sagas might be seen as having been written in the earliest period of Irish literature. However, 'most of our saga material belongs' to 'the end of the seventh century onwards' in a 'period of revision and new creation', 'part of a constant policy in early Irish monastic schools of revising early traditions for either religious or political reasons'. Carney admits his *Studies* was written in reaction to the domination of prevailing orthodoxies regarding the date of Patrick and the nature of early Irish saga. However, he reinforces his view (with Thurneysen and Miles Dillon) that the *Iliad* influenced the seventh or eighth century compilation of *TBC* (128-130). This influence is noteworthy to our present debate in that firstly it continues to reinforce the criticism of Plummer being too ready to attribute to Irish sagas what are universal marvellous features. Secondly, it traces (at least some) marvellous influence in the Irish sagas to the same Greek milieux from which Christianity fought to distinguish itself from its inception onwards. Marvels formed an integral part of first century Palestinian world-view. However, Christians, from the model of their founder, did not, and would not accept that the marvellous aspects of their faith and practice cohered with pagan magic (e.g. Origen, *Contra Celsum*, etc.) This distinction is still evident in the *VC*. It makes the possibility of blind adoption of pagan magic in the work of so eminent an author as Adomnán improbable.

Stokes does not like the morality, may originate in the eighth century. The probability must be that any influence would have been from *VC* to it.[134] The remaining sources cited by Plummer are of such remove chronologically from *VC* that any similarities in style of description cease to have bearing in making them evidence for pagan influence on Adomnán. There is thus no unquestionable current chronological evidence from the manuscripts that Adomnán had any written secular tradition from which to draw his mirabilia.

Similarity of Description, and Vector of Influence

The probability that the scribes would have been Christian monks seeking to record entertaining tales, probably under the patronage of a local ruler, makes it likely that Christian supernatural motifs could have been interpolated into the tales as they were codified, if not before as they were told around monastic refectory tables. *VC* shows how far the Christian imagination was prepared to be entertained, with stories such as the teleporting bachall (ii.14); the beast of River Ness (ii.27); and the magic stake (ii.37), which have perhaps less than obvious Christian origin.[135] Could it not be that extant secular hero tales could have been fertilized by an imagination fed by constant daily exposure to the Christian scriptures and other Christian literary traditions? We will compare the phenomena under the three headings in which the parallels of Plummer fall: prophecy, healing, and cloak of invulnerability. These three coincide with phenomena detailed in the first two books of the *VC*.

Christian Prophecy or Druidic Sight

Plummer states that 'Many of the prophecies ascribed to the saints have a striking analogy with the phenomenon of second sight.'[136] Using Adomnán's *Life of Columba*, and the examples of prophecy there presented as a paradigm, we will attempt an investigation of the viability of Plummer's links. I hope to demonstrate that Adomnán's description owes nearly everything to Christian tradition, and little which is identifiably, or necessarily, of pre-Christian paganism. First, then, we must identify any available characteristics of pagan 'Celtic' foresight against which to compare Adomnán. As we have seen, Plummer includes various references to druidic foresight in the *VSH*.

---

134 The identity of the woman who foreknows the arrival of the voyagers may be worth investigating here; it should be noted that Columba is not the only individual described as acting 'supernaturally' in *VC*.

135 Though note the great monsters Leviathan (Job 3:8, 41:1; Pss 74:14, 104:26) and Behemoth (Job 40:15).

136 *VSH*, clxx.

(i) Rhys' tradition is cited as evidence of the presence of the phenomenon of 'second sight' in Celtic folklore. It could reflect the continuation of a pagan phenomenon such as that postulated by Plummer as an influence on the Christian writers, representing a pagan tradition with which the Christian tradition had to deal as it developed.[137] However, Plummer concedes that accounts of seeing the whole world by Adomnán and others, one example of the phenomenon, were probably influenced by 'our Lord's temptation on the mount, Luke 4:5'.[138] While reasonable at first sight, a problem here is that the biblical incident is enabled by satanic, not divine power, whereas Columba is described as being empowered by God

> And the *devil* took him up, and showed him all the kingdoms of the world in a moment of time... (Lk. 4:5).

> ...this holy man of the Lord...in some speculations made *with divine favour* the scope of his mind was miraculously enlarged, and he saw plainly, and contemplated, even the whole world as it were caught up in one ray of the sun (*VC* i.1, 10b, my italics.)

Adomnán makes it clear that this gift is analogous to that written of by Paul, who told '...of such visions revealed to himself...' (*VC* i.43:45a). The tradition of revelatory vision was clearly, from *VC*, an important feature of Columba's life to emphasize. We may conjecture, in contrast to Plummer, that the secular tradition in Rhys could perhaps have its origin in the Christian prophetic tradition, the description of which has developed over time to its emergence as a rather different phenomenon in Rhys' tale. The early church practice of the laying on of hands for the empowering of the Holy Spirit could even be postulated as the origin of the touch conveying the power to 'see' magically, as the story of Simon the *magus* shows

> Now when Simon saw that the Spirit was given through the laying on of the apostles' hands, he offered them money, saying, 'Give me also this power, that any one on whom I lay my hands may receive the Holy Spirit' (Acts 8:18-19).[139]

(ii) Again, in Plummer's references to foreknowledge of the arrival or safe return of visitors,[140] we have no need to look any further than

---

137 Again, this is the familiar controversy in Christian history, from biblical accounts of apostolic dealings with magicians, through Origen's refutation of Celsus' accusations, and so on.

138 *VSH*, clxxi note 10.

139 Touch is also important in Deut. 34:9; Mt. 9:21//, 14:36//; Mk. 6:56, 8:22, 10:13//; Lk. 6:19; Acts 9:17, 19:6 etc.

140 *Immram*, Stokes (1888, 490); *Do Fogluim*, Stokes (1908, 120); *Maige Léna*, Curry (1855, 39); *Tocmarc*, Curry (1855, 158-9).

the Bible to find adequate precedent for prophetic knowledge of the arrival of guests in *VC*

> And while Peter was pondering the vision, the Spirit said to him, 'Behold, three men are looking for you. Rise and go down, and accompany them without hesitation; for I have sent them.' And Peter went down to the men and said, 'I am the one you are looking for; what is the reason for your coming?' (Acts 10:19-21).

(iii) In *TBC* the foreknowledge of Medb's druid[141] parallels that of Columba in its directness, and even in the manner of asking, see for instance *VC* i.15: King Rhydderch of Strathclyde sends to ask Columba if he will be slain by enemies or not. Columba said he would not. However, other instances in *TBC* where riddle or poetic lay-forms of prophecy are given show a distinctively different style and influence in play. Given a seventh-century codification of the *TBC*, during which century the prophecies of Columba were themselves being codified by Ségéne and Cumméne, the possibility of an influence from the Columba tradition, rather than the reverse, is perfectly feasible. The embellishments in prophetic style given to the druids in the *Táin*, not seen for Columba in the *VC*, act as confirmation of this revised direction of influence. Thus *TBC* retains traditional elements, while its Christian scribes add elements from the Judao-Christian tradition. The prophecy of Colum Cille's arrival suggests either a post Colum Cille (i.e. post-sixth century) composition, or Christian interpolation.[142] The Christian colophon appended to the tale in *LL* is of special interest in the context of this investigation.[143] Here we see firm evidence of both the copyist's rejection of the mythological phenomenology of the tale as either demonic deception, or poetic figments, and thus of his own acceptance of a cosmology which coincides with that of Adomnán. We can observe his own awareness of a differentiation between the pagan magic tales he records, and the non-figmentary, non-demonic mirabilia with which we must presume he is contrasting them.

(iv) *The Death of the Sons of Uisnech (sic)*,[144] not cross-referenced to *VC* in *VSH*, records the following prophetic actions:

> And Fergus sent forth a mighty cry in the harbour, so that it was heard throughout the farthest part of the districts that were nearest to them.

---

141 *TBC*, O'Rahilly (1970, 142).
142 *TBC*, O'Rahilly (1970, 173).
143 *TBC*, O'Rahilly (1970, 272).
144 *Ed.* Stokes (1887, 109f). Plummer (clxii.7, and cxlviii.1) also cites *Oitte (sic)* 14 and 22 (Meyer's 1906 edition) as examples of druidic prophecy of Christ's coming, plainly a Christian interpolation, and of druidic floods. See dating information above.

He sends out three such cries, and the third identifies him to Deirdre, who had had a vision the night before

> to wit, three birds came to us out of Emain Macha; and three sips of honey they had in their bills, and those three sips they left with us, and with them they took three sips of our blood.

She explains to Naisí the meaning

> Fergus has come from our own native land with peace; for not sweeter is honey than a (false man) message of peace; and the three sips of blood that have been taken from us, they are ye who will go with him, and ye will be beguiled.[145]

The first section of quotation is reminiscent of Columba's miraculous voice (*VC* i.37), which is one sign of a prophet in the Fathers.[146] This in itself might indicate Christian influence on the secular saga. However the poetic metaphorical style of the prophecy is wholly unlike the straightforward un-veiled language Adomnán records for Columba's prophecies. Indeed it is more reminiscent of Samson's riddle in Judges 14. It must therefore be unlikely that this tale could have been an influence on Adomnán, if it existed in his time, for which we have no evidence. Thus this reference is further evidence for the difference in prophetic style recorded of the druids being based on OT hero figures.

(v) A further example can be observed in *Da Choca's Hostel*.

> 11. Now the wizards [*druid*] were foreboding evil and uttering ill omens to Cormac mac Usnech. They declared that the journey would be neither easy nor speedy.

In Druim Airthir, they saw a 'red woman' wanting her chariot

> 15. When she lowered her hand, the bed of the river became red with gore and with blood. But when she raised her hand over the river's edge, not a drop therein but was lifted on high; so that they went dryfoot over the bed of the river.

> 16. ...then, standing on one foot, and with one eye closed, she chanted to them saying... 'I was the ? of a king who will perish...'[147]

Again, Plummer does not give any parallels in *VC*. However it is possible to discern in this story of the red woman a set of images

---

145 Ed. Stokes (1887, 156).

146 E.g. Ignatius *To the Philadelphians*, VII: 'I spake with a loud voice, with the voice of God...but it was the Spirit who kept preaching in these words.' Srawley (1900, 86). *The Death of the Sons* says: 'And Conchobar uplifted his loud king's voice on high...' Stokes (1887, 153, line 19). This is an example of the loud voice of authority, which may derive from Patristic ideas on prophecy. See chapter 4 below.

147 *Da Choca*, Stokes (1900, 154-5), cited in *VSH*, clxii note 6.

strongly suggested by the biblical story of Moses and the Pharaoh's *magi*, an influence Plummer himself suggests elsewhere;[148] of Israel crossing the Red Sea (Ex. 14:16, 21-22); or of Joshua and the crossing of the Jordan (Josh. 3:13-17). This clear biblical influence confirms McCone's view of this saga being influenced by biblical borrowing, mediated via *Scéla Muicce Meic Da Thó*.[149]

These passages[150] demonstrate both some of the similarities and the differences between the accounts of druidic 'prophecy' and that of Columba. Common elements include the foretelling of the conditions of a journey (c.f. *VC* i.4, 5, 6, 19, 20, 45, 47, ii.42); the use of a hand movement in demonstration of power (c.f. *VC* ii.2, 11, 12, 28, 29, 31, 35); foreboding evil and uttering ill omens (c.f. *VC* ii.22-25). At the same time there are distinct differences. Foreknowledge of a husband is not seen in *VC*. A peculiar posture is adopted by the druids, but not recorded of Columba. The style of ecstasy in *VC* appears markedly different, with Adomnán giving the impression of a quiet, un-induced state, which he parallels with Paul's being taken to the third heaven, 2 Corinthians 12:2 (though staring eyes, and druidic frenzy,[151] have possible OT archetypes in Numbers 24:16 and 1 Samuel 10 and 19). The gore, absent in *VC*, is prominent in the sagas (though not absent in OT prophecy cf. Isa. 34:6). Druids, but not Columba, made claims of 'highest knowledge' or 'great knowledge' (though cf. 'knowledge from the Most High', Num. 24:16). The skin of the druid, but not the saint, shines through the garment (though cf. Moses at the foot of Mt Sinai (Ex. 34:29f), and the transfigured Christ (Mt. 17:1-8//)). The druid chants a lay rather than Columba's plain talk, and prophesies in obscure riddles (though cf. OT prophets' poetic oracles). No source of druidic foresight is declared other than druidic ability, (though again those who practice divination in OT (Deut. 18:14) have no source attributed). Charms termed 'path protection' are delivered by the druids with foreknowledge of safe return,[152] as distinct from standard prayers for safety, (though the evolution from prayer to charm is

---

148 *VSH*, clxvi.
149 McCone (1990, 32).
150 (And see note 140 above).
151 C.f. MacCulloch (1911, 247). 'Staring eyes' is the TEV translation.
152 *Maige Léna*, Curry (1855, 36-7). Curry mentions a path protection poem attributed to Columba (*Misc. Ir. Arch. Soc.*), also cited by Plummer here, and a number of what he calls 'Latin Coimghi' (TCD Class, B.3.17, page 672). The latter is a conventional Trinitarian prayer with an Irish legend naming it an 'encircling safeguard of the angel'. This illustrates a possible amalgamation of tradition; the Irish pagan encircling, and a Christian prayer for help. It would appear to be the Irish legend which turns it into an automatic charm, rather than a supplicatory prayer.

straightforward). Though Plummer cites these tales as evidence for the pagan influence on the *Lives*, closer examination suggests influence may have flowed in the reverse direction, and particularly from the OT to the druid.

A possible avenue for elucidating an explanation for Adomnán's preoccupation with the prophetic is suggested by the context of the struggle with the clairvoyant powers and consequent influence of the *magus*. Is he seeking to show Columba as the more powerful seer, free of the need for the druid's mummery, and representative of the true God rather than the shady world of the *Síde?* For Adomnán, direct encounters are with a *maleficus* (ii.17), with the *magi* (i.37c) and Broichan, the *magus* of the King of Picts (ii.33-4). Indirect challenges also occur (ii.11, 32). All are in Pictland. The encounter is not about who is the more powerful prophet, but who is more powerful in the ability to perform miracles (with a possible exception in i.37c where the *magi* seek to prevent the *gentiles populi* hearing the praises of the brothers). Adomnán is concerned to distinguish Columba's divinely sourced power from that of the magic of the *magi,* and thus shows himself as both aware of the accusation, and concerned to correct any reader's mistaken view, that Columba is a magician.[153] He is the one who brings true salvation, who carries the power of the true God. That pagan adherents should follow Christ is the object. Patrick is presented as mortal enemy of the *magi* in the seventh-century *Lives*. Plummer records that Patrick's biographer makes prophecy the chief function of the *magi,*[154] and acknowledges biblical influence. Testing this thesis would require an assessment of the prevailing influence of the *magus* in Ireland and Scotland in both Columba and Adomnán's times. This detailed analysis has yet to be attempted, and may prove problematic in the light of Carney. Again, we may be seeing druidic character fashioned according to the model of some of the characteristics of some OT magicians, witches, and prophets, and of the intransigent Pharisee of the gospels.

If Adomnán is not influenced detectably by the prophetic in the sagas, where might other influences come from? Apart from the druidic, three traditions of prophecy may be outlined on which Adomnán could reasonably have modelled his description of Columba, and, indeed, on which Columba could have modelled his ministry. The first is that of the early Hebrew prophets, Moses, Samuel, Elijah and Elisha. Their prophecies are presented in narrative form, often accompanied by miracles, and directed at

---

153 C.f. *VSH*, cxxxiv; 'Christian teachers never took the line of denying [pre-Aryan magic's] existence. It was gentile or diabolic knowledge, powerfully ranged against themselves...'

154 *V.Tr.* (Stokes 1887, 273).

individuals. A second group are the more political preacher-prophets whose writings and records are dominated by poetic oracles of judgment or promise for the Jewish nation, but whose personal works, and references to individuals, are much less recorded. The third group are from the Christian era, and include Jesus of Nazareth, the Apostles, and others operating in the *charisma* of prophecy. Here, prophecy relates almost entirely to individuals and local situations, as we shall see.[155] Adomnán's references to Elijah and Elisha, with his known use of Gregory's *Dialogues* which make the same links, suggests an adoption of Gregory's ideas about prophecy, particularly as he adopts Gregory's explanation of Benedict's gift of the knowledge of remote happenings.[156] Adomnán has been selective in his allusions to Elijah, Elisha, and Moses, to coincide with recording Columba as an example of a prophet in a New Testament and patristic model, dealing by and large with individual, local, and immediate situations. From this division, we can observe quickly that Adomnán sees Columba as identifying strongly with the first and third type of prophet.

The immediately striking character of the instances of the prophetic Adomnán records is their application in the main to individual persons as distinct from groups such as families, tribes, or 'nations'. Adomnán never employs what Von Rad calls the 'messenger formula' in which a prophet delivers a message prefaced by the 'thus says the Lord' formula so characteristic of the later OT prophets who saw themselves acting as ambassadors for God.[157] Did Adomnán see Columba as such an ambassador? It seems not in this way, though as we shall see, he certainly saw him as one through whom God revealed his divine will and knowledge, though primarily for individuals not 'nations'. There is no collective eschatological view here either, i.e. bearing on the future of the whole nation / people/ *cenél*, and thus little in the way of the sort of testamentary deposit left by many OT prophets intended to be read in time to come, or to be recognised in retrospect as prophetic to a nation in its fulfilment.[158] Adomnán has not recorded such testimonies either because it did not suit his purpose in writing, or because Columba never delivered such. This was not his rôle as a post incarnation prophet, though it would be a style Adomnán (or Columba) could

---

155 ...including prophets of the early church up to Columba's day? We know Iona was familiar with the scriptures and some patristic writings, but not how known accounts of post-biblical prophets were; see chapter 5 below.

156 See *VC* 1.43b; Gregory, *Dial* 2.35 and 4.7. Note also the earlier less developed account in *VA* 34 and 59, and chapter 4 below.

157 Von Rad (1968, 18f.).

158 Von Rad (1968, 24).

reasonably have adopted, given the putative advantages such pronouncements could have had in the political situation of the day. There could have been prophecies of judgment over the more southerly Irish, Saxons or British who threatened dynasties favourable to Iona; or, if Picard's argument relating to competition with Armagh is to be adopted, such prophecies against competitor *familiae*. Given Adomnán's advantage of a century of hindsight, it would have been simple in the extreme to include prophecy on Columba's lips promising success to groups who had shown signs of 'divine blessing' as their history unfolded to Adomnán's day. In actual fact, such prophecy as is recorded with a putative political function appears to have little direct propagandist character. It appears rather to record the historical development, with little obvious advantage to Iona, or to Columba's repute as one who pronounced divine curses or blessings. He is presented rather as a neutral who spoke God's foreknowledge as and when God chose so to reveal, and to human view perhaps rather arbitrary in selection of subject. It is this neutrality which lends weight to the argument that Adomnán was including known stories simply to illustrate the life and ministry of this man of God, rather than that his purpose was primarily political. This observation also helps us to answer the oft heard query regarding the uniquely special nature of *VC*. The main purpose maybe that of presenting a man of God cutting through political and geographical divisions to bring the unifying power of the kingdom of God into being wherever and with whomever it is received. It also helps us to assess these stories as reflective of a genuine tradition of prophecy in the Ionan church, against which to compare the 'pagan' equivalents. Turning Plummer on his head, we might say that many of the instances of second sight ascribed to the wizards have a striking analogy with the phenomenon of Christian prophecy.

Healing

The tale of Eochaid from the *Dindsenchas* confirms the presence of healing motifs in the secular literature. We might ask if the background to this late tale may be the Christian tradition of healing, rather than the pagan tradition referred to in Adomnán. In the case of *The Battle of Ventry/VC* ii.11, we confirmed a clear parallel between the two works, but is Adomnán betraying pagan influence in his thinking here? Plummer believed this was 'one of the departments in which the Christianization of localities and customs originally heathen can be most clearly traced.'[159] Certainly this story is a good example of such a process under way. Sharpe says

> While the worship of the well is condemned here, both this story and the previous one demonstrate that Adomnán approved the continuous reverence for miraculous holy wells. Pagan well worship was easily transmuted into Christian practice, and still continues....[160]

It is important to note what Adomnán actually says here.

> [Columba] heard that the fame of another well was widespread among the heathen populace, and that the insensate [stupid] people venerated it as a god, the devil deluding their understanding [blinding their senses].[161]

He describes the cause of infirmities brought by touching the water as devilish art *(daemonica arte)*, but permitted by God, and continues: 'Led astray by all this, the heathen gave honour to the well as to a god.'[162] On learning this, Columba engages in a spiritual power encounter, expelling demons from the well by, 'raising holy hand in invocation of the name of Christ.' He washes and drinks, and the well is transformed. As Sharpe observes, Adomnán condemns the worship of the well. He uses fairly strong language in so doing, and is careful twice to condemn treating the well as a god, and worshipping a god in it. It would thus be inconsistent were we to interpret his words regarding the healing properties of the water after Christ's cleansing as implying that he approved of its continued worship, albeit under new management. He condemns well worship as a product of devilish deception, and shows himself acutely aware of the different tradition in which he stands compared to this heathen practice, which has been here defeated as the restoring values of Christ are established, repelling destructive demonic deceit. The well is not described as now inhabited by Christ, or Columba, but as a place where the healing power of God may be accessed. Adomnán is more careful in his use of language than to allow the well to be worshipped in its newly cleansed state.

Now the question as to why Adomnán took up what looks like a pagan motif, i.e. the healing well, remains to be answered. We see in the preceding discussion that he demonstrates acute awareness of the different tradition in which he walks, and he has a straightforward ancestor for his story of Columba's action in one of the models on which his presentation of his hero is based, namely Elisha.

---

159 *VSH*, cxlix.
160 Sharpe (1995, note 234), following Reeves (1857, 119, note b).
161 ...*audiens in plebe gentili de alio fonte deuulgari famam, quem quasi deum stolidi homines diabulo eorum obcaecante sensus uenerabantur* (*VC* 61b).
162 *Ob quae omnia seducti gentiles diuinum fonti deferebant honorem* (*VC* 61b).

Now the men of the city said to Eli'sha, 'Behold, the situation of this city is pleasant, as my lord sees; but the water is bad, and the land is unfruitful.' He said, 'Bring me a new bowl, and put salt in it.' So they brought it to him. Then he went to the spring of water and threw salt in it, and said, 'Thus says the LORD, I have made this water wholesome; henceforth neither death nor miscarriage shall come from it.' So the water has been wholesome to this day, according to the word which Eli'sha spoke (2 Kgs. 2:19-22).

The precise vehicle adopted to convey God's healing, and the state of the afflicted people are different, but the problem well and the outcome are the same. We know Adomnán had Elisha in mind as he composed his portrait of Columba from *VC* ii.32. Thus, while Adomnán may be seen to confirm the existence of the pagan practice of well-worship in his era, his story can be seen to have a clear source in his own tradition, a tradition which was in his day consciously exposing pagan practice as satanically inspired, and thus to be exposed and defeated. The record of the process in the *VC* thus identifies a function of the *Life* in recording a success of the new faith in eclipsing paganism.

Cloak of Invulnerability

In the case of parallels with *VC* ii.24 in *The Combat of Cú Chulainn with Senbecc* and the *TBC* we noted Plummer's view that these are examples of the pagan motif of a magical 'cloak of invulnerability'. Adomnán describes Findlugán as 'clad in the covering / cap / cowl *(cucula eius indutus)*' of the holy man, and that this vestment represented a miraculous most protective and impenetrable *lurica*. The picture conveyed is thus of a physical vestment normally worn by the saint (or hero/magician in secular tales) which, by virtue of its ownership is imbued with a magical protective quality. Plummer talks of the analogy with the *congancness*, lit. 'horn-skin'. Thus Adomnán wishes to portray the saint as superseding the pagan hero and he, rather un-discerningly, borrows the vestment from the back of a secular hero in circulation at his time, and places it straight onto the shoulders of his own hero Columba. This is a clear example of Plummer's hypothesis as applied to *VC*, and a potentially serious indictment of Adomnán's discernment of what he thought may be allowable as a Christian motif of power and authority.[163] However,

---

163 Ó Floinn (1997, 149-150) notes the continuation and development of the tradition concerning Columba's cloak, or cowl, *cochall*. This relic gained the reputation of magical protective powers. Fragments of cloth possibly linked survived to 1814, but were subsequently lost, and are thus unavailable for radiometric dating. Clancy (1997b, 22) avers the substantial destruction of the *cochall* in the sixteenth century. That such a legend developed later is not material to the origin of the tradition as discussed above, but nor is it entirely

there may be an alternative interpretation that could be applied in Adomnán's defence. His description of the *congancness* reads

> Findlugán, wearing his [Columba's] cowl, came between, ready to die for him. But miraculously that garment of the blessed man, like a coat of well-fortified and impenetrable armour (*munitissima et inpenetrabilis lurica*), could not be pierced even by a strong man's powerful thrust of a very sharp spear, but remained uninjured; and he (Findlugán) that was clad in it was shielded by that covering (*munimentum*) from hurt or harm.[164]

The transfer of power by cloak is clearly pre-figured in the story of Elijah and Elisha (2 Kgs. 2:8-15). More interesting is a reference in Ephesians 6:14. The Vulgate reads: 'Stand therefore...clad in a breastplate of righteousness *(State ergo...induti loricam justitia)*'. We know Adomnán was familiar with this passage from his reference to 'the armour of the apostle Paul' in *VC* iii.8. The context of this phrase is a passage concerning armour to be worn to resist the devil's tactics (Eph. 6:10), and Paul uses the metaphor of conventional Roman body armour for his description of spiritual armour, representing the protective strength of the power of God to resist such satanic assault. In the *VC* tale under discussion, the malefactor is described as being 'prompted by the devil' into his attack on Columba. He is also called a 'strong man' (*...fortis uir*). Given the reference to the prompting of the devil this might conceivably carry a metaphorical meaning. The evangelists' accounts of the riposte of Christ to the Pharisees as he was accused of casting out demons by Beelzebul includes the phrase

> Or how can one enter a strong man's house and plunder his goods, unless he first binds the strong man? (Mt. 12:29 // Mk. 3:27 // Lk. 11:21.)[165]

The strong man is a metaphor for Satan.[166] Thus in Adomnán's story, the spear thrust comes as an assault of Satan on Columba, but an assault which fails on account of the *lurica*.

---

out of harmony with a biblical tradition that includes such tales as the healing handkerchief of St Paul (Acts 19:12).

164 *Findluganus nomine, mori paratus pro sancto uiro cucula eius indutus intercessit. Sed mirum in modum, beati uiri tale uestimentum quasi quaedam munitissima et inpenetrabilis lurica, quamlibet fortis uiri forti inpulsione acutioris hastae, transfigi non potuit, sed inlessum permansit. Et qui eo indutus erat intactus et incolomis tali protectus est munimento* (*VC* 72a).

165 *Vulg: Aut quomodo potest quisquam intrare in domum fortis ...nisi prius alligaverit fortem?*

166 Jerome uses the term *fortis* as a substantive, while Adomnán adds a subject, thus his phrase is not clearly derivative. However, Adomnán is clearly rendering the sense of the metaphor, while using a different construction.

A further conjecture with bearing on the question is that the immediate sequel to the biblical discourse on the strong man is a warning against blaspheming the Holy Spirit, by whom Christ claims he cast out demons. Adomnán consistently portrays Columba as a bearer of this Spirit,[167] and as we have seen, the section might have reference to the Pauline armour of God, which enables its wearer to resist spiritual attack. Thus we may discern the assault by Satan, using Lam Dess as his instrument, upon the bearer of the Spirit. This acts out in cameo the persecution of the church, as bearer of the Spirit, by the spiritual powers of darkness,[168] here encountered working through the human agency of the sons of Conall Domnall. For this blasphemy against the Spirit, which is not forgiven, (Mt. 12:31//), Lam Dess suffers judgment a year later, as Adomnán recounts. It is not certain that Adomnán would have been familiar with this application of his phrase *uiri fortis*, though with his description of the prompting of Lam Dess by the devil, it is tempting.

We may thus have two new alternative possibilities open. The tale may have begun as a reference to the armour of Paul, originally of a spiritual battle as in *VC* iii.8, but now transformed into a physical encounter. Alternatively, it may be an account of a tradition that the spiritual armour described by Paul was wielded so effectively by Columba as to provide protection against satanically driven physical assault. Indeed the protective power of the holy man's divine *lurica* could be appropriated by a third party, for it is the companion of Columba, the monk Findlugán,[169] who put on the protective covering, and so was protected from harm. Assuming Adomnán is differentiating between 'the man who was clad in (the *lurica*)' and 'the holy man', there is also a clear suggestion of disguise in the covering, as the attacker withdraws believing he has speared Columba himself. Thus it may be that the physical garment represented the spiritual armour sacramentally. Taking in the final part of the tale, the revelation of Lám Dess' death, Adomnán might additionally have had Isaiah 59:15-20 in mind as he wrote, with the bringing of the persecutors, foiled by a human / divine intervention, to justice by God's chosen instrument in the islands of the West, with Iona as the local expression of Zion, and the breath of God, the Holy Spirit, working through the dove of the church.

---

167 See my section on this feature of the *VC*, chapter 4.

168 'For we are not contending against flesh and blood, but against the principalities, against the powers, against the world rulers of this present darkness, against the spiritual hosts of wickedness in the heavenly places' (Eph. 6:12).

169 For whom see Reeves (1857, 136).

Truth is lacking, and he who departs from evil makes himself a prey. The LORD saw it, and it displeased him that there was no justice. He saw that there was no man, and wondered that there was no one to intervene; then his own arm brought him victory, and his righteousness upheld him. He put on righteousness as a breastplate, and a helmet of salvation upon his head; he put on garments of vengeance for clothing, and wrapped himself in fury as a mantle. According to their deeds, so will he repay, wrath to his adversaries, requital to his enemies; to the coastlands he will render requital. So they shall fear the name of the LORD from the west, and his glory from the rising of the sun; for he will come like a rushing stream, which the wind of the LORD drives. 'And he will come to Zion as Redeemer, to those in Jacob who turn from transgression', says the LORD (Isa. 59:15-20).

There is thus no compulsion to interpret the tale as representing a magic cloak. Adomnán may be seen to have maintained biblical orthodoxy in describing the physical manifestation of a conventional Christian motif. Indeed, the *congancness* might itself find an origin in this biblical usage.

Plummer's Presuppositions

The question of the probability of the existence of these sagas in oral form in Adomnán's time remains open. However, dipping into their recorded forms stimulates an interesting question. Both the Bible and *VC* record the rejection of sacrifice to demons, idols, and other gods, and of magic, divination etc., all features of pagan religion.[170] Thus, the commonness of the inclusion of such motifs in the secular saga materials, written almost certainly by Christian monks, is strange. If they edited the tales so as to remove references to putative pagan Irish deities, as is commonly suggested, why did they allow these examples of the actual activities of pagan religion to remain? The record of such actions would have a greater immediacy for the adherents of pagan religion even than the mysterious existence of gods in the pantheon. They would also be, as actions bearing on the nature of the old religion, rather more important for the bearers of the new, superseding religion, to suppress.

Is there an explanation for this? Could we in fact be reading fair codifications of the sagas as they existed, unexpurgated by Christian scribes? Is the early existence of pagan Irish gods a product of an inappropriate eagerness on the part of scholars to transfer known religious systems outside of Ireland to the somewhat misty Irish period of pre-history? Could Carney's hypothesis that the writers of the secular sagas have been more dependent on twelfth-century

---

170 E.g. *VC* ii.11 and Deut. 12:29f., etc.

imagination shaped by seven centuries of Christian influence, than on genuine ancient pre-Christian tradition, bear re-examination? The pursuit of answers to these questions, though relevant to the development of this book as background, would take us beyond its central interest and competence, and must remain for others more qualified to explore.[171]

Substantial solid ground is agreed as being available in Adomnán's *Life of Columba.* Yet there seems to be more willingness in Plummer *et seq.* to accept the anonymous and, if Carney *et seq.* are correct, fabricated testimony of the sagas on the nature of pre-Christian Irish religions. This testimony is allowed to control interpretation of the hagiographies, despite these having been written in many cases before the sagas were codified. Adomnán claims to be writing the facts as he knows them. Is the problem that his major evidence, the marvellous, is unacceptable?

Plummer, in common with all of us, held presuppositions as he engaged in his research. Is it possible to identify what these were in relation to the question of the place of supernatural *mirabilia* in the *Lives* of Irish saints? Amongst the numerous authorities cited in *VSH,* Plummer refers to the foremost church historian of his day, Adolf von Harnack (1851-1930), and to his *Die Mission und Ausbreitung des Christentums.* There are sufficient references to warrant an entry for the work in his list of abbreviations.[172] These show clearly that Plummer accepted Harnack as an authority.[173] Harnack inherited from Ritschl (1822-1889), the leading theologian in Germany of the time, 'an approach which stressed the humane and ethical elements in Christianity at the expense of the metaphysical and supernatural,' in the Kantian tradition.[174] We may thus suggest that Harnack's de-supernaturalizing theology influenced the view Plummer is here

---

171 See, for example, McCone (1989), who suggests *Cath Maige Tuired* could be understood as having three models: an ancient pagan tradition; a reaction to contemporary Viking attack; and a partial imitation of biblical models. McCone says, 'The greater the significance attaching to such contemporary factors in an extant text's compilation, the less faith one will have in the minimalist assumptions of nativists regarding the creative and manipulative impact of monastic *literati* upon the form and contents of those early medieval Irish sagas and their various recensions surviving in manuscript' (137). McCone argues, following Carney, for an understanding of the sagas as composed deliberately and carefully for their contemporary milieu, under the by then formative influence of the Bible, and, quoting Carney, 'their total literary experience' which includes a knowledge of Greek epic (139, citing Carney (1955, 321).

172 *VSH,* cxxx notes 3 and 4; cxxxiv note 2; cxxxvi note 4; clxvi note 3; clxvii note 6.

173 He follows and/or applies Harnack's views in each of the above references.

174 Colin Brown (1971, 154).

espousing, i.e. that pagan religious influence on the saint's *Lives* is the source of their emphasis on the supernatural phenomena, rather than their own unpolluted tradition. Harnack followed Ritschl in regarding metaphysics and mythology as an alien Hellenistic intrusion into Christian thought. Did Plummer regard the miraculous attributes of the Irish Christian writings as also alien to Christian orthodoxy, though here derived from Irish pagan mythology?[175]

We must return to examine his discredited attitude towards the early Irish Christian scribes. Plummer appears to have believed that the scribes were either unaware of their heathen 'substratum' as he terms it, or that they 'toned down' the alien material in the secular tales by finding ecclesiastical parallels, or 'omitted its most characteristic features.'[176] They wrote both saga and *Life*, and incorporated stories from one to the other, with the main influence being pagan corruption of Christian ideas. As Gwynn suggests, it is possible to imagine a mediaeval antiquarian monastic scribe wishing to record the entertaining folk-tales of his day for their preservation in the developing medium of manuscript. Tolerance it may have been, but if so, it was tolerance from a position of security and strength. The more important question is that regarding the discernment employed by our hagiographers, and by Adomnán in particular. Was he so undiscerning in his tolerance as to simply incorporate the pagan substratum into his writing? And did the substratum actually contain the supernatural elements Plummer is so keen to explain as deriving therefrom? If the scribes excized the 'most characteristic features' as they wrote the records from which we are constrained to characterize pagan mythology, how can this influence be traced at all?

We must examine further Plummer's underlying attitude, which is illustrated in part IV in two passages which must be quoted in full

> *Unfortunately* too, the almost universal idea of these writers was that the best way of honouring their saintly patrons was to *heap* as many miracles as possible upon them. It is true that many of the lives, both Latin and Irish, conclude with a list of the superhuman virtues of the saint. But this moral tribute is purely perfunctory, and is very largely 'common form' (Delehaye pp.28-29). *The real interest of the writer is in the thaumaturgy.* Another *unpleasant characteristic* is the way in which spiritual blessings, including *salvation* itself, are made to depend on purely material conditions, on external circumstances and *acts*... both these characteristics come from the pagan amalgam in these lives which it is one of the main purposes of this introduction to trace. The saint is

---

175 In the same way as he had borrowed Harnack's view of the Christianization of Asia Minor, noted above.

176 *VSH*, cxxxiii.

regarded as the more powerful druid, *the forces underlying his religion are conceived as magical* rather than spiritual and moral, and the objects and ceremonies associated with his creed and worship are only a very superior kind of 'medicine'... Meanwhile it may be noted that the very points which give *offence* to the hagiologist in search of edification are often the things which most interest the student of mythology and primitive modes of thought.[177]

And in the same way [as bells and bachalls] other objects and formularies connected with the new (Christian) religion came to be regarded as having not a spiritual and sacramental value, but a *magical* and material force.[178]

In looking at the whole collection of saints' *Lives* as he does, Plummer has good reason to reach these conclusions. The hagiographical corpus could be thus criticized justly. However, Plummer takes the approach of treating the corpus *in toto* regardless of individual variation in character, date, authorship etc. He treats the marvellous images contained in the *Lives,* folklore and Bible as a single set of phenomena without distinction of function, nature, or claimed source. They are all 'magic'. In looking, as we are, at the singular *Vita Columbae*, we have seen the weakness of this approach in general. In particular, though Adomnán could be said to 'heap' miracles upon his patron; his claims are frequently substantiated by testimony. The 'miracles' are, as we shall see, differentiated carefully at various levels of organisation: the three books, types of prophecy, posthumous miracles, etc. He does not conclude with a list of superhuman virtues. The 'points which give offence to the hagiologist in search of edification', the 'magic', fails to take account of the equivalent points presented in the scriptural record. Here, for instance, objects are used to convey a spiritual blessing, 'miracles' are cited as evidence of the coming of the awaited Messiah, 'miracles' found the faith, and 'miracles' accompany both the words of commission, and the acts of mission of those sent to proclaim the kingdom. In rejecting them all as 'magic', hence with a pagan origin, Plummer by inference rejects the scriptural record of the same images. He renders the authorized source of the new faith as itself subject to the same interpolation. The canon thus loses its authority as a standard by which practice may be measured, a wholly anachronistic approach applied to the early mediaeval mind of Adomnán however acceptable today.

Two consequences flow out from this treatment: Firstly, the attitude of the sixth/seventh century Ionan church towards the canonical authority of scripture is overlooked. For them, the

---

177 *VSH*, xcii-xciii (my emphasis).
178 *VSH*, clxxviii.

appearance of a practice in the scripture would be adequate authority for both the emulation of the practice in ministry, and for the recording of such a practice in the literary record, perhaps regardless in the latter case of the question of actual occurrence.[179] If it was acceptable to the writers of the sacred word to record such as showing the activity of God through his saints (i.e. disciples) then it was acceptable, perhaps even required, for later writers to emulate. The major question here becomes that of the point at which the use of these miracles, and indeed of the whole corpus of the marvellous, crosses over from the acceptable signs of the kingdom of God to the unacceptable counterfeiting of these signs by other means, i.e. where Christian miracle does become magic. It is evident that our seventh-century Irish Abbot had a rather different idea of where this line was crossed as compared to our nineteenth-twentieth century critic.

This introduces us to the second consequence of Plummer's attitude, 'another unpleasant characteristic is the way in which spiritual blessings, including salvation itself, are made to depend on purely material conditions, on external circumstances and acts...' He might here be seen to articulate a bias against meritorious salvation, and against saintly miracles as part of this doctrine. True spiritual blessings, he infers, are not dependent on material manifestation. He dismisses these as polluting with mythological magic the original 'spiritual' faith in which the early Irish saints, whose reputation he seeks to defend, must have believed.[180]

---

179 As Herbert and Picard have suggested. Though it is accepted that these writers were not writing history in the modern sense, I think we must be careful in accepting too readily the idea that they did not care about the actual occurrence of these events in history. Adomnán shows himself to be so concerned, and to undergird his record of historical miracles by both the recording of witnesses, and of contemporary miracles which show their possibility. See chapter 1 above.

180 We could repeat the earlier conjecture here that Plummer's late nineteenth-century Anglicanism might have put him in a position to be defensive in the context of the recent re-establishment of the Roman Catholic hierarchy (1849), and the disestablishment of the Anglican Church of Ireland (1871). (He was made Deacon in 1875 and was Chaplain of Corpus Christi College, Oxford. He had numerous links with Ireland (he held Hon. DLitt, Dublin (1923) and Celt. Nat. Univ. Irl. (1925), Hon MRIA (1925), and holidayed there annually.) He might thus himself have been partly motivated by a desire to demonstrate a non-Roman Catholic nature in the original church of Ireland, viz. one which did not accept salvation by 'works', including any sort of strange miracle. The Catholic Church of course has not ever rejected its belief in miracles as some liberal Anglicans had by this stage. Plummer was no low-church Protestant however, as can be seen by his negative description of Hardy's *Wells* as written from a 'strongly Protestant point of view', and his deliberate selection of prayers for the deceased in his *Book of Devotions* (1916).

If we were to posit the adherence to and practice of a biblically based supernaturalism in sixth-seventh century Ireland / Scotland, in accordance with Adomnán's record, an interesting possibility would present itself. With Carney *et seq.*, we could propose a late composition of the Irish sagas, incorporating elements of the secular Irish folk-tales, elements of the Christian supernatural, and elements of the Greek myths and sagas. Here we might find an explanation for the form in which the Irish sagas have been received, with their surprisingly Christian cosmology, and for the virtually non-existent documentary record for such material before ca.1100. The proposal would thus be that though there may be an element of influence from oral saga and myth in the Christian writings, which grew with time, the strongest influence was actually from the Christian stories of the miracles of the saints to the secular tales as they became written. Thus reports of prophecy, nature miracle, vision, and healing in the sagas had as their inspiration the miraculous gifts of the Spirit of Christ, and the sub-Christian element in their nature as described in the sagas was the result of imaginative redaction with pagan Irish and Greek mythological influence. It is possible that that documents preserving earlier manuscripts of the secular sagas were destroyed by the depredations of the Scandinavians. However, as Chadwick has said, it is possible that the Vikings were not as universally destructive as the monastic writers, who bore the brunt of their attentions, have tended to portray them,[181] and that thus we ought to expect to find at least fragmentary evidence of earlier manuscripts. Secondly, while saga manuscripts are in very short supply for the period 600-1100, Christian and other secular texts do exist. It seems strange that all evidence of the existence of early saga manuscripts is lost.

A second corollary of the position, if established, would not be acceptable to the theological school of Ritschl and Harnack, which I suggest was an influence upon Plummer. This would be that in the hagiographical record, there might after all remain evidence for the continuation in Christian history of marvellous manifestations. That the seventh-century Ionan church should describe herself as in full possession of prophetic and apostolic supernatural accreditation, in full accordance with the biblical record, would, if demonstrable, be itself evidence for an alternative view of the miraculous in scripture than that proposed by Ritschl *et al.* This could be, as Herbert suggested (above), that the seventh-century church accepted the record of scripture as a standard by which to fashion her own practice. Around this she built her expectations of what was both possible in miraculous terms, of what she should expect to observe as

---

181   See Chadwick, (1971, 104).

Christians practiced their faith, and of what she selected to record as important in her own history. If this was shown to be the case here, it would potentially be interpreted as a continuation of 'alien' Greek supernaturalism introduced into Christian thought in the first century on into the supposedly isolated culture of seventh-century Ireland. However, Ritschl's case as to the origin of the mirabilia in Christian thought remains open to question.[182] On the other hand, the biblical record is firm as a known authority for seventh-century Irish Christian belief; the mirabilia would appear to them as an important element in the spread of the faith. Establishing a biblical model for the record of *VC* would thus form an alternative view to that propounded by Plummer and his followers for the main formative influence on the marvellous in the *Lives*. There would then be little need to posit a formative influence on the *VC* from the Irish sagas. Rather we could see the formative influence as the biblical record, with perhaps a secondary influence from sagas which may themselves have been influenced by the same biblical mirabilia, as well as retaining reflections of pagan Irish religious belief and practice.

Plummer and Biblical Influence

At various stages in his vast collection of references, as we've seen, Plummer himself concedes the occasional influence of the church, rather than pre-Christian religion, on some of the marvellous motifs in Irish hagiography. He even admits occasional biblical influence in the secular tales which he's arguing are providing the *Lives* with their marvels. Collecting and reviewing these references will show how mysterious is Plummer's view of the vector of influence.

He records 'ecclesiastical matter imported into secular tales', citing Simon Magus, Paul, pharaoh's dream, the golden calf, and four 'small christianizing touches'.[183] He refers to 'purely biblical miracles,' of which he says, 'But in our lives they are not so common': druids bless; are unable to curse cf. Balaam; a body flux is healed.[184] Later he mentions others: Saints' spittle cures disease or blindness: 'this shows biblical influence'.[185] 'The idea of food which has the taste of any dainty which the individual eater may desire is

---

182 The field of pre-Christian miracle traditions remains a fruitful source of interest, see for instance Lynn Li Donnici (1995).
183 *VSH*, cxxxii note 4: *Simón drúi* in *TBC* (1905, 355); St Paul in Windisch (*Irische Texte* III: ii, 190); pharaoh's dream in *Magh Lena* (1855, 4); the golden calf in *Keating* (1908, ii.346); and the 'christianizing touches' from *LL* (114b 21; 115a 4; 117b 6; 123a 4).
184 *VSH*, cxxxiii note 4: druids bless, *Tr.Th.* (1847, 416a); body flux healed, *Noua Legenda* (ii 319).
185 *VSH*, clxxviii note 5.

very common, but may have been derived from, or at least been influenced by, Jewish-Christian sources, for the rabbis had the same fancy with reference to the manna in the wilderness.' He gives secular parallels alongside saintly occurrence, and compares the motif with Wisdom 16:20-1.[186] A sudden appearance within closed doors 'may be due to biblical influence, Jn. 20:19, but it has analogies in the secular literature'.[187] Of saints or objects '...transported from place to place in an incredibly short time,' Plummer says: 'The biblical parallel of the transport of Habakkuk is sometimes cited.'[188] Regarding the phenomenon of seeing the whole world spread out before the seer, he concedes: 'Our Lord's temptation on the Mount has probably had influence here', citing Lk. 4:5.[189] These are surely all 'biblical miracles'.

He notes numerous instances of the influence of the 'cult of the Celtic water deity' in tales of saints walking on water. Having furnished the list, he concedes 'Of course this is a case where biblical influence is possible' and gives examples of the motif in the secular tales, though without further comment, so we are left unclear as to whether he believes the possible biblical influence reached them.[190] He lists five saints dividing water: 'here again biblical influences may be at work.'[191] Of the numerous tales of producing a fountain from the rock, he says more certainly: '...here the biblical parallel of Moses smiting the rock has clearly been at work'.[192] He notes in two *Lives* 'The demand of a druid for a human victim to still the raging of the sea', conceding that it 'may be modelled on the Jonah story.'[193]

Discussing the view that the saints' success in combating the druids was the triumph of a more powerful kind of 'medicine', he says

> ...it must be admitted that the biblical story of the contests of Moses with the magicians of Egypt gave colour to this point of view. Indeed many of the accounts of Patrick's conflicts with the druids have evidently been influenced by the narrative of Genesis.[194]

On the punishment of criminals condemned to wandering round and round, numerous in the *Lives*, he says, 'I believe, however, that these stories owe their origin not to popular tradition, but to fanciful

---

186 *VSH,* clxxxv note 13: RC 9:486, 490; *Acc Sen* 153.
187 *VSH,* cxxxix, *VTr* 52.
188 *VSH,* clxxxvi note 6. (Habakkuk from the apocryphal *Bel and the Dragon*).
189 *VSH,* clxxi note 10.
190 *VSH,* cxlvii, and note 6; *TBC* (1905, 159); *Da Choca* (1900, 156); *Magh Rath* (1842, 84).
191 *VSH,* cxlvii note 10.
192 *VSH,* cl note 2.
193 *VSH,* cxlix note 3.
194 *VSH,* clxvi.

interpretation of a verse of scripture' (Ps. 12:9).[195] Some saintly imprecations cause a hand or arm to fall off as judgment. Plummer notes: 'Dr Reeves suggests that Job 31:22 may have suggested the idea.'[196] Of the violation of the folk-tale sex taboo, common in secular literature, but rare in the *Lives*, Plummer says 'We find it in the OT' (1 Sam. 21:4-5).[197]

Of these references, most refer to Old Testament influences. That there are so very few such places of biblical influence noted is itself a noteworthy feature of Plummer's collection, and we may wonder, given the commentaries above, if he was looking at all diligently for them. Very many rather obvious influences are overlooked. For instance the transportation of Philip from the Judean desert to Caesarea in Acts 8:39-40 is a more obvious biblical example of teleportation than that of Habakkuk, and perhaps gives some background in the Christian tradition for the strange story of the teleporting bachall in *VC* ii.14.[198] Again, hands being made skilful by the saint's touch must be prefigured by the examples in Exodus 35:31 of the Holy Spirit gifting folk with skills of various kinds. Plummer says of the latter: 'I cannot produce any secular analogue' which may well be true, but the biblical analogue *is* clear.[199] Plummer's conclusion regarding the vector of influence does not accommodate the comments collected above.

Plummer is not alone in seeing the malign influence of secular marvels on the *Lives*. As we saw at the opening of the chapter, the view Plummer espoused reached the early D.A. Binchy. He later admitted to Hughes' influence in tempering his earlier 'over-statement' of his case against the historicity of early Irish hagiography on the basis of its pagan mythological content.[200] A more recent student of Irish miracles, Stancliffe, acknowledges the folkloric as the third source of the miracle stories in Irish hagiography, but after the biblical and apocryphal. She draws a parallel between the druids' magical ability to raise a wind, and that of Patrick and Columba.[201] Plummer was criticized for imputing to Irish folklore features that were common to the Indo-European genre. Stancliffe falls into the same trap. Similarity in appearance does not of itself indicate dependence without correlative evidence. The motif of storms opposing the servants of God has a wide

---

195 *VSH*, clxviii note 6.
196 *VSH*, clxxiv note 2.
197 *VSH*, clxxxiv note 2.
198 (A reference Plummer misses in his section on this motif, *VSH*, clxxxvi).
199 *VSH*, clxxxv note 14.
200 Binchy (1982, 165).
201 Stancliffe (1992, 92 and note 30; 31); *VC* ii.34; *VSH*, clxxiii-iv.

occurrence in the Judaeo-Christian tradition, as well as in non-Irish folklore. She notes one example from Plummer: 'that the Irish saints took over from the druids their fearsome curses,' but notes in caveat documented Irish care to cite biblical and patristic authority for the practice.[202] This casual observation demonstrates clearly that for these Irish writers of the *Hibernensis*, a key document in Irish church polity, this aspect of the marvellous had scripture and the Fathers as authority and foundation, not pagan myth, though these last may also rely on scriptural motifs for the druidic characteristics.

In summary, we can say with growing confidence that the accounts of the marvellous in the secular sagas look like those in the *Lives*, rather than the other way round. The answer to the question of chronological priority, and of probable source thus finds a more secure evidential foundation in the Christian tradition. We have seen that it may not be viable to interpret the marvellous phenomena associated with Columba as borrowings or unconscious references to secular saga material, nor as the literary appropriation by Christian authors of pagan magic, on grounds of the unreliability of the source materials, the uncertainty of the congruence between saga descriptions of pagan marvellous and their historical reality, and the congruence, at first sight, with accounts in the Christian tradition of similar manifestations. It is tantalising to imagine that in Adomnán we have one of the last descriptions of an active Christian tradition of marvellous phenomenological activity captured 'in print' as it were just coinciding with the onset of the practice of writing pre-Christian Irish history. This practice might subsequently itself come to influence the writing of Christian histories of saints in a synergistic amplification of thaumaturgical hyperbole. Pursuing the reliability of this theory of the influence of the Christian tradition upon Adomnán's description of the marvellous will engage us for the remainder of this discussion. Described against the biblical account of the marvellous, the standing of these phenomena as recorded by Adomnán in this tradition is increasingly clear. For Adomnán, Columba is a prophet in the biblical tradition, and not a clairvoyant.

---

202 E.g. Job 27:21; Isa. 41:16; Jer. 18:17; Ps. 48:7; Jonah 1:4; most importantly Mk. 4:37-41; storms hindering St Germanus on his mission to England (*V. Germ.* xii) etc.

CHAPTER 3

The Flowering of the Kingdom of God in the Isles of the Ocean: Eschatological Nature and Function

> The kingdom of God stands not on the flow of
> eloquence but in the flowering of faith.

Introducing the Servant of the Divine Gardener

The fundamental purpose of establishing the sanctity of a saint is established as the primary reason that the hagiographers performed their task. The political and didactic purposes of the author, over which there remains an element of debate, depended on the foundation of establishing his saint's position as an earthly representative of God, and as one who spoke God's word into the contemporary and subsequent historical situation. Without the authority established through the proof of sanctity, political and didactic purposes would have no weight. Thus it was essential, for an effective hagiography, to demonstrate the saint's (and thus in this case his successor's) virtue, in both its senses of ethical righteousness and spiritual power. The task for us here is to go beneath the surface level of understanding the function of this life as proof of sanctity, however this is then employed, to seek elucidation of the question of what it was that the writer believed he was using to demonstrate this authority; what categories did his theological understanding hold which he employed to the task; and thus what did he believe to be the nature of the phenomena he records. We are not so much here searching for literary sources for Adomnán, as seeking to trace the conceptual and theological background to the way in which he presents the marvellous in this *Life*. We are seeking to determine if he is simply 'following the trend', as it were, in hagiographic fashion, in which case his examples and descriptions will find their source only in these predecessors. The thesis being pursued is that Adomnán was operating out of a much older tradition than the hagiographic, a tradition which goes back to the earliest days of Christian history.

The Kingdom of God and the Flowering of Faith

Following a conventional apologia, Adomnán opens his work with a warning for his readers to concentrate on the substance of the work rather than on its lexicography. Reeves (followed by Fowler and Sharpe) noted that this passage was 'a paraphrase of 1 Corinthians 4:20, suggested by the passage in Sulpicius Severus' Preface to his *Life of St. Martin.*[1] The three passages are:

Vulgate: Non enim in sermone est regnum dei, sed in virtute.[2]

VSM: ...quia regnum dei non in eloquentia, sed in fide constat. Memerint...[3]

VC: Memerintque regnum dei non in eloquentiae exuberantia sed in fidei florulentia constare.[4]

While the distinction is conventional in Christian writing, Adomnán embellishes the phrase uniquely: '...the kingdom of God

consisteth not in the richness of eloquence, but in the blossoming of faith. (B)

standeth not in abundance of speech, but in excellency of faith. (F)

inheres not in exuberance of rhetoric, but in the blossoming of faith. (AA)

...stands not on the flow of eloquence but in the flowering of faith. (S)

Though Adomnán has borrowed the paraphrase from Sulpicius Severus, it is not a slavish copy. He has indicated the function for which he employs the phrase, and his understanding of the meaning of it, by his own additions in what we might correctly call flowery language.

We should also notice particularly both the *Life of Antony* and Patrick's employment of the same idea. *VA* records Antony arguing that God's deposit in a Christian is 'the power of faith', not worldly wisdom, nor 'the emptiness of eloquence'. It is faith which results in the marvels they see. He taunts the Greek sophists that their beautiful language does not impede the Christian mission, whereas the

---

1   Reeves (1857, 3 note a); Fowler (1894, 1 note 1); Sharpe (1995, note 1). Sharpe does not acknowledge earlier notes. Sharpe sees the process as a borrowing direct from the *VSM*, 'Adomnán's primary literary model', the model having itself depended on Paul.
2   *Vulg.*, 1 Cor. 4:20.
3   *VSM*, first preface.
4   *VC* 1a.

power supplied by God through faith in the cross weakens magic and sorcery.[5] Similarly, Patrick says

> How much more ought we to seek, we who are, he affirms, the letter of Christ for salvation as far as the furthest part of land, and if not learned, yet valid and very vigorous, written in your hearts, not with ink but by the Spirit of the living God.'[6]

Patrick, whose learned sophistication Howlett has recently demonstrated, defends himself by insisting not that the message of salvation has been spread by learned eloquence, but by the strength of the Spirit demonstrated in the vigorous mission of establishing the faith in Ireland. He goes on to describe this mission in part IIII of the *Confessio*. It was a mission guided by prophetic vision, and accredited by 'signs and wonders'.[7] Patrick's thesis will be seen to have major relevance in Adomnán's presentation of the ministry of Columba. Jerome expounds Paul's passage

> I shall not regard the *pomp of eloquence*, but the *results of conduct*, where the *power of faith* is an issue.[8]

Significantly to Adomnán's flowery metaphor, the hymn *Altus Prosator*, widely regarded as being from the pen of Columba himself, carries a vivid picture of the flowery midst of paradise where the tree of life bears leaves for the healing of the nations (cf. Rev. 22:2)

> Paradise was planted from the beginning... in whose *flowery* midst is also the Tree of Life whose leaves, bearing healing for the nations, do not fall; whose delights are indescribable and abundant[9]

---

5 '...*non in sapientia mundi habemus repositum, sed in virtute fidei*'; '...*eloquentiae vanus*' (*Vita Antonii*, tr. Evagrius, *PL* 73 0160D: XLIX).

6 *Conf. i.11, tr. Howlett*. '*quanto magis nos adpetere debémus qui sùmus inquit "Epistola Xristi in salutem usque ad ultimum terrae." Et si non diserta sed ráta et fortíssima 'scripta in cordibus uestris non atramento sed Spiritu Dei uiui*' (Howlett, 1994, VII lines 37-41 =ch. 11), cf. 2 Cor. 3:3, and Cassian (*Coll.* 1:20).

7 Patrick, *Conf.* See Howlett (1994, XX.1-53 =chs. 37-40); and (XX.121-2 =ch. 45) for Patrick's refs. to signs and wonders; and (p. 111f.) for visionary refs.

8 '*Et cognoscam non sermonem eorum, qui inflati sunt, sed virtutem. Examinabo non eloquentiae pompam, sed conversationis effectum, ubi virtus fidei esse probatur*' (Auctor incertus, Hieronymus Stridonensis? *Comm. I Cor.* IV.19-20, *PL* 30 0729BC).

9 C&M, 49, stanza P. '*Plantatum a prooemio paradisum a Domino... cuius etiam florido lignum vitae in medio cuius non cadunt folia gentibus salutifera cuius inenarrabiles deliciae ac fertiles.*' They argue for sixth-century composition, and see no reason that it should not have been written by Columba, as early tradition asserts (39-40). They link this stanza to the concept of the kingdom of God (62). It should be noted that in most place where C&M refer to 'the kingdom', they are referring not to an earthly, pre-

These sources demonstrate various foundations of Adomnán's
opening phrase, and of the method of the *VC*. He does not derive his
additional vocabulary from Jerome, but Jerome may have suggested
Adomnán's imaginative adjectival couplet in his *eloquentiae
pompam* and *conversationis effectum*. It may be from *VA* that he
derived the *eloquence*, and from Columba himself that he derives the
flowering. It must be unlikely that Adomnán would have borrowed
this phrase from the *VSM* if it had not fitted his purpose in writing
the *Life*, so it may be that he has in mind a particular source of
exuberant rhetoric which he seeks to counter. Could it be the claims
of Armagh, of the Ionan conservatives, of the Pictish rulers, of
Northumbria? Political possibilities here have already been discussed
above. Or is it a more spiritual, theologically loaded observation,
arguing that there is more to the faith than intellectual
understanding? The question we wish to answer in this section is what
are the contents of Adomnán's concepts of the 'kingdom of God
(*regnum dei*)', and of the 'blossoming of faith (*fidei florulentia*)' in
which this kingdom is inherent, or on which it stands? We will take
the phrases in reverse order.

The Flowering of Faith

Adomnán uses a term related to *florulentia* in the angel's
annunciation to Columba's mother in iii.1: '...you will bear a son of
such flower (*filium floridum*) (S) that he, as though one of the
prophets of God, shall be counted in their number...' Biblical
references to flowers, flowering, blossom, and blossoming are few,
and in the main refer to an ephemeral object representing
temporariness, something which though beautiful, fades quickly. This
is evidently not Adomnán's allusive intent, as for him, the flowering
of faith represents the coming of the kingdom of God. It would be
impossible to imagine this to be, in Adomnán's theology, a
temporary, fading phenomenon. Thus he is using the image in a way
which is practically the opposite of the general biblical usage, but
directly in line with the idea in the *Altus Prosator* of the flowery
paradise created by the Lord.

---

parousia manifested kingdom, but to the heavenly kingdom wherein the
blessed dead reside with God. Their focus is thus, in a sense, upward. I am here
investigating whether Adomnán demonstrates familiarity with a 'horizontally'
manifest kingdom, anticipating the eschatological heavenly kingdom where
all is new (though see chapter 4 below for a different nuance in their
understanding).

The adjective *florulentia* is very rare in this ending.[10] Cassian describes abbot Moses as among the most beautiful of the 'flowers of holiness' (*Conf.* 1.1). It provides a metaphor whose meaning can be illustrated from the Greek root, *ek-flainw*, to stream forth'; 'putting forth; the visible manifestation of the purpose of a living system'. L&S give 'abounding in flowers' as a post-classical rendering,[11] Souter suggests 'having flowers' or 'flourishing'. The flower is the typical manifestation of a flowering plant's nature, and the crowning achievement of its existence. The morphology of the flower is also critical to the definitive taxonomy of the plant which produces it. Hence, for Adomnán, faith coming into flower manifests the presence of the kingdom, which, if he has the *Altus* in mind, is the heavenly paradise. The flowers for which he is looking, which demonstrate the nature and incontrovertible arrival of the kingdom, are described in the stories he is about to relate.

In the Old Testament, the prophets looked forward to the establishment of the new heaven and earth. The book of Isaiah has passages particularly redolent of Adomnán's thought concerning Columba's repute and status as he presents him.

> There shall come forth a shoot from the stump of Jesse, and a branch shall grow out of his roots. And the Spirit of the LORD shall rest upon him... And his delight shall be in the fear of the LORD. He shall not judge by what his eyes see, or decide by what his ears hear; but with righteousness he shall judge the poor... with the breath of his lips he shall slay the wicked. Righteousness shall be the girdle of his waist, and faithfulness the girdle of his loins... The sucking child shall play over the hole of the asp, and the weaned child shall put his hand on the adder's den. They shall not hurt or destroy in all my holy mountain; for the earth shall be full of the knowledge of the LORD as the waters cover the sea (Is. 11:1-9).

The eschatological vision of the blooming of the desert may provide biblical background to Adomnán's descriptive metaphor here.

---

10   Diarmuid Ó Laoghaire cites a usage of a similar image, a 'fertile field with many flowers', referring to the church, from an unpublished section of the later (late ninth/early tenth century) *Catechesis Celtica* (CC 42rb, Ní Chatháin and Richter (1987, 148)). The application is to the church as a field of flowers of martyrdom, red flowers of their blood; white of incorruptibility; 'viola' of humility. Although Adomnán is concerned to present Columba as incorrupt and holy ('his pure heart' is a commonplace), he has no interest in the *VC* of presenting the flowering of faith as martyrdom as such. He sees ascetic holiness demonstrated in marvellous acts which demonstrate the presence of the kingdom of God. The flowers on his robe are also of every colour (iii.1), an entirely more comprehensive floral banner than the martyrological tricolour.

11   L&S, 761.

In days to come Jacob shall take root, Israel shall blossom and put forth shoots, and fill the whole world with fruit (Isa. 27:6).[12]

The wilderness and the dry land shall be glad, the desert shall rejoice and blossom; like the crocus it shall blossom abundantly, and rejoice with joy and singing. The glory of Lebanon shall be given to it, the majesty of Carmel and Sharon. They shall see the glory of the LORD, the majesty of our God... Then the eyes of the blind shall be opened, and the ears of the deaf unstopped; then shall the lame man leap like a hart, and the tongue of the dumb sing for joy. For waters shall break forth in the wilderness, and streams in the desert (Isa. 35:1-2, 5-6).

In Adomnán's Christian world-view, it is the new Israel, the kingdom of God established by Christ, which blossoms where once there was wilderness. We see here and in related passages that the flower has a further function in reproduction, vital to the establishment and propagation of the species through the production of fruit. By this extension of the content of Adomnán's metaphor to include fruit, it may be possible to understand further how it is that he works out the ramifications of his statement in the rest of the *VC*. 'By their fruit you will recognise them' (Mt. 7:16). Fruit bearing is not the result of human action, but of the working of the power of the Spirit (Mt. 3:8//). Eschatologically, every tree without fruit will be condemned (Mt. 3:10; 7:19; Lk. 13:6). Close, obedient fellowship with Christ is seen as the secret of the power to bear fruit (Jn. 15:2ff). The fruit counts and abides for eternal life (Jn. 4:36; 15:16). Paul recognizes that walking in the light, characterized as the fruit of the Spirit, in goodness, righteousness and truth (Eph. 5:8-9), is required in order to inherit the kingdom of God. This is fruit, which again appears as a result not of unaided human effort, but of the activity of the indwelling Spirit on the will. Paul also uses the term to refer to the results of his own missionary work (Rom. 1:13; Phil.

---

12   '*Qui ingrediuntur impetu ad Jacob, florebit et germinabit Israel, et implebunt faciem orbis semine.*' This suggested source for the metaphor of the kingdom, taken with the tale of the robe of Columba's mother's vision (see below on iii.1) brings with it a geo-political connotation: could this be taken as background to a suggestion that Adomnán is subtly presenting the spread of the power of one or other of the nations of his day? It seems highly unlikely in the literary context that Adomnán could have such a purpose in mind. The most obvious group to whom this could feasibly apply is the dynasty of Dál Riata. Herbert has argued for the support of Adomnán for his sept of the Northern Uí Néill (see my summary above). His attention to various of the contemporary dynasties, declining openly to favour any of them, combined with his direct, open, and heavily substantiated account of the spread of the spiritual kingdom of God in this book incline one to take Adomnán's interpretation of Isaiah, if it exists, at the eschatological and not contemporary geo-political level. The question would bear closer scrutiny in another study.

1:22). The fruit of the fig tree is included in Messianic prophecies (Mic. 4:4; Zech. 3:10); and in reference to the coming of the kingdom, when coming into leaf anticipates the coming summer, and subsequent fruit (Mt. 24:32f//). Finally Revelation 22:2 records that in the eschaton all hindrances to the production of fruit are removed, and we see the tree of life in constant production, as in the original, and recreated paradise.[13]

Book two contains numerous marvels of a similar nature to these biblical motifs. The gushing forth of water (Is. 35.6, cf. *Altus* §P) has a direct parallel in ii.10, and healing miracles, albeit different in detail, constitute signs of the coming kingdom, produced by Columba's blessings. So, the etymology of Adomnán's embellished borrowed phrases here appear to denote that in his abbatial opinion, the kingdom of God is established in what we might term manifest ontological reality when, and only when, faith is exercised in such a way that tangible evidence of its exercise are manifestly observable in ways beyond the unaided ability of human resources. We might expect this evidence to demonstrate the glory of the system from which it derives, the nature of this system, the identity of the system, and a reproductive function.[14] And we might assume that as Adomnán addresses a contemporary audience in terms of their expectation of the content of the kingdom in their experience, that he himself expects such evidence to be available in his own time. Adomnán does not answer at this point what he would accept as evidence for such flowering, instead he appeals to his readers to concentrate on the deeds which represent this flowering, deeds which were dependent on God for their achievement

> Let them not despise the publication of deeds that are profitable and that have not been accomplished without the help (*opitulationes*) of God').[15]

In his recording this, we have a clear indication of his view of the phenomena he is about to describe: they were not the product of

---

13   Following Hensel (*NIDNTT*, 1:722-3) and Motyer (*NIDNTT*, 1:724-5). The eschaton here is the concept of a 'real' future state whose fulfilment is awaited, as prophesied in the OT, and inaugurated in the NT. Adomnán's belief in such an awaited heaven is demonstrated incontrovertibly in his writing, and in his era, as O'Reilly shows (1997, 80-106). Again, note the reference above from the *Altus* to these motifs.

14   By 'system' I am referring for instance to a plant which gives rise to a flower as the system which produces the flower; in this application, the system is the kingdom of God.

15   *Vulgate*, 1 Cor. 12:28 is another example of the use of *opitulationes*; here Paul is listing the various *pneumatikoi* i.e. gifts and ministries empowered by the Spirit: '...gifts of healings, helps, governments, diversities of tongues (*gratias curationum, opitulationes, gubernationes, genera linguarum...*)'.

human activity or human words, but are dependent on the assistance, the intervention, of divine agency, as Antony had insisted.

> For as the rain and the snow come down from heaven, and return not thither but water the earth, making it bring forth and sprout, giving seed to the sower and bread to the eater, so shall my word be that goes forth from my mouth; it shall not return to me empty, but it shall accomplish that which I purpose, and prosper in the thing for which I sent it (Isa. 55:10-11).

The identification of the saint with Divine intervention on his or her request is nothing new to our understanding of the hagiographer's method. However, we are interested in the content of Adomnán's concept of the nature of this intervention. The rest of his work forms an exposition of the evidence he would consider to constitute a manifestation, a flowering, of the faith which may educe the manifestation from God. Before exploring Adomnán's argument, his presentation of Columba's marvellously accredited life, we need to examine the second phrase of Adomnán's embellished borrowing: the kingdom of God within the eschatological view of his milieu.

The Kingdom of God in the Life of Columba

Adomnán quite deliberately demonstrates throughout *VC* that actions, and in particular supernaturally powerful, marvellous actions, are the true proofs of faith, and that the flowering of this faith manifests the kingdom. He records very little indeed of Columba's preaching, or other eloquence, recording only the fruitful words of his prophetic revelations, and small selections of significant conversations. In his opening statement, the participle of *consto* has the sense of something which is established, manifest, or evident. This manifestation is especially of something which consists in, or rests in something else, in order to become what it is.[16] Thus we can safely assume he is referring to the manifest establishment of this kingdom by virtue (i.e. through the power or agency of) the flowering of faith. Biblical theologians over the last century have rediscovered the importance of eschatology as an important substrate in the thought of the biblical writers, and the concept of 'the kingdom' as a central eschatological concept in the evangelists' accounts of the life of Christ.[17] The gospels present Christ as coming

---

16 L&S, 439.

17 From Klappert, *NIDNTT* 2:372-389. In the Old Testament, the kingdom primarily comes to be associated with the rule of God as expressed through the immanent rulers of his people, and refers to the power of God manifested in this way. 'In later texts, Yahweh's kingship is interpreted in an eschatological sense' (2:376), looking forward to Yahweh's rule over the whole earth at the

to inaugurate the establishment of the kingdom of God (or for Matthew, the kingdom of heaven [18]) on the earth in the present age. The disciples of Jesus were sent out by Him to further the establishment of this kingdom; an establishment which will, in this age, only ever be partial, but will nevertheless manifest the conditions of the coming eschaton. This is an eschaton in process of being 'realized'. Building on Ritschl, the early C.H. Dodd saw this as an already established ethical kingdom which proceeds inexorably to a summit of ultimate evolutionary achievement. Plummer, as we've seen, writing under Harnack's influence, after explaining the miraculous as folk-tale, was interested primarily in the ethical dimension of the portrait of the saints presented in the *Lives*. Adomnán goes further. He does mention Columba's pure heart on many occasions, but the ethical content of this pure heart is never significantly developed. Where it is, the accompanying proof is not ethical activity on the natural level, but the miraculous phenomena which flow from the ethical heart. Neither is it Columba's human wisdom which is the focus. What interests Adomnán is rather the direct contact this man has with the source of wisdom; the source of ethical rectitude; the source of power to incarnate that eschatological ethical wisdom. In other words it is the in-breaking of the rule of God, making, by direct action as it were, the conditions of the eschatological kingdom present the pre-fulfilment age. This feature, if present in Adomnán's thought, coincides with the so-called 'inaugurated' eschatological view in the NT a view that McGrath recognises as held by most biblical theologians today.[19] G.E. Ladd developed this view, significantly to our study, taking notice of the

---

end of time. In Rabbinic Judaism, the kingdom is a purely eschatological concept (2:377), and in LXX apocrypha, it is identified with the four cardinal ethical virtues (4 Mac. 2:23, and Wis. 6:20: 'The desire for wisdom leads to a kingdom'), a shift of meaning completed in Philo. Jesus is not recorded as claiming kingship, but named as king by others, 'we may suppose that the basis of the charge is to be seen and found largely in the way Jesus behaved' (2:379). 'We should note that Jesus himself saw his miracles of healing, his casting out of demons, and his preaching of the gospel to the poor as the fulfilment of Isaianic prophecies (cf. Isa. 29:18f; 35:5f; 61:1f). 'The Kingdom of God is a term of central importance only in the Synoptic tradition; It will come: it is coming; is guaranteed by Jesus' actions as the leaves of the fig tree show the nearness of summer (Mt. 24:32f; Mk. 13:28f; Lk. 21:29f), and will break in suddenly. It is present (as shown by expulsion of demons, Mt. 12:28, Lk. 11:20; shows Satan has been bound by one stronger than he, Mt. 12:29; Mk. 3:27; Lk. 11:21). 'In the works of Jesus the kingdom of God is already a present reality' (2:382). I am interested to trace any similar eschatological function in Adomnán's view of the marvellous.

18 Cf. *Altus Prosator*, *'Caeli de regni'* (C&M, 44).
19 McGrath (1997, 547).

marvellous manifestations in scripture which seem to make present
on earth, in part, conditions of the eschaton. He describes this
present age, after the resurrection and ascension, but before the
return of Christ, as an 'already but not yet' experience of conditions
of the kingdom of God (Ladd 1974 and 1975). The view is developed
amongst others by Max Turner (1996).

ESCHATOLOGY IN THE MILIEU OF SEVENTH-CENTURY IRELAND

Patrick shows himself to have held a clear view of the approach of
the end of the world, realizing the call to preach the kingdom to the
ends of the earth, and the Joeline promise of the outpouring of the
Spirit.[20] The last seven stanzas of the *Altus Prosator* present a firm
interpretation of the biblical description of the day of the Lord
meaning the end of time and space, the coming judgement, and
return of Christ from heaven.[21] Columbanus believed the world to be
in its last days; e.g. 'The world is already in its latter days'.[22] As we
have noticed, Adomnán adapts a phrase of Sulpicius, and thereby
adopts his eschatology, as the context confirms. Important to our
study here, Hillgarth believes a function of Gregory the Great's
record of miracles, visions and signs is 'to show how the future age
had broken into Italy'.[23] He also sees one of two principle legacies of
the seventh century being their perception 'less often noted today
but perhaps the greatest novelty of the age... of the constant
interpenetration of this world and the next'.[24] From his presentation
of the journeys of souls of the departed, Adomnán, it seems, shares
what Hillgarth describes as Gregory's central conviction, 'that an
immortal soul is the only essential thing a man possesses and that the
whole of life has to be lived in the light of the approaching
judgement', and also, 'There seems no doubt that one of the main
aims of the *Dialogues*, as a whole, is to make men see heaven as
their true home (*patria caelestis*); this is stressed from the preface
onwards.'[25] Whether Hillgarth's next sentence also applies to

---

20 *Conf.* chs. 14, 17, citing Mt. 24:14, Mk. 16:15-16, and Acts 2:17-18. These
      views of these early mediaeval writers must be held in tension with some
      recent New Testament research which suggests its writers may not have
      intended an end of time and space as such (see e.g. N.T Wright, 1996, 145-end).
      If not, our early mediaeval writers did not get the message, though see Altus
      §U which shows clearly an acceptance of figures in eschatological writing.
21 C&M, 55-53.
22 Columbanus, *Ep.* v, 4:23-4, Walker (1970, 41).
23 Hillgarth (1987, 325).
24 Hillgarth (1992, 230-1).
25 *VC* iii6, 7, 9-14. Hillgarth recapitulates R.A. Markus (1985, 92f.), and his own
      (1987, 324f.).

Adomnán forms part of the question this present book seeks to answer

> The miracles are intended to demonstrate the transient, transparent nature of the visible world and so to instil a longing for the future life.[26]

He notes the shared nature of this world-view in Late Antique thought

> The Christian thinkers whom we see as living in Late Antiquity hardly thought of themselves as doing so. For them man's history was divided into ages and they were in the sixth age, that had begun with the birth of Christ and would see the conversion of all peoples to belief in Him. Theirs was a theology that envisaged history as progressing, with remarkable speed, towards a definite goal. The conversion of the world would shortly be followed by its end.[27]

This was a view developing across the old empire, largely through the influence of the Bible and the works of Gregory the Great in the growing and influential monastic movement: 'a new transcendent view of the world was already emerging in the seventh century', and, 'A new hierarchy of values was at war with an older system, based on pagan values... The true *patria* was now no longer Rome... it was situated in the heavens.'[28] Isidore addresses the subject directly if briefly: 'How should the kingdom of God be understood? Answer: five ways: that is, Christ, faith, the gospel, the church present, indeed the kingdom of heaven itself' and he refers to John the Baptist's proclamation of its advent in Mt. 3:2.[29] Bede was certain the end would come soon; Christ had been preached even in Britain,[30] and Columba worked 'in a remote corner of the world'.[31] Although Adomnán shows no interest in the advent of antichrist shown by Gregory in his *Moralia* and letters,[32] he does share in the conviction of the approaching end, though perhaps without Gregory's urgency. Herbert notes the link of this process of conversion with miraculous demonstrations of the gospel: 'From his hagiographical reading, Adomnán no doubt was familiar with the convention that miraculous

---

26 Hillgarth (1992, 220).
27 Hillgarth (1992, 221).
28 Hillgarth (1992, 228; 230).
29 '... *regnum Dei quibus modis intelligitur? Respondit: Quinque: id est, Christus, fides, Evangelium, Ecclesia praesens, vel ipsum regnum coelorum... Poenitentiam agite; appropinquavit enim regnum coelorum.*' Isidorus Hispalensis: *De Veteri et Novo Testamento Quaestiones.* Quaestio XXXIII, *PL* 83 0205B.
30 Hillgarth (1992, 221).
31 Bede *HE* V.15.
32 Hillgarth (1992, 222).

signs assisted the process of conversion of a heathen people.' She
notes the final sentence of *VC* ii.34

> Let the reader reflect how great and of what nature was the venerable man,
> in whom almighty God made manifest to the heathen people the glory of
> his name through those signs of miraculous power described above.[33]

This view was not unique; Jonas reports the missionary vision of
Columbanus as an image of the round world with great spaces still left
for him to work in.[34] Thomas O'Loughlin's important work on the
seventh-century Irish mental map of the world, with (what we now
call) Ireland / Scotland on the furthest edge, at 'the ends of the
earth',[35] lends weight to the probability that Adomnán, if not
Columba himself, saw their mission to the Picts as the final vital
enactment of the Matthaean missionary commission.[36] We should
also note, from the immediate milieu, references in the *Amra* to
Christ as 'the King's son' (VII.23), and to Columba turning the tribes
of the Tay to 'the will of [God] the King' (VIII.6). These show the
currency of the idea of God as King, inferring the existence of his
kingdom.

THE KINGDOM IN THE MONASTERY

The realization of the kingdom in the environment of the Christian
community, and the monastery, in its rituals, liturgies and rules of
life, resulting in renewed inter-human, human-creation and human-
deity relationships is an element of monastic thought. Gregory of
Tours' episcopal city provided a 'model for the kingdom of the
people of God'.[37] For him, the Christian hold over Gaul remained
fragile, and the civic realization of the kingdom acted as bulwark
against persistent paganism. Could this too be detected in Adomnán's
writing, and therefore be part of the reason for writing as he does?
Eucherius sees the ascetic community of Lérins as a retreat from the

---

33 Herbert (1988, 140). We should note R.A. Markus' caution on the conceptual
    consideration of conversion, 'The awareness of the conceptual problems
    involved to be found in Wallace-Hadrill's chapter 'From Paganism to
    Christianity' is, alas, rarely to be found in the work of historians.' (1992, 158
    note 6), and see McCone's discussion (1990, 21f.).

34 *V.Col* i.27, though Wood (1982, 75) suggests Columbanus' interest in
    missionary work may have been exaggerated by his biographer.

35 O'Loughlin (1997, 11-23).

36 Mt. 28:18-20. One example from the end of the eighth century in Ireland
    suffices to show the process viewed nearing completion: The *Martyrology of
    Oengus* records: 'Paganism has been ruined, although it was illustrious and
    widespread. The kingdom of God the Father has filled heaven, earth and sea'
    (Stokes, 1905, 215-6). For the date, see Breatnach (1996, 74-5).

37 Hillgarth (1992, 214).

fallen world, 'a placid harbour far removed from the breakers'.[38] The desert retreat moreover was the place where God's light was manifested, and the grace of the heavenly kingdom poured out in miracle, as seen in the lives of Moses, Elijah, David, and pre-eminently of Christ. Eucherius notices from Matthew 3 and 4 that it was in the desert where Christ first mentions the kingdom of heaven (*in deserto primum mentio regni coelestis infertur*) (21), where the angels ministered to him (21, 23), where he was first seen to receive the Spirit (21-2), where food was multiplied (24), and where the transfiguration occurred (25).

Each of these motifs is important in Adomnán's presentation of Columba, as we will see.[39] This may represent at least a partial recovery of lost paradise; the kingdom realized there to some extent. Hilary followed Honoratus as Eucherius' abbot. His *Life* describes Lérins as an 'earthly paradise'.[40] Cassian shows us that the kingdom of God, by which he means eternal life, is the aim of the holy life, of purity of heart.[41] For Cassian, the kingdom is established where the pure heart is established. In *Conference* 10, Cassian brings together the concepts of union with God, spiritual vision (see chapter 4 below), purity and the eschatological kingdom. He sets his description on the high mountain of solitude, removed from the turbulence of sin, as on the mount of transfiguration. The mount forms a possible type of Iona, and though Columba was not removed from others' sin, he did withdraw there and to other islands to pray, as Cassian recommends.

> While we still hang around in this body we must reproduce some image of that blessedly eternal life promised for the future to the saints so that among us it may be a case of 'God-all in all' All a monk's striving must be for union with God, that he may deserve to possess in this life an image of future happiness and may have the beginnings of a foretaste in this body of that life and glory of heaven.[42]

Cassian holds the kingdom as a future reality, contemplation of which can bring joy in the discipline of maintaining purity in preparation for its promised blessings. As we shall see, Adomnán goes beyond this internal, invisible definition.

---

38 Eucherii Lugdunensis, *De Contemptu Mundi*, *PL* 50, 0726.
39 Eucherii Lugdunensis, *De Eremi*, *PL* 50 passim. See esp. §21-26 0706B-0707A for Christ's eremitic sojourn.
40 *VS Hilarii Arelatensis*, 5:7 (Carallin, 1952, 86).
41 *Coll.* 1, see esp. 1.13.
42 *Coll.* 10:6-7 (Luibheid, 1985, 128-30).

Both Gilbert Márkus and Jennifer O'Reilly have recently considered the eschatological element in Adomnán's thought.[43] Márkus noted the particular character of the zoological miracles taking place on Iona, where incidents show an unnatural harmony between Columba and animals (horse (iii.23), snakes (ii.28, iii.23), knife blunted (ii.29). Márkus thought the blessings here create a sort of paradise, a centre of harmony, a glimpse of heaven on Iona. 'Adomnán paints a picture of his monastery almost as if it were a foretaste of heaven where the peacefulness of God's reign is already apparent.'[44] There may here be a reference to Isaiah's prophecy, and to the monastery as a foretaste of heaven, but it was only to be so while the monks maintain God's commandments. In her exploration of Adomnán's use of the monastic tradition of *lectio divina* O'Reilly identifies various eschatological elements. The story of Oswald's envisioned victory is an image of the continuing fulfilment of Joshua's prophecy.[45] The fragrance and savour of paradisean flowers, and the fruit of heaven, is foretasted in the monastery,[46] and monastic life prefigures the heavenly sanctuary.[47] The image of the eschatological Jerusalem is foreseen in Columba's blessing of Iona; the sacramental foretaste of eternal life may be discerned in the bread of angels taken at mass before his death; and Adomnán's exposition of the patristic octave relating to salvation history and Columba's entry into eternal rest on the eighth day, reveals his learned approach to it.[48]

THE KINGDOM IN THE WORLD BEYOND THE VALLUM

However, as well as affecting much within, the concept we are here investigating goes far beyond the vallum,. The concept looks forward to a new age when the kingdom will have been completely established in a new heaven and earth, and all destructive elements of the present age are done away with (see e.g. Cassian, *Conf.* 1:13). God's perfect writ will run freely, and will result in a perfect existence without hunger, thirst, disease, without sin of any kind, without conflict, broken relationships either between humans, between them and the rest of creation, or between the creation and the creator. In short, it is the concept of a future when all will be in peaceful, harmonious co-existence, creation and creator in a state of 'rest'

---

43   O'Reilly (1997), Márkus (1999), and O'Reilly, paper at the conference Spes
        Scotorum, Edinburgh, 7th June 1997. O'Reilly interpreted some of the images
        contained in the Book of Kells as having an eschatological element.
44   Márkus (1999, 119).
45   *VC* i.1, O'Reilly (1997, 85).
46   *VC* i.37, O'Reilly (1997, 90), ii.44 (92) and iii.23 (96).
47   *VC* ii.44, O'Reilly (1997, 93).
48   *VC* iii.23, O'Reilly (1997, 96-end).

together under the rule of Christ the King. This 'eschaton' is thus the concept of a 'real' future state whose fulfilment is awaited as prophesied in the OT, and inaugurated in the NT. Adomnán's belief in such an awaited heaven is demonstrated incontrovertibly in his writing, and in his era, as O'Reilly (1997) shows. He has a definite concept of the new earth, describing Columba as a leader of innumerable souls to the heavenly country (*ad caelestem patriam*, iii.1), i.e. the fully consummated kingdom of heaven of the eschaton.

A number of early poems associated with Iona take us closer to the time of the 'historical' Columba. *Amra Choluimb Chille* is interpreted as recording Columba's evangelistic success in turning the tribes of the Tay, 'to the will of the King'.[49] The context strongly suggests this to be the heavenly king, and thus records the establishment of God's kingdom, the place where God's will rules, on earth. Similarly, the seventh-century Irish poet Beccán says

> To heaven's king he [Columba] was known... the king who ends evil... the king of fire... On the loud sea he cried to the king who rules thousands who rules... kings and countries.[50]

Each of these kings must refer to God.

O'Reilly identifies linkage between various patristic and other early Christian sources, and the ideas she traces here, showing Adomnán to be presenting a sophisticated contemporary theological presentation of Columba's life, rather than a simplistic collection of a series of hagiographic commonplace narratives simply demonstrating sanctity. There are many more indications of the eschatological in the *VC*. O'Reilly does not link this eschatological awareness with Adomnán's mentioning of the kingdom of God, a concept I believe may be shown to act as a unifying key to the interpretation of Adomnán's presentation of Columba's life, and particularly for our purpose here, of his use of the marvellous. O'Reilly has demonstrated that Adomnán clearly had a keen awareness of the eschaton in his thought; I hope to demonstrate that Adomnán distinctly understood the realization of the eschatological kingdom, in part, in his personal and familial experience.

Thus by 'kingdom', we see that Adomnán is referring to a rule of God which is conceived as being fulfilled in the eschaton, but made partially present in the age before, through miracle. Adomnán, like the evangelists, holds a concept of miracle as an eschatological realization, understood as an in-breaking of the future state into the

---

49 *Amra* viii.5-6 (C&M, 119). For the *Amra*, see C&M, 96f., and their conclusion (122).

50 *Fo Réir Choluimb*, 9, 24-5, and *Tiugraind Beccán*, 8 (C&M, 129-31). They argue for a seventh-century date for Beccán's poems.

present, thus this might form a category which helps to interpret at least some of the phenomena in the *VC*. I recognise that there is much debate here, but wish to employ Ladd's 'already but not yet' framework in an attempt to make sense of the purpose of Adomnán in including the stories we will look at in the *Life*. We will now need to review some representative examples of the tales to illustrate the major aspects of Adomnán's concept of kingdom of God as expressed in *VC*.

The Coming Kingdom in the *Life of Columba*

There are in *VC* various conventional borrowings from the Bible or duplications of biblical miracles: water into wine (ii.1), resuscitation (ii.32), healing by touching the hem of his robe (i.3), calming of storms (ii.13), water from the rock (ii.10). If With Adomnán's eschatological awareness, if he is understanding an eschatological content in these stories, and associating this with Columba, we might suggest that he is importing the eschatological view of the biblical originals. Our difficulty here of course is that these very close-to-biblical tales do not help us to see into Adomnán's theological mind as he may simply be adopting biblical stories and re-fashioning them with Columba as the central character, and placed in a Gaelic context. We cannot determine directly with *these* tales that he has an eschatological kingdom in process of realization in mind. However, there are a number of stories with no obviously direct origin in biblical narrative, or in other extant early Christian writings. Given no demonstrable secular origin (see chapter two above), and the accepted importance of the Bible on Iona, we may posit that the stories are selected, and/or shaped, by Adomnán's patristic biblical theology.

The Kingdom of God as Good News to the Poor

According to Luke, Jesus of Nazareth announced the agenda for his mission of establishing the kingdom by quoting the prophet Isaiah: 'The Spirit of the Lord is upon me, because he has anointed me to preach good news to the poor...' (Lk. 4:18, c.f. Mt. 5:3-10, the Beatitudes; and Mt. 14:13f., feeding the 5000). The tales of the stake (ii.37), cows (ii.20, 21), and thief (i.41), can be read straightforwardly as material translations of this good news into divinely empowered action. The hungry are fed. The humble lifted. These characteristics were reflected in the *Amra*: 'he was a shelter to the naked, he was a teat to the poor' (VI.26-7). Thus Adomnán's description of the ministry of Columba includes this inaugural element of the conditions of the kingdom.

The Kingdom of the God of the Marvellous Harvest

A group which most obviously contain an eschatological reference, and which may therefore contain the concept of a kingdom in process of realization are those concerning nature in the process of perfection. Book two opens with a triplet of tales of the marvellous transformation of nature; we will consider two of them.

THE FRUIT TREE

In *VC* ii.2 we have a tale which may relate directly to the etymological discussion concerning flowers and fruit above. Columba is described as responding to a complaint of the people living on the southern side of the Ionan foundation of Durrow. Here was a tree which bore much fruit, but fruit which was bitter and hurtful. Columba goes to the tree in the autumn, its natural season for fruiting, and, raising his holy hand, blesses it, saying,

> In the name of almighty God thou bitter tree, may all thy bitterness leave thee, and thy fruit, hitherto most bitter, now become most sweet.

The fruit becomes wonderfully sweet, '*more quickly than words, and at the same moment*'. Adomnán's primary concern is, as ever, to show the saint's sanctity, this time manifested in power over nature. However, Adomnán shows his customary care over the source of the transformation being not the power of Columba himself, but that of the God whom he invokes. The saint is a channel through whom God works in creation. The point of particular interest here is the form of this manifestation as the transformation of nature from bitterness to sweetness. More especially its application to the fruit of a flower should be noted, the possible reference of this being to the fruitfulness of life lived by active faith which manifests the kingdom, and the linked eschatological reference to the transformation of nature which will come about as the kingdom is realized fully in the eschaton. A first-fruit example is the physical transformation of the fruit on the tree. Amos 9:14 is an example of eschatological expectation linked to fruit

> I will restore the fortunes of my people of Israel, and they shall rebuild the ruined cities and inhabit them; they shall plant vineyards and drink their wine; and they shall make gardens and eat their fruit.

Moses was instrumental in God's transformation of the bitter lake of Marah into sweet water (Ex. 15:23ff.), which may be a model from which Adomnán is working. However, apart from the adjectival change, there is little else of similarity here. Adomnán is keen to stress that it was not anything so naturalistic as the ripening of the fruit over time that he records here. On the contrary, the transformation is instantaneous, at the point of invocation of God. An ecclesio-political conjecture here could be that Adomnán is referring allegorically to a church or community not owing allegiance to Iona proximal to Durrow, which Columba brings into his *familia*, thus sweetening the fruit, as it were. Alternatively, and perhaps with more congruence with similar encounters in Pictland, this could be the remnant of a contest with the druids. The Song of Moses contains a reference to the enemies of Israel

> For their vine comes from the vine of Sodom, and from the fields of Gomor'rah; their grapes are grapes of poison, their clusters are bitter; their wine is the poison of serpents, and the cruel venom of asps (Dt. 32:32-33).

Now the response to this bitterness in the song of Moses is not healing, but punishment, so though this passage might provide a clue to a further allegory, it does not explain the 'healing' of the fruit. The story of Jesus' curse of the fig tree is another possible reference model, but again, though a fruit tree is involved, the fig tree had no fruit, and was out of season, the evangelist's point being the unfruitful nature of Israel that would lead to its being passed over by God, and Jesus is not pictured as transforming it. No other literary source has thus far been suggested as Adomnán's model, so we may take this as his own tale, and as either reporting a received tradition, or at the very least his own idea of what Columba's ministry demonstrated. Even if he did have a source, as yet unidentified, outwith the Columban tradition, he has adopted this image for his own purpose.

Biblical eschatology anticipates a time when the earth will be transformed or re-created (e.g. Mt. 19:28), and all that is in it restored or transformed to perfection as the kingdom of God is finally fulfilled. The earth will be released from the curse under which it suffers as a result of rebellion against the creator (Rom. 8:19-23). Wolves eating with lambs (Is. 11:6, 65:25); mountains flowing with sweet wine (Joel 3:18, Amos 9:13); abundant crops, fruit (Amos 9:13); etc., represent a fraction of the available biblical imagery of this new heaven and earth. As we have seen, the New Testament writers present the marvels of Jesus as in-breakings of this kingdom into the present age, as first-fruits of the heavenly kingdom; as its works and signs. Jesus himself is the eschatological God coming into the world, and his death and resurrection act out man's ultimate destiny. The age of the church is the age of the Spirit, in whom Christians participate in the eternal life of the age to come. By the

Spirit they make the eschatological future of creation known in proclamatory mission to the ends of the earth, so all men may hear and receive, as the kingdom is being established. As Richard Bauckham puts it, 'The Spirit is the first fruit of the full harvest'.[51]

> and not only the creation, but we ourselves, who have the first fruits of the Spirit, groan inwardly as we wait for adoption as sons, the redemption of our bodies (Rom. 8:23).

It must be significant to our understanding of Adomnán that he opens his work with a direct reference to the establishment of the kingdom, as consisting in the flowering of faith, and in his second preface, carefully and deliberately presents Columba as a bearer of the Spirit, as a bearer of the one who makes the presence of the kingdom manifest in this age, while pointing to the age to come. In presenting this marvel of the transformation of bitter, damaging fruit into sweet, beneficial fruit, and given its originality *vis á vis* scripture, Adomnán may be seen to be standing in the tradition of the New Testament writers, and is showing Columba as one who continues to demonstrate the incipient presence of the kingdom. In him and in his acts, says Adomnán, the kingdom is seen to flower, to be manifested, to be bearing fruit which points towards the awaited day of the Lord when Christ returns and completes the work he began.

> ...on either side of the river, the tree of life with its twelve kinds of fruit, yielding its fruit each month; and the leaves of the tree were for the healing of the nations. There shall no more be anything accursed, but the throne of God and of the Lamb shall be in it, and his servants shall worship him (Rev. 22:2-3).

That he appears to be presenting an original mode of manifestation of this eschatological concept suggests that the theology of an inaugurated, partially realized kingdom is embedded in his own theological makeup, and also points to the genuineness of the tradition he records. Now, my task is to show that this reading of Adomnán is not overly subjective, and that it can be identified clearly in the rest of the *VC*. Thus, we will proceed to an examination of other tales in order to test the hypothesis. In this way, I hope to confirm that in Adomnán there was a more sophisticated purpose behind the collection of marvellous stories than the conventional accreditation of the sanctity of a saint. The strong link to the activity of the Spirit will be followed up in chapter four.

---

51 Bauckham (1982, 343). See chapter four below. Bauckham's article makes a useful introduction to eschatology. For an extensive treatment, see Moltmann, *Theology of Hope* (1968).

RAPIDLY GROWING GRAIN (ii.3)

Adomnán presents the tale of the supernaturally rapid growth of grain. It is after mid-summer. As recompense for bundles of withies taken from the land of the layman Findchán, Columba sends six measures[52] of seed-grain from the Ionan storehouse, with instructions to sow it in ploughed land. Adomnán explicitly mentions Findchán's doubt about the sense of sowing so late in the season, as being 'against the nature of this land', thus showing his own awareness of the unusual nature of the miracle he is to describe. However, his wife encourages him to follow Columba's bidding, 'to whom the Lord will grant whatever he may ask of him.' The messengers deliver a word of prophecy from Columba, who had foreknown the incredulity, saying, 'Let that man trust in the omnipotence of God. His crop, although sown after fifteen days of the month of June have passed, will be reaped in the beginning of the month of August'. Having obeyed, though Adomnán says, 'against hope (*contra spem*)',[53] he reaps a harvest after only six weeks of growth. The marvel is perhaps the more to be noted if we take Sharpe's suggestion for the identity of the location as 'thorn headland',[54] which may suggest land of poor quality.

Here the eschatological element is clearly present, the result of Columba's prayer, and of 'trust in the omnipotence of God'.[55] The biblical background can be seen in the following examples:

> They shall come and sing aloud on the height of Zion, and they shall be radiant over the goodness of the LORD, over the grain, the wine, and the oil, and over the young of the flock and the herd; their life shall be like a watered garden, and they shall languish no more (Jer. 31:12).

> 'Behold, the days are coming,' says the LORD, 'when the ploughman shall overtake the reaper and the treader of grapes him who sows the seed; the mountains shall drip sweet wine, and all the hills shall flow with it' (Amos 9:13, and see Hos. 2:21-22).

However there is no direct biblical source for the tale Adomnán relates, but he is presenting the concept of a condition of the eschatological kingdom being made present in his own age. An interesting contrast is shown by the following verse

---

52   '[S]ix measures (*bis terni modii*)'. A&A make a Roman measure equivalent to 'a little under 2 English gallons', making a little less than 12 gallons, or 54.6l. The quantity also occurs in i.41 in Columba's funeral gifts to a thief.

53   This is perhaps better understood as against natural possibility, or against nature, unlike A&A who have 'without hope' which suggests the man did not trust in God's omnipotence as instructed by Columba.

54   Sharpe (1995, note 214).

55   Adomnán refers to the omnipotence of God in five places, all in book II: ii.3, 12, 34, 42, 43.

They have sown wheat and have reaped thorns, they have tired themselves out but profit nothing. They shall be ashamed of their harvests because of the fierce anger of the LORD (Jer. 12:13).

In Adomnán's tale, the opposite condition is pertaining. Sharpe's suggestion of the meaning of the name of the place, 'thorn headland', leads us to an interesting conjecture of a possible reference to the overturning of the condition of this prophecy of doom awaiting an unrepentant, disbelieving Israel. The tale presents the opposite in Columba, who brings the kingdom, and the trusting Findchán who accepts the omnipotence of God, and thus ceases his rebellion against the source of life. As a result, he 'sows among thorns, and reaps wheat', as it were, as a result of God's grace, a thought reminiscent of Isaiah's prophecy of the eschaton

Instead of the thorn shall come up the cypress; instead of the brier shall come up the myrtle; and it shall be to the LORD for a memorial, for an everlasting sign which shall not be cut off (Is. 55:13).

The Kingdom of God in the Kingdom of Animals

Adomnán relates a number of tales which show Columba or his colleagues interacting with the animals illustrating a complex relationship to the non-human creation: a whale, with which they recognise common creatureliness (i.19); a crane is given shelter (i.48);[56] praising cows (ii.4); a milk-bull (ii.17); transformed snakes (ii.28, iii.23); scary sea creatures (ii.42); and Columba's horse (iii.23). While not espousing cruelty or unnecessary harm, the tales allow repulsion of a river-beast (ii.27); and slaughter for food, resource, or protection: wethers and seals (i.41); fish (ii.19); cattle (ii.20, 21); a boar (ii.26); wild animals caught on a stake (ii.37); and there is the incongruous exception of the knife that will not wound (ii.29). I wish to suggest that incorporated in these tales of interaction with the animal creation, is an eschatologically oriented element which makes the conditions of the new earth partially present. In other words, the conditions of the consummated kingdom of God are being presented as being manifested by the blossoming of faith.

---

56 Kelly (1988, 60) notes from the *Law Tracts* that druidic sorcery may be effected through *corrguinecht*, a 'term which means "heron (or crane) killing".' It involves standing on one leg, one arm raised, one eye closed, mimicking the crane's posture. The similarity of this with druidic prophetic practice from *Da Choca* (above) is striking. This may form a background to Adomnán's tale here, showing Columba as the anti-Druid, reviving rather than killing the sacred bird, another eschatological feature. See Márkus (1999) for further discussion.

WATER MONSTERS (i.19; ii.27; ii.42)

The story of the great whale (i.19) deals ostensibly with Columba's gift of prophetic foreknowledge, and the wisdom of heeding his warnings. The brother Berach and his crew foolishly ignore Columba's warning not to sail to Tiree across the passage but to proceed around the Treshnish islands, and are nearly sunk by the prophesied huge whale. A second party led by Baithéne, prior of Iona's daughter abbey on Tiree, also receive the prophetic information, but he answers: 'I and the beast are in God's power.' Columba does not warn them to avoid the whale, but says, in contrast, 'Go in peace, your faith in Christ will protect you from this danger.' When Baithéne encounters the whale, which of course terrified his companions, he 'without a tremor of fear raised his hands and blessed the sea and the whale', which wisely withdrew without harming anyone.

The blessing with which the undaunted Baithéne greets and repels the whale may be compared with the similar repulsion of the water beast of the Ness in ii.27. Here Columba raises his holy hand, draws the saving sign of the cross in the empty air, and in the name of God, commands the beast to proceed no further. It complies, but in contrast to Baithéne's whale's peaceful departure is described as fleeing terrified 'as if pulled back with ropes.'

A third encounter with monstrous animals is contained in the tale of Cormac's voyages (ii.42) where Cormac encounters exceedingly dangerous small creatures, about the size of frogs, with a powerful, thrusting 'sting'.[57] Here the danger is averted neither by destruction of the objects of terror, nor by repulsion, but by the omnipotent God changing the direction of the wind at the imprecation of the brothers

---

57   These creatures have never yet been identified satisfactorily, perhaps because they are simply mythical. However, granted that most myths are grounded in some form of historical event, the hunt can continue legitimately. Fowler suggested they were jellyfish (1895, 117 note); A&A thought the stings were to the front (1991, 168). Three species of fish fit the description, given an unusual shoal: Lumpsuckers (*Cyclopterus lumpus*) gather in shallow coastal waters in Feb.-May, and their young spend summer in the seaweed zone. They are dark coloured, covered in bony denticles, with a pronounced dorsal ridge. The larva of the sunfish (*Mola mola*) fits the description beautifully, with elongated spines in four directions, though are rather too small. The young swordfish (*Xiphaias gladius*) would certainly have had the equipment the Andersons see, and are recorded as 'lashing out wildly' with their sword when catching prey. Finally, a species of hypotremata, the stingray (*Dasyatis pastinaca*), which is black, has a long barbed poison spine on their dorsal side. A large shoal at the surface, slapping the water with their pectoral fins and barging the boat, looking for food might be sufficiently disturbing (for an introduction and excellent illustrations, see Muus (1974, 168-9; 194-5; 148-9; 58-9).

on distant Iona, and thus rescuing the beleaguered sailors. So, in each of these three encounters with danger brought by animals, the response has been to return the two parties to a safe distance where danger will be averted, rather than to curse and destroy. The attitude has been conservative towards nature, but in each case, God's relationship with man and beast has played a central part in the response. In the first, the common relationship of the creaturely to God is acknowledged. Thus the place of both man and beast as cocooned in God's power was recognised as reason enough, when accepted, for the voyage to proceed in safety. There are echoes of Psalm 104:24-26 here.

> O LORD, how manifold are thy works! In wisdom hast thou made them all; the earth is full of thy creatures. Yonder is the sea, great and wide, which teems with things innumerable, living things both small and great. There go the ships, and Leviathan which thou didst form to sport in it.

The encounter itself brought the response of blessing as distinct from cursing, and the result was peace. This peaceful outcome is perhaps emphasised by Adomnán's use of the term *'(a)equor'* for the sea, which may contain the idea of the flat calm surface of the sea which Baithéne blesses.[58] In this, we may discern the partial prefiguring of the eirenic eschatological relationship between man and beast towards which Christian thinkers such as Adomnán were hoping. (See Isaiah 11 above, and, '[You]... shall not fear the beasts of the earth. For... the beasts of the field shall be at peace with you' (Job 5:22-23).) This is the first indication of an eschatological element in Adomnán's animal tales. The commonplace encounter with wild beasts, represented in ii.26 where a wild boar is slain (in contravention of the myth of animal-loving Celtic Christians), is replaced by the hand of blessing and harmony. A subsidiary note is that the hand raised to bless belongs not to Columba, the subject of the *Life*, but to Baithéne. Adomnán thus shows his understanding of the benefits of eschatological pneumatic power to be not restricted to his hero alone, but present in the ministries of others.

The tale of the river Ness water beast fits less well in this light as the beast is repelled in terror. However, as Márkus notes, the tale is set in the context of the account of Columba's bringing the (new) kingdom of God into flower within the (old) Pictish kingdom of Bruide. Adomnán demonstrates the conditions of the new kingdom in the manner in which Columba brings the beast under control in the name of its creator, with the saving sign of the cross by which this kingdom was established. The ropes may echo God's reply in Job 40-41. He is also depicted as offering God's protection to Luigne in the

---

58 L&S, 58.

face of danger, which may be pre-figured by the eschatological promises of the psalmist, now applied by Adomnán to the one who brings the kingdom of God into Pictland, as protection from danger is demonstrated

> He who dwells in the shelter of the Most High, who abides in the shadow of the Almighty, will say to the LORD, 'My refuge and my fortress; my God, in whom I trust.' For he will deliver you from the snare of the fowler and from the deadly pestilence; he will cover you with his pinions, and under his wings you will find refuge; his faithfulness is a shield and buckler. You will not fear the terror of the night, nor the arrow that flies by day, nor the pestilence that stalks in darkness, nor the destruction that wastes at noonday... You will only look with your eyes and see the recompense of the wicked... For he will give his angels charge of you to guard you in all your ways. On their hands they will bear you up, lest you dash your foot against a stone... Because he cleaves to me in love, I will deliver him; I will protect him, because he knows my name. When he calls to me, I will answer him; I will be with him in trouble, I will rescue him and honour him (Ps. 91:1-15).

THE SNAKES OF IONA (ii.28; iii.23)

An illustration of Adomnán's concept of the eschatological kingdom is provided by his account of the fate of snakes on Iona at Columba's hand (ii.28, iii.23). In the primary tale, amongst an apparently random collection of tales about the boar, the water beast, and the dagger (ii.26-ii.29), Columba comforts the brothers saddened by his prophecy regarding his own imminent death by blessing the island, and specifically affecting the snakes thereupon. Aspects of this tale in relation to the sagas have been discussed above. The prophecy over Niul in the Irish origin myth is that snakes in Ireland would not have venom, while recording the total absence of snakes from Ireland from Patrick's time onward. Reeves notes Solinus' third century reference to the absence of snakes in Ireland. Fowler corrects Reeves' dating, notes Bede's reference, and discusses Ireland's herpetology. Jocelyn makes Patrick the one who expels all snakes and many reptiles from Ireland as a whole.[59] Sharpe notes the commonplace of the removal of snakes by a saint's blessing, noting Florentius' prayer that kills snakes in his area and has their corpses

---

59 Fowler (1894, xxxii) places Solinus correctly in the third century (*Polyhist.* xxii), cf. Reeves (1857, 142 note d), Bede (*HE* i.1). Fowler also mentions Ussher having given the credit to Joseph of Arimathea (*Works*, vi.300); and a full discussion of the subject in Messingham, *Florileg. Insulae SS* (1624, 127-134), and Colgan, (*Tr.Th.*, 255).

carried away by birds.[60] In contrast, snakes simply flee from Honoratus on Lérins.[61]

Commentators up until O'Reilly and Márkus have assumed similar fates for Ionan snakes, but these observers have seen more clearly. Márkus notes the event as a prevention of snakes from harming other creatures, as a demonstration of the unnatural harmony between Columba and animals on Iona.[62] O'Reilly agrees

> Columba does not banish snakes but renders them harmless to all creatures on the island – men and beasts – evoking the paradisal peace of the new creation (Is. 11:8-9).

She sees the two references as an example of a Gregorian ethico-spiritual allegorical miracle. The narrative forms a spiritual and allegorical exegesis of the biblical eschatological narratives concerning snakes. Adomnán testifies to his community's continued faithfulness to Christ's command, and recapitulates the calling. [63] Adomnán's tale, however, is more subtle still.

> ...raising both his holy hands [Columba] blessed all this island of ours, and said: 'From this moment of this hour, all poisons of snakes shall be powerless to harm men or cattle in the lands of this island, so long as the inhabitants of that dwelling-place shall observe the commandments of Christ.'[64]

The effect is confirmed in the final chapter of the *Life*

> And from then to the present day, as has been written in the above-mentioned book, the poison of three-forked tongues of vipers has not been able to do any injury to either man or beast.[65]

Adomnán records the result of Columba's blessing as being not the extermination of snakes on Iona, nor the complete elimination of their venom, nor the prevention of their harming *any* other creatures. Rather the blessing brings about the future inability of the venom of snakes to *harm man or cattle/beasts* on the island. Venomous snakes deprived of effective venom with which to paralyse their natural prey would be unlikely to survive; they would starve to death and die out rather cruelly. Hence O'Reilly's and Márkus' improvement on their predecessors, while noting the

---

60 Sharpe (1995, note 276); GG *Dial.* iii.15.
61 *Life* by Hilary ch. 15, Hoare (1954, 260).
62 Márkus (1999, 118-9).
63 O'Reilly (1997, 95-7).
64 *VC* ii.28: '...*omnia viparum venina aut hominibus aut pecoribus nocere poterunt*'. Translators are unanimous in rendering 'men or cattle' here.
65 *VC* iii.23, 125a: '...*aut homini aut pecori*'. Translators are unanimous in rendering 'men or beast' here.

evocation, miss Adomnán's subtlety, and the true nature of Adomnán's eschatological kingdom.

If snakes became harmless to *all* creatures, they would cease to exist, at least in their 'old' earthly habit. This story accepts the presence of venomous snakes on Iona, and their retention of venom necessary for their own habit in the 'old' earth. But divine grace brings through Columba divine protection against the harmful affect of snake venom on man *or cattle*,[66] the latter being important to the insular economy, which has to continue in the inaugurated but not-yet consummated kingdom. O'Reilly sees Adomnán as writing symbolically, Columba's blessing 'makes present... Christ's work of redemption which fulfilled the prophecy of the [Genesis] serpent's defeat'.[67] The redemption of Christ establishes the kingdom on Iona. This has a completely different point to the concept of expulsion, extermination, or de-venoming. The habit of the Ionan venomous snake is not interrupted; his presence is not terminated; only the effect of a strike on an animal not the normal prey of the snake is affected.

O'Reilly notices Antony's and Gildas' depictions of Arianism, and Bede / Prosper's denouncement of Pelagius as snakes spreading the poisonous discord of heresy. She conjectures that Adomnán's tales, set in the context of the divisive Easter dispute, call for a return to the original harmony established by Columba, paralleling Antony's similarly structured call to his followers.[68] These metaphors are, of course, all prefigured by Christ, and his herald, to the intransigent Pharisees (Mt. 3:7, 12:34, 23:33//). If this is the correct interpretation, and it looks attractive, we must take it that Adomnán is saying that there were/are snakes on the island, dissenters, heretics, threats to harmony, but that their power to harm was once blocked by Columba, and it has never been harmful to his day. It is an act of bravado, a declaration that unorthodoxy will not damage Iona's life. That Iona had resisted change to the catholic dating of Easter for much of the century, and that Adomnán was personally unsuccessful in his desire to bring about conformation make his preaching, if such

---

66 Adomnán's other uses of the term (i.38, ii.4, ii.28, ii.29, ii.37) refer to cattle, so we can take it he means domestic herds in both of these instances, not 'all creatures' as O'Reilly and Márkus make it. Souter records that from Tertullian onwards, *pecus, pecoris* was used to refer to a foetus. Though there is no context for it in the *VC*, it may be possible that we see Adomnán here saying it was neither men *nor their offspring* who were harmed, cf. Gen. 15, where the curse bringing enmity between man and serpent applies to the offspring, and the eschatological promise of Is. 11:8 when a baby shall put her hand by a viper's nest but not be harmed?

67 O'Reilly (1997, 96).

68 O'Reilly (1997, 96-7).

it is, somewhat hollow, if finally prophetic, in that paschal conformity finally arrived in AU 716. An alternative allegorical interpretation would make the snakes the priests of the old religion, the druids whose magic Columba neutralized. This would harmonize with Carney's theory of the fashioning of these priests in Irish literature after the likeness of their biblical counterparts (see chapter two above), and would not give Adomnán any difficulty in that their influence on Iona was evidently gone.

Difficulties with these spiritual, allegorical understandings of Adomnán here are two fold. Firstly his models, if such they are: John, Christ, Gregory, Athanasius's Antony, Gildas, Bede, Prosper, are all explicit in their use of a serpentine metaphor for intransigent heresy or heretic. Adomnán openly refers to Columba's struggle with druids in Pictland, but without the metaphor, and makes no decipherable hint here or anywhere of 'heresy' on Iona. Secondly, if the hint is contained here, its extreme subtlety makes one wonder at how effective it could be as a didactic tool. It may be that it is the interpreter reading-in such an explanation so as to bring the narrative into an interpretative epistemological framework which accords not with seventh-century Christian, but modern categories.

The clear precedent can be found in a tradition which certainly preceded Adomnán, and which we can be virtually certain he would have known, as both Márkus and O'Reilly recognise in what they see as symbolic form in the text. I cite further biblical precedent which shows the tale as an eschatological declaration, one of many signs of the coming of the kingdom

> 'For behold, I create new heavens and a new earth... behold, I create Jerusalem a rejoicing, and her people a joy... The wolf and the lamb shall feed together, the lion shall eat straw like the ox; and dust shall be the serpent's food. They shall not hurt or destroy in all my holy mountain,' says the LORD (Is. 65:17a, 18b, 25).

> And I will make for you a covenant on that day with the beasts of the field, the birds of the air, and the creeping things of the ground; and I will abolish the bow, the sword, and war from the land; and I will make you lie down in safety (Hos. 2:18).

Both Isaiah and Hosea here look forward to the New Earth, partial signs of which are inaugurated, in Adomnán view, on Iona: joy is known (see below), the serpent does not destroy, but it is not yet eating dust. The conditions of this New Earth are seen to be established in partial form at the coming of Christ in a passage particularly important to reading the *VC*, as we will see

> And he said to them, 'Go into all the world and preach the gospel to the whole creation... And these signs will accompany those who believe: in

my name they will cast out demons; they will speak in new tongues; they will pick up serpents... it will not hurt them; they will lay their hands on the sick, and they will recover...' And they went forth and preached everywhere, while the Lord worked with them and confirmed the message by the signs that attended it. Amen (Mk. 16:15, 17-18, 20).

One of the earliest apostolic delegates is recorded as experiencing the power of the new kingdom in which he is working as precisely the effect Adomnán describes for Iona

Paul had gathered a bundle of sticks and put them on the fire, when a viper came out because of the heat and fastened on his hand... He, however, shook off the creature into the fire and suffered no harm (Acts 28:3-5).

For protection to be maintained on Iona, the commandments of Christ will need to be followed, but the protection appears to have been limited to this island, and not to extend across a whole territory of influence, as with Niul or Jocelyn's Patrick. Thus we have Adomnán claiming that on this holy mountain of *I*, the in-breaking eschatological conditions of the kingdom of God have been made present through Columba, but that their continuation depends on the maintenance of a holy relationship with their true source. Venomous snakes, as part of the creation, are not exterminated, but now live in heaven-like harmony with man and his domesticated beasts. Adomnán may be employing an exquisitely subtle code to proclaim a non-material, spiritual message. He might also be seen to be recording his belief in the coming of the kingdom to the ends of the earth, proclaimed, with signs following.

THE MULTIPLICATION OF COWS (ii.20,21)

An intriguing couplet of tales concerns the marvellous multiplication of the few cows of two poor laymen (ii.20, 21). In the first, Nesán is rewarded for the hospitality he offers Columba. The latter raises his holy hand and blesses five little cows, prophetically declaring their increase to 105, and the blessedness of the man's seed. In the second very similar tale, which Adomnán insists is a distinct occurrence,[69] Colmán also provides hospitality, and is similarly blessed. This time his sons and grandsons are also blessed with 'fruitfulness'. The opening of the sequel ii.22 confirms that, 'the power of [Columba's] blessing raised [Colmán] from poverty to wealth.' Adomnán adds the note that the predetermined number of cows could not be increased by any means; unless used by the respective households, any surplus beasts were lost. Both tales also attract sequels which show: the

---

69   Scholarly opinion dismisses Adomnán's insistence, believing the two to have derived from a single folk-tale.

penalties of rejecting the values of the kingdom (Vigen was parsimonious; Ioan oppressed Colmán, and sacked his house three times); the penalty of rejecting Christ and his bearers (Vigen slighted Columba and did not receive him as a guest,[70] and '[Ioan] despised Christ in his servants'); and the consequent withdrawal of any blessing that reception of the kingdom might otherwise have brought.

In the first case, a contrast is drawn between the poor man who became wealthy as a result of receiving the blessings of the kingdom, with a tenaciously rich man who refused hospitality to Columba, whose judgement was to become poor, and who would suffer a violent, unprotected death.[71] Colmán himself is the focus of the sequel to his story which again concerns a detractor of Columba in a story with political connotations. Ioan son of Conall, son of Domnall, oppresses Columba's ward Colmán, and refuses to yield to Christ's bearer, scorning him. As a result of Columba's prayer 'to the Lord', Ioan and his crew came under near immediate judgement, and, having refused the kingdom of God, were snatched away (see 'Judgement' below).

THE WHITE HORSE (iii.23)

We must make reference to the closing tale of the *VC* wherein Adomnán describes Columba's relationship with the white horse (iii.23, 127b-128a).

> It went to the saint, and strange to tell put its head in his bosom, inspired, as I believe, by God, before who every living creature has understanding, with such perception of things as the creator himself has decreed; and knowing that its master would presently depart from it, and that it should see him no more, it began to mourn, and like a human being to let tears fall freely on the lap of the saint, and foaming much, to weep aloud. When he saw this, the attendant began to drive away the weeping mourner; but the saint forbade him, saying, 'Let him, let him that loves us, pour out the tears of most bitter grief here in my bosom. See, man though you are, and having a rational soul, you could by no means know anything of my departure except what I myself have even

---

70 E.g. 'If anyone will not welcome you or listen to your words, shake the dust off your feet when you leave that home or town' (Mt. 10:14). Luke's parallel has, 'But when you enter a town and are not welcomed, go into its streets and say, "Even the dust of your town that sticks to our feet we wipe off against you. Yet be sure of this: The kingdom of God is near"' (Luke 10:10-11). The latter clearly links the nearness of the kingdom with the refusal of hospitality and refusal to accept its messengers. Thus Adomnán has a clear biblical model for the two cautionary tales, and both may be seen to be linked to Jesus' teaching on the coming of the kingdom in its bearers.

71 A&A note their opinion that, though absent from MS A, this insertion was very possibly by Adomnán himself, so I treat it here as such.

now disclosed to you. But to this brute and unreasoning animal the Creator has, in what way he would, revealed clearly that its master is going to depart from it.' Thus speaking, he blessed his servant the horse, as it turned sadly away from him.

The tale forms part of what Smyth describes as 'one of the most moving narratives in the whole of Dark Age historical literature.'[72] Although this is the earliest prophetic horse in the extant Irish record,[73] and the tale is mainly illustrative of the prophetic in Adomnán's conception, I have included it here as a final though rather tentative example of the eschaton breaking out on Iona in Adomnán's zoological thoughts. Negatively, the tale is of bitter grief at the loss in this life of the horse's beloved master, and thus is focused not on the eschaton, but in the present. However, we should not miss Adomnán's description of the horse coming to put its head in Columba's bosom and weeping, which Adomnán describes as 'strange to tell (*mirum dictu*)', using one of his stock phrases for a marvellous event. Adomnán discerns the cause as God's revelation of non-rationally discernible knowledge to the 'brute and unreasoning animal'. So, we have a special relationship between man and beast, one of the images of the eschaton already discussed, plus supernatural revelation to a beast, which has resonance (albeit fleeting) with the marvellous talking ass of Balaam (Num. 22:28). On its own, this tale would not present a strong case for the presence of the kingdom on Iona, but taken with the foregoing as guides to interpretation, may be seen to add something to my case.

THE DISABLED DAGGER

As we follow the establishment of the eschatological kingdom in Adomnán's collection of interactions with the animal creation, we consider the curious tale of the disabled dagger (ii.29), which closes a small series before Adomnán moves on to a consideration of Columba's healing ministry. In this tale, brother Molua comes to Columba, who is engaged in copying a book, to ask a blessing on an iron tool. Columba absent-mindedly reaches out his pen,[74] makes the sign of the cross, and says a blessing, all without taking his eyes off the page. After Molua has gone, Columba asks his attendant what it was that he'd blessed. On hearing that it was a knife for slaughter, he replies

I trust in my Lord that the implement I have blessed will not hurt either man nor beast (*nec homini, nec pecori nocebit*).

---

72   Smyth (1984, 115).
73   See Sharpe (1995, note 408), on Mayer.
74   O'Reilly has pointed out the significance of the pen as an instrument of the application of God's word, referring to Ps. 45:1 (Spes Scotorum 1997).

This proves to be the case, and as a consequence, the monks overlaid other tools with the metal of the first, rendering them harmless to flesh, 'because the efficacy of that blessing of the saint continued.'[75] The sense of the tale would suggest that from this time on, no more beasts were slaughtered on Iona, and indeed that no more meat was eaten if it had been eaten previously.[76] Molua had presumably supposed that the blessing would make his knife more effective, for a cleaner and quicker slaughter. On discovering the actual effect, and presumably assuming Columba's, and God's will to be the general disabling of tools to hurt flesh, they go to the trouble of distributing the blessed blunting metal around the whole monastic 'armoury'. The tale contradicts others which suggest that slaughter was normal practice on Iona, e.g. i.41, and on Columba's travels, e.g. ii.19, ii.20-1, ii.26, ii.37. The timing of the tale is unknown, the only information being that from the time of the blessing onwards, the tools were unable to harm flesh, (though their continued use in harvesting grain and other horticulture or culinary use would not, by this stricture, be affected). This inconsistency and possible lack of attention to circumstantial detail contrasts with Adomnán's accustomed care.

The question left to my mind, however, is whether we have here another example of Adomnán presenting a condition of the eschatological kingdom being inaugurated through Columba, but one which, unusually, does not take account of the effect of the story on wider conditions. Hosea 2.18, cited above, refers to abolishing the sword from the land, and the image recurs in Micah.

> It shall come to pass in the latter days that the mountain of the house of the LORD shall be established as the highest of the mountains, and shall be raised up above the hills; and peoples shall flow to it, and many nations shall come, and say: 'Come, let us go up to the mountain of the LORD, to the house of the God of Jacob; that he may teach us his ways

---

75   Fowler (1894, 97 note 4), believes the knife in question was actually of bronze thus allowing literalness in Adomnán's description. Sharpe insists that *ferrum* must mean iron. A&A (1991, 136 note 166), following Sharpe (1995, note 282), note using Scott the probability that Adomnán's description of distributing melted iron should be taken as a terminological transfer from bronze work, and must only actually refer to softened iron. The puzzle remains as Adomnán unostentatiously but definitely refers to a hot fire (*ignis calore*) and says the monks distributed the iron of the knife melted (*liquefactus*). Could it be that Adomnán has another nature miracle in mind? This is unlikely as he makes nothing of the fact, except its occurrence. If however *liquefactus* is taken to mean 'softened' (see L&S 1069, *liquefacio* IIB), then the knot is slackened. However, the practicality of distributing a thin coating of softened iron onto all the tools in the monastery remains to be investigated.

76   See MacDonald's debate with Sharpe in MacDonald (1997, 35-6), and the archaeological evidence discussed by McCormick (1997, 56-60 and 62).

and we may walk in his paths.' For out of Zion shall go forth the law, and the word of the LORD from Jerusalem. He shall judge between many peoples, and shall decide for strong nations afar off; and they shall *beat their swords into ploughshares, and their spears into pruning hooks*; nation shall not lift up sword against nation, neither shall they learn war any more (Mic. 4:1-3).

The image here is not, of course, at all precise. This eschatological promise is rare in the scriptures, coming in the overwhelming context of multiple metaphorical references to the sword being used to refer to coming judgements of various sorts both on the people of God, and on their enemies in return for unrepentant sinful living. Micah, and most other references to the sword in the scriptures, refers to human carnage, rather than to the slaughter of beasts for food. Adomnán's tale refers not to war or judgement at all, but is rather set in a domestic insular context. He speaks of melting the iron blade and applying it to others in order to convey the blessing, in an imputation of anachronistic iron working skills.[77] The carrying of a blessing in material objects is common in Adomnán's thinking, so the concept is no more or less magical than his other references to similar *eulogia*. We may conjecture that the original tale, depleted by the time it reached Adomnán, was of blades which miraculously did no accidental or criminal harm. We can not know. Despite these objections, we may yet be seeing another reference, albeit perhaps unconscious, to the conditions which are promised for the mountain of the Lord in the future kingdom. Many come to the house of the Lord's representative to learn God's ways (Mic. 4:2). The blessing of God is transmitted through the holy one so in tune with the divine that an absent minded shake of the pen is enough to convey it the island community. The promise of the word of God is thereby applied. Blades are made unable to do damage to man or beast (Mic. 4:3), and man and beast are at peace.

The Kingdom of God in the Healing of Creation

The marvellous healings of the *VC* provide a further set of images which conjure up the picture of the establishment of the kingdom in Columba's time, as they do for the New Testament. Christ inaugurated his ministry with the words from the LXX Isaiah

The Spirit of the Lord is upon me, because he has anointed me to preach good news to the poor. He has sent me to proclaim release to the captives and recovering of sight to the blind, to set at liberty those who are oppressed, to proclaim the acceptable year of the Lord (Lk. 4:18-19).

---

77   Sharpe (1995, note 282).

The motif of release from oppression is commonly interpreted to mean, in part, healing from illness, and the year of the Lord's favour to refer to the coming of the kingdom. When asked by John's disciples if he was the one who was to come, Jesus replied

> Go and tell John what you have seen and heard: the blind receive their sight, the lame walk, lepers are cleansed, and the deaf hear, the dead are raised up, the poor have good news preached to them. And blessed is he who takes no offence at me (Lk. 7:22-23).

Jesus sends out his own disciples, twelve, and seventy-two, to proclaim the kingdom and heal the sick

> ...and he sent them out to preach the kingdom of God and to heal (Lk. 9:2).

> ...heal the sick in it and say to them, 'The kingdom of God has come near to you' (Lk. 10:9).

Thus there are irrefutable grounds for associating healing with the presence of the kingdom in the Synoptic gospels, and we know of the importance of these documents to the Ionan church.[78] Athanasius likewise presents Antony as one through whom God healed. He emphasises that it was not Antony himself who healed, but God in answer to his prayer and calling on the name of Christ (*VA* 84). A factor hinting at the possible veracity of the tales of healing in *VC* is that Adomnán is not at all exhaustive in the biblical echoes he collects, suggesting that those he does collect come from genuine traditions, and not from the imagination of his mind soaked as it would have been in biblical imagery. He records a whole range of non-biblical 'ailments': an unloving attitude (ii.41), a bleeding nose (ii.18), an inflammation of the eyes (ii.7), a broken hip (ii.5), a life-threatening childbirth (ii.40). Some conditions echo the biblical: mortal sickness (ii.30, 31, 33), and even death itself (ii.32). However, Adomnán misses healing from blindness, demonization, fever, leprosy, paralysis, and dumbness, which are obvious biblical conditions he could have adopted. Adomnán is careful in each case to record that the source of healing is divine: God, the Lord, Christ. We can take the healings he records then, as being further examples of 'the flowering of faith'.

THE PESTIFEROUS CLOUD AND THE PRAISING COWS (ii.4)

Our first example focuses on a marvellous healing in a complex tale containing an eschatological image of the righting of all of creation, not simply restricted to humans, but to beasts of the field as well. The 'pestiferous cloud' deposits disease on man and beast alike, and

---

78   See Turner on healing in the NT (1995, 240-261).

the healing gift is conveyed, via the *pane benedicto / salubri pane* carried by Silnán, to both, as Columba specifically instructs. Thus many are healed.

> And immediately recovering full health the men, saved with their cattle, praised Christ in Saint Columba, with very great rendering of thanks (*VC* ii.4).

Sharpe alone translates the sentence differently: 'At once men and beasts regained their health, and praised Christ in St Columba with exceeding gratitude,' suggesting an amusing prospect of the beasts joining the men in praising Christ for their deliverance. This sense is perfectly acceptable to Adomnán's text, and in tune with a biblical eschatological view of nature

> Beasts and all cattle, creeping things and flying birds!... Let them praise the name of the LORD, for his name alone is exalted; his glory is above earth and heaven (Ps. 148:10, 13).

The economic importance of the cattle is surely a further element to be considered in understanding the impact of the healing on the human recipients. The people of the area were not only saved from a terrible suffering and death from disease, but their economy was also rescued from disaster. They have encountered the power of a God who was interested in their whole lives, and their response is spontaneous gratitude.[79] As is his habit, Adomnán does not tell us if this means the conversion of the people from a pagan to the Christian faith specifically, but whatever the situation, Christ, and Columba, were glorified through the manifestation of the kingdom, which was Adomnán's interest. Again, Adomnán has no direct models from the scriptures, but his story clearly contains biblical imagery of the eschaton as it is manifested by Christ through Columba, and as it is so manifested, it brings glory to the one who is its source, namely Christ, and also to his servant. The tale may also be seen to contain the eschatological element of demonstrating the kingdom being carried to the ends of the earth / to all the world, as the power of Christ is shown in Ireland. There may be political purpose here, as yet unidentified, but there is no need to turn to such devices to make sense of the tale; a higher administration is more clearly in view.

A TALE OF RESUSCITATION (ii.32)

This is a rather formulaic tale set in Pictland, with strong reminiscences of both the Widow of Nain's son, and Jairus' daughter

---

79 Adomnán refers to 'man and cattle' in five chapters in the *VC* illustrating their importance in his thought: ii.4, ii.28 and iii.23, ii.29, ii.37.

(Lk. 7:11-15; Mt. 9:18-25//) and Acts 26.16. Adomnán may here be presenting a picture of the continuing earnest of God to bring salvation to eternal life in the history of his own immediate *familia*. Paul calls the resurrection of Jesus a first fruit anticipating that of believers (Rom. 8:23, 1 Cor. 15:20, 23). Irenaeus believes the translation of Elijah, the preservations of Jonah and of Daniel *et al.*, and the resurrection of Lazarus were earnests of God's promise of resurrection, acting as empirical confirmation of his power, promise and fidelity to unbelievers.[80] Thus the presence of this power, which is an earnest of the future eschatological resurrection, is demonstrated as being present significantly in Pictland, the land of the heathen, in the face of outright opposition to the gospel.

Messengers of the Kingdom: Angels

Columba's encounters with angels (and demons), are recorded in the second preface, and chapters i.1, i.3; ii.33; iii.(intro.), 1, 3-16, 22, and 23. Adomnán seems only to consider two major categories of angel, namely 'angelic messengers' with whom Columba had discourse, and their fallen counterparts, the demons. A differentiation between 'angels from the highest heaven' (iii.14, 16, 19, 22) denoting their origin in the throne room of the king of heaven, a claim of Columba's status, and others, is evident,[81] but in the absence of any further subdivision it seems likely that he was not influenced by Dionysius.[82] Thus his angelology can be regarded as going back to a more primitive foundation. Bietenhard understands the NT to have taken over the Jewish concepts of angels as

---

80 Irenaeus, *Adv. Haer.* (v.v.2 and v.xiii.1). The latter also includes Irenaeus' exposition of the idea of earnest reception of a portion of the Holy Spirit, which causes a man to cry Abba. Complete grace of the Spirit will render men like Him.

81 Cf. *Altus Prosator:* 'He created good angels and archangels, the orders of Principalities and Thrones, of Powers and of Virtues (*Bonos creavit angelos ordines et archangelos principatum ac sedium potestatum virtutium*' and 'From the summit of the Kingdom of Heaven, where angels stand (*Caeli de regni apice stationis angelicae*)' C&M, 44.

82 The Pseudo-Areopagite's *Celestial Hierarchy*, which became a formative influence on mediaeval angelology only became widely know in the West after Erigena's translation, though he was approved by Gregory I and Lateran IV (AD 649). Dionysius' / Gregory the Great's nine-fold hierarchy of angels is not in evidence in *VC*. For a recent discussion of seventh century Irish cosmology, see Marina Smyth, *Understanding the Universe in Seventh-Century Ireland,* (1996). Pages 88-93 contain her discussion of heavens. Adomnán would not appear to be familiar with the physical characteristics of the heavens in *Liber De Ordine Creaturarum,* nor of Isidore's *De Natura Rerum.* His highest heaven may, of course, derive from e.g. Psalm 148.4: 'Praise him, you heavens of heavens (*laudate eum caeli caelorum*)'.

...representatives of the heavenly world and God's messengers. When they appear, the supernatural world breaks into this one. Because God is present in Jesus, his way on earth is accompanied by angels.[83] At his coming again they will be at his side...[84] They act on behalf of the Apostles[85] and make God's will known to them.[86]

In this light, we might understand Adomnán's presentation of Columba as one who shared the company of angels, who sent them to do his bidding, and who was apprised of God's will by them, as being in full conformity with biblical practice. He was showing Columba as one around whom the supernatural world broke into this world, in whom God, by his Spirit, was present. Thus, the kingdom of God becomes present where the apostolic Columba is present.

IN THE COMPANY OF ANGELS

Picard interprets the motif of showing a saint in the company of angels as undeniable proof of sanctity in hagiography.[87] He gives no reason for so saying. Picard has gained the impression that Columba 'passed his entire life in the company of guardian angels', perhaps rather an over interpretation of Adomnán's presentation. Book three is the shortest of all, collecting nineteen of the twenty-one examples of angelic appearances in the *VC*. iii.1 concerns a vision of his mother; i.3, ii.33, iii.6, 7, 9, 10, 11, 12, 13, 14 are visions of angels operating elsewhere than his presence; only iii.3, 4, 5, 8, 15, 16 record direct encounters between the saint himself and angels. Now, in the epilogue to iii.16, Adomnán mentions visits indiscernible to (ordinary) men, while Columba lay awake, or prayed alone. However, while believing the visits to be numerous in extent Adomnán clearly believes them to be limited especially to these occasions when Columba is alone. Even in the example he gives of Columba's guardian angel (iii.15), Adomnán records him as saying not 'my angel' but '*Angelo domini qui nunc inter uos stabat*'. The introduction to *VC* book three records,

> ...in this third book, concerning angelic apparitions, that *were revealed to others* in relation to the blessed man, or to him in relation to others, and concerning those that were made visible to both, though in unequal measure (that is to him directly and more fully, and to others indirectly and only in part, that is to say from without and by stealth)...

---

83   Mt. 1:20; 2:13,19; 28:2,5; Mk. 1:13; Lk. 1:19; 2:9,13; 22:43; Jn. 1:51; cf. Acts 1:10.
84   Mt. 13:49; 16:27; 25:31; 2 Thes. 1:7.
85   Acts 5:19; 12:7-10.
86   Acts 8:26; 10:3-8; 27:27f. (Bietenhard, *NIDNTT*, I:102-103).
87   Picard (1981, 94).

This process is illustrated in Columba's youth, trial, and on visit to Clonmacnoise

> During those days in which the saint was a guest in the monastery of Clóin, he prophesied... by revelation of the Holy Spirit... concerning some angelic visitations revealed to him, in which certain places within the enclosure of that monastery were frequented by angels at that time (*VC* i.1).

The tale is interpreted by Sharpe as propaganda. Columba's sanctity is being demonstrated as he visits another *familia*. This perhaps misses the reference to the presence of angels in 'certain places' in the monastery, known to Columba, but showing the kingdom as supernaturally present there. It is not certain that their presence is only due to that of Columba; he merely makes their presence known. Two tales of angels as travelling-companions (iii.3-4) are perhaps somewhat more obviously political in intent, showing the saints Bréndan of Birr and the venerable bishop Uinniau/Finnbarr seeing, apparently not in the natural, angels accompanying Columba in his pre-peregrinatory life in Ireland. The second is set during his youth; the first at his trial at the synod of Teltown, and includes a further reference to Adomnán's concept of Columba as a missionary saint who would, in words recorded as from Bréndan, 'be a leader of nations into life.' Both the Andersons and Sharpe chose here to translate *populorum* to refer to 'nations', thus, perhaps, rendering a political interpretation onto Adomnán's statement. Both Forbes and Fowler choose the more neutral 'people', which sits more naturally with the 'innumerable souls' of iii.1. Adomnán intends to show Columba as a missionary saint who brings people into the salvation of the kingdom of God, and his accompaniment by God's supernatural messengers once again illustrates his point that where Columba was, there did the supernatural kingdom break in.

In ii.16, Adomnán records the meeting with Columba of a large company of angels, as illicitly observed by one of the brothers

> For holy angels, citizens of the heavenly country, flew down with marvellous suddenness, clothed in white raiment, and began to stand about the holy man as he prayed. And after some converse with the blessed man, that heavenly throng, as though perceiving they were watched, quickly returned to the highest heaven.

'*Sancti angeli caelestis patriae cives*' is translated by Sharpe as 'citizens of the heavenly kingdom', thus the alternative translations bring together the concepts of the new heaven and earth, and the kingdom. The inclusion of the observer is a device Adomnán uses to illustrate that many other visitations happened unobserved by others, a note with which he closes the chapter. Once again, Adomnán has adequate scriptural background to the scenario, which explicitly presents Columba's credentials as a man of renown, on the basis of his sharing in the society of the eschatological kingdom.

Are they not all ministering spirits sent forth to serve, for the sake of those who are to obtain salvation (Heb. 1:14)?

But you have come to Mount Zion and to the city of the living God, the heavenly Jerusalem, and to innumerable angels in festal gathering (Heb. 12:22).

For the Son of man is to come with his angels in the glory of his Father, and then he will repay every man for what he has done. Truly, I say to you, there are some standing here who will not taste death before they see the Son of man coming in his kingdom (Mt. 16:27-28//).

This is evidence of the righteous judgement of God, that you may be made worthy of the kingdom of God, for which you are suffering, since indeed God deems it just to repay with affliction those who afflict you, and to grant rest with us to you who are afflicted, when the Lord Jesus is revealed from heaven with his mighty angels in flaming fire (2 Thes. 1:5-7).

AGENTS (iii.15)

Adomnán gives us a splendid tale of Columba on Iona commanding an angel in the shortest prayer he records, '*Auxiliare, auxiliare*', to rescue a monk whom he sees, by divine revelation, falling from a tower in distant Durrow (iii.15). The holy man describes the wonder of what he sees as the angel speeds to catch the fortunate brother. Here, once again, we see Columba being presented as sharing characteristics with Christ, who himself had authority to command angels

Do you think that I cannot appeal to my Father, and he will at once send me more than twelve legions of angels (Mt. 26:53)?

Psalm 34 talks of rescue by the Angel of the Lord, who will not allow the bones of the righteous man to be broken. In this tale of Adomnán, this is quite literally interpreted.

The angel of the LORD encamps around those who fear him, and delivers them... He keeps all his bones; not one of them is broken (Ps. 34:7,20).

And again in Psalm 91, a further background appears

For he will give his angels charge of you to guard you in all your ways. On their hands they will bear you up, lest you dash your foot against a stone (Ps. 91:11-12).

The conditions of the kingdom are once again present. Conversely in ii.33, an angel strikes Broichan, *magus* of the King of Picts, in divine response to his unyielding obstinacy (see section on 'Judgement' below).

MESSENGERS

The King's Robe

VC iii.1 describes the appearance of an angel to announce the birth of the saint in a commonplace hagiographical device, with little significance in itself. However, the use Adomnán makes of the tale is important eschatologically, and may be seen to link closely with the reference in his preface to the kingdom of God consisting in the flowering of faith, discussed above. The angel appears to Columba's mother in a dream, and gave her

> ...as it seemed, a robe of marvellous beauty, in which there appeared embroidered splendid colours, as it were of all kinds of flowers. And after some little space, asking it back, he took it from her hands. And raising it, and spreading it out, he let it go in the empty air. Grieved by losing it, she spoke thus to that man of reverend aspect: 'Why do you so quickly take from me this joyous mantle?' Then he said: 'For the reason that this cloak is of very glorious honour, you will not be able to keep it longer with you.' After these words, the woman saw that robe gradually receded from her in flight, grow greater, and surpass the breadth of the plains, and excel in its greater measure the mountains and woods. And she heard a voice that followed, speaking thus: 'Woman do not grieve, for you will bear to the man to whom you are joined by [the bond] of marriage a son, of such grace that he, as though one of the prophets of God, shall be counted in their number; and he has been predestined by God to be a leader of innumerable souls to the heavenly country (S: kingdom).' While she heard this voice, the woman awoke.[88]

Peplum is a term used generally to denote a wide upper garment, but is specifically used to refer to the splendid robe of state of the gods or human dignitaries; emperors or kings,[89] and with this would denote majesty, dominion or rule. The second term Adomnán uses for it, *sagum,* is less conclusive in itself as perhaps denoting the coarse woollen blanket of a servant, but *hoc sagum alicuius est tam magnifici honoris* would suggest Adomnán has in mind a military cloak used as a sign of warfare,[90] and to be worn by one of great or noble honour. Thus the image is of a robe, a vestment denoting rule, the ultimate ruler being the Lord God, King of Kings, who would one day come.

---

88   A version of the tale appears in the *Annals of Clonmacnoise,* 590 (Murphy, 1993, 91-2), though it lacks the reference to flowers.

89   L&S, 1332.

90   L&S, 1617.

The LORD reigns, he is robed in majesty; the LORD is robed, he is girded with strength (Ps. 93:1-2).

I saw the LORD seated on a throne, high and lifted up; and his train filled the temple (Is. 6:1).

The day of the LORD, most righteous King of Kings, is at hand.[91]

Psalm 45, which Columba chanted outside Bruide's palace (i.37c) is filled with royal imagery, relating an earthly king to the Heavenly King. God's throne is eternal (Ps 45:6). The earthly king's robes (*vestimentum*) are of myrrh (*murra*), and myrrh-oil (*gutta*) and wild cinnamon (*cassia*) (Ps. 45:8). This description primarily refers to the king's anointing with fragrant oils, but also evokes the image of the trees from which the oil is derived. It is a small step to imagining their blooming. Thus, the image of the robe decorated in flowers of all colours may be seen to represent kingly rule. Adomnán is not interested in presenting Columba with temporal jurisdiction, thus this image must represent the concept of the kingdom of God, and is thus symbolic of the kingdom which will be spread in conflict with opposing forces,[92] by one, predictably, of honour. In extraordinary beauty, a concept of the kingdom fully conversant with a Christian eschatological outlook, it depicts the bringing into being of all kinds of blossoming faith, i.e. conditions of the eschatological kingdom with which Adomnán opens his work, nurtured through the ministry of this mother's son. The taking of the mantle away from the mother is both a sign of her need to let her son go on his pilgrimage away from Ireland, and of the impossibility of her holding on to the kingdom of God which will be established over an area extending well beyond the confines of her son's homeland, and which cannot be possessed by any human being. It spreads out beyond the confines of Ireland, indeed beyond the confines of the physical earth. In presenting this picture, Adomnán shows us that his conception of Columba's significance was far greater than a peregrination into ascetic exile. Rather, his leaving home and family is essential to the spreading of the kingdom of God, which will itself, as it grows and flowers, render the bringing of many souls into its membership. Adomnán presents Columba as the one through whom God, as represented by his divine messenger in this instance, will accomplish this task which is unquestionably missionary in focus, as distinct from eremitic. We may also read a political element in this image, as

---

91   *Altus Prosator*, Q, (C&M, 51).
92   That the coming of the kingdom is envisaged as bringing conflict, see Lk. 4:34-5; Mt. 10:34; Jesus and his disciples' conflict with Satan and the religious rulers; Paul's conflict with paganism etc. This conflict is reflected often in the *VC*.

showing Columba's 'international' influence and importance, but again, this importance is founded upon the concept of a mission to establish a kingdom which transcends the earthly territories, and which has the effect of 'saving' people embroiled in the temporal, for the far more significant eternal realm.

Trance Encounter

VC iii.5 records an encounter with angels shared by numerous biblical characters, gathered around possibly the first record of a Christian ordination of a monarch.[93] Adomnán relates that the angel was seen 'in a trance of [Columba's] mind', instructing him to read the book of ordination of kings. When Columba refuses to ordain Áedán, he is struck by the angel, producing a physical scar on his side which remained all his life. The incident is repeated on two successive nights, and the angel emphasises that his command is from God. After the third vision, Columba is convinced it is of God, not his own imagination, and 'submitted to the word of the Lord'. He ordains, and blesses Áedán, whom he now accepts, though not his own original choice, as God's choice as king. That there is a political element in the tale is accepted. What is more interesting to this discussion, however, is the precision with which Adomnán describes the encounter. The angel is seen 'in a trance of mind', i.e. it is an ecstatic experience, unlike most of the other angelic appearances. As such, Columba is recorded as having treated it in a different way. Though apparently having received the scar on the first night, he is not ready to accept the vision as genuinely of God until it is proved by triple repetition; it is not, apparently, the scar which makes him accept the divine source. Adomnán is familiar with the concept of angels smiting men, as he shows in the tale of Broichan (ii.33, above), and it is not unknown in scripture, e.g. 'Then they struck the men who were at the door of the house, young and old, with blindness so that they could not find the door' (Gen. 19:11). Adomnán is thus concerned to show that Columba is not a credulous mystic, but one who knows the wisdom of 'testing the spirits',[94] and who is wary of deception.[95] Columba is one who follows the tradition of Samuel, Gideon, Jeremiah, Zechariah, and Peter, all of whom struggled with

---

93 For which, see Sharpe (1995, note 358), responding to Michael Enright; and Meckler (1990) who deals with the religious/political ramifications of the tale, dismissing the marvel in line with usual historian's line: 'whatever one wishes to make of the angels...'

94 'Beloved, do not believe every spirit, but test the spirits to see whether they are of God; for many false prophets have gone out into the world' (1 Jn. 4:1).

95 'And no wonder, for even Satan disguises himself as an angel of light. So it is not strange if his servants also disguise themselves as servants of righteousness. Their end will correspond to their deeds' (2 Cor. 11:14-15).

visions; Gideon and Zechariah specifically with mediating angels. Once again, Adomnán is showing Columba as one who shares experience with these prophets and apostles of the biblical tradition, and places him directly in line of succession to the same type of experience of the in-breaking of the kingdom of God. At the same time, in this instance, Columba is shown to be firmly in this world, and in need of his sanctified wits.

Foes of the Kingdom: Demons

Expulsion of demons in the *VC* is not directly from people (ii.11, 16, iii.8). O'Reilly interprets Antony's discourse concerning demons to be an allegory for the achievement of ascetic discipline.[96] It is 'spiritual combat', tramping the demonic serpents of ethical vice underfoot. This allegorical interpretation of the *Vita Antonii* sidesteps the question of why the writer seems to refer to a real struggle with the demonic. Biblical and early-Christian demons bring temptation, flattery, and false prophecy. Antony sees Christ's words in Lk. 10:19 as an allegory referring to doing battle with very real demons. Virtue is the defence.[97] This interpretation of demonic reality fits Adomnán's account of Columba. The ascetic virtues are certainly in place, and form the ground upon which the marvellous manifestations are built, but the 'spiritual combat' takes place in a higher arena than the human soul.

iii.8 is unique in the *VC*, describing a battle with demons which is founded upon Paul's description in Ephesians 6:10-18. The Pauline concept of principalities and powers against which the faithful contend is clear in the *Altus Prosator*.[98] The feature of note in this context is the way in which Adomnán describes the battle as proceeding. Columba goes off to pray in seclusion, another open reference to the similarity with Christ in his servant, e.g. 'And in the morning, a great while before day, he rose and went out to a lonely place, and there he prayed' (Mk. 1:35). He saw an array of innumerable demons making war on him, which the Spirit revealed to him were wishing to assault his monastery, to kill his brothers with the iron spits which they held. The battle raged back and forth most of the day, neither side being able to prevail, until 'angels of God' came to Columba's support. Fear of them drove the demons off the island. The Spirit further reveals to Columba that the repulsed demons proceed to harry the monasteries on Tiree, intending to afflict the brothers with pestilential diseases, and that many would be

---

96   O'Reilly (1997, 95); *VA*, Gregg (1980, 21-43).
97   *VA*, Gregg (1980, 30).
98   *Altus Prosator*, B (C&M, 44-5), see above, note 79.

killed. So it happened, with the exception of Abbot Baithéne's monastery, where as a result of his leadership, the community was defended by prayer and fasting, and only one died 'on this occasion'.[99]

The whole account both shows a familiarity with scriptural accounts of spiritual warfare (cf. Ps. 91:6, above), and suggests a familiarity with its contemporary continuation, including a defensive strategy. The most obvious reference to the 'armour of the apostle Paul' which Columba took up, as Sharpe notes, reads

> Finally, be strong in the Lord and in the strength of his might. Put on the whole armour of God, that you may be able to stand against the wiles of the devil. For we are not contending against flesh and blood, but against the principalities, against the powers, against the world rulers of this present darkness, against the spiritual hosts of wickedness in the heavenly places. Therefore take the whole armour of God, that you may be able to withstand in the evil day, and having done all, to stand. Stand therefore, having girded your loins with truth, and having put on the breastplate of righteousness, and having shod your feet with the equipment of the gospel of peace; besides all these, taking the shield of faith, with which you can quench all the flaming darts of the evil one. And take the helmet of salvation, and the sword of the Spirit, which is the word of God. Pray at all times in the Spirit, with all prayer and supplication. To that end keep alert with all perseverance, making supplication for all the saints (Eph. 6:10-18).

However, though the image of spiritual war, and of the demonic 'arrows', must have their home here, Paul has more weapons in his armoury

> But, since we belong to the day, let us be sober, and put on the breastplate of faith and love, and for a helmet the hope of salvation (1 Thes. 5:8).

> ...for the weapons of our warfare are not worldly but have divine power to destroy strongholds (2 Cor. 10:4).

---

99   This account may be another place where we can observe a ecclesio-political element, in that it is ostensibly the Columban monastery on Tiree that is protected, whereas other foundations there probably owing allegiance to other founders are ravaged. The element is also present in Adomnán's concern over the regime of a Tiree monastery in his account of Artchain (i.36). Two contrary views complicate the picture however. Adomnán is quite clear that Mag Luinge is protected by the action not of Columba himself, but of Baithéne his colleague who is presented as acting independently. Secondly, the posthumous protection of Pictland and Dál Riata from the late seventh-century plague depicted in ii.46 is not restricted to Columban houses, but is viewed as a general benefit of the establishment among those peoples of Columban establishments, a factor that, apparently, does not protect Ireland.

This is the armour of the eschatological kingdom to which believers belong, employed in its defence. Adomnán's tale is not a slavish copy of any of these images, but the basics remain. The struggle is against spiritual forces of evil in the heavenly realms. Columba, having done everything to resist, stands in the face of attack. His ascetic purity is demonstrated. Adomnán is less interested than Paul in the metaphorical panoply, and even the little he has differs. The demonic weapons iron spits / stakes (*ferreís aciem / sudis*) are not burning, and the terms are not *Vulgate*.[100] Nevertheless, they bring death, as Reeves noted from the Tiree experience, by disease,[101] and it is their offensive capability which Adomnán wants to note. He makes no specific mention of an ethical dimension to the battle, though this must be assumed in his readers' understanding of the armour of the apostle Paul. As we have observed, although a constant presence in the *VC*, Columba's ethical virtue is never dwelt upon. Adomnán's interest, as in the rest of the work, is on spiritual virtue as power exercised by the Spirit's activity in and through Columba. Here he takes up the armour of God, and the kingdom is manifested

> The Lord will rescue me from every evil and save me for his heavenly kingdom. To him be the glory for ever and ever. Amen. (2 Tim. 4:18).

Adomnán does, however, describe precisely the essentially defensive nature of the armour, which enables the holy man to stand firm despite massive assault. The context of this tale in the third book must suggest that Adomnán had in mind his patron's association with the light of God (Rom. 13:12; 1 Thes. 5:8). Adomnán goes further than Paul in describing the intervention of the angelic host to repulse the demonic array. However, this too has an adequate scriptural model in Psalm 91.

Adomnán is concerned with sketching the spreading out of the kingdom of God, of which the expulsion of demons is a repeated New Testament image, 'But if I drive out demons by the Spirit of God, then the kingdom of God has come upon you' (Mt. 12:28). It is also a major apostolic commission, 'When Jesus had called the Twelve together, he gave them power and authority to drive out all demons and to cure diseases, and he sent them out to preach the kingdom of God' (Lk. 9:1-2). It is thus curious that he does not present Columba as himself able to repulse the demons, even while deploying the armour of God. In fact, in common with other early Irish

---

100 Cf. Ps. 90:6. *Vulgate* gives 'fiery darts/javelins (*tela ignea*)', i.e. hand held and thrown weapons, for Paul's *beleh...pepurwmena* which can represent a bow-fired arrow or throwing dart.
101 Reeves (1857, 206 note b).

hagiography, the expulsion of demons from people does not occur at all in the *VC*, an apostolic credential we would expect a composite Columba to have been given.

Stancliffe interprets this as the result of the ascetic, Eastern/British pre-Pelagian, and biblical (especially OT) background of Irish Christianity and of the development of the concept of the ascetic predestined to sanctity, and thus in no need of temptation. She describes the *Life of Antony* and Cassian as the major channels through which this eastern 'more optimistic' anthropology came to Ireland (103). What she seems to mean is that the early Irish church had little or no demonic interest as pre-Christian Irish cosmology explained evil without resort to it: the mischievous *áesside* played their rôle. The demonic was a Christian category introduced by those such as Adomnán reading continental *vitae*. *VA*, and Cassian however, give considerable attention to the demonic. Why would the hagiographers not record conflict with the *síde*, pagan equivalent of demons? In the light of Carney, were the *síde* a Christian interpolation? Her analysis of the demonic in 'the Irish church' as applied to Adomnán, though she recognises his differences cf. Muirchú, Tírechán and Cogitosus, is in need of further examination.[102]

Further notes of interest here are Baithéne's own success in defeating the attack on his own monastery, achieved, according to a revelation of the Spirit, by his God-aided management of prayer and fasting. Here is the clearest example of an apparent familiarity with the business of spiritual warfare, perhaps founded on the synoptic story of the failure of the disciples to drive out a demon, Mt. 17:21, Mk. 9:29, 'this kind does not go out except by prayer and fasting'. The spiritual wisdom of Baithéne is evidently not shared by his fellow Tireean priors, whose communities succumb to the attacks. Finally, both Columba, as head of the *familia*, and Baithéne as his lieutenant and successor, are only able to defend their own immediate community, a factor which might have bearing on our understanding of the exercise of authority and responsibility in the ecclesiology of the *familia*, though I will not pursue this here. This section of the tale contrasts with the posthumous miracle of protection of Columban establishments and their surrounding peoples/nations from the plague (ii.46), with no hint of the lack of protection for non-Columban houses in the territory. (Evidently, Columba was regarded as more effective when operating from the throne room of God, than when on his old holy mountain, perhaps a feature which shows

---

102 Stancliffe (1992, 97; 102-110), see her p.106, cf. *VC* ii.11, 16, 17, 24, 34, 37; and p.108 where she misses i.39, ii.24, ii.37. Space does not permit this examination here.

the developing cult of this saint; his power expands with his reputation, and with his importance to the cult.) This tale is thus a further piece of evidence for the moving image Adomnán is creating of the spread of the kingdom of God as it overcomes opposing spiritual forces. Here it is the powers direct, as it were, perhaps metaphorically representing a plague of some sort which assaulted the *familia*; elsewhere, it is disease, injustice, hiddenness, sin, pagan religious adherence etc. which is defeated. They are all on the kingdom inaugurating agenda of Lk. 4:18f.

The Glory of the Kingdom: Heavenly Light

The curious phenomenon Adomnán records as 'heavenly', or 'angelic light' occurs, apart from an advertisement in the second preface, only in book three: in its introduction, iii.2, 3, 11, 18, 19, 20, 21, 23:130a, 131b, 132b, 135a. The purpose of including these tales is made explicit in the epilogue appended to iii.23. The writer[103] draws attention to the significance of the phenomenon to Columba's standing, in a commonplace ascription to his merit

> After the reading of these three books, let every attentive reader observe of how great and high merit, how greatly and highly deserving of honour, our venerable superior... was esteemed in the sight of God... how frequent was the *brightness of divine light* that shone about him, while he still lived in the mortal flesh. And even after the departure... this same *heavenly brightness*... does not cease, down to the present day, to appear at the place where his holy bones repose; as is established through being revealed to certain [unnamed] elect persons (*VC* iii.23:135a-b).

Once again, we are seeking to discern the nature of the phenomenon employed in making this otherwise routine hagiographical tribute. In this selection, the brightness is not visible to all comers, only to the elect, who, like Moses, Peter, James, John and Paul before, responded to the call to holy life. It is a light which Patrick looked forward to

> in that day we shall rise in the sun's brilliant light (*cláritáte sólis*), that is, in the glory of Christ Jesus our redeemer (*Conf.* 59).

The presence of this motif early in the Columban tradition is shown in the poem *Adiutor Laborantium* (O Helper of Workers), tentatively identified as Columba's own composition. Among the forms of address to God, which Clancy and Márkus recognise may

---

103 The writer may be alluding to himself as an observer of this light, using a Johannine construction which is unlike Adomnán's more direct style elsewhere: cf. i.1, 49, ii.45, iii.23 (see Reeves 224-5 note b) where he employs the first person.

later in the tradition have been transferred to Columba himself, lines 12 and 13 read

> *Lumen et pater luminum* (light and father of lights)
> *Magna luce lucentium* (shining with great light)[104]

If this *is* Columba writing, this is perhaps the most interesting of all these phenomena. We might here have clear first-hand evidence of the background to the phenomenon Adomnán describes in the thought of Adomnán's subject himself. These lines clearly reflect the common idea of God as light, but line 12 also has the less common phrase from James 1.17

> Every good endowment
> And every perfect gift
> Is from above
> Coming down from
> *The Father of Lights (Patre luminum)*
> With whom there is no variation
> Or shadow due to change

Pushing out into the shadows, the tradition attached to Columba, grounded as it may be in the thought contained in the poem, clearly surrounds him with this phenomenon of visible light. It is important enough to form part of the title of the third book of the *Life*. If Columba experienced anything at all like the phenomenon ascribed to him, and we are seeing more than the imaginative over-development of a metaphor, we might even in this poem have Columba's own reflection on what it was he experienced.

SIGN OF THE PARACLETE (iii.2,3,17)

This sign is seen at the beginning, at the point of peregrination, and at the end of Columba's life

(i) Two luminary accounts relate to the pre-peregrinatory Columba. The first is an annunciation

> One night, this blessed boy's foster-father... found his whole house *illumined with clear light*; for he saw a *ball of fire* standing above the face of the sleeping child. Seeing this, he began at once to tremble; and marvelling greatly bowed his face to the ground, and understood that the *grace of the Holy Spirit* had been poured from heaven upon his foster-son (*VC* iii.2).

Trembling and bowing in the manifest presence of God and in reverence toward the boy, Cruithnechán reacts in accord with biblical tradition. Trembling is scripturally most often associated with the eschatological coming of God, thus here we have a further example

---

104 C&M, 69-70.

of the inauguration of the kingdom. We see clearly the content of Adomnán's imagery, as the light is said to demonstrate the pouring of 'the grace of Holy Spirit' on the boy.[105] All of the marvellous phenomena surrounding Columba have the same source; here, the presence of the divine Spirit is manifested more directly as the glory of God seen as 'clear light (*clara lux*)', and as 'a ball of fire (*globum igneum*)', which the title describes as 'a ray of light (*radius luminosus*)'. These last are non-biblical images, though they occur in other hagiographies,[106] and are intended as theophanic.

(ii) Later in Columba's career, at the trial of excommunication before he leaves for the desert, he is protected by an image from Exodus 13:21-2 (cf. 14.24; Num. 14:14; Ne. 9:12,19).

> 'I have seen a *pillar*', Brénden said, '*fiery and very bright* going before that man of God... therefore I dare not humiliate this man, whom I see to have been predestined by God to be a leader of nations into life' (*VC* iii.3).

The same image occurs later as a sign of the connection through Columba between the heavenly and earthly realms

> Saint Brénden mocu Alti saw (as he afterwards told Comgell and Cainnech) a kind of *fiery ball, radiant and very bright, that continued to glow* from the head of Saint Columba as he stood before the altar and consecrated the sacred oblation, and to *rise upwards like a column*, until those holiest ministries were complete (*VC* iii.17).

These two references to pillars of light form further typological devices,[107] and again are concerned to show the saint as the bringer of people into the promised land of the eschatological kingdom, as Moses brought his people into Israel accompanied by the pillar of fire, and as Jesus brought the presence of the eschatological kingdom manifested as the bright light of the transfiguration.

SIGNS OF THE GRACE OF THE HOLY SPIRIT (iii.18,19,20)

Three tales of this phenomenon are worth quoting rather more fully in order to set the context. They show clearly the connection between these outpourings of heavenly light, and the abundant

---

105 See iii.18 in the next chapter. Dunn sees Lk. 1:35 as an allusion to the *shekinah*, implying the manifestation of divine glory in Jesus (*NIDNTT* 3:697; see notes 108 and 114 below). Adomnán seems here to adopt such an allusion, making its implication physically manifest in connection with the messiah's representative in Ireland.

106 See Reeves on SS Declan and Mochaomhoc (1857, 192 note d), and St Martin (222 note h), who share similar phenomena. And see *VSH*, cxxxv-cxxxviii.

107 Both are associated with Bréndans, though the first is he of Birr, the second is the Navigator of Clonfert (see Sharpe 1995, notes 131, 354).

presence of the grace of the eschatological Spirit in Columba's life
The emphases are mine, making the point self explanatory.

> At another time when the holy man was living in the island of Hinba, the
> *grace of the Holy Spirit* was poured out upon him abundantly and in
> incomparable manner, and continued marvellously for the space of three
> days, so that for three days and as many nights, remaining within a house
> barred, and filled with *heavenly light*, he allowed no one to go to him,
> and he neither ate nor drank. From that house *beams of immeasurable
> brightness* were visible in the night, escaping through chinks of the door-
> leaves, and through the key-holes. And *spiritual songs, unheard before*,
> were heard being sung by him. Moreover, as he afterwards admitted in
> the presence of a very few men, he saw, *openly revealed, many of the
> secret things* that have been hidden since the world began. Also
> everything that in the sacred *scripture is dark and most difficult became
> plain*, and was shown more clearly than the day to the eyes of his purest
> heart (*VC* iii.18).

> One winter night... Virgno, fired with the love of God, entered the
> church alone for the sake of prayer, while others slept... Columba entered
> the same sacred building; and along with him there entered a *golden light*
> descending from highest heaven and wholly filling the inside of the
> church. Also the enclosed space of the exedra, in which Virgno tried to
> conceal himself as well as he could, was filled with the brightness of *that
> heavenly light*, which streamed through the partly-open inner door... not
> without some effect of terror. And just as none can look can look with
> direct and undazzled eyes upon the summer midday sun, so also Virgno,
> who saw that *heavenly brightness*, could not at all endure it, because the
> *brilliant and incomparable radiance* greatly dazzled his sight. When he
> saw this *flashing and terrifying effulgence*, that brother was so greatly
> overcome by fear that no strength remained in him (*VC* iii.19).

> On another night... Colcu... chanced to come to the door of the church,
> while others slept, and standing there prayed for some time. And then he
> saw that the whole church was suddenly filled with *heavenly light*.
> Quicker than speech, this *flash of light* vanished from his eyes. He did
> not know that Saint Columba was at the same hour praying within the
> church, and after this sudden *apparition of light* he was much afraid...On
> the following day, the saint summoned him, and sharply reproved him,
> saying: 'Henceforth take great care, my son, not to attempt like a spy to
> observe *heavenly light* that has not been granted you, for it will flee from
> you' (*VC* iii.20).

Both Virgno and Colcu are charged not to divulge their experience
during Columba's life, conventionally interpreted as a comment on
saintly humility. If we grant seventh-century belief in the reality of
the phenomenon, it becomes a wise precaution, given the danger
unauthorised viewing of the glory of God brings. As it was, the two

here described were filled with awe-full fear/terror; Virgno was frozen to the spot. Again, this has a scriptural background.

> And when the priests came out of the holy place, a cloud filled the house of the LORD, so that the priests could not stand to minister because of the cloud; for the glory of the LORD filled the house of the LORD (1 Kgs. 8:10-11).

The light manifested in a variety of forms: 'golden light (*aurea lux*)',[108] 'immeasurable brightness', and 'brilliant and incomparable radiance', could last three days, or flash for an instant. It was stopped by physical barriers (cf. Is. 4:5, 'Then the LORD will create over the whole site of mount Zion... the shining of a flaming fire by night'). Whilst bathed in the light, Columba fasted, sang spiritual songs unheard of before;[109] had secrets from since the world began, and difficult scriptural exegesis, revealed. Given the identification of scripture as the word of God in Iona, this last is reminiscent of the Psalmist: 'The disclosing of your words gives light...(*declaratio sermonum tuorum inluminat...*)' (Ps. 119:130), interpreted by Adomnán literally. The benefits of thus bathing are evidently conditions which will pertain in the eschaton, thus further inauguration is in view.

> For our knowledge is imperfect and our prophecy is imperfect; but when the perfect comes, the imperfect will pass away (1 Cor. 13:9-10).

> Then he showed me the river of the water of life, bright as crystal, flowing from the throne of God and of the Lamb ... And night shall be no more; they need no light of lamp or sun, for the Lord God will be their light, and they shall reign for ever and ever (Rev. 22:1-5).

THE LIGHT OF ANGELS (iii.11,23)

The story of Columba's passing provides a tripartite witness to a final description of a manifestation of light, associated with angels, (iii.23: 129b, 131ab, 132b, 135a).

> ...at midnight, [Columba]... went to the church... in advance of the others... In that moment, Diormit, the attendant, saw from a distance the whole church filled inside with *angelic light* about the saint. As Diormit approached the doorway, the light that he had seen quickly faded. A few more of the brothers also had seen it, when they too were a little way off (*VC* iii.23:129b).

---

108 (*VC* iii.19). The colour of the *shekinah* here should be noted. I can only find this description occurring before Adomnán in a paschal hymn Migne uncertainly attributed to St Ambrose '*Aurora lucis rutilat*' (*PL* 17 1203).

109 See chapter 4 below.

A group of three stories from Columba's death further illuminate Adomnán's conceptual understanding of what he's reporting. In the monastery called *Cluain Finchoil*,[110] a holy old man named Luguid had a vision which Adomnán says he 'not only found... set down in writing', but also heard from elders who had themselves heard it from the one to whom Luguid had described it, namely Virgno, an anchorite of Hinba. It is described thus,

> ...in the hour of [Columba's] blessed departure I saw *in the Spirit* the whole island of Io (where I have never come in the body) lit up with the *brightness of angels*; and all the spaces of the air, as far as the ethereal skies, *illumined by the shining of those angels*, who, sent from heaven, had come down without number, to bear aloft his holy soul (*VC* iii.23:131a-b).

The tale has a parallel with an earlier one of Bréndan's departure.

> For in this past night I have seen the sky suddenly opened, and companies of angels coming down to meet the soul of Saint Brénden. Their *shining and incomparable brightness* in that hour *lit up the whole circle of the world* (*VC* iii.11)

Ernéne, an old soldier of Christ, described a third vision of the same event directly to the youthful Adomnán himself. It is interesting to note that these observers apparently saw only the light of the angelic escort 'in the natural', as it were, with their physical eyes, whereas Luguid saw 'in the Spirit' a more detailed picture.

> In that night... I and other men with me... [fishing in Glen Finn, Donegal][111] saw the *whole space of airy heaven suddenly lit up*. Startled by the suddenness of this miracle, we raised our eyes and turned them to the region of the rising sun [i.e. to Iona];[112] and behold, there appeared what seemed like a *very great pillar of fire* which, rising upwards in that midnight, seemed to us to *illumine the whole world* like the summer sun at midday. And after *the pillar pierced the sky*, darkness followed, as after the setting of the sun (*VC* iii.23:132a-b).

These four motifs can be seen as further typological devices to illustrate the closeness of the life of Columba with that of Christ. His gestation, commission, mission, and final journey to glory are all accredited by the glorious light of the presence of the Spirit of God whose glorious kingdom, and even person, is made present.

THE GLORY OF THE KINGDOM

The key to understanding Adomnán's concept is given in iii.21.

---

110 Un-located, see Sharpe (1995, note 414).
111   A&A (1991, 229, note 254).
112 A&A (1991, 229, note 255).

And craftily spying [Berchán] set his eyes opposite the holes for the keys, supposing that within [Columba's] house some heavenly vision was being manifested to the saint, as the event showed to be true. For in that hour the blessed man's lodging was filled with the *glory of heavenly brightness*; the youthful transgressor could not bear to look upon it, and immediately fled away.

Berchán is severely reproved by Columba, who tells him that he knew, by the Spirit, that he was spying, and prayed to prevent him from either falling and dying, or from having his eyes torn from their sockets. What he observes illicitly is 'the glory of heavenly brightness', the light of glory accompanying angels, a phanerosis of the divine presence as experienced pre-eminently by Moses (Ex. 33:19-23); the transfigured Christ with Abraham and Elijah, and the apostles Peter, James and John (Mt. 17:1-6//); and Paul (Acts 26:13); and a potentially dangerous experience. These, with the exception of Abraham, are, of course, figures with whom Adomnán wishes explicitly to identify Columba.

The Judao-Christian tradition in which Adomnán writes is firmly established. Light clothes the LORD God as a garment of majesty and honour, displaying his glory (Ps. 104:1-2). Stewart states that the concept (which we see Adomnán encapsulating) 'saturates both Testaments', though the 'glory of God' is present in a special way in the eschatological temple and city (Rev. 15:8 and 21:23). The Targums and Rabbis use a post-biblical term *shekinah*, derived from the Hebrew root verb *sakan*, 'to dwell', for 'the radiance, glory or presence of God dwelling in the midst of his people... to signify God himself'. It is the 'nearest Jewish equivalent to the Holy Spirit', and a 'bridge between man's corporeality and God's transcendence'.[113] The Hebrew concept may be important in the Irish context in view of the interest amongst Irish translators and exegetes in Hebrew meaning.[114] Adomnán, observing these phenomena from his Christian tradition, presents a similar view, though is more clearly equating the light and the grace of the Spirit. Ellis describes this light as signifying in the Bible: 'God's presence and favour (Ps. 27:1; Is. 9:2; 2 Cor. 4:6)' and his holiness (1 Tim. 6:16; 1 Jn. 1:5), and in John's gospel, denotes the 'revelation of God's love in Christ (8:12; 9:5; cf. 12:46)'.[115] Hahn records: 'The sphere of God's rule is characterised in the Synoptic gospels (Mt. 17:5//Mk. 9:5; Lk 9:34) by the use of the OT image of the bright cloud which overshadows

---

113 Stewart (1982, 1101-2).
114 See Ní Chatháin and Richter (1987) passim. *Shekinah* occurs in Ex. 16:10; 24:16; 29:43; 33:18. Barclay (1957, 132) calls it 'the divine splendour of light which descended when God was visiting his people.'
115 Ellis (1982, 701).

Jesus and his disciples on the Mount of Transfiguration'.[116] Thus the concept is inextricably linked to the presence of the kingdom. Aalen records that the concept of angels being endowed with glory is widespread, since Ezekiel. It is found in manifestations from heaven of visible light (Lk. 2:9; 9:31; Acts 22:11). The Christian hope is the 'hope of glory' (Col 1:27; cf. Eph 1:18; 2 Thes. 2:14; 2 Tim. 2:10) 'the eschatological glory will take the believers and the whole creation up into itself by a new creation or transfiguration' (Rom. 8:18,21; 1 Cor. 15:43; 2 Cor. 3:18; 4:17; Phil. 3:21; Col. 3:4; 1 Pet. 5:1, anticipated in Is. 66:19,22).[117]

An eschatological reference to the light of God's glory in Isaiah may provide a link into Adomnán's image of the flowering kingdom

> The sun shall be no more your light by day, nor for brightness shall the moon give light to you by night; but the LORD will be your everlasting light, and your God will be your glory. Your sun shall no more go down, nor your moon withdraw itself; for the LORD will be your everlasting light, and your days of mourning shall be ended. Your people shall all be righteous; they shall possess the land for ever, *the shoot of my planting, the work of my hands, that I might be glorified...* I am the LORD; in its time I will hasten it (Is. 60:19-22).

Hopes for the new age are plainly being realized through Columba's Spirit-empowered ministry, which brings the blessings of the eschaton into partial reality. These words of Isaiah would happily sit with Adomnán's Columba,

> Listen to me, my people, and give ear to me, my nation; for a law will go forth from me, and my justice for a light to the peoples (Is. 51:4)

> And nations shall come to your light, and kings to the brightness of your rising (Is. 60:3).[118]

The light in the *VC* is thus a sign of the presence of the soteriological kingdom, and of hope of the coming eschatological kingdom already evident in and around other parts of Adomnán's record of Iona's founder. His sanctity is seen thus to be grounded on firm biblical theological foundations.

Judgement

As we've seen, in ii.33, an angel strikes Broichan, *magus* of the King of Picts, in divine response to his unyielding obstinacy. Adomnán

---

116 Hahn (1971, 555).

117 Aalen (1976, 46-8).

118 Hahn (1976, 492) cited in reference to the missionary outlook of the prophecies concerning the Messiah.

does not say Columba prayed for this response, rather that the response was revealed to him. However, the response is mediated, uniquely in this case, by an 'angel from heaven'. Here we have a clear manifestation of a further aspect of the coming of the kingdom not hitherto mentioned. The book of Revelation is replete with visions of angels bringing God's judgement upon the unrepentant and intransigent. The same sign of the presence of the kingdom is seen in the various manifestations of what are conventionally termed 'vengeance miracles' (ii.20-25, from Adomnán's own description *de terrificis ultionibus,* ii.25). Columba dispenses divine justice in an outworking of Christ's promise and declaration to the apostles

> ...he breathed on them, and said to them, 'Receive the Holy Spirit. If you forgive the sins of any, they are forgiven; if you retain the sins of any, they are retained' (Jn. 20:22-23).

This is a further aspect of apostolic ministry, bringing the rule of God into the pre-eschatological age, demonstrated in Acts 5.1-11, in fulfilment of OT prophecies (e.g. Isa 11).

Conclusion

Adomnán's presentation of Columba as one who brings the eschatological kingdom of God into partial realization supersedes and eclipses the petty politics of earthly rulers of his day. It is difficult to imagine that, in most of these tales, Adomnán is being deliberately obscure and subtle in his imagery. To his monks, to whom he ostensibly writes the *Life,* the images may well be familiar. However, to the infinitely less well-schooled secular authorities of the day, any very subtle reference which may be supposed to be contained in these tales would surely have been lost and inaccessible, unless of course the tales were told by those who elucidated the subtle connections for the ears of the secular rulers. Imputing delicate power plays from one ruler to another would appear to have demanded a form of superlatively sly subtlety. It must be mined from the text with consummate dedication and care, looking for cat's hairs of evidence in the microscopic side-strokes of this politician's cunning pen.

The evidence of this *Life* however allows an alternative, and more obvious overarching interpretation. This biblically-literate theologian announces the coming of ultimate rule into the area over which he presides, and makes a plea for all rulers to submit to it in order that they might receive its blessings, and not, as a consequence of its rejection, be lost. In making this claim, it might be possible to see Adomnán attempting to lift his patron, and himself, out of the muddy swirling of seventh-century politics, and into the clear waters of the heavenly realms.

As we noticed early in this chapter, Max Turner's analysis of the canonical understanding of the miraculous forms part of his recent contribution on the gifts of the Spirit, and follows Fee's expository foundation, and Grudem's analysis of the prophetic, among many others.[119] In summary, he wants, with Richardson, to move beyond a Thomist extrinsic evidentialism, which makes the gospel miracles simply argue for the divine nature of Christ, or the godliness of a disciple, to seeing them as intrinsic eschatological revelations, where the eschaton is contained within the miracle. The miracles are a vital, inescapable, and undeletable part of the message as outlined in Jesus' programme (Is. 61:1-2 /Lk. 4:18-21). We might compare this in Adomnán's own corpus with the ethical kingdom exemplified in his *Law of the Innocents*. Turner says

> For Luke, as recorded in the gospel and Acts, salvation is not merely forgiveness of sins, contentment of soul, and a bright future hope; it is holistic liberation and social renewal of God's people... To this programme, deliverance from evil powers and healing of the sick are not merely extrinsic factors, they are themselves very much part of the salvation announced... They are concrete expressions of the message.[120]

Turner argues that John builds on the theological stance that 'the miracles are expected to invite towards faith because they embody the kingdom of God that is preached.' It is not a crude extrinsic proof; Jesus refuses the attention of those who believe merely because of the miracles (Jn. 2:23,24; 3:2; 6:14-15). In Adomnán, as a result of his lack of chronological structure, there is no sense of a building eschatological presence, i.e. it is not evolutionary, progressing towards an ultimate age of achievement. However, I believe that from the above collection of cross-references to biblical imagery and principles, the awareness in Adomnán of the kingdom being inaugurated in the ministry of his patron is evident. However, the manifestation of the presence of the kingdom, its flowering, requires to be recorded for posterity, hence the collection of incidences. These stories then themselves act as carriers of the teaching and presence of the kingdom. In his introductory summary, i.1, Adomnán is claiming that the life of their blessed patron was spent in establishing the kingdom of God not so much in words, and he includes very little of Columba's preaching, but in power. The teaching of the kingdom, the word of the Lord, is a scriptural given,

---

119 Turner (1996); Fee (1994); Grudem (1992). Others, e.g. Ruthven (1993, chapter 3).

120 Turner (1996, 248; 249).

and is not added to. In this he follows Athanasius, Gregory and Sulpicius very closely. The coming into being of the product of faith, is, for Adomnán, a kingdom of followers of Christ who experience the blessings of his kingdom in the present age as they anticipate the future fulfilment. This important clue to Adomnán's thinking links closely to the commentary he provides at the end of ii.32 where he likens Columba to the apostles and prophets, specifically naming Peter, John and Paul, the three apostles most associated in the New Testament with miraculous confirmatory signs of the in-breaking of the kingdom. Adomnán's accounts are not so much showing us *a* church in charismatically-accompanied activity, as *the* church in the act of establishing a kingdom ruled under the authority of the God of Elijah and Elisha, the Father of Christ, the God of the Apostles and prophets. And this kingdom was being established in Dalriada, Connacht, the territories of the Uí Néill and Cruithne, in Dál Riata, Pictland, and Britain alike. (It remains curious that Adomnán makes no reference to Northumbria apart from Oswald's battle).

Adomnán explicitly records concern for the eschatological destination of the soul, and of souls across the geographical area for which he is responsible as abbot of Iona, as shown in a number of the visions of book three. If we may take Abbot Adomnán at his word, the monks who had requested the recording of Columba's life were living at a period when the political fortunes of their church were on the wane, at a time when the missions of Lindisfarne and possibly Armagh were claiming to be more effective. In the face of this putative loss of confidence, it could be that the monks wanted assurance of the Godly foundation of their own mission, and to ask why their founder had been so successful in his establishment of that mission. Adomnán's answer is to record this set of foundation-stories, as if to say: 'This is how the holy Columba worked. This is why he was so successful. Let us emulate him, seeking God's supernatural power for the task of continuing the establishment of his kingdom.'

CHAPTER 4

The Indwelling Outworking Eschatological Spirit:
Pneumatological Nature and Function

God anointed Jesus of Nazareth with the Holy
Spirit and with power...
he went about doing good and healing all that were oppressed by the devil,
for God was with him.[1]

Manifestations of the Eschatological Spirit

In his first preface, as we've seen, Adomnán gives us a clear image of
his conception of the kingdom of God as consisting in the flowering
of faith. With the analysis of the evidence amassed in the body of his
writing, we have seen how his concept of the kingdom is woven into
the fabric of his presentation of the life and ministry of his hero
Columba. In this chapter, I wish to proceed by applying the category
of the coming eschatological kingdom to further analysis of the
understanding of Adomnán as to the nature of the marvellous
phenomena he describes. He sees their function as showing the
coming of the kingdom in Columba's work. Are we able to probe still
deeper into the descriptions he gives, taken with the influences upon
him that we have identified, so as to identify at least some of his
conception of the functioning nature of the phenomena he uses with
such striking effect?

Operating with this eschatologically oriented understanding,
established in chapter three above, Adomnán seeks to portray his
hero's ministry. His organisation of the life into the three books of
types of marvellous phenomena is unique in extant writings to his
period, as we've seen. He has at his disposal, we assume, a set of
various tales of this life with which to build his case. His formulaic
insistence on the availability of a wide number of tales does not help
us to know how finite his sources actually were, nor the extent to
which his own imagination, that of the compilers of his sources, and
that of his informants, was involved in furnishing the tales he uses.

---

1   Acts 10:38, spoken by Peter called bar-Jonah (Jn. 1:42; 21:15-17). The
     significance of this name may not have been missed by Adomnán, as we shall
     see.

The important point here is that the record he leaves has been fashioned by the thought processes of the era, and he pays unique attention to organising the tales he does use. Picard argues that the progression of the three books towards higher forms of the marvellous presents a sequential argument for Columba's nature as a man of God, in the style of a grammarian. First he is depicted in the superior prophetic / contemplative tradition. Then his miracle working ability emulates Christ and the apostles. Finally, the divine origin of his power as a soldier of Christ is confirmed by his accompaniment by angels and heavenly light, which also shows him to be part of the heavenly world. Picard describes the prophetic 'words' as inferior to thaumaturgical 'acts', apparently mirroring Adomnán's use of 1 Corinthians 4:20 (see above).[2] His scheme has the merit of accommodating Adomnán's divisions. However, Adomnán himself evidently regarded Columba's prophetic ministry not simply as words, but as a flowering of faith, i.e. acts of dynamic power energized by God through faith, and we have seen that it is not only angels that show Columba to have been 'part of the heavenly world', but also these and other kingdom inaugurating marvels.

Picard sees a classically trained Adomnán following the biographical tradition of Plutarch and Suetonius. Plutarch 'dismissed the value of deeds', dwelling on 'the signs of man's soul', in order to immortalize the virtues of the hero. They wrote to encourage emulation. In the tradition of Aristotle, they saw a man's disposition, his *ethos*, given at birth, as determining his life. Thus the life was presented as a response of *ethos* to circumstance.[3] Adomnán does dwell on the signs of Columba's soul, as it were, but sees these being manifested by acts empowered by faith in God, not initial disposition. Thus for him the marvellous, God-empowered act is the vital sign. It is not unaided human act.

Picard's description of the Judeo-Christian tradition being 'a progression towards God, allowing for possible mutations of the personality'[4] recognizes the break with the philosophers, but only hints at the rôle of the Spirit in Christian tradition in the death of the old self, and the re-birth and spiritual empowerment of the new (cf. John 3, Romans 8 etc). Though Columba may have been called before birth, and maintained a pure heart, his 'heroic' sanctity, and his holy nature is dependent not on his initial disposition, but on the transforming empowerment of the *Spiritus Sanctus*, as we will see.[5]

---

2   Picard (1985, 76-7).
3   Picard (1985, 69-71).
4   Picard (1985, 79).
5   Picard's note of the correspondence of saintly with Irish secular heroism (79) should be seen in the light of the discussion in chapter two above.

In this, Adomnán follows the model of his exemplar Gregory, who, as Hillgarth notices, sees the 'men of God' as 'full of the Spirit of Christ'. 'In this they represented the New Age'.[6] The static character of saintliness may determine hagiographical representation, but the growing repute of an individual identifies one who fits the character.

What Adomnán does not do is to set out in any detectable manner to present a sequential argument for the nature of the marvellous. I wish to proceed to use the eschatological category identified above in elucidating Adomnán's concept of the nature of the marvellous, specifically of the prophetic, the major category of marvellous phenomenon to which Adomnán gives attention. In this way, I aim to consolidate and corroborate my eschatological interpretation by testing its application to a category of the marvellous which we have yet to investigate.

The kingdom of God is seen by Adomnán to flower in three distinct ways: firstly it flowers in prophetic revelations; secondly in miracles of power; and thirdly in visions of heavenly light and of angels. Columba is the focus around whom this blossoming occurs, but, as we shall see, he is not its only locus. An important key to this three-fold classification might be found in the prophet Joel, repeated by Peter in his address on the day of Pentecost.

And *in the last days* it shall be, God declares,
that *I will pour out my Spirit* upon all flesh,
and your sons and your daughters shall *prophesy*,
and your young men shall see *visions*,
and your old men shall dream dreams;
yea, and on my menservants and my maidservants in those days
I will pour out my Spirit;
[and they shall *prophesy*.]
And I will show *wonders* in the heaven above
[and *signs*] on the earth beneath,
blood, and *fire*, and vapour of smoke...[7]

The writer of Acts records the emphasizing addition of 'and they shall prophesy' accompanying the outpouring of the Spirit, and the classification of earthbound wonders as 'signs'. Awareness of the Joeline promise is not uncommon in Latin Christian authors before Adomnán.[8] Perhaps the most interesting occurrence to this

---

6   Hillgarth (1987, 325), citing Gregory, *Dial.*, (II:8, 9 and III:38, 3).
7   Acts 2:17-19 cf. Joel 2:28-30. Additions in Acts are shown in [square brackets]; emphasis is mine.
8   Standard works on the treatment of the Holy Spirit in the patristic and mediaeval eras are H.B. Swete (1912), *The Holy Spirit in the Ancient Church*, and H. Watkin-Jones (1922), *The Holy Spirit in the Medieval Church*. A more

discussion is that in the *Confession* of Patrick, where he defends his part in the mission of the church to make disciples. He explicitly quotes the evangelists' anticipation of the consummation which will follow preaching to the ends of the earth, thus demonstrating his awareness of the eschatological orientation of this mission. He cites Joel's prophecy from Acts to v.18, then shows how signs of the outpouring include turning from idol worship, calls to celibacy, divine words delivered by angels, and steadfast faith despite persecution. He summarizes with a refusal to deny these 'signs and wonders *(signa et mirabília)*' which God showed him. This clearly demonstrates the awareness of two significant categories to our investigation: first, the eschatological promise of the outpouring of the Spirit being realized in fifth-century Ireland, as manifested here in 'signs and wonders', and second, the recognition of the imminence of the eschatological consummation which will follow preaching the gospel to the ends of the earth.[9] Patrick is explicit in his ascription to the Spirit the source of power for this mission, and claims to have had seven (prophetic) visions.[10]

The citations of the Joeline eschatological promise of the Spirit, especially in Patrick, and non-insular works Adomnán is likely to have known,[11] show the likelihood of his own awareness of the promise, even if he himself does not quote it. It may well be that he uses the categories of manifestations in the Joel/Peter promise in shaping his own three categories of 'proof'. Adomnán's three categories cohere. Peter reminds his hearers of the promise of the outpouring of the Spirit resulting in prophecy and visions, wonders and signs, and fire. Adomnán's major categories of marvellous phenomena are prophecy, miracles (i.e. some 'signs and wonders'), and visions of angels and heavenly light, including fire. The conceptual link is clear, as we will see below, between the outpouring of the Spirit and the accompanying manifestations, all, as we have seen, linked with the coming new creation. Adomnán's groupings are not exclusive or identical, (prophecy occurs throughout the *VC* and

---

recent summary is provided by William G. Rusch (1978): 'The Doctrine of the Holy Spirit in the Patristic and Medieval Church'. These works, as those upon which they report, major on the doctrinal questions of the Spirit's person and origin, rather than the Spirit's manifestation.

9   Patrick (*Conf.*, 40-45). The rejection of Patrick's marvels is recognized as a sign of opposition, perhaps from disapproving British ecclesiastical authority. It might also indicate resistance to the acceptance of marvellous phenomena from those who laugh and insult his intelligence in claiming such, a resistance Adomnán is concerned to counter (see chapter one).

10   Patrick (*Conf.*, 11*)*, see Howlett (1994, 111-113).

11   E.g. Jerome (*Ezek.*, XI); Augustine (*Civ. Dei*, XVIII:xxx) see O'Loughlin (1994a) and C&M (1995, 211-222).

in his introduction to book three; wonderful appearances of angels
are called visions), but he does not try to force the manifestations of
the Spirit into discrete categories where a combination is recorded.
Events during and after Pentecost, when Peter reminded observers of
strange manifestations of the Joeline prophecy, showed that the new
age had dawned. Subsequent chapters of Acts, and the remainder of
the NT record the continued outpouring of the same Spirit manifested
in various ways, including prophecy, healing, demonic expulsion,
dreams and visions, etc.[12] Joel's prophecy is interpreted in Peter's
speech as emphasizing the rôle of the prophetic in the age of the
outpoured Spirit, in that he repeats the formula. In the primary and
pervading place Adomnán gives to the prophetic in the *VC*, we see a
parallel emphasis in understanding the rôle of prophecy in the
realization of the eschaton through the life of the holy man of God.

What then is the place Adomnán gives to the operation of the
third person of the Trinity in relation to his view of the coming of
the kingdom in Columba's life, and what place prophecy? New
Testament documents clearly link the present reception of the Spirit
with the eschatological life of believers, as Peter explains using the
prophetic promise. Paul sees the same link

> We know that the whole creation has been groaning in travail together
> until now; and not only the creation, but we ourselves, who have the first
> fruits of the Spirit, groan inwardly as we wait for adoption as sons (Rom.
> 8:23).

> [God] has put his seal upon us, and given us his Spirit in our hearts as a
> guarantee (2 Cor. 1:22 //5:5).

> …[those] who have tasted the heavenly gift, who have become partakers
> of the Holy Spirit, and have tasted the goodness of the word of God and
> the powers of the age to come… (Heb. 6:5).

(And see Rom. 8:1-17; Eph. 1:13, 4:30). Having the Spirit now is
thus a first fruit of the new creation, 'the Spirit is the first fruit of
the full harvest', as we have already observed.

Sherry notes that New Testament writers felt that Christ was 'still
amongst them through the presence of the Holy Spirit, because his
personality seemed to be manifested in this presence.' He quotes E.J.
Tinsley

> St Paul is most aware… of a life and an activity which is working in and
> through him moulding him into the shape of the vision of the image of
> God which he has seen. This life and activity was the action of the Spirit
> bringing about the birth of Christ in the Christian, and sustaining the

---

12 See Gordon Fee (1994), *God's Empowering Presence,* or Max Turner (1996),
    The Holy Spirit and Spiritual Gifts, for recent treatments of the topic.

growth of Christ in the believer to maturity. In the Christian *imitatio Christi* the Lord Christ is at one and the same time the object of the *mimesis* and, through the Spirit, the means of it.[13]

In their lament at the lack of explicit reference to the third person of the Trinity in *Altus Prosator*, Clancy and Márkus record a discourse worth repeating in full in the present context

> The church teaches that Christians can already begin to share the life of God, here and now, through the gift of the Spirit. Rather than simply obeying in the present world in order to receive their eternal reward in the next, they are, so to speak, already citizens of the kingdom of God, members of the Body of Christ, by virtue of this Holy Spirit which is poured into their hearts.[14]

It is not clear whether this excursus sees the activity of the Spirit as implicit in the *Altus*, though they do confirm that it is not explicit. However, what the *Altus* may contain implicitly of this Spirit mediated life of the kingdom, *VC* may contain explicitly. If this is true of the New Testament writers, and of what 'the church teaches', how far is it also true of Adomnán? Did his pneumatology include such notions of the Spirit as the means by whom Christians became imitators of Christ, not merely by behavioural emulation of truth communicated by the Spirit, but by dynamic transformation actually wrought by the effectual presence of the Spirit? Adomnán stresses the fellow-ship of Columba not just with the apostles, who experienced Pentecost, but also with the Old Testament prophets. Illustrating a fifth-century continental view, Leo the Great has this to say

> ...when on the Day of Pentecost the Holy Spirit filled the disciples of the Lord, it was not so much the beginning of a gift as it was the completion of one already bountifully possessed: because the patriarchs, the prophets, the priests, and all the holy men who preceded them were already quickened by the life of the same Spirit... although they did not possess his gifts to the same degree.[15]

I wish to proceed to examine Adomnán's view with a more detailed analysis of the ways he describes the Spirit as working in the life of Columba, with special reference to the prophetic, Adomnán's major category of the marvellous. I will seek to trace the background to his interpretations of the traditions he records, and will thus probe more deeply into the question of if, and how, Adomnán reflects the Christian tradition of the activity of the eschatological, kingdom

---

13 Sherry (1984, 72), citing Tinsley (1960, 165).
14 C&M, 67-8.
15 *Sermon* 76, ch. 3 (*PL* 54:405f) and see de Lubac (1969, ch. 4).

inaugurating Spirit. The question we are seeking to answer is, does Adomnán see the kingdom coming in Columba's activity? A subsequent question, which will be raised by the evidence we will examine, takes us into controversial territory; namely, can this coming properly be described as 'mission' in the Christian sense? The reasons for this last question being identified at this stage will, I hope, be becoming apparent as we proceed.

'Spirit' in the *Life of Columba*

Adomnán shows himself to be Trinitarian in his theology, in accordance with the doctrine of his day. He recognizes the place of the Spirit in the Trinity (ii.32, iii.23:134b). The Spirit of God is third person of the Trinity, and not an impersonal supernatural power or force. He has silently adopted the Trinitarian description of the Spirit as God. However, his pneumatology is focussed not ontologically, but on the manifest activity of the Spirit. He uses the terms 'Spirit', 'Lord', 'Christ' interchangeably to describe the manifest intervention of God in his own contemporary world, and in that which he describes for Columba. I am here limiting myself to an examination of the references made explicitly to 'S/spirit'.[16] The Spirit acted in and through Columba to produce manifestations that, for Adomnán, had their explanation in the dynamic presence of God working in and through the life of the holy one. The phenomena were super-natural. They were near-contemporary manifestations like those recorded for Jesus and the early disciples, yet they are not simply copies of biblical examples. Significantly, he does not mention the Spirit in connection with Columba's ethical sanctification in the production of the fruit of the Spirit (Gal. 5:22), though running through the whole work is a refrain referring to 'the holy man', or 'his pure heart'. This ethical sanctity is, for Adomnán, the ground upon which the spiritual manifestations flourish, and which they in their turn accredit. As we shall see, it provides a dwelling place for the Spirit in Columba himself. Adomnán's silence on this process of Spirit-empowered sanctification cannot be taken as indicating the absence of this concept in his theology, but neither will it permit us to elucidate ethical sanctification as a spiritually empowered manifestation in Adomnán's thought.

We will consider firstly the opening description of the Spirit dwelling in Columba, and other visitations; secondly the rôle of the Spirit in Columba's prophetic ministry in its various nuances; thirdly

---

16 I employ the convention of referring to the third person of the Trinity in upper case, and to other references to spirit in lower case. It is not always straightforward to interpret Adomnán's intent.

the more miscellaneous references to the Spirit's activity in and through Columba.

The Spirit in Columba

Columba's name refers to the Spirit (sp:2a). The descent of the Holy Spirit in the form of a dove on Jesus is the opening reference (sp:2a), thus 'often in sacred books', says Adomnán, 'a dove is understood to signify mystically the Holy Spirit' (sp:2b).[17] Columba 'offered to the Holy Spirit a dwelling in himself' (sp:2b). He was filled with the joy of the holy Spirit[18] (sp:5a). Citing Paul (1 Cor. 6:17), he records the union of Columba and the Lord as 'one spirit' as the rationale for his supernatural abilities (i.1:10b). He was visited by the Spirit, whose grace was poured out on him as a child (iii.2), and later 'abundantly and in an incomparable manner' (iii.18). In this visitation he sang spiritual songs unheard before (iii.18). He recognized the place of the Spirit in the Trinity (ii.32, iii.23:134b).

Adomnán opens his second preface by recording how Columba received his name

> There was a man of venerable life and blessed memory, the father and founder of monasteries, who received the same name as the prophet Jonah. For although sounding differently in the three different languages, yet what is pronounced *iona* in Hebrew, and what Greek calls *peristera*, and what in the Latin language is called *columba*, means one and the same thing... According to the truth of the gospels, moreover, the Holy Spirit is shown to have descended upon the only-begotten son of the eternal Father in the form of that little bird that is called a dove. Hence often in sacred books a dove is understood to signify mystically the Holy Spirit.

Adomnán explicitly links his subject with the dove in which form the Spirit descended upon Christ (Mt. 3:16 // Mk. 1:10 // Lk. 3:22 // Jn. 1:32), and reminds us that *columba* mystically signifies the Holy Spirit in sacred books. The direct association with the meaning of the name, dove, with Jonah, which is plainly Adomnán's point here, needs further elucidation. The dove as a sign of the Spirit is the primary explicit association which Adomnán records. He follows it by reference to the purity and simplicity of doves as referred to by 'the Saviour himself' (Mt. 10:16), but the reason this feature is mentioned is not to expound on Columba's own purity, which is

---

17   'Sacred books' would include pre-eminently the four gospels, then commentaries of Jerome, e.g. on Mt. 3:16.

18   Von Hügel calls the stipulation of Pope Benedict 14th that there should be a note of joy in the lives of those put forward for canonisation 'nothing short of spiritual genius' cited in Sherry (1984, 34).

simply a stated given, but to establish that it is as a result of this simplicity and purity of heart that he offered the Spirit a dwelling in himself

> [Columba] with dovelike disposition offered to the Holy Spirit a dwelling in himself.[19]

Thus there are two questions: why did Adomnán make the link between Columba, the prophet Jonah, and the Spirit, and how are we to understand what he means by the Holy Spirit dwelling in Columba's dove-like heart?

COLUMBA, JONAH, DOVE, SPIRIT

Jonah, as Adomnán knows, means 'dove' in the Hebrew. Jonah is something of an anti-hero in scripture. He is not a shining example of one either open to the working of the Spirit generally, nor of the Spirit of prophecy specifically. We do not know that Adomnán refers to the Jonah of the Old Testament directly; it could simply be with reference to the evangelists' references to him on the lips of Jesus that Adomnán has him in mind. From the gospels onwards, the primary sign of Jonah was of the resurrection of Christ. The sign of Jonah is seen as one of the inauguration of the kingdom in the coming resurrection. The Holy Spirit descended upon Jesus in the form of a dove. He later breathed the Spirit onto his followers after the resurrection in fulfilment of the eschatological promise of Joel (above). Huyshe reminds us of the many epithets that the dove of the church attracted, including 'the Wise', and, 'the Meek'.[20] It is to this sense of the dove with which Columba is popularly associated. However Adomnán sees this meekness as the condition for his being filled with the Holy Spirit of prophecy, miracles and visions. While the sign allows for both applications, the *VC* as a whole argues unquestionably for Columba as man of the Spirit, as we will see.

Columbanus mentions his own connection with the prophet three times in his letters: in the first, he introduces himself 'son of Jona (poor dove) (*Bar-iona (vilis Columba)*)'; in the fourth, he likens his possible shipwreck to that of Jonah 'who is called Columba in Hebrew', cf. Jerome's allegorical interpretation

> Jonah, fairest of doves, whose shipwreck shews in a figure the passion of the Lord, recalls the world to penitence, and while he preaches to Nineveh, announces salvation to all the heathen.[21]

In Columbanus' third letter, he says

---

19 '...*in sé columbinís moribus spiritui sancto hospitium praebuit*' (sp:2b).
20 Huyshe (1905, lv).
21 Jerome (*Ep.*, tr. *NPNF*, Series II, Vol. VI, 53:8).

I am called Jonah in Hebrew, Peristera in Greek, Columba in Latin, yet
so much is my birth-right in the idiom of your language, though I use
the ancient Hebrew name of Jonah...[22]

However, he gives little away to help us to read any more than that
he shared the name and the maritime adventures of the prophet, and
that he was aware of the linguistic pedigree of his name. This linkage
was thus known in seventh-century Hiberno-Latin, but this does not
answer the prominence given to the link for Columba, nor its link
with the Spirit. Likewise, Isidore comments on the name, 'Jonas
means dove, that is one weeping / sorrowing,'[23] and equates it not
with the Spirit, but in common with many patristic references, as a
reference to sadness.

A major clue to the construction Adomnán places on the epithet
is furnished by his near contemporary, Bede, who says

Jesus beheld him, saying, 'You are Simon son of Jonah'... Jonah,
rendered Columba in our language. You are therefore son of Jonah, you
are son of the Holy Spirit. Son, that is to say, of the Spirit, who accepts
in humility the Holy Spirit.[24]

Bede's construction shows the seventh/early eighth-century currency
of the association of Spirit and Jonah,[25] but not a source for
Adomnán's link. We may ask, parenthetically, if Bede has derived
his association from Adomnán? Gregory may furnish a clue to
understanding Adomnán's thinking here, in mentioning the sign of
Jonah

Benedict... had the same Spirit who, through the outpouring grace of our
redemption, has filled the hearts of his elect servants, of whom John
writes, '...of his fullness we have all received' [Jn. 1:16]. For God's holy
servants might have miraculous ability from the Lord, but not to bestow
them upon others. Therefore it was he that gave the signs of miracles to

---

22   '... quam facienti mihi Ionae hebraice, Peristerae graece, Columbae latine,
      potius tantum vestrae idiomate linguae nancto, licet prisco inter hebraeo
      nomine...Columbanus (*Epist.*, I.1; IV.8; V.16; Walker 2-3; 34-5; 54-5).
23   '*Jonas interpretatur columba, sive dolens,*' Isidorus Hisp. (*Etymol.*,
      VII:viii:18).
24   '*Intuitus autem eum Jesus, dixit: Tu es Simon filius Jona... Jona, lingua
      nostra dicitur columba. Tu es ergo filius Jona, tu es filius Spiritus sancti.
      Filius ergo dicitur Spiritus, quia humilitatem de Spiritu sancto acceperat*',
      Bede (*Comm. Jn.*, 1.42; PL 92:653A).
25   His reference to the 'son of the Holy Spirit' is in turn prefigured by Augustine
      of Hippo, who writes of Jesus as '*filius Spiritus sancti*' in the context of his
      birth of an inviolate virgin. Bede (*Serm.*, CCXIV.III.6; PL 38:1069).

his servants, who promised to give the sign of Jonah to his enemies [Mt. 12:39].[26]

Although Gregory again rehearses the standard meaning of the sign as pertaining to the resurrection, he associates the giver of the Spirit with the giver of the sign of Jonah. Adomnán also apparently wishes to associate his Columba not only with the name, but also with the prophet who bore the name of 'dove', *viz*. Jonah, and all this in context of a discussion of Columba's association with the Spirit. He has made the etymological link, Jonah equals dove, dove equals Spirit, and therefore Jonah equals Spirit. We may conclude a link extant in seventh/eighth-century Christian thought between dove, Columba, Jonah, and the Holy Spirit, and thus in emphasizing Columba's link with the prophet, we see him making an epithetic link between the saint and the Spirit-bearing prophet who is a sign of salvation. Thus Columba's name marks him as a man of the Spirit, just as Jonah was a man of 'the Spirit of prophecy'. In Adomnán's thought, the Irish term *Colum Cille* might better be understood not simplistically as 'dove of the church', meaning man of peace or meekness, but 'Spirit-bearer of the church', the one who demonstrated the life and ministry of one in whom the Spirit dwells. While recognising scholarly dissent from the idea, it would accord with Adomnán's intent of association if a modification of the island name gave this location an association not only with the famous founder, but also with the Spirit who was, as we shall see, the source of the founder's ministry, and thus ultimately of his fame. Iona was thus the place where the dove of the Spirit of God was poured out in the Provinces, almost as a new Pentecost. This leads us to the second question.[27]

THE SPIRIT OFFERED A DWELLING IN COLUMBA'S DOVE-LIKE HEART

Hilary describes Honoratus as 'this dwelling place of the Holy Spirit'.[28] The sixth/seventh-century *Alphabet of Devotion* records a similar motif

> In whom does the Spirit dwell?
> In the one who is pure without sin

---

26 *'Benedictus... unius spiritum habuit qui per concessae redemptionis gratiam electorum corda omnium impleuit. De quo Iohannes dicit: "...De plenitudine ejus nos omnes accepimus". Nam sancti Dei homines potuerunt a Domino uirtutes habere, non etiam aliis tradere. Ille autem signa uirtutis dedit subditis, qui se daturum signum Ionae promisit inimicis...'*, Gregory (*VB*, VIII.9; *SC* 260:166).

27 A further element in the association with Jonah will be noted below, in chapter 5 on the Mission of Columba.

28 *Life of Honoratus*, tr. Hoare (1954, 272).

It is then that a person is a vessel of the Holy Spirit, when the virtues have come in place of the vices. It is then that desire for God grows in a person, when worldly desire withers.[29]

Clancy and Márkus believe the alphabet was written by Bishop Colmán mac Béognae (Colmán mac Elo), a student of Columba's, and may thus give a second-hand version of Columba's own philosophy.[30] How are we to understand this? Part of the answer is provided by Adomnán himself. In i.1:10b, he quotes from Paul, 1 Cor. 6:17

For according to the words of Paul, 'he who adheres to the Lord is one spirit.'[31]

The verse is set in the context of Paul's argument as to who will and will not possess the kingdom of God.[32] He reminds his readers that the immoral and indulgent will not possess the kingdom, and that those who are members of Christ (v. 15) by the Spirit (v. 11) should keep free from entanglement with the sinful. As ones bought at a price (v. 19), they should honour God with their bodies (v. 20). In verse 19, Paul reminds his readers that as those united to the Lord, their body is a temple of the Holy Spirit, thus the Spirit is in them, and they should keep themselves pure. The concept has clear foundation in another of Paul's eschatologically oriented passages, reminding the Ephesians of their status as fellow citizens with the saints in the household of God, built on the foundation of the apostles, prophets and Christ (Eph. 2:19-20). He concludes the section

...in whom you also are built together for a dwelling place of God in the Spirit (Eph. 2:22).

The concept is echoed in the *VC* as we have seen. Other scriptures which present the same image, and which may be seen to have influenced Adomnán's view include 2 Cor. 1:21-22 (quoted above), and

But you are not in the flesh, you are in the Spirit, if in fact the Spirit of God dwells in you. Any one who does not have the Spirit of Christ does not belong to him. But if Christ is in you, although your bodies are dead

---

29 C&M, 207.
30 C&M, 195.
31 Forbes, and Sharpe, translates this: 'He who is joined (Fowler has 'cleaveth') to the Lord is one Spirit.' Gregory quotes the verse in his discussion of knowing God's secret counsel by revelation of the Spirit (*VB* XVI); see below.
32 1 Cor. 6:9. We should note the nearby location of the other key verse we have been considering concerning the kingdom, 1 Cor. 4.20, and see C&M on the *Altus* quoted above.

because of sin, your spirits are alive because of righteousness. If the Spirit of him who raised Jesus from the dead dwells in you, he who raised Christ Jesus from the dead will give life to your mortal bodies also through his Spirit which dwells in you (Rom. 8:9-11).

All who keep his commandments abide in him, and he in them. And by this we know that he abides in us, by the Spirit which he has given us (1 John 3:24).

Cf. By this we know that we abide in him and he in us, because he has given us of his own Spirit (1 John 4:13).

These biblical ideas must lie behind the comment about the home in Columba's pure heart. In quoting 1 Cor. 6.17, Adomnán explicitly claims his patron as one such person, cleaved to the Lord in death to self, and resurrection to the new life. As a result he has the Spirit of God in him, and is one in spirit with God. This does not make him divine, as Adomnán makes clear in his following comments regarding enlarged vision being a result of God's grace, not a new found magical ability. It means that Columba shares in the life of the Spirit of God. In part, by grace on each occasion, as we shall see, he is able by this union to share in the supernatural attributes of the divine such as sight, power, presence, as well as ethical purity, i.e. both senses of the term 'virtue'. As such, he is living the kingdom, inaugurated in his day. Adomnán is making sure that we appreciate that his subject is not merely a good man, a human hero energized by human altruism or human goodness, but that he was born by the Spirit of God into the kingdom, as John described in what is a conventional understanding of the spiritual dynamic of baptism

Jesus replied, 'Amen, amen, I say to you, unless anyone will have been reborn of water and the Spirit, he cannot enter the kingdom of God.'[33]

That the concept of spiritual re-birth and indwelling of the Spirit is important in the Irish context is shown by Patrick's own words

He has poured out abundantly among us the Holy Spirit, a gift and pledge of immortality, who makes those who believe and obey to be sons of God (*Conf.*, 4);

...on account of his indwelling Spirit (*Conf.*, 33);

...many people through me should be reborn to God (*Conf.*, 38);

---

33 '...*respondit Iesus, Amen amen dico tibi, nisi quis renatus fuerit ex aqua et Spiritu non potest introire in regnum Dei*' (John 3:5).

...we do not know the numbers of our family [i.e. his converts to Christ]
who have been born there (*Conf.*, 42).[34]

Adomnán does not mention this indwelling in connection with
baptism, but in connection with Columba's life and ministry.
Augustine has a similar idea in his *Confessions* (IX.vi), and elsewhere
returns to this indwelling as the essential basis to spiritual life. He
'broke new ground' in patristic theology in 'his understanding of the
Spirit as a gift and love, the sanctifying inhabitant of the just soul.'[35]
Thus we may deduce that Adomnán is claiming such a status for his
hero; he belongs to Christ, the sign of which is the manifest presence
of the Spirit shown both in his righteousness, which makes him a fit
vessel of the Spirit, and more significantly for the *VC*, in the
marvellous phenomena which surround him, manifesting the Spirit's
presence. His being inhabited by the Spirit is the rationale,
motivation and the power source for these manifestations. In this
Adomnán's pneumatology goes beyond Athanasius' Antony.[36]

THREE OPERATIONS OF THE SPIRIT IN COLUMBA

Joy

His closing statement at the end of the second preface shows a
further nuance to the understanding Adomnán has of his subject's
membership of the kingdom, brought by the inhabiting Spirit

> he was happy in his inmost heart with the joy of the Holy Spirit (sp 5a).

As Clancy and Markus notice, the *Amra* records that for Columba,
'His choice poured out joy and quiet peace)',[37] thus Adomnán
continues the earlier tradition. Joy is an eschatological condition, a
fruit of the Spirit available in this age of first fruits.[38]

> And the disciples were filled with joy and with the Holy Spirit (Acts
> 13:52).

> For the kingdom of God is not food and drink but righteousness and
> peace and joy in the Holy Spirit (Rom. 14:17).

---

34   *Conf.* ed. Howlett (1994): *'propter inhabitantem Spíritum eíus'* (33); *'populi
      multi per me in Déum renàsceréntur'* (38); *'de genere nostro qui íbi náti sunt
      nescimus númerum eórum'* (42).

35   W.G. Rusch (1978, 81-2), citing Augustine (*Ep.*, 194.18; *Serm.*, 71, 187:16,
      267).

36   See above, chapter 3; Antony attributes the power to Christ.

37   *'A rogu ro-fer subai sámsid'*, *Amra* (IX, C&M 115, 126). They point to the
      analogy with political literary ideas of just kingship, and to 'biblical
      teaching', which I suggest is focussed around Gal 5.22, the fruit of the Spirit.

38   Gal. 5:22. The term appears 'particularly where there is express mention of the
      eschatological fulfilment in Christ, of being in him, and of hope in him'
      (*NIDNTT*, II. 357).

> May the God of hope fill you with all joy and peace in believing, so that
> by the power of the Holy Spirit you may abound in hope (Rom. 15:13).

Cassian emphasizes joy as a product of the presence of the kingdom,
as brought by the Holy Spirit.[39] He records Isaac's comment on this
manifestation in a passage echoed in the *VC* (and see below)

> ...because of a visit of the Holy Spirit my heart is unspeakably glad and
> my mind ecstatic (*Coll.* 10:10:135).

Thus the presence of the kingdom, in the presence of the Spirit, is
an aspect of the flowering of faith, and the reality of that presence
brings joy. The Spirit's presence is also an earnest or deposit,[40]
securing the resurrection to eternal life promised to believers. God's
ability and certainty to provide the promised eternal life to believers
is demonstrated by his tangible donation of the life transforming
Spirit in the present age, as he also promised.[41]

> In him you also, who have heard the word of truth, the gospel of your
> salvation, and have believed in him, were sealed with the promised Holy
> Spirit, which is the guarantee of our inheritance until we acquire
> possession of it...(Eph. 1:13-14).

> He who has prepared us for this very thing is God, who has given us the
> Spirit as a guarantee (2 Cor. 5:5).

Adomnán does not explicitly refer to this rôle for the Spirit in
salvation, either for Columba or others. However, in recording the
occurrence of marvellous attributes to both Columba himself, and to

---

39   *Coll.* 1:13.
40   (Rom. 8:11; 2 Cor. 1:22 quoted above). We might use a musical metaphor such
      as the first chord of a symphony to illustrate the need to differentiate the
      deposit from the thing purchased; there is likeness, and even some sense of
      portion (Lightfoot (1895, 323)), but the thing anticipated will be of a different
      order of magnitude to the first chord prefiguring it.
41   Jn. 3:36, 5:24, 6:40,54. Sherry (1984, 56) takes this argument further in
      arguing for the necessity of the continuous presence of saints who
      demonstrate the fruit of the Spirit's transforming presence (which he
      explicitly identifies as change beyond natural causation, and allows appeals
      to miracles which we may take to include the gifts of the Spirit) in order to
      give perpetual earnests of Gods faithfulness to the promise of eternal life. If
      saints, having once been present in post first-century history, ceased to be
      visible, then evidence for God's faithfulness would begin to look less
      maintained, and lose credence. Sherry wants to take account of saints'
      existence right up to modern times, and argues this as a logical corollary of
      God's desire continuously to demonstrate his faithfulness. He only refers to
      the fruit of the Spirit, but we might reasonably argue that the two expressions
      of the Spirit's presence belong together. Thus Sherry's account suggests
      further theoretical evidence for the possibility that the *pneumatika* could still
      be in operation in Columba's day (see ch. 5 below).

others (chapter 5), and we will see that he believes the source of these to be the indwelling Spirit, he implicitly makes the connection between the possession of the Spirit, demonstrated by marvellous phenomena, and the possession of eternal life, or to put it another way, membership of the kingdom. That he records the phenomena for those other than Columba himself must argue for his belief in a link between salvation and the reception of the marvellously active Spirit in the believer.

Light

Columba was visited by the Spirit, whose grace was poured out from heaven on him as a child, and was manifested in visible form to his foster father as clear light shining from 'a ball of fire standing above the face of the sleeping child' (iii.2). Here, the origin of the manifestations of light considered in the previous chapter is traced explicitly to the activity of the Spirit. It thus reflects a rich biblical background, including the Joeline promise and its inaugural consummation in the manifestation of fire at Pentecost. The background to the precise mode of the manifestation, a ball of fire, remains to be elucidated. Later in Columba's life, while living on Hinba, 'the grace of the Holy Spirit was poured out upon him abundantly and in an incomparable manner and continued marvellously for the space of three days' (iii.18). This visitation is manifested again by heavenly light, but also this time 'spiritual songs, unheard before, were heard being sung by him', and as he later disclosed, by exegetical revelations (see below).

Spiritual Songs

> And spiritual songs, unheard before, were heard being sung by him (iii.18).[42]

This is an intriguing phrase. We observe that the songs come as a result of the visitation of the Spirit, that they are 'spiritual', and that they have never been heard before. Their appearance is either as compositions learned elsewhere, new to the brethren, and prompted by the Spirit from memory for the occasion; or they are original songs, newly inspired by the Spirit as Columba's composition; or they are an invasively inspired voicing of the Spirit. This reference is likely to have endorsed the tradition of attributing the various so-called 'songs of Columba' to the saint's composition. The *Amra* associates him with the heavenly 'custom of music', and depicts him going to heaven with 'two songs', (or 'a sad song'), though this is

---

42   *Carmina quoque quaedam spiritualia et ante inaudita decantari ab eo audiebantur (VC 119a).*

not the output of a prolific songster.[43] Adomnán makes it more than one song, but does not say if it is in discrete packages, or a sustained spiritual doxology. Adomnán uses *'carmen'* and *'canticum'* in i.42 to refer to a composition of the poet Crónán, thus for him, we can deduce the terms are interchangeable. In iii.23:131a, *'carmen'* refers to the singing of the heavenly angelic host. Either sense could be in mind here. The *Vulgate* mentions *'canticis spiritalibus'* as the third of Paul's options for thanksgiving, with psalms and hymns

...be filled with the Spirit, addressing one another in psalms and hymns and spiritual songs, singing and making melody to the Lord with all your heart (Eph. 5:18-19 cf. Col. 3:16).

Though the contexts do not insist that these are previously unheard spiritual songs, the Ephesian instruction is preceded by a command to be 'filled with the Spirit.' The *Vulgate* uses Adomnán's term in Job 35:10: 'Where is God my Maker, who gives songs (*carmina*) in the night,' clearly a similar concept to that which Adomnán describes. Turner notes one category of OT/Jewish encounter with the Spirit manifested in what he calls 'invasively inspired charismatic praise', and cites this as the closest Old Testament analogy to the phenomenon of tongues (*glossolalia*).[44] One category of *glossolalia* could be angelic (1 Cor. 13:1).[45] We might thus conjecture here an example of the pneumatic practice of 'singing in tongues', in the language of angels whose company he keeps. This is a charism which acts as a sign of the kingdom of God: 'I will sing with the spirit' (1 Cor. 14:15); '...tongues are a sign not for believers but for unbelievers' (1 Cor. 14:22; and see Acts 2). It is otherwise unmentioned in the selection Adomnán presents. With no confirmatory evidence, the conjecture is most tentative, but within the bounds of possibility.

---

43   *Amra* III.4, VII.2; C&M, 245.
44   Turner (1996, 11, 312).
45   As Turner suggests (1996, 314). For an introduction to tongues in the post-apostolic church, see: Maloney and Lovekin (1985), *Glossolalia*; Kelsey (1968), *Tongue Speaking*; Murray (1978), *Voices from the Gods: Speaking in Tongues;* and Kydd (1973), *Charismata to 320 A.D;* (1984), *Charismatic Gifts in the Early Church.* Interestingly, Kelsey observes that the practice of tongue speaking has remained current in the Eastern monastic tradition, a tradition often linked as an influence on the character of 'Celtic' Christianity.

Columba and the 'Spirit of Prophecy'

WHAT SORT OF PROPHECY?

First, we must examine what Adomnán meant by 'prophecy' in the *VC*. Adomnán begins his first book (in the Schaffhausen manuscript 'A') with the phrase, *'de profeticis reuelationibus'* (6a), and as part of the conclusion to the first chapter, a summary of the whole work, he reports

> ...he began from his youthful years to be strong also in *the spirit of prophecy*; to foretell future events; to declare absent things to those present, because although absent in the body he was present in spirit, and able to observe what took place far away. For according to the words of Paul, 'he who clings to the Lord is one spirit' (i.1:10a).

Adomnán gives prominence to the prophetic not only by making it one of the three major divisions of his treatise on Columba, but also by making it first in order, and predominant in terms of number of references to the exercise of the gift compared to the rest, comprising over sixty per cent.[46] Making sense of the presentation is exercising. In book I, which Adomnán describes as being in 'inverted order' (i.1, final para.), after two initial groups concerning major saints (i.2-i.6), and various kings (i.7-i.15), it is very difficult to discern any system to the order, though other small groups exist.[47] In books II and III, the occurrence of the prophetic is even less systematic, it only being recorded as it applies to, or as it arises within stories regarding the main interests of these two books. It is possible to discern recurring themes in the prophecies. It may concern the persons of other saints, kings, or lay folk; regarding their sin, death, success or failure in battle. It might predict various activities such as the arrival of visitors, of a storm, or of an animal; or outcomes such as glory to God or marvelling or even repentance. We may also discern significance regarding the place, both of delivery of the revelation, and of its effectual destination.

The faith of Adomnán's subject is shown to flower pre-eminently in prophecy. As an apparently formulaic passage, we might pass over the introduction as immaterial to our investigation. However,

---

46   62.2%. My analysis reveals 85 manifestations of predictive prophecy (35.3%), 51 of knowledge (28.5%), and 14 of spiritual sight/vision (10.4%), making 150 in all, out of a total of 241 citations of all examples of lifetime miraculous phenomena recorded (see appendix 1).

47   Chapters 17-32 largely concern minor saints; 23-25 are nature miracles with a weak prophetic element; 23-28 are linked by the introductory phrases, and concern various prophetic foresights; 33 and 34 are in Pictland; 35-6 concern the eschatological destiny of two sinners; 38-43 concern sin and obitual predictions.

experience with the formulaic annunciatory narrative should make us more careful. The phrase Adomnán uses here, 'strong in the spirit of prophecy (*profetiae spiritu pollere*)', is important. In i.3, he describes the phenomenon: 'he prophesied... by revelation of the Holy Spirit (*reuelante profetauit sancto spiritu*)'. He later (i.37:37b) uses a similar term as a description of the collection: 'revelations of the prophetic spirit (*profetici spiritus profetationes*)'. We could perhaps render this somewhat clumsily as 'prophesyings of the prophetic spirit'?[48] As noted above, Adomnán's own overall term for this phenomenon appears to be 'prophetic revelations'. He was about to record some of the stranger manifestations (spiritual refreshment, and the voice: see below), so he emphasizes the source of the prophecy as being the Holy Spirit at this point to reinforce his message that Columba's gifting was not an innate 'magical' ability, but a gift from God. He uses this term at the close of book I; '...of the blessed man's prophetic gift (*de beati uiri profectica gratia...*)' (i.50:52a).

Reeves records the opinion of Giraldus Cambrensis that Columba was one of four Irish saints believed to have been endowed with the gift of prophecy.[49] Fowler notes many spurious prophecies being attributed to Columba in later times, and says he may only at first have been called 'prophet' in the sense of 'preacher'.[50] This divergence of interpretation in two of the foremost Columba

---

48 Cf. Forbes: 'manifestations of prophetical spirit'; Huyshe: 'manifestations of prophetic spirit'; Fowler: 'utterances of the prophetic spirit'; and Sharpe: 'revelations of the spirit of prophecy'.

49 Reeves (1857, 17 note g). He also records the attribution to Columba of the *Buile Coluim-cille* in *Tr.Th.* 472b, a series of ecstatic predictions of Irish sovereigns. Kenney (220:l, lxxiii-iv, 439-41) includes a number of collections of prophecies of 'respectable age'. While no reliability can be assigned to these collections, they do show the repute of Columba as a prophet continuing in the developing tradition.

50 Fowler (1894, 4 note 6). He refers us to 'Dölinger, *Prophecies*'. This is not the place to enter into the debate over the question of differentiating prophecy in the two senses of preaching and ecstatic utterance (for a recent assessment of the debate and bibliography see Turner (1996, 185-187). Turner finds three main views: 1. Packer *et al.* see all prophecy as preaching: forth telling God's pre-sent word to his people, applying previously revealed truth. 2. Farnell *et al.* see prophecy as authoritative, inspired, special revelation of God's truth, which ceased with the canon. 3. Grudem *et al.* hold the latter in canonical prophets and apostles, but recognize a weaker concept, described first by Philo and Josephus, which can be 'as little as a flash of divinely given knowledge about a person or situation, or being given insight or discernment from God'. Turner rejects the view that NT doctrine was delivered prophetically (220), but affirms the continuation from OT times into the age of the church of the 'weaker form' of prophecy.

scholars helps us to focus the study. Richard Sharpe touches the debate from a different angle, writing

> [Adomnán] presents St Columba as a man whose vision was not limited by time and space, for he could see events far away or in the future. His prophecies are not like those of the Old Testament prophets but they show him as a man joined to the Lord in spirit (I 1 p. 112). Adomnán explains this cosmic vision (I 43), citing St Paul, but has silently adapted a passage from another model, Gregory the Great's Dialogues.[51]

Sharpe's first sentence here is a paraphrase of Adomnán's own description of Columba's prophetic gifting (i.1:10a-b). His second appears to misunderstand the range and the source of prophetic practice in the Old Testament as we shall see, and again paraphrases Adomnán, who himself uses Paul. Sharpe mentions without comment that 'Prophecy and the working of miracles are gifts of the Spirit',[52] these being two of Adomnán's three proofs of Columba's status as a man of God. Thus the questions we will hold as we enter the investigation are: Did Adomnán see Columba as strong in innate predictive ability (clairvoyance), or strong in the dynamic presence of the Holy Spirit-who-speaks. Is it spirit or Spirit of prophecy? If the latter, was it that the Spirit strengthened his homiletic ministry, or that he revealed new truth, or that the Spirit revealed personal or circumstantial knowledge or insight, or gave discernment? In other words, did Adomnán see Columba as a specially gifted preacher, an ecstatic canonical prophet, or as one operating in the *pneumatikon* of prophecy? We will investigate his preaching first.

COLUMBA AS PREACHER

Adomnán clearly and explicitly records Columba as a preacher of the word of God to the unconverted, most directly in ii.32, which refers to some days Columba and his companions spent in the Province of the Picts.

> ...a certain layman with his whole household heard and believed the word of life through an interpreter at the preaching of the holy man; and believing, was baptized, the husband with his wife and children, and his household.

---

51 Sharpe (1995, 57). Sharpe (note 49) has a very useful note to Adomnán's *'quamis absens corpore praesens tamen spiritu'* (i.1:10a), pointing out two similar occurrences at ii.39:90b and ii.42, and the Pauline source (1 Cor. 5:3), with the related incident of refreshment in i.37.

52 Sharpe (1995, 58).

The account records that a particular household responded to 'the word of life' which had been proclaimed by the holy man.[53]

> ... the things which have now been announced to you by those who preached the good news to you through the Holy Spirit sent from heaven, things into which angels long to look (1 Pet. 1:12).

Although we can discern a temporal element here – the word was delivered prior to the conversion – Adomnán does not make the word of life predict or see remotely the response by precognition or divine revelation. We only read of the response of one family, but this does not necessarily mean others were not addressed. Given the sense of public proclamation in the term *predico*, we may also read here a preaching that was general in terms of its audience. We see that Columba employed the services of an interpreter through whom he proclaimed the word of life, and from later in the tale that he had companions with him ('*suís comitibus*'). We may only conjecture, but it is not unreasonable to infer that whatever their ultimate travelling objective was, Adomnán wishes to suggest that the party

---

53 There is a tantalizing echo here of scripture: In 1 John 1:1-5, *verbo vitae* refers to Christ, who was declared ('*adnuntio*') to the recipients of the letter. (The other occurrence in the Bible is Philippians 2:16, a reference within a passage on sanctification rather than evangelization.) Believing responses of households are found in John 4:46-53 and also Acts 11:14; 16:15,31; 18:8. The context of the Johannine reference is especially interesting. Jesus is on a journey. He has just chided an official whose son is ill for not believing until he sees *signa et prodigia*, but following further supplication prophesies that the boy will live. The official believes what Jesus said. The boy begins his recovery at the exact hour Jesus prophesied it; as a result, the man and his household believes (i.e. that Jesus is literally the 'word of life'). Here soteriological belief *follows* Jesus' restoration of the boy from the point of death. In *VC*, preaching the word of life (Christ) *and* belief come *before* the confirmation by marvellous sign and the restoration is from death itself. It is just possible that we may here find Columba's text(s), or at least Adomnán's idea of the message proclaimed. Now, Adomnán's version of the story may be interpreted as his wanting to demonstrate the superiority of Columba even over Christ (as suggested by Owen Dudley-Edwards' comment at Scottish Univs. Eccles. Hist. Reading Party, Perth, 1998), i.e. Columba's converts do not require signs and wonders to believe. However, this is to ignore the inauguratory rôle which Jesus plays in the establishment of the kingdom. His whole ministry was significatory, with the cross as the transition point from the ages of the old to the new covenant. In Acts 11:14, Peter is described as having words whereby a pagan household will be saved; as he preaches, confirmatory signs of the Spirit are manifest; the result is that the Jerusalem elders recognize the granting of repentance also to the pagans; in Acts 16:13-15, Lydia heard the proclaimed word and believed; in Acts 16:31-34, a wonder is followed by preaching the word of the Lord and conversion. None of these makes the preachers superior to Christ; their preaching depended on Christ's revelation of God, and the same may be said for Adomnán's Columba, who does not at this point move outwith scripturally attested practice.

from Iona were taking the opportunity to preach the gospel to the people they encountered along the way. There is nothing to deny that a preaching mission was their objective here (the debate over how many journeys Columba made into Pictland does not affect this conclusion). They were sufficiently organized to find, or bring along, the interpreter, and were evidently listened to. Their message was accepted (by this family and household) without prior marvellous accreditation. Indeed the fact of their need for the interpreter demonstrates that here, Pentecostal gifts of preaching by pneumatic simultaneous translation were absent. (The same need for translation is also mentioned for Skye, i.33). This is thus evidently speaking the word of God *qua* preaching. Adomnán does not call it prophecy, nor describe it as ecstatic, though he would no doubt have seen it as inspired by the Spirit.

The second example of Columba as preacher comes in the record of another explicitly evangelistic occasion, this time on the Isle of Skye.

> And as soon as he had, through an interpreter, received the word of God from the saint, he believed and was baptized by him.[54]

Although here a prophetic word of knowledge (see below) is involved in anticipating the arrival of the convert-to-be, once again an interpreter is employed to communicate the word of God by unaided natural means. There is no mention of anyone other than Artbranan receiving the word, though it is unlikely his two young helpers would not hear, but again, this is evangelistic preaching, not prediction, and again, Adomnán does not call it prophecy. The *Amra* confirms this view of Columba as a preacher: Clancy and Márkus cite the phrases, '...leader of nations who guarded the living', and '... the restraint of nations' as so indicating.[55]

Later in ii.32, Adomnán says Columba was 'roused with zeal for God', and went to the house of the new convert where a son had died.

> Seeing that they were in great grief, the saint addressed them with heartening words.[56]

This is now a pastoral setting, with the shepherd feeding his new, and distressed flock with the word of God. They are encouraged not to doubt God's omnipotence; he is thus expounding Christian doctrine to them. No marvellous 'revelation' is communicated; Columba does

---

54   '*Qui statim verbo Dei a Sancto per interpraetem recepto credens ab eodem babtizatus est*' (i.33).

55   C&M 120, 122, referring to *Amra* I.10 and VI.29.

56   '*Quos sanctus ualde tristificatos uidens confirmans dictis conpellat consulatoriis*' (ii.32:78b).

not predict anything. It is not 'preaching' as addressing a large group, nor evangelistic, but it is nevertheless a dogmatic homily. The *Amra* confirms this view, speaking of Columba as teacher, 'For he does not return to us, he who would explain the true Word'; 'For we do not have the teacher who would teach the tribes of Tay'; and, 'The teacher wove the word, By his wisdom he made glosses clear'.[57] The description in *Amra* I.14 relieves some of the frustrated tension left by *VC* iii.18 where Columba is described as receiving profound expository revelations, but having not written them down in the absence of his amanuensis. Adomnán may here be recording his own frustration that the benefits of the teachings of his patron had not been passed down in written form, whereas his predecessors evidently did benefit from it.

However the *Amra* also explicitly records Columba's prophetic reputation: 'the prophet has settled at God's right hand in Sion', and 'for we do not have the seer who used to keep fears from us.'[58] Thus if the composition of the *Amra* within a few years after Columba's death is accepted, we see that he was *not* only at first called 'prophet / seer' in the sense of 'preacher'. Indeed, though there is evidence that he engaged in homiletic activity, the record we have may suggest he was called 'prophet' and 'teacher' more explicitly than 'preacher'. We can thus agree with Fowler in so far as we do see evidence of Columba the preacher of the word of God. However, this does not confirm Fowler's opinion that Columba was *only* at first called 'prophet' in the sense of 'preacher.' It is to his rôle as prophet that we now turn.

COLUMBA AS PROPHET

We must first clarify whether Adomnán saw Columba as a prophet who revealed new truth. There is one tale in the *VC*, just referred to, which may claim the revelation of such new truth, iii.18.

---

57   *Amra* (I.14, I.15, V.2-3). In noting Columba's teaching rôle, Clancy and Márkus quote from *VC* iii.18, (mistakenly referred to in the footnote as *VC* iii. 19).

58   I.7 and 13. C&M note the *Amra* record of him as a having 'a reputation for visionary powers, especially for converse with angels' (125), saying this makes Adomnán's interest in the angelic visions 'more easy to comprehend'. The RIA *Dictionary of the Irish Language* (fasc. III, 154-5) gives both 'seer' and 'prophet' as possible renderings of *fáith*, saying it is 'used in a wide sense, both of heathen seers and druids and of prophets of scripture.' We might add '...and of early Christian Gaeldom.' *Fissid* has two main groups of meaning, which may further resolve: (a) learned, well-informed / seer, soothsayer, versed in druidic science, one who knows, visionary, and (b) physician. Columba is never referred to as a physician, though he is involved in healing. That he is a *fissid* my mean he is simply well educated, but the third group of possibilities as one able to 'see' or 'know' by other than ordinary sense seems most likely.

> ... he saw, openly revealed, many of the secret things that have been
> hidden since the world began. Also everything that in the sacred
> scriptures is dark and most difficult became plain, and was shown more
> clearly than the day to the eyes of his purest heart ... mysteries, both of
> past ages and of ages to come, mysteries unknown to other men; and also
> a number of interpretations of the sacred books.

Columba bemoans the absence of his senior associate Baithéne who
therefore could not record the revelations for posterity, in what may
be a convenient device, as the revealed secrets are not revealed to us.
The attempt to place Columba in the rôle of the canonical prophet
is thus unconvincing, and sniffs strongly of typology. However, this
event bears a marked similarity to Cassian's category of the
illumination of the Holy Spirit, who in *Coll.* 1:19 opens up the
mysteries of heaven to us, as described of Isaac the monk

> ... because of a visit of the Holy Spirit my heart is unspeakably glad and
> my mind ecstatic. Here is a great overflow of spiritual thought, thanks to
> a sudden illumination and to the coming of the Saviour. The holiest
> ideas, hitherto concealed from me, have been revealed to me. And so if I
> am to deserve to remain thus for much longer, I must anxiously and
> regularly cry 'Come to my help, O God; Lord, hurry to my rescue (*Coll.*
> 10:10:135).

The experience also has clear scriptural precedent

> But [Stephen], full of the Holy Spirit, gazed into heaven and saw the
> glory of God, and Jesus standing at the right hand of God; and he said,
> 'Behold, I see the heavens opened, and the Son of man standing at the
> right hand of God' (Acts 7:55-56).

> [the secret plan of redemption] was not made known to the sons of men
> in other generations as it has now been revealed to his holy apostles and
> prophets by the Spirit (Eph. 3:5).

Stephen the deacon, not one of the twelve apostles, saw the secret
things of heaven openly revealed by the Holy Spirit, as did the
apostles John (Rev. 1 etc.) and Paul (in the reference Adomnán
acknowledges as prefiguring Columba's visionary experiences, 2 Cor.
12:1-4). Adomnán may however not be claiming here the revelation
of new truth on the measure of biblical revelation; he clearly
mentions the elucidation of biblical mysteries, and all the categories
he records could fit into this exegetical process, a process promised
of the activity of the Spirit by Christ

> When the Spirit of truth comes, he will guide you into all the truth; for
> he will not speak on his own authority, but whatever he hears he will
> speak, and he will declare to you the things that are to come. He will
> glorify me, for he will take what is mine and declare it to you (Jn. 16:13-
> 14).

Thus, though Adomnán may appear to be engaged in typological hyperbolae, he might protest that he simply shows Columba to be in receipt, like others, of the promised gift, as the *Amra* claims (see I.14, V.2-3 above). Although Adomnán wants to present Columba as typologically linked with these famous groups, it is thus not clearly in the truth revealing sense. Columba does not write new law, nor show anything previously unrevealed about God (except in the sense that the kingdom can come to Pictland, but this is fully predicted). Nor did he pronounce judgement on a national scale.[59] In these senses he is not like the OT prophet.

Prophets in the OT did more than reveal new truth, and proclaim national judgement. They also engaged in what Grudem terms a 'weaker form' of prophecy (note 50 above), and in this they were joined by prophets of the NT, and in Adomnán's view, by Columba. Adomnán's phrase *profetiae spiritu* in i.1:10a occurs as a biblical term only in the apocalypse of John, and there not precisely

> ... the testimony of Jesus is the spirit of prophecy *(... testimonium enim Iesu est spiritus prophetiae)* (Rev. 19:10).

Interpretation of this verse is complicated with a similar question to that which we have been asking of Adomnán,[60] so though it *may* provide a biblical source, it does not help us to determine Adomnán's usage. However, the Spirit is clearly linked to prophecy elsewhere in scripture, e.g.

> Then the LORD came down in the cloud and spoke to [Moses], and took some of the Spirit that was upon [Moses] and put it upon the seventy elders; and when the Spirit rested upon them, they prophesied. But later they ceased (Num. 11:25).

> Then the Spirit of the LORD will come mightily upon you, and you shall prophesy with them and be turned into another man (1 Sam. 10:6).

> ... on my menservants and my maidservants in those days I will pour out my Spirit; and they shall prophesy (Acts 2:18).

These examples, and many more (for some of which see below) would be understood to refer to variations of ecstatic prophecy, where a revelation is conveyed by the direct intervention of the Spirit into the life of the prophet, who becomes the mouthpiece, or demonstrator of the message. This understanding is a familiar term to various of Adomnán's influences, e.g. Gregory on Benedict

---

59 That is, he is not on record as having pronounced national judgement, though the reference in the *Amra* referred to above to his rôle as 'the restraint of nations' must be borne in mind.

60 Again, is it spirit or Spirit of prophecy?

King Totila heard that the holy man had the spirit of prophecy ... he
undertook to discover if the man of God had the spirit of prophecy.[61]

Gregory explores the concept further: Peter asks whether Benedict
always had the spirit of prophecy when he wished or only at certain
times. Gregory replies

> The spirit of prophecy does not always illuminate the minds of the
> prophets, because as it is written of the Holy Spirit: 'He breathes where
> he wills,' [Jn. 3:8] so it is known he breathes because and when he
> wills.[62]

He illustrates from the stories of Nathan and Elisha (2 Sam. 7:3 and
2 Kgs. 4:27), that it is only when God reveals that they 'know'. He
continues

> Which thing Almighty God of great pity so disposes: for giving at some
> times the spirit of prophecy, and at other times withdrawing it, he both
> lifts up the prophets minds on high, and yet preserves them in humility;
> that by the gift of the Spirit, they may know what they are by God; and
> at other times, not having the Spirit of prophecy, may understand what
> they are of themselves.[63]

Turner identifies the predominant understanding of the Spirit in
the Jewish context of New Testament writings as 'the Spirit of
prophecy', this being the Spirit's primary (but not only)
manifestation in the pre-Christian era.[64] From the earliest NT
writings onward, the same Spirit empowers those in whom he dwells
with a wide range of supernatural manifestations of his presence.
Thus the term has a wide precedent in the tradition. Each
manifestation has an eschatological, and sometimes a soteriological
reference (this last in the process of purification and drawing closer
to God through understanding; see the discussion of iii.18 below). We

---

61   '...rex ...Totila sanctum uirum prophetiae habere spiritum audisset, ...an uir
     Dei prophetiae spiritum haberet explorare conatus est' (Gregory I, Vita
     Benedicti XIIII; SC 260:180).

62   'Prophetiae spiritus... prophetarum mentes non semper inradiat, quia sicut de
     sancto Spiritu scriptum est: "Ubi uult spirat," ita sciendum est quia et quando
     uult adspirat' (vʙ XXI, SC 260:200).

63   'Quod omnipotens Deus ex magnae pietatis dispensatione disponit: quia dum
     prophetiae spiritum aliquando dat, et aliquando subtrahit, prophetantium
     mente et eleuat in celsitudine, et custodit in humilitate, ut et accipientes
     spiritum inueniant quid de Deo sint, et rursum prophetiae spiritum non
     habentes cognoscant quid sint de semetipsis' (vʙ XXI, SC 260:200).

64   Turner (1995, 5-18) lists charismatic revelation and guidance, wisdom,
     invasive speech, and praise as the four chief manifestations of the activity of
     the Spirit in ITP Judaism (6-12), and shows that the targums and rabbis
     recognized activity wider than prophecy, including miracles, as empowered by
     the Spirit. And see for example Beasley-Murray (1978, 276).

must proceed to a study of what Adomnán says of the operation of this gift in order to elucidate his understanding of the term, and thus its significance. If the term means extraordinary homiletic prowess, then there is little to link it to the eschatological realisation we have been considering. Columba then takes his place in an honourable line of distinguished teachers. If we see the Spirit-empowered ecstatic prophet in action, what is Adomnán claiming?

Adomnán's presentation of Columba's prophetic ministry is not confined to book I, but plays an important part in the whole work. In his introductions to books II and III, Adomnán makes clear his understanding that the miracles of power he describes therein are 'often accompanied by prophetic foreknowledge' (ii intro.) or 'the grace of prophecy' (iii intro.), and numerous examples follow. In the summary (i.1), he explicitly differentiates two modes of the prophetic: firstly, foretelling future events (*uentura praedicere*); secondly, declaring absent things to those present (*praesentibus absentia nuntiare*). Both are described as manifestations of Columba's strength in the spirit of prophecy from the years of his 'youth' (*ab annis juvenilibus coepit etiam prophetiae spiritu pollere*).[65] The two modes could be seen as relating to the same phenomenon: the future may be described as being absent to those in the present, and perhaps temporally 'far away'.[66] However in his second phrase, Adomnán appears to have in mind not a temporal, but a spatial displacement (*longe acta peruidere poterat*), as we shall see his presentation making clear. Thus, before we begin closer investigation, we must take note of Adomnán's keen awareness of these two modes of the functioning of the prophetic in Columba's ministry. A second feature to note is that Adomnán is presenting the phenomenon as something beyond normal, beyond even extraordinary, human ability. He implicitly infers that people cannot ordinarily foretell the future nor see remote events, and explicitly attributes Columba's so doing as resulting from his strength in the 'spirit of prophecy'. Thus as the game opens, we detect a stratagem which orients us towards the 'ecstatic' interpretation.

This phenomenon will be considered then in the two distinct subsections which Adomnán clearly differentiates:

---

65 The formula is conventional, though we must bear in mind that Latin youth lasted until the age of 42, the age when Columba left Ireland on his mission. It is the description of the prophetic we are here interested to pursue.

66 Some at least of the predictive prophecies refer to the immediate future, thus not temporally far away; some of them refer to immediate contemporary events, thus only distant in spatial terms. There are still other tales which relate to factors immediate in both senses, e.g. a boy in Coleraine (i.50).

Foretelling future events. Columba was strong in the 'spirit of prophecy' (i.1:10a). The Spirit prophesied through him (i.2). He prophesied by revelation of the holy/prophetic Spirit (i.3, i.37). He foresaw (i.41), and foreknew in the Spirit (ii.42, iii.23:131a).

Prophetic disclosure of absent things. Columba and others received revelations through the Spirit (sp:3a, i.1:7b, iii.8 (two occurrences)). Like Paul he had visions in the spirit (i.43). He recognized that nothing could be hidden from the Spirit (iii.21). He, and others, saw in the Spirit (i.3, ii.13). He, and Cainnech, heard in the Spirit (i.29, ii.13). He was inspired by the Spirit (iii.14). By the grace of the divine Spirit, his voice was heard at 1000 paces (i.37:39b).

Prophetic Foretelling of Future Events

As we have seen, Adomnán refers to his collection as accounts of revelations of the *prophetic* spirit (i.37), and he saw/wanted to present Columba as 'strong in the spirit of prophecy' (i.1:10a). Here we will focus on those accounts Adomnán explicitly links to the agency of the Holy Spirit, though many other accounts of the operation of this prophetic gift are recorded in the *VC*.[67]

i. The Holy Spirit Prophesies the Future through Columba: Carefully attested by Adomnán, Fintán arrives on Iona shortly after Columba's death, i.e. ca. 597, wishing to become monk to Baithéne, Columba's successor. The new abbot remembers a private conversation with his predecessor. He says to Fintán,

> I cannot profane the command of Saint Columba ... *through* whom the Holy Spirit prophesied of you (*per quem spiritus sanctus de te profetauit*) (i.2:13a).

He explains that Columba told him this privately 'speaking with prophetic lips [i.e. voice]'. Thus the Spirit spoke *through* Columba of an event which was yet to happen, the young man's future coming to Iona, and that it was God's will and foreknowledge that it was not predestined for Fintán to be a monk of any abbot, rather that he had been elected by God to himself be an abbot of monks in Leinster, where he would both pastor a flock of Christ's sheep, and be 'a leader of souls to the heavenly kingdom'.[68] Adomnán's record makes it posthumously verified. The Bible provides Adomnán with explicit foundation for the idea of the Spirit speaking *through* the prophet, e.g.

---

67 Some type of prophetic activity, including spiritual sight /vision occurs in all but 24 chapters of books II and III (see appendix).

68 '...*animarum dux ad caeleste regnum.*' The meaning of this phrase will be discussed in chap. 5.

... the law and the words which the LORD of hosts had sent by his Spirit through the former prophets.[69]

... you spake by the Holy Spirit through the mouth of our father David.[70]

The Holy Spirit spoke through Isaiah the prophet.[71]

These all describe OT prophets, and show that the pedigree for this description of how Columba prophesied may also be found in earlier records than the NT, although the prophecies themselves may not, as Sharp recognizes, have the same style. New Testament references are fewer, but give similar pedigree, e.g.

... prophets came ... one of them named Agabus stood up and foretold by the Spirit that there would be a great famine (Acts 11:28).

... a prophet named Agabus ... said, 'Thus says the Holy Spirit' (Acts 21:10-11).

Fintán's commission is for himself as abbot to set up a mission-station in Leinster (he would lead many souls to heaven). We need only impute backdating of Fintán's actual later position as Abbot, as Sharpe puts it,[72] if we reject the possibility of the prophetic *per se*, a position Adomnán would not identify with. Discounting for a moment the claim of prophetic foreknowledge, we see here a concern for the building of a non-Ionan *paruchia*. As abbot, Fintán would not operate under the authority of Iona. Rather, it was building the kingdom of God. Indeed, the imperative is not to keep this important evangelist in the islands, but to commission him, with Iona's blessing and in peace (twice mentioned) to the work of mission. Commentators seeking political aims may claim here an ulterior motive in Adomnán's including this tale. He connects Iona with a Leinster saint of repute, and establishes his mission upon the blessing of Iona. However, any such reading of the text does not allow us to ignore Adomnán's explicit description either of the source of the prophecy as being the Holy Spirit, nor the reported outcome which was the extension of the kingdom.

---

69 Zech. 7:12, '...*legem et verba quae misit Dominus exercituum in spiritu suo per manum prophetarum priorum*' (*per manum* = through the instrument of).

70 Acts 4:25, '*Spiritu Sancto per os patris nostri David ...dixisti,*' (cf. Mt. 22:43).

71 Acts 28:25. '...*Spiritus Sanctus locutus est per Esaiam prophetam,*' and see Num. 11:26 (of the elders); 1 Sam. 10:6 (above), cf. 10:10; 19:20 (of Saul and his men); Neh. 9:30, 'didst warn them by the Spirit through thy prophets'; Ez. 11:5 (of Ezekiel); Lk. 1:67 (of Zechariah); Lk. 2:26 (of Simeon); 2 Pet. 1:21, '...no prophecy ever came by the impulse of man, but men moved by the Holy Spirit spoke from God.'

72 Sharpe (1995, 255, note 53).

(A minor point of interest deriving from this tale is that of
Baithéne's lack of prophetic knowledge of both the young pilgrim's
identity on his arrival, and of a missing 'I'. His patron frequently
knew the identity of visitors to the islands, and as Plummer
recognized, the added preface to the *Amra* recorded that the
foreknowledge of guests never left Columba

> And it was revealed to Columba that they were anear, for no company
> ever came to him without his knowing of it beforehand.[73]

Poor Baithéne is depicted as again unenlightened in relation to the
missing 'I' in i.23. He is not lacking all pneumatic virtue, viz. his
calming the sea and whale (i.19), and his Ephesians 6 style defence of
the monks of Mag Luinge (iii.18), and he is venerated highly as
Columba's successor, with the same feast day etc. However,
Adomnán does not know him as one who ministered in the
prophetic, which is a gift he does know of others (see chapter 5
below). The single possible exception to this is Baithéne's
explanation of the marvellously fragrant, load lifting joy which
comes upon the monks as they return from the work of the fields
(another eschatological reference to the flowering of the kingdom,
which brings relief (Mt. 11:28-30)). However, Adomnán gives us no
reason to suppose that he attributes Baithéne's knowledge to other
than conversation with Columba in the natural, in the same way we
read of the prophecy regarding Fintán being communicated. There
would surely be advantage to presenting the successor of the great
Columba as one who also was strong in the Spirit of prophecy, as
Elisha follows Elijah, thus maintaining the divine authority of the
Ionan *familia*. Adomnán does not do this, despite Baithéne's thirteen
appearances, an observation which contributes to the impression that
he does not easily allow his imagination to supersede his reasoned
weighing of received evidence.)

ii. Columba Prophesies by Revelation of the Spirit: A second nuance
Adomnán records of direct intervention of the Spirit revealing the
future comes in i.3, where Columba pronounced prophetically
(*profetice profatur*) about the gift of both healthful doctrine and
eloquence which God would give to Ernéne in the future. In
explanation and extension to other instances, including his only
explicit reference to the Easter debate, Adomnán describes this
incident as having been 'by revelation of the Holy Spirit'.[74] He

---

73   *VSH*, clxx note 7, Plummer refers to *Amra*, Stokes (1899, 140), which is the
     preface added at a later date than the poem itself.
74   '*reuelante profetauit sancto spiritu*' (15b). This tale also includes an example
     of the second type of prophecy, for which, see below, and Adomnán uses this

records that it was from the testimony of Ernéne himself to fifth abbot Ségéne (d. 652), made in the presence of Faílbe who became eighth abbot (669-679), and who was Adomnán's predecessor and interlocutor, that the words of the prophecy were learned.[75] In sp:3a, Adomnán uses this same construction in describing the origin of the prophetic foreknowledge of Columba's coming. Patrick's disciple Mochta is depicted as foretelling the coming of Columba by 'revelation of the Holy Spirit (*spiritu reuelante sancto*)'. Laying aside the question of veracity, the point to note here is that Adomnán describes the prophecies as having come by revelation of the Holy Spirit, adding confirmation to our understanding that the prophetic was seen as a pneumatic, not human activity. It may be Adomnán who interprets the prophecy as having been by revelation of God the Spirit, not the testimony itself which states this, but again, Adomnán is on clear scriptural ground as the following examples show

And it had been revealed to him by the Holy Spirit that he should not see death before he had seen the Lord's Christ (Lk. 2:26).

... it has now been revealed to his holy apostles and prophets by the Spirit (Eph. 3:5).

But, as it is written, 'What no eye has seen, nor ear heard, nor the heart of man conceived, what God has prepared for those who love him,' God has revealed to us through the Spirit. For the Spirit searches everything, even the depths of God (1 Cor. 2:9-10).

---

term to refer to a revelation 'by the Lord' in iii.23, one of the examples of his Trinitarian ascription of the marvellous.

75 It is conceivable that we read here of an instance in the process of Adomnán's compilation. Herbert has suggested that Ségéne recorded formal testimony which formed Cumméne's account of Columba's life (1988a, 16-26). Sharpe (1995, 247, note 15) questions the hypothesis that Ségéne necessarily produced such a vehicle for the preservation of the tradition. If Adomnán did learn the words of the prophecy from Faílbe, he did so up to twenty years before the accepted date for the completion of the *VC*, and before he himself succeeded Faílbe as abbot. This sharing may have occurred during Faílbe's visit to Ireland in 673-676 (A&A (1960, 91)), if Adomnán was late in coming to Iona, or more likely in Iona, if as Sharpe suggests he had been there since ca. 640 (1995, 46). Adomnán was thus perhaps undertaking the task of composing the *VC* at that stage, with abbatial sanction, and going over extant traditions with his abbot, who, as Sharpe suggests (*op cit*) saw him as 'a trusted bearer of Columban tradition'. Faílbe either provided entirely the individual tales Adomnán explicitly mentions him as doing (here and in i.1), or perhaps provided the detailed narrative which Adomnán wrote down to enrich a less full written account of Ségéne/Cumméne which they were using as a source.

The latter is quoted by Gregory in his discussion on knowing the secret counsel of God. Benedict discerns a demonic affliction, and knows the future outcome should the victim seek holy orders (*VB* XVI). Prophecy of the future is involved. Adomnán may be reading scripture via Gregory. Knowing the secret counsel of God is a product of union with God, available to any so joined as holy men. However the almost total circumstantial differences of these tales suggest independence at this point. Adomnán has taken the concept of revelation by the Spirit out of the scriptural source, where Gregory leaves it, and employed it in his own explanation of the phenomenon. We see that the Spirit who reveals temporal happenings, is also the Spirit who reveals the eschaton, who searches the deep things of God, who reveals to the prophets and apostles, and whose revelation the angels can only aspire to (1 Pet. 1:12). All these things may be present in Adomnán's presentation of the holy man who himself also receives revelation of the Spirit. The gifting which is prophesied for Ernéne is itself an important spiritual endowment, linked both to the Spirit who will lead into truth (Jn. 14:17; 15:26; 16:13), the office of teacher (Eph. 4:11), and the gifts of wisdom and discernment (1 Cor. 12:8,10 etc.), all brought by the Spirit whose coming as demonstrated in these gifts is itself a sign and earnest of the coming kingdom. Such revelations are spoken of in Paul's writings as being given as, or with, prophecy for the edification of the church (1 Cor. 14:6,26). Of interest here is Adomnán seeing the gift of eloquence as positive; we should contrast this with his opening statement regarding the kingdom not consisting in exuberant eloquence. Thus we can assume that what is meant for Ernéne is not the latter, but the ability to expound doctrine in a healthful, healing manner.

iii. Columba Foresees in the Spirit: A third nuance of predictive prophetic ability is recorded in i.41, where Columba foresees in the spirit (*in spiritu praevidens*) the death of Erc the thief. The advanced knowledge of death is shared, among others, by Adomnán's senior biblical models, the prophet Elijah (2 Kgs. 1:4), and Christ himself (Jn. 11:11). One example from the prophet Elisha clearly recalls our previous discussion

> And Elisha said to him… 'The LORD has shown me that Ben-Hadad shall certainly die' (2 Kgs. 8:10).

The *Vulgate* only uses *provideo* in this sense in two places: Acts 2:31 in reference to David's foresight of Christ's resurrection, and Galatians 3:8 of the foresight of salvation going to the gentiles.

There are no references to foreseeing 'in the Spirit'.[76] Thus here we have a form that Adomnán must have derived from elsewhere. The Fathers use the phrase of biblical characters and writers. Ambrose describes John as 'the Apostle foreseeing in the Spirit'.[77] Augustine refers to the intent of the writers of Genesis to show in the people of God the prefiguring and foretelling of the city of the eternal kingdom. This was 'foreseen, by inspiration of the Spirit'.[78]

The ability to foresee the future is thus clearly linked to activity expected of prophet and apostle. It is also a result of the eschatological outpouring of the Holy Spirit, as specified by Joel whose understanding of prophecy would clearly have included such a category. It was reiterated by Peter, who was, with the writer of the Acts, to have experience of predictive prophetic activity in the period following Pentecost. Jerome shows his understanding of this activity of the Spirit to be by virtue of the grace of Christ, and linked to other promises of the coming kingdom.[79] By providing a dwelling for the Spirit of God in a pure heart, Columba is joined to the omniscient God, and thus, in a degree, shares, by grace, the ability to see beyond the normal constraints of time and space. He is living in the eternal eschatological kingdom, and given access to its conditions, in part, by his union with the Spirit.

iv. Columba Foreknows in the Spirit: Closely related to foreseeing, in ii.42 Columba 'foreknew in the spirit (*in spiritu praecognouit*)' that Cormac, voyaging in search of a desert place in the ocean, would land in the Orcades. Columba sought protection for him there from Bruide, suzerain of the islands. Adomnán has the only precise instance of his phrase in *PLD*, and here again we face the problem of the case of the 's'. Gregory, Isidore and Bede record various instances of the Spirit being involved in human precognition.[80] Bede connects

---

76   '*...in spiritu*' does occur, but not in reference to foreseeing, e.g. Eph. 6:18: praying in the Spirit; Col. 1:8: love in the Spirit; Rev. 1:10, 4:2, 17:3, 21:10: being 'in the Spirit'.

77   '*...in Spiritu praevidens Apostolus*' (Ambrose, *De Spirito Sancto*, I.ii.31; *PL* 16:712A).

78   '*...in Spiritu praevidebantur*' (*Civ. Dei*, XV.8), and see Ambrose (*Apologia Prophetae David*, VII; *PL* 14), on foreseeing Christ in the Spirit, repeated in Isidore, below; Cassian (*Coll.*, XXIV.I.iii.vii; *PL* 49), on Paul foreseeing in the Spirit); Isidore (*Mysticorum in II Reg.*, IV.2; *PL* 83), on David seeing Christ in the Spirit.

79   Jerome (*Comm. Job*, XL; *PL* 26), referring to Mk. 16.

80   '*In tempestae noctis cuncta sub silentio, quasi sub solis radio omnem mundum conspexit. Ant: Benedictus Dei famulus per Spiritus sancti indagia praecognoscens quae ventura sunt omnia*' (Gregory I, *Resp. & Antiph.* '*Ant. in matutinis Laudibus*'; *PL* 78:0794B); '*Maligni spiritus hoc, quod intra nos mundare cupimus, sine intermissione tentant iterum sordidare. Sancti autem*

the tale of Simeon seeing his death, with foreknowing by grace of the Spirit, seeing with the eyes of his heart the heavenly Jerusalem, and coming to the spiritual temple wherein dwells God.[81] The Bible does not use the phrase 'precognition in the Spirit' as such, though obviously as a variation of prophetic foreknowledge, as Bede shows, it is not to be regarded as absent from Christian experience. The above instances of the practice as described by the near contemporaries of Adomnán show it as a familiar, if rare, description of the activity of the Holy Spirit, and most notably for our purpose from Gregory's responses, an activity referred to in contemporary holy living.

v. Columba is Inspired by the Spirit: The final description of the Spirit's involvement in foretelling the future also acts as an example of seeing things distant. In iii.14, Columba is said to have been 'inspired by the Holy Spirit (*inspiratus spiritu sancto*)'. During a journey with companions along Loch Ness, he sees ahead, in the farmland of Airchartdan, a group of angels who have been sent from heaven to conduct the soul of a pagan thither. The Pict awaits baptism before the ascent can occur. Thus the revelation is of both the present spatially distant, and the future temporally (slightly) distant. Again, the revelation is explicitly the work of the Holy Spirit who this time *inspires* the holy man. As we have seen, Columba rushes to the scene of his vision, preaches the word of God; the pagan hears and believes, and receives baptism. His son Virolec also hears, believes, and is baptized with his whole house. This is unmistakably evangelistic 'mission' in the pattern of the Acts of the Apostles, as inspired by, we might say directed by, the Holy Spirit. Here is, as it were, a divine appointment between the bearer of the good news, and one whom the Lord has prepared to receive it, an appointment intimated by the Spirit, who is also the one who brings new life to those being received into the kingdom of heaven.

We should note in concluding this section the observation that one of Adomnán's chief models refuses to regard future prediction as signifying sanctity. Athanasius' Antony does not regard this ability as a sign of moral virtue (see *VA* 33-4). We have already established that Adomnán was not, in essence, seeking to make such a case for Columba. His sanctity was a given, out of which the possibility of the marvellous grew. Antony's strictures serve to confirm my thesis that what was important to Adomnán was to present his patron as a man

---

eorum insidias praesago spiritu praecognoscunt, et quidquid in semetipsis terrenum sentiunt, indesinenter operibus sanctis exhauriunt, ut de intimis puri inveniantur' (Isidorus Hisp., *Sententia* III.v.21, PL 83:0664A).

81   Luke 2:26-27; Bede (*Comm.*, PL 92:0344B-D).

living in The Coming Kingdom which was being realized by the work of the Spirit.

Prophetic Disclosure of Absent Things: Revelations of Knowledge

The second division of the prophetic Adomnán discerns is what he calls the disclosure of things absent to those present. This prophetic activity does not foretell future events. Rather it revealed to the recipients events or circumstances which were occurring simultaneously, but which were not perceptible to unaided natural senses. Again, I will consider initially only those examples of the exercise of this gift which are explicitly recorded as having involved the Holy Spirit in their functioning.

i. Seeing/Knowing by Revelation of the Spirit: Columba is reported to have received revelations of current affairs by revelation of the Spirit. In the summary of the *VC* (i.1:7b) Adomnán says of Columba seeing the final journeys of souls (portrayed also in iii.6, 7, 9-14): 'he saw by revelation of the Holy Spirit (*sancto reuelante spiritu uidebat*)'. In iii.8, the Spirit revealed to him the assault of an array of demons on his monastery on Iona: 'as was revealed by the Spirit (*per spiritum revelatum*'(iii.7:110a)). Two days later he describes 'by the revelation of the Spirit (*reuelante spiritu* (iii.8:111a))' the outcome of their subsequent assault on Baithéne's church community on Tiree. The way in which the revelation is perceived as being given by the Spirit is thus differentiated. In the case of the emigrating souls, their journey is described as being visible, by revelation of the Spirit, to the observer. We are not told how Adomnán perceives this as having occurred, whether by vision, supernaturally aided natural sight; or in some other way. Of this, more below. This type of seeing souls is, however, one of the more frequent phenomena listed in the *VC*. By contrast, in iii.8, Columba is described as acting out of knowledge which the Spirit has revealed first of demonic intent, and later in the two day long attack, of the progress resulting from Baithéne's apposite defence, and of the reverse suffered by other monasteries without such able leadership.[82] It is followed by a prophecy foretelling the future. The record of both the defence of Columba and his subordinate have, once again, clear scriptural precedent, as Adomnán for once makes explicit, in Ephesians 6. There may also be recognition in Baithéne's defence of the words of

---

82 This last point is made so briefly and with such lack of flourish that its mention as a way of denigrating the other monasteries of other *paruchiae*, if such they were, lacks credibility. The record appears rather as a statement of reported fact, as testimony to the accuracy of Columba's prophecy, and the preparedness of Baithéne.

Jesus following the failure of his disciples in an encounter with a demonized boy

This kind cannot be driven out by anything but prayer (Mk. 9:29).

Whether we take Adomnán's account of demons seriously or not, Columba is described as knowing that his monastery was about to be attacked by a fatal disease, and that Baithéne has prevailed. This knowledge came by revelation of the Spirit while Columba was engaged in solitary prayer.[83] It is not this time analogous to sight (or hearing); he simply comes to know, to be aware of what he could not have come to know by his ordinary senses or intuition. This observation has important implications for understanding the phenomenon described. It has strong resonance with the gift of knowledge, 1 Cor. 12:8.

ii. Inspiration to Seek Divine Appointment: As we have seen, in iii.14, walking in the Great Glen along the banks of Loch Ness with his companions, Columba is 'suddenly inspired by the Holy Spirit (*subito inspiratus spirito sancto*)'. Adomnán uses *inspiratus* three other times in the *VC*: In Ireland, the young Fintán mac Tulcháin, later St. Munnu, burned with desire to join Columba in pilgrimage on Iona (i.2); his desire is said by Colum Crag to have been inspired by God (*a deo inspiratum*). Columba is said to be divinely inspired (*diuinitus... inspiratum*) in counselling pilgrims to take the monastic vow (i.32). He is inspired with manifest joyful, exultant gladness (*inspiratae laetationis*), as he observes the nature of an angel sent to retrieve the deposit of his soul (iii.23:125b).[84] In these three examples, the inspiration is primarily a conventional divine influence or stimulation. While true also of the instance we are considering, Adomnán's reference to the Holy Spirit, who is in biblical terms the breath of God, may permit a further nuance to the meaning of the term here, calling on its etymological foundation. It is the only such example in the *VC*, so must remain tentative, but we could here be seeing a reference to Columba being 'blown into' by the

---

83   Another Christological allusion. Jesus is described in the gospels as seeking lonely places to pray.

84   Anderson (1991, 237) and Sharpe (1995, note 399) note the close transcript from Evagrius of the passage *sanctorum...infundit*, which leads to the question containing this phrase. However this must not be allowed to prevent us from noticing the different contexts of the experiences so described. In *VA*, the gladness is a sign of heavenly angelic presence, as contrasted with demons disguised as angels, given as an aid to discernment. The soul observing them is overcome with desire for future reality. In the *VC*, the presence of the angels brings the discerning Antonine joy, but is focussed on Columba's anticipation of the eschatological fulfilment of his hope, as he looks forward to imminent transportation into the heavenly kingdom.

Spirit, in other words, to use a biblical phrase, he is at this point filled with the Spirit.[85] Now, no such phrase in the *Vulgate* uses *inspirato*, however there are clear examples of the link between God breathed inspiration and the inflowing of the Spirit.

> And when he had said this, he breathed on them and said to them, 'Receive the Holy Spirit'... (*hoc cum dixisset insuflavit et dicit eis accipite Spiritum Sanctum*) (Jn. 20:22).

> All scripture is inspired by God (lit. God-breathed)... (*omnis scriptura divinitus inspirata*) (2 Tim. 3:16).

In Luke 1:67, Zechariah is described as being 'filled with the Holy Spirit' and prophesying. Patristic examples include Augustine, who in a distantly related discussion refers to John 20:22, disclosing his understanding that the Spirit can be breathed into a person.[86] Others, more directly relevant include John Cassian

> Since he says this, since he asserts that nobody can show forth the fruits of the Spirit unless he has been inspired by God and has worked with God, it would surely be foolish, indeed sacrilegious, to attribute any actions of ours to our own effort rather than to the divine grace.[87]

Cassian refers more closely to the linkage of inspiration and prophecy in a comment on the prophet Micah being willing 'to be excluded from the inspiration of the Holy Spirit *(ab inspiratione sancti Spiritus alienum)*.'[88] Eucherius of Lyon regarded Moses and the prophets as being inspired by the Spirit, who acted as the finger of God.[89] Bede suggests inspiration may refer to an entering of the Spirit into a person, rather than simply mental quickening, as in his comment on the Virgin conception

> The holy Virgin being chosen to have conceived for our redemption by inspiration of the same Holy Spirit (*Virgo sacra inspiratione Spiritus sancti eumdem Redemptorem nostrum concepisse legitur*).[90]

These last references refer to biblical texts and situations, though the categories used to describe the activity of the Spirit are evidently current to the writers' thinking. In the case of *Coll.* III, this activity is current to the writer's own day. Thus God's empowering presence

---

85 Ex. 28:3, 31:3, 35:31; Dt. 34:9; Mic. 3.8; Lk. 1:15, 41, 67; Acts 2:4, 4:8, 31, 9:17, 13:9, 52; Rom. 15:13; Eph. 5:18. None of these references in the Vulgate uses *inspiro*.
86 *Civ Dei* XIII.24.
87 *Coll.* III.16, tr. Luibheid (1985, 96).
88 Cassian (*Coll.* IX.18; Luibheid 112).
89 Eucherius (*Instr. ad Sal.* I.i, PL 50:0780D; *Form. Spir. Intell.* I.i; PL 50:0732C).
90 Bede (*Exp. Jn* XII; PL 92).

by the inspiration of the Spirit is clearly part of the tradition which Adomnán would inherit.

That the continuation of this same inspiration was expected in Adomnán's contemporary church is illustrated by the following example from the writing of Columbanus. Here Columbanus is expounding on Christ as the fountain of the water of life. Drinking will never consume him; the more that is drunk, the more thirst grows

> O Lord, Thou art Thyself that fountain ever and again to be desired, though ever and again to be imbibed...
> We pray for nothing other than Thyself to be given to us. Inspire our hearts, I beg thee, O our Jesus, with that breath of Thy Spirit... *(Inspira corda nostra, rogo, Iesu noster, illa tui Spiritus aura...)*[91]

This technical interpretation of Adomnán's possibly casual description of the involvement of the Spirit in prophetic knowledge can, without internal supporting evidence, only hint at his understanding of what he is describing being a 'filling of the Spirit', but external evidence demonstrates such an understanding as being in concord with the non-hagiographical tradition. We see the coming into Columba of the Holy Spirit, this time bringing a word of knowledge to be of use in an evangelistic encounter.

iii. Seeing in the Spirit: At Clonmacnoise a boy seeks to touch the hem of Columba's cloak

> But this was not concealed from the saint. For what he could not with bodily eyes observe, done behind his back, he discerned with spiritual sight (*spiritalibus perspexit*) (i.3).

This appears to be a very rare description. Bede's description of Simeon's sight, though of the future, is resonant, and of course the incident is clearly based in the gospel story of Jesus and the haemorrhaging woman (Lk. 9:43-48). Adomnán adds the detail of the mode of seeing, and makes it a result of the Spirit's presence, by revelation of whom he prophesied also many other things there (i.3:15b).

The second incident occurs in ii.13 which describes the prayers of Cainnech and Columba working together to deliver the latter from marine peril.

> Then saint Columba, miraculously seeing in the spirit (*in spiritu uidens*) although... far away...

---

91   Columbanus (*Instr. XIII*, tr. Walker (1970, 118:38-9; 120:3-4)).

Columba had prophesied that it would be Cainnech who would be the instrument of their salvation. Cainnech hears this prophecy by revelation of the Holy Spirit. Columba then sees Cainnech abandoning breaking the *eulogium*, and running with one shoe to pray for him and his companions at sea, whereupon the sea was becalmed. Adomnán makes the seeing occur in Columba's spirit, or it may be that he sees in the Spirit. Certainly the Spirit is involved in Cainnech's hearing. Prosper of Aquitaine describes David as having seen in the s/Spirit (*in spiritu uidens*).[92] Augustine believed the prophets (Old and New Testament, including those mentioned in Acts 10:11 and 1 Cor. 13:2) saw in the Spirit.[93] He deals at length with spiritual sight and visions in the final book of *De Genesi ad Litteram*, as we will see, in what may be an important influence on Adomnán.

iv. Hearing in the Spirit: In an analogue of another of the natural senses, Columba, and Cainnech, hear in the Spirit (i.29, ii.13). i.29 has a series of pneumatic manifestations. Columba is on Iona. He is distressed as he sees (presumably 'in the s/Spirit') the hard labour in bad weather of his exhausted monks building in far away Durrow. Their taskmaster Laisrán is 'impelled... kindled by an inward fire' (surely a reference to the standard metaphor of the Spirit as fire acting in this case in response to the tearful concern of his superior[94]) to order rest and refreshment. Columba 'hears in the s/Spirit (in spiritu audiens)' their taskmaster Laisrán ordering a rest, in response to the activity of the Spirit convicting him of his monk's need. In ii.13, as we have noted, Adomnán explicitly makes the Holy Spirit the one who reveals Columba's words to Cainnech who hears 'in the inner ear of his heart'.

The Holy Spirit's activity associated with hearing beyond the natural occurs unequivocally in Ezekiel 2:2, 'And when he spoke to me, the Spirit entered into me and set me upon my feet; and I heard him speaking to me.' Less conclusively, in Revelation 1:10, John says 'I was in the spirit on the Lord's Day and heard behind me a loud voice', most likely referring to John being in an ecstasy of the Holy Spirit. Ambrose writes of David hearing in the s/Spirit,[95] and in a passage referring to the kingdom of God, he says that the witnesses

---

92 Prosper Aq. (*Exp Ps*. CIX; *PL* 51:0318B).

93 '*Utroque autem munere prophetiae donantur hi qui et rerum imagines in spiritu vident*' (Aug. *Div. Quaest. ad Simpl.*, Q.1; *PL* 40:0130).

94 Tearful concern is itself mentioned by Augustine (*Conf.*) among others, as a needful response of the saint (i.e. Christian) to ungodly action.

95 *Exp. Ps* XI, XXII; *PL* 15.

to its spiritual law cannot be heard by bodily ears, only by those who hear in the s/Spirit.[96] Augustine describes Peter as hearing the Spirit speak to him during the vision of the vessel (Acts 10:13) not with bodily senses but '*in spiritu*'. Augustine emphasizes that the Holy Spirit spoke within the spirit of Peter, which is also the location for images formed in spiritual visions.[97] Thus from the NT canon onwards, being 'in the Spirit' and hearing God's revelation 'in the Spirit' are associated. Columba is not, however, hearing God, rather he hears in the s/Spirit the words spoken remotely by a human agent. Again, this finds a precursor in scripture. An early commentator sees such a process occurring between Paul and the Corinthian Christians. He comments on 1 Corinthians 1:11 that Paul, though absent in body, hears the Corinthians in the Spirit.[98] In this comment, the writer refers to Colossians 2:5, a further feature of Adomnán's pneumatology to which I shall refer below. He equates 'hearing in the Spirit' with 'knowing in the Spirit', a phenomenon Adomnán evidently ascribes to Columba.

v. Visions of the Spirit: Adomnán asserts that in company with the apostle Paul, Columba had 'visions of the spirit (*spiritalium uisionum*)' (i.43). The chapter containing this reference acts as a key to our interpretation of Adomnán's understanding of the whole group of phenomena involving spiritual perception. Brüning first elucidated the Gregorian influence on Adomnán at this point in clear borrowings from *Dialogues* II.35 and IV.7.[99] Sharpe adds that Adomnán wished to ascribe to Columba this 'rare' gift, thus bringing him silently into the contemplative tradition of Benedict.[100] Is Gregory the sole interpreter of the tradition upon whom Adomnán builds his picture of Columba's visionary experiences? What exactly did Adomnán understand the phrases concerning spiritual perception to mean, and how did he understand the operation of this spiritual gift, if gift it is?

---

96   '*Non illam audit Judaeus, qui audit corporaliter; sed ille audit, qui audit in spiritu. Habent illi libros, sed sensum librorum non habent. Habent prophetas, sed non habent quem illi prophetaverunt*' (Ambrose, *Ps. Exp.*, XXI.12; PL 15:1506C).
97   *De Gen. ad Litt.* 12.11.24; PL 34:0563, tr. Taylor (1982, 192). See further discussion below.
98   Jerome (*Comm. I Cor*, PL 30:0719B).
99   Brüning (1916, 250) followed by Anderson (1991, 79 note 99) and Sharpe (1995, 57 and note 189) 'Adomnán explains this cosmic vision, citing St. Paul.' For an extended comment on the Gregorian borrowing, see Appendix 2. Citations from Gregory *Dial.*
100 Sharpe (1995, 57).

Spiritalium uisionum has been rendered variously 'visions of the Spirit (B) / spirit' (A, S), or 'spiritual visions' (F, H). The case of the 's' is again important in determining which spirit it is to which Adomnán is referring here. Is it the human spirit of Columba which sees unaided, or the Spirit of God which enables Columba to see beyond normal ability, or a combination of the Holy Spirit enabling Columba to see in his spirit? Is he confused as to which, or does he regard both the human and divine spirits to be involved? My discussion above has argued that Adomnán's constant thrust is to insist that the marvellous phenomena in which Columba moves are not attributable to some marvellous ability he naturally possesses, but to the dynamic action of God in or through Columba's human spirit. Adomnán confirms that the source is divine in the first part of Columba's explanation of the visions

> There are some, although very few, on whom divine grace (*diuina...gratia*) has bestowed this: that clearly and most distinctly they can see even the entire orb of the earth with its surrounding of ocean and heaven at one and the same moment, as though under one ray of the sun; the inmost place of mind being marvellously enlarged.[101]

Thus he wishes to emphasize that the source of the vision is divine grace. Grace and the Spirit of God are linked in scripture: O T eschatological prophecy promises: 'And I will pour out... a spirit of grace (*spiritum gratia*)' (Zec. 12:10). The Holy Spirit is called the 'Spirit of Grace (*Spiritui gratiae*)' (Heb. 10:29). There are 'varieties of gifts (*divisiones vero gratiarum*)' one of which is 'the gift of healings (*gratia sanitatum*)', all given by the Spirit (1 Cor. 12:4,9). If we render *gratia* here by the English 'free granting' or 'gift(s)', we see that the vision of Columba is granted by the Spirit of God. For Adomnán, following Gregory, the arena of the vision is in the 'marvellously enlarged scope of the mind'. The Holy Spirit makes the vision possible in the recipient by enlarging the scope of the mind from its natural, earthly mode of operation, to one operating partially under the conditions of the eschaton.

In this, Adomnán is entirely in line with mainstream Christian tradition. He explicitly claims this in citing Paul as precedent to Columba's talking in the third person out of humility. The whole Pauline section reads

> I will go on to visions and revelations of the Lord. I know a man in Christ who fourteen years ago was caught up to the third heaven–whether in the body or out of the body I do not know, God knows. And I know that this man was caught up to Paradise...he heard things that cannot be told, which man may not utter (2 Cor. 12:1b-4).

---

101 *VC* i.43:44b-45a, my transliteration.

Adomnán's knowledge of this passage is an important piece of evidence to hold as we proceed. A further scriptural passage can be seen as a clear example of the same phenomenon in operation, with examples of some of Adomnán's other modes of delivery of prophetic knowledge

> When Balaam saw that it pleased the LORD to bless Israel, he did not go, as at other times, to look for omens, but set his face towards the wilderness. And Balaam lifted up his eyes and saw Israel encamping tribe by tribe and the Spirit of God came upon him, and he took up his discourse, and said, 'The oracle of Balaam son of Beor, the oracle of the man whose eye is opened, the oracle of him who hears the words of God, who sees the vision of the Almighty, falling down, but having his eyes uncovered...' (Num. 24:1-4).

Gregory says that for Benedict, first a light brighter than daylight shone in the dead of night, representing the presence of God, then, 'the whole world, gathered as it were together under one beam of the sun, was presented before [Benedict's] eyes'.[102] Benedict sees the soul of Germanus in a fiery globe being carried up to heaven by Angels. Gregory explains that it is

> by means of that light that the capacity of the inward mind is enlarged, and is in God so extended, that it is far above the world; yea and the soul of him that seeth in this manner, is also above itself; for being rapt up in the light of God, it is inwardly in itself enlarged above itself... the man of God... could not see those things but in the light of God... what marvel, then, is it if... he was at that time out of the world?[103]

Benedict saw light with his outward eyes, while 'the inward light which was in his soul ravished the mind of the beholder to supernal things, and showed him how small all earthly things were.'[104] In *Dial.* IV, Gregory returns to the theme following Peter's questioning the immortality of the soul. Gregory asserts that the soul's immortality and posthumous presence is demonstrated by the miracles associated with the corpses of the martyrs; the visible miracles assert the real presence of their invisible souls. He goes on

> A little before, you complained for that you could not see the soul of one when it departed out of the body: but that was your fault, who desired with corporeal eyes to behold an invisible thing, for many of us, that by sincere faith and plentiful prayer, have had the eye of our soul purified, have often seen souls going out of their bodies... examples may satisfy our wavering and doubtful minds, which reason can not so fully persuade... I told you how venerable Bennet (as by relation of his own

102 *Dial.* II.35 (de Vogüé (1979 and 80, 25-6), tr. Gardner (1911, 97)).
103 *Dial.* II.35.53-64, tr. 98.
104 *Dial.* II.35.68-71, tr. 98.

monks I learned) being far distant from the city of Capua, beheld the soul of Germanus... at midnight to be carried to heaven in a fiery globe. Who, seeing the soul as it was ascending up, beheld also, in the largeness of his own soul, within the compass of one sunbeam, the whole world as it were gathered together.[105]

He gives the example to aid belief, to 'satisfy our wavering and doubtful minds which reason can not so fully persuade', and infers that he has himself seen such visions. Here we must have the understanding that Adomnán adopted for the function and nature of the visions he describes. Comparing these passages with the *VC*, we see that Gregory has a much fuller explanation. However, close parallels include both referring to a man of God being the recipients of the visions; both reported on the vision afterwards; both experience rapture / ecstasy; both are insistent that the envisioning is not a natural ability, but a direct intervention of God in enlarging the capacity of the mind. Gregory, like Adomnán elsewhere, is conscious of rationalistic objections to the evidence he presents; both received the story through monastic interlocutors. There are numerous differences in circumstantial detail, as well as application. Benedict stood in the dead of night, Columba sat during the day; Benedict saw light here, followed by, or at least accompanying the vision, Columba saw only the vision on this occasion. There is no attempt at secrecy with Benedict, indeed, he calls another to witness the event. The immortal soul is the focus for Gregory, part of his proof of the existence of the invisible seen only by spiritual vision; for Adomnán, the tale functions as a vehicle for explaining Columba's experience of these visions. However, an important difference is that Adomnán links the visions specifically to the activity of the Holy Spirit. This simultaneous dependence upon and independence from Gregory should make us further question the thesis of Adomnán simply creating his *Life* of Columba in the hagiographical gathering of good tales from elsewhere. It shows a developed pneumatological understanding of the basis of the marvellous phenomena as products of the grace of the Spirit.

However, the tradition regarding seeing in the s/Spirit is not only biblical and Benedictine. Athanasius' Antony recognizes that as in Elisha (2 Kgs. 5:26) the pure soul can 'become clear sighted, to see more and farther than the demons, since it has the Lord who reveals things to it' (*VA* 34). Spiritual vision resulting from purity of heart is noted by Augustine in his treatise *De Genesi ad Litteram*.[106] The

---

105 *Dial.* IV.7-8, tr. 187.
106 *DGL* 12.27.55. He also notes demonic ability to see over distance (12.17.34). Marina Smyth (1986) has shown the influence of this treatise elsewhere in the Irish context.

twelfth and final book investigates this phenomenon in attempting an explanation of Paul's rapture to the third heaven. This, as we have seen, is Adomnán's text for Columba's explanation. Augustine ranks three types of vision: the corporeal, seen with bodily eyes and imagined in the human spirit; the spiritual, imagined in the human spirit; and the intellectual, a direct encounter with truth unmediated by an image of an object.[107] The last is the highest form, exemplified in Moses' face-to-face encounter with God.[108] Augustine considers the apocalyptic vision of John a spiritual vision, not of the highest order.[109] Importantly for us, he explicitly links the phenomenon to prophecy, again discerning three orders.[110] The lowest class sees and communicates images in dream or ecstasies, but with no understanding (e.g. Pharaoh). The second interprets images revealed to others (e.g. Joseph). The highest order both receives the revelations, and interprets them (e.g. Daniel, Moses, Paul).

In both these classifications, we can see Adomnán presenting Columba as a practitioner of the highest orders, as well as the lower. He both receives revelations, and explains their meaning. In the visions of heavenly light, he sees the glory of God as did Moses, and receives hidden knowledge.[111] Augustine also has the concept of seeing things absent.[112] He sees the visions and dreams as fulfilments of the Joeline promise, adding weight to my suggestion above of this passage's relevance to Adomnán's explanation.[113] He sees the visions mediated by the love of the Spirit of God through the spirit of man, confirming the interpretation I suggest above for *VC* i.43.[114] He describes the phenomenon as a gift of the Spirit, confirming Sharpe's classification (and see chapter 5 below).[115] Finally, he interprets the vision of the third heaven as a vision of the life to be the believer's forever after this life, that is to say a vision of the heavenly kingdom. As we have seen, Adomnán wants to show Columba as being involved in its realization.[116] Given Augustine's influence upon Gregory, this book thus forms the original patristic foundation of both Gregory and Adomnán's explanations, and of many of Adomnán's themes. We see Adomnán operating out of a mainstream tradition.

---

107 *DGL* cc. 6-8, 11, 12, 14, 24.
108 Num. 12:27; *DGL* 12.27.55.
109 *DGL* 12.26.53.
110 *DGL* 9.20.
111 *DGL* 26.54.
112 *DGL* 12.25.
113 *DGL* 21.44.
114 *DGL* 12.26; 34.67.
115 *DGL* 13.28; 26.54.
116 *DGL* 28.56.

Cassian too refers to the seat of this phenomenon, 'everything lies at the innermost recess of the soul' and links purity here with the establishment of the kingdom.[117] Only the pure soul of high virtue with Peter, James and John is able to see the glorified Jesus

> with the inner gaze of the soul, it sees the glorified Jesus coming in the splendour of His majesty...to those worthy to look upon it with the clear gaze of the s/Spirit (*Coll.* 10.6)

The tradition concerning Columba has an early record in the Irish context. Clancy and Markus refer to the *Amra*'s note of his visionary powers, with which they include converse with angels. They take the refrain; 'our hero used to speak with the apostle' as such a visionary encounter.[118] Another interesting phrase here is in I.16, 'The whole world, it was his'. This may be a reference to his gift of extended vision. Finally, we should note that Columba is not the only Irish Christian claiming such visionary experience. Patrick states explicitly that he heard and saw in dream or waking vision the Spirit praying inside his own body, which he observed from a position outside himself, and he heard the Spirit praying over his inner man.[119] Thus although Adomnán uses Gregory's words, the concept can be seen to be present in Ireland's earliest Christian history. While Gregory is evidently a direct influence, he is not the only source for the concept Adomnán is discussing. This deeper tradition perhaps explains why Adomnán includes so little of Gregory's explanation to Peter, and why he adds alternative material in its place.

Augustine's treatment of Paul's rapture, visited en route from scripture to Adomnán by Gregory in his explanation of Benedict's gifting, is thus instructive in elucidating what this spiritual vision, or vision 'in the Spirit' was to Adomnán. Other tales he records without using the term 'spiritual vision', but which clearly involve supernatural perception include the three days in the Spirit where the secrets of difficult scripture were revealed to him (iii.18); angelic visions (i.1,3; iii.3-16,19,22,23); visions of souls of the deceased departing for heaven (i.2; iii.1,14); his tears over hard working monks (i.29); the Italian volcano (i.28), etc. At one point, Adomnán makes Columba call these visions a '*darkest mystery* (*obscurissimum sacramentum*)' (i.43). Reeves notes the reference to a similar '*sacramentum*' in the *Life of Brendan*,[120] where it signifies a 'solemn secret or deposit'. The occurrence of the phrase 'spiritual visions' going back to Augustine and Jerome, and their attribution of the

---

117 *Coll.* 1.13.
118 *Amra* VI.21, C&M 120; 125.
119 *Conf.* §24-25, and see Howlett (1994, 13; 113-114).
120 Reeves (1857, 84 note k), referring to the *Codex Kilk.*, cap. 18.

phenomena to the biblical record, show this to be a phenomenon familiar to, and integral to Christian tradition. In entering a relationship with the omniscient Creator, and in being filled with the very presence of the same, by the Holy Spirit, the *sanctus*, one made holy by this indwelling, is given (limited) access to the view of the creation, as it were through the eyes of the Creator. Such vision is granted by the grace of God to those whose communion with God is refined by the ethical lifestyles in which they live; there is less of this world to get in the way, as it were. The granting of visions of creation in this way is itself a sign of the location of the person so seeing. They are above, to use Gregory and Patrick's description, i.e. in the heavenly world, the kingdom of God. They observe the world from this perspective and with divinely empowered spiritual eyes that are able, with God's help, to see beyond the intellectual and physical vision of those not so gifted (and I emphasize the view held by Adomnán that the gift is God's donation of the temporary, first fruit ability to see in this way at certain restricted times. Complete heavenly perspicacity will not be available until the kingdom is entered fully at death.) The relationship of the presence of God and light accompanying Columba's devotions is a major theme of Adomnán in the *Life*, and to which he returns in book three as we have seen, but it is the union of the spirit of the man with the Spirit of God which makes the prophetic visions possible. Columba is to be seen as one who sees from the vantage point of the eschatological kingdom.

Thus yet again we see Adomnán the hagiographer using terminology which has respectable precedent in the serious writings of the doctors of the church, describing a phenomenon associated with the activity of the Spirit of God in the holy person. Columba's place in the procession of such in Christian history is thus further confirmed.

vi. Nothing can be Hidden from the Spirit: A closely related aspect of Adomnán's pneumatology is found near the close of the work, in iii.21. An *alumnus* of Columba's, one Berchán Mes loen, is cautioned not to approach his master's lodging that night, as he had apparently done before.[121] However, he disobeys once more, and spies through a keyhole in the door of the house, presumably hoping that the heavenly vision he expected would give him wisdom. He saw the glory of heavenly brightness (which may be the brightness accompanying the granting of vision as in Benedict, above). He cannot bear to look on this divine glory, however. Perhaps it

---

121 Anderson (1991, 215 note 234), suggests part of the tale relating this repeated occurrence is omitted.

convicts the youth of his sin in wilful disobedience of the abbot's caution, and terrified, he flees. The next day, he is severely objurgated for his repeated defiance. He, being of impure heart and motive is not able to look upon the manifest glory of the presence of God without mortal danger. The saint in the Spirit (we assume) sees the sinful spy, and pleads for God's mercy, which is granted. Columba also prophesies of Berchán's future, a future which comes to pass.

Here Adomnán explicitly names the source of this phenomenon that is described frequently in *VC*. Supernatural sight comes as a result of union with the Holy Spirit, from whom nothing can be concealed or hidden. We have examined the aspects of fear and purity in connection with heavenly light above. The point for our purpose here is that Adomnán explicitly shows us his understanding that Columba's ability to see 'things absent' and 'things future', to return to his description, is again not his natural unaided ability, but one granted by the Spirit. It is thus given to him to see, on this occasion as on other particular occasions, that which the Spirit reveals.

vii. The Marvellous Voice: By 'the grace of the divine Spirit', Columba's voice was heard at distances up to 1000 paces (i.37b:39b). Adomnán calls this a rare miracle in a report which at first sight appears to attribute to the activity of the Spirit something beyond the wide bounds of Christian tradition. This is not a naturally loud voice; those standing next to Columba were not apparently aware of any raised volume. However, those far away were able to hear every syllable he sang clearly. 'His voice sounded alike in the ears of those that heard it, near or far.' We have considered the miraculous voice above in context of the saga *The Death of the Sons of Uisneach (Oided mac nUisnig)*. There is more to notice as here we consider Adomnán's pneumatology. Adomnán introduces i.37 with the *divisio*, 'Among these memorable revelations of the prophetic Spirit it seems not out of place to record...' and then relates the tale of Columba's spirit bringing comfort; this tale of the voice; and a third regarding his voice terrifying Bruide and his people. It is an unusual triplet of incidental stories, more naturally to be thought of belonging to book II. No previous comment has been recorded as to why this collection has been recorded here, as it seems, deliberately, but with Adomnán's recognition of their appearing out of place. Neither i.36 nor i.37 are given place in the contents lists of mss A or B. i.37c is again strangely out of place in the first book. Columba's miraculously amplified voice, like thunder, roars in response to the prohibitions of the druids against singing vespers outside Bruide's palace, resulting in this pagan king and people being struck down with intolerable fear. No further affect is recorded. This would very naturally go with the Pictish mission accounts in ii.33-5, though evidently brought here to follow the previous voice miracle. But why is *that* recorded here?

Kydd notices the reference in Ignatius' *Letter to Philadelphians* where Ignatius says he 'spoke with a loud voice', thus adopting the contextual hallmark of a prophet.[122] In scripture, the loud voice is often a sign that it is God's powerful voice speaking, with information gained from no man, but given by the Spirit (e.g. Isa. 5:25ff, Ezek. 3:12; Rev. 1:10 etc.). In these linked stories from Iona and Pictland, Columba's marvellously audible voice is thus the voice of the prophet, produced by the grace of the Spirit, enabling the word of God to be heard and responded to by God's intended audience. In the first, the voice is not loud as such, but it is heard at a distance. In the second, the voice of God, mediated through his word and his prophet, rings out judgment in thunderous roars (see e.g. Job 40:9). Thus the tales are seen to be placed quite rightly in the book of prophetic revelations, even if, as Adomnán acknowledges, they are unusual. The lack of clear scriptural or ecclesiastical precedent for the actual miracles marks these prophetic tales out as perhaps indicating an ability on the writer's part not merely to ape his predecessors, but to record original phenomena, though ones which do not do violence to the concept of prophecy conveyed therein. The phenomenon described is comparable, in an inverted way, to that of spiritual sight. Here, instead of the mind of the subject being enlarged so as to encompass a marvellous viewpoint, the voice of the subject is enlarged, and others are enabled to hear it. Adomnán insists 'it could not have happened at all, without the grace of the Holy Spirit.' We may well be seeing here an example of Adomnán own creativity in bringing yet another eschatological reference. Paul's metaphor for the hope of the eschaton where believers will see clearly (1 Cor. 13:12) is here transferred to hearing clearly in a first-fruit experience of the kingdom brought by the Spirit.

Actions Ascribed to the Spirit of Columba

In these final references to 'spirit', Adomnán is unquestionably referring to the human spirit of Columba. Like Paul, Columba could be present in spirit though absent in body (i.1:10a, ii.39:90b, ii.42:96b), and his spirit provided spiritual refreshment (i.37). Finally, Columba is described as the father, and teacher, of spiritual sons (iii.23:128b), and at the last, he breathed out his spirit in death

---

122 Ignatius, *Ep. Phil.* (7.1,2), tr. Kydd: Kydd (1973, 151).

(iii.23:130b cf. Mt. 27:50; Acts 7:59). These last are commonplace descriptions which I merely note.

Adomnán has adopted a Christian anthropological idea of the existence of a human spirit which constitutes part of the human being. This study's direct interest is not to investigate the anthropological relationship and or differentiation of spirit and soul, intellect or mind in the *VC*, but Adomnán is evidently close to equating the human spirit with the animating power of the mind, as in Augustine's *De Genesi ad Litteram* (12.7.18). I am assuming a view where the action of the person's spirit is identified with the action of the person rather than an external agent. In two examples here, action is removed spatially from the fleshly location, but it is still expressly identified with the man, and not the divine. We will not investigate either soteriological questions of the regeneration of the human spirit by the inspiration of the soteriological Spirit discerned by Luke, profitable though such studies would prove. Here my interest is to introduce Adomnán's use of the category to show his awareness of both the differentiation between human and divine spirits, and the possibilities opened up by their coming into relationship.

COLUMBA COULD BE PRESENT IN SPIRIT THOUGH ABSENT IN BODY

In the summary (i.1:10a) this is presented as a rationale for Columba's prophetic ability both to declare absent things far away to those present, and to foretell future events (as above described), because, says Adomnán, he was able to observe what took place. Biblical precedent for this phenomenon is claimed by Adomnán explicitly in a verse we have already considered for another purpose

> For according to the words of Paul, 'he who clings to the Lord is one spirit'.

He quotes 1 Cor. 6.17, the context of which is Paul's ethical discussion of life in the kingdom, in the church, and in the body of Christ. He emphasizes the spiritual union with Christ which derives from being part of his body, and the consequent need to use the body towards God's glory. However, Paul does not develop his thought at this point along the line which Adomnán does. He has done so already in this letter in a section Adomnán must clearly have had in mind

> For though absent in body I am present in spirit, and as if present, I have already pronounced judgment in the name of the Lord Jesus on the man who has done such a thing. When you are assembled, and my spirit is present, with the power of our Lord Jesus... (1 Cor. 5:3-4).

Paul repeats the idea in another letter

For though I am absent in body, yet I am with you in spirit (Col. 2:5).

Paul returns to a consideration of the human spirit in 1 Corinthians 14, where he considers this to be the organ which prays in tongues ('uttering mysteries', vv. 2,16) and which can pray, praise, and sing independently from the mind (vv. 14,15), all features we can recognize in Adomnán's account of Columba. (e.g. iii.18, see above). Paul's earlier comment regarding the spirit may also be echoed in Adomnán's presentation

> For what person knows a man's thoughts except the spirit of the man which is in him? So also no one comprehends the thoughts of God except the Spirit of God (1 Cor. 2:11).

As one whose spirit is united with God through the indwelling of the Holy Spirit, the spirit of Columba is, by grace, occasionally given glimpses into the mind of God. Thus in Christian theological terms, there is nothing unusual in Adomnán's claim. One who is joined to Christ is one spirit, as Adomnán explicitly records; the Spirit is omnipresent, and makes himself especially 'present to bless' in particular locations of space and time.[123] That this belief was held in the Columban tradition is confirmed in the tales of Librán (i.39:90b) and Cormac (ii.42:96b), who speak to Columba, present in the Spirit, while they themselves are distant from his physical location. The saint responds to the pleas by prayer to God, and thus obtains changes of wind. This belief is clearly preparatory to the belief in speaking to deceased saints, invoking their help.

COLUMBA'S SPIRIT PROVIDED SPIRITUAL REFRESHMENT

The spirit of Columba is said to have met some of his monks on their way from hard work in the fields (i.37). Something marvellous and strange was felt by them at the same place and vesper hour each night. Baithéne called it a miracle; it was reportedly accompanied by a marvellous floral fragrance and a pleasant heat, and an inspired joyousness of heart, all of which brought miraculous revival and gladness such as to forget the hardship of labour, and to lighten any burden then being carried. All felt the same independently. Baithéne explains that it is Columba's spirit meeting them; he being unable to meet them physically. They respond by 'worshipping Christ in the holy and blessed man'. Again this idea is not unknown in scripture, though in a slightly different form

> ...for they refreshed my spirit as well as yours. Give recognition to such men (1 Cor. 16:18).

---

123 See Grudem (1994, 634 note 1).

Therefore we are comforted. And besides our own comfort we rejoiced still more at the joy of Titus, because his mind has been set at rest by you all (2 Cor. 7:13).

We have ready understanding of the floral fragrance, and joyousness from our eschatological and pneumatological discussions above. Here Columba's disciples are smelling the fragrance of the flowering kingdom. Again we note Adomnán's refusal to mix up the persons of the saint and of God in his description of their worshipping Christ *in* Columba, and not Columba himself, nor his spirit.[124] We could accuse Baithéne, or his commentator, of theological naïvety in the explanation he is reported to have given, making the human spirit able independently to move around as it wills. Taken with all of Adomnán's understanding of the interplay of the human and divine spirits, however, this is incorrect for Adomnán, and unfair to Columba's successor.

Conclusion

We are seeking an understanding of the nature and function of the marvellous phenomena in the *Life of Columba*. In chapter two, we challenged their nature as pagan survivals, and identified instead a clear biblical pedigree. In chapter three, we recognized their biblical eschatological nature. Their function was traced as an outworking of the biblical concept of the partial realization of the conditions of the eschatological kingdom of God in the present age.

In this chapter, we have applied these earlier findings to a study of prophecy, which is the major class of phenomenon in the *VC*. We have concluded, contra Fowler, that though Adomnán notices Columba as a preacher of God's message to the unconverted, the notice is only casual, whereas he sought quite deliberately to present him as one operating in the biblical model of the prophet; as one empowered by the various operations of the Spirit of prophecy; as one strong in the pneumatic gift of prophecy (i.50: *prophetica gratia*); as no superman; and finally as one involved in establishing the kingdom of God as the Spirit is outpoured. Adomnán's understanding is sophisticated, and has a broad range of description. We thus have in Adomnán a rich and diverse account of the range of expressions that this outpouring might take.

Firstly, the pre-eminent manifestation for Adomnán is prophecy, following on from the biblical prophets, operating in the 'weaker'

---

124 Fowler (1895, 48 note 4) noted that fragrance is a commonplace at saints' tombs, though Columba has not yet been buried; perhaps we see a further prefiguring of the development of shrine worship in the Ionan *familia*.

gift of both testaments, and in two main divisions: prediction, and knowledge of things absent. Columba hears, sees, knows, and is made aware of these things, either of the future, or of things in the present unseen by natural senses. Adomnán does not artificially classify the results of his observations of prophetic activity from the witnesses, but his understanding flows implicitly from the narratives he does record.

Secondly, for Adomnán, it is the Holy Spirit, the Spirit of prophecy, who empowers and enables this prophetic activity, and the accounts of prophecy play a dominant part in Adomnán's presentation of the rôle of the Spirit in the life and ministry of Columba. We have observed his explicit linking of the operation the eschatological Spirit with prophetic activity, and the eschatological function of prophecy. We have thus clearly identified the operation of the eschatological Spirit, prophesied in the Old Testament, poured out in the New, now continuing in the age of the inaugurated kingdom of God, at the ends of the earth.

Thirdly, this rôle has identified the nature of some of the marvellous phenomena as gifts of that same Spirit. Paul provides the only extended discussion of the early Christian's experience of these phenomena operating amongst them, albeit in a discussion skewed by its corrective function. He refers to prophecy amongst a list of various *pneumatika*, all of which derive from the Holy Spirit. Adomnán regarded Columba's exercise of prophecy and word of knowledge as the major sign of the work of the Holy Spirit in his life. As such, it confirms the standing of Columba as one in whom the eschatological gift of the Spirit has been poured out, and as one who sees with the perception of the kingdom of God. In this he follows the NT evaluation of the *pneumatika*, so in Ephesians 4, those who had the office of 'prophet', were regarded as second only in precedence to those with the office of apostle, and in 1 Cor. 14:1-5 prophecy is named as the superior gift.

Fourthly, we have recognized Adomnán's insistence that Columba was not operating as some sort of talented superman, with marvellous innate abilities of his own. Rather, he makes it clear that the activity described is not human, but a gift of the divine. Columba was one whose human spirit was joined to the Spirit of God; the human and divine spirits were united into one, and thus could operate as one, the human sharing characteristics of the infinitely greater divine. The Spirit of God, as third person of the Trinity, is co-equal in the omnipotence of God (which Adomnán explicitly recognizes in ii.3,12,34,42,43), the omniscience of God, and the omnipresence of God. Thus in being intimately united to this God, the spirit of Columba, and thus the man animated by this spirit, was able to operate in accordance with the grace and mercy of God, that is to say in God's characteristics, albeit in a limited way. In this, we can perceive clear echoes of the teaching of bishop Paphnutius, as recorded by Cassian. Paphnutius follows scriptural teaching in insisting that it is God's initiative and enabling that produces virtue of every type. In this he is saying it is the 'flowering' of faith in the God who provides, and life lived in dependence on that God, that produces the virtues. This faith is itself a gift, and needs God's intervention to maintain it, as the story of Jonah shows.[125]

In each of the examples of the prophetic gift we have examined, Adomnán shows how the Spirit brings a marvellously augmented perception to those who receive the revelations. The perception may be directly to the mind, or received in terms understood of the natural senses, but not by natural ability. The explicit linking of the Spirit's activity in each of the instances which we have studied suggests this same implicit functioning nature for all the remaining reported instances of prophetic activity. In this, Adomnán can be seen to share a style with biblical writers who, having established the agency of the Spirit in both the life of Jesus and of the disciples, do not then always mention the Spirit in connection with these phenomena. There are very many more instances of the same phenomena in the *VC* which do not have this explicit description, but in that there are no recorded instances of the prophetic which do not fit into the above series, it is difficult to infer that Adomnán could see the nature and functioning of the gift as being anything other that the operation of the eschatological Spirit in his patron's life. The prophetic activity in which he is so fully described as engaging is the first and most important sign, for Adomnán, of this presence.

Finally, none of the oracles Columba utters have an eschatological reference as such. He is not recorded as referring directly to the Day of the Lord, the last days, the judgment, the new creation etc. However we do see in them the inexorable progress of the establishment of the rule of God amongst those who come into contact with this harbinger of the kingdom, and we see that in the very act of prophesying by the Holy Spirit, Columba is realizing the biblically prophesied conditions of the kingdom themselves foretold by the prophet Joel and claimed by the apostle Peter.[126] All of these

---

125 *Coll.* 3: see 15-20 especially, and note the reference to Jonah in the light of our discussion of Columba's name above.

126 Given Adomnán's presentation in this light, a question we are left with is, what went wrong; why when the gospel had reached to the ends of the earth did Adomnán not see the ushering in of the kingdom? This question, as challenging today as it may have been to Adomnán himself, must be left to another to answer.

manifestations / phenomena are fully in accord with the biblically prophesied and reported results of the eschatological outpouring of the Spirit that would occur as the kingdom was established. In Columba we see the kingdom of God, in an 'already but not yet' mode. As Paul puts it in 1 Cor. 13:12, seeing partially, but not yet fully, like a dim image in a mirror…

CHAPTER 5

The Marvellous Growth of the Eschatological Garden: Missiological Nature and Function

Columba converted the Picts to the faith of Christ
by his words and example.[1]

I have been arguing that Adomnán's presentation insists that the flowering of the kingdom of God is to be found firstly in marvellous, eschatologically oriented manifestations, which, secondly, are of the dynamic presence of the Spirit, who empowers these manifestations in Columba, and thirdly, which are manifested pre-eminently in the exercise of the *pneumatika* of prophecy. We have been seeking a determination of the function and nature of the marvellous, and have found that the two are tied together:

Their conventional function in demonstrating that he was a man of faith in God is confirmed, but we can add that their nature make Columba one in whom the Spirit of God worked to bring the kingdom of God into being in the Provinces. They function as signs of the presence of the kingdom; their nature is seen as miniature realizations of the conditions of that kingdom in the age. They function as signs of Columba's membership of the kingdom; their nature is as flowering of his faith, energized we see now by the work of the Spirit. They function as signs of the presence of the Holy Spirit in Columba; their nature is that of manifestations of the operation of the Holy Spirit, the *pneumatika*. The saint is thus himself a sign of the presence of the eschatological Spirit in the Provinces.

These observations enrich our understanding of the content of Adomnán's hagiographical portrait, but are we able to identify more of the landscape within which he places the figure? Changing the metaphor, is there more to the function of the marvellous blooms that has yet to be noticed and described so as to trace the overall picture which will locate and bring sense to the various pieces of the jigsaw that we have been identifying.

---

1   *HE* III.4.

Columba the Missionary Re-Examined

Bringing the Picts to Faith?

It is well known that Bede describes Columba as one who came to Britain to preach the word of God in the provinces of the northern Picts. In contrast, Adomnán says Columba came as a 'pilgrim for Christ'. This is conventionally taken to mean that Adomnán saw his patron as one who spent his exile in seeking the perfect contemplation of God in ascetic, ethical rigour, following the monastic stereotype of Cassian. Comparison with Adomnán's exemplars appear to show the *VC* as closer in flavour to the *Lives* of contemplatives Antony and Benedict than to missionaries Martin, Germanus and Patrick. There is little account of preaching tours. Columba is not recorded as founding churches. He visits the King of the northern Picts, Bruide mac Maelchon, in cordiality, to seek asylum on Orkney for his monk (ii.42). He leaves the stone which protects Bruide to his dying day (ii.39), but is not recorded as baptizing this the last pagan northern king, an event which couldn't have been missed. But is this impression true at a deeper, background level? Columba certainly engaged in a power contest with the *magi,* as did St. Martin in Gaul. He ministers the gospel to the leader of a Skye war band (i.33). Is Columba's singing of Ps. 45 (i.37) a wooing of Bruide? Márkus points out the significance of its words, the second last verse especially regarding the inheritance of the king's sons. Adomnán's record allows honouring Columba's God as the outcome, but how significant is this in evangelistic terms? Peter Brown says of the early Christian missionaries that they proceeded: 'negotiating an honourable surrender of the old gods'. It is likely that Columba and his companions are only part of the story of the conversion of Pictland. Dál Riata and British Christians probably played a rôle, but how much of a rôle did Iona have, given the current tentative consensus that its mission was focused on asceticism.

The rôle played by Columba in the evangelization of the Picts based on Bede's account has come under scrutiny. Kenney calls Columba 'greatest of Irish missionaries', and Huyshe calls his visit to Pictland 'mission'.[2] Hughes believes Bede to be inaccurate: 'if Columba really had come, as Bede's informants told him, in order to preach to the Pictish people... Adomnán... would surely have recorded his successes'. She notes the stories concerning Pictland, but regrets 'it is surprisingly little for one who was supposed to have converted the northern Picts...' She observes that Adomnán *does* say that Columba was received at court, with respect and fear, and

---

2   Kenney (1968, 425); Huyshe (1905, 145).

that he does *not* say that Bruide, or the Pictish aristocracy was converted formally.[3] *If* they had been; *if* Iona had sent a powerful mission; *then* the evidence of conversion *would* be found. The literary and archaeological evidence leads to a rather negatively expressed conclusion that, 'there were undoubtedly christians and some christian communities in seventh-century Pictland', albeit, 'as minor cells, established without royal patronage, exercising little influence on society'. She summarizes: 'contrary to Bede's report... Ninian and Columba only started the work of evangelisation... it proceeded slowly'. 'Success' came with the conversion of the later Pictish king Nechtan.[4] Sharpe further doubts Bede's accuracy regarding the progress of any mission, i.e. converting Bruide, thence to Iona, saying Bede is giving a politically adjusted view of the conversion, and that we can only guess whether Ionan monks of Columba's era were engaged on mission.

> Adomnán does not really help either to confirm or refute Bede's depiction of Columba as a missionary to Pictland... For the most part, Adomnán makes no attempt to describe the work of missionary preaching.

However Sharpe does acknowledge the conversion of two families, and two references to preaching, and remembers that it was as their missionary 'for which Columba was remembered by the Picts who were Bede's informants'.[5] Macquarrie is of a similar view, but suggests the anointing of Aedan (iii.5) may have been part of a baptism, and that Columba went on to Pictland, before returning to establish Iona.[6] Clancy and Márkus give a more positive assessment. They note the thirteen years left to Columba for Pictish 'contact' after Bruide's death in 584, and the founding of Abernethy by Pictish kings who were thus likely to be Christian before 620. This royal patronage would indicate that evangelistic progress may not have been as slow as Hughes thought. This is supported by evidence from the *Amra*

---

3   Hughes (1980, 48). I will not be the first to note the error introduced into the reprint of the 1970 paper which makes Hughes say, 'what Adomnán does and does not say is worth *nothing*'.
4   Hughes (1980, 51-2).
5   Sharpe (1995, 18; 22; 31-2).
6   Macquarrie (1997, 77-8). He bases the suggestion on similarities with i.10, the blessing of Domnall, which 'it would be natural to read...as part of a baptismal ceremony.' Adomnán mentions baptism of both infant and adult elsewhere explicitly. Given the sacrament's importance in Christian initiation, it must be highly unlikely that he would miss the opportunity to mention it. The similarities of i.10 and iii.5 to each other are not evidence for the events having been baptism, so in the absence of liturgical evidence to the contrary, the suggestion must remain merely a suggestion.

His blessing turned them…
who lived on the Tay,
to the will of the King,
from the dark journeys of man (VIII.5-7).

As we've recognized, here Dallán must mean The Heavenly King, and thus again the concept of the heavenly kingdom is present. Columba is also described as 'messenger of the Lord' (I.12); that 'His work poured out saints towards ladders for the city' (VI.4-5); that he prepared 'crowds…under the holy law' (VII.11); and that he died 'guardian of a hundred churches' (VII.3).[7] Thus, though it is an idealized portrait, with the hundred churches perhaps meaning many, one of the features of this man's life, which Dallán wishes to celebrate, is his evangelistic mission.

Columba may not have converted the entire northern Pictish people to the faith of Christ. Adomnán may not record the formal conversion of a king and court in Pictland. The process of evangelization may have been slow, and only started by Columba. His pilgrimage may have been, like Fursa, seeking salvation and solitude, not motivated by the call to evangelize.[8] Adomnán does not explicitly present a mission of the type associated with Martin or Patrick. Evidently he did not see it as important to present his patron as having been involved in such systematic church planting in his own region. That Tirechán and Sulpicius Severus had ecclesio-political reasons for their constructions of saintly missionary itineraries should, however, cause us to question their literary model of mission for the period. *VC* does not fit their model, thus it is not seen to present mission, but is their model of mission the only one?

The debate raises questions over our previous discussion in which we have traced Adomnán's description of Columba as one through whom the eschatological kingdom comes. As we have seen, an essential component of this concept is the spreading of the kingdom, following the great commission, as identified here in the vision of the robe. What then was the nature of Columba's pilgrimage; was the rôle of Columba seen as that of an apostolic missionary saint to Dál Riata and Pictland at all? Was the kingdom restricted only to Columba himself, or did faith blossom for other individuals and in other communities? How unusual was slow evangelization; how usual was the early conversion of aristocrats? How should Bede be understood? Have the marvellous phenomena anything to contribute

---

7   C&M (1995, 119 and *Amra* translations). The lower case 'f' in VIII.7 is my deliberate misquotation of the translation in a speculative contribution to 'unravelling the meaning'.

8   Hughes (1970, 39).

to our understanding of these questions? We will consider the evidence Adomnán presents.

Peregrinatio in the Vita Columbae

One of the important assumptions upholding the received view is the understanding commonly brought to the term *peregrinatio*, on which Adomnán says Columba is engaged. Peregrination is a common practice of early Irish Christians, and normally taken to refer to a religious, ascetically oriented journey into isolated exile,[9] 'getting away from it all', as it were, to spend time in rigorous mortification of the flesh, with the object of obtaining salvation. Hughes wonders whether Bede's 'very unusual' record of Columba as an evangelist rather than the standard ascetic saint is a product of Pictish propaganda.[10] What is the content of the term *peregrinatio* and its cognates as used by Adomnán? *VC* uses fall into two groups:

The first group comprises those describing the years Columba spent in Britain. Adomnán describes Columba as 'a pilgrim for Christ (*pro Christi peregrinari*)' (sp); who 'sailed away to be a pilgrim (*peregrinaturus... enauigauit*)' (i.7) from Ireland. Columba was 'living in pilgrimage in Britain (*in Brittaniam peregrinantem*)' (i.13). ii.10 is set 'during the saint's life in pilgrimage, while he was making a journey (*cum sanctus in sua conuersaretur peregrinatione*)' to Pictland, and iii.22 marks the beginning of the end, 'Thirty years have been completed of my pilgrimage in Britain (*...meae in Brittania peregrinationis*).' Columba is looking for what he calls release from his residence, and he 'crossed over to the heavenly country from this weary pilgrimage (*...de hac tediali perigrinatione*).' Thus Adomnán sees Columba as having spent 34 years in *peregrinatio*. In addition, in ii.33, we read of the 'pilgrim captive (*peregrinam captivam*)', an Irish woman ('*scoticam*') held by Broichan as a slave. Anderson suggests she 'had been living as a nun in Britain'. Her plight is strongly reminiscent of the maidservants of God to whom Patrick refers, 'who were detained in service (*quae seruíto dètinéntur*)', and she could constitute a female predecessor to Columba as a missionary to the Picts.[11]

The second group are others described as on peregrination of some sort. Seven visitors to Columba have the term applied to them, one of which is the famous crane of i.48. It came to rest, perhaps as a sign of the eschatological rest realized in Columba's presence, itself a sign of the presence of the eschatological Spirit. Its peregrination,

---

9   Charles-Edwards (1976, 43-59); C&M (1995, 157-8).
10   Hughes (1988a, 39).
11   *Conf.* 42, ed. and tr. Howlett (1994, 80-1).

with that of the incognito Bishop Cronán (i.44) is thus a 'sojourn in the Spirit' in the company of the Spirit bearer. Two brothers (i.32), and an Irishman (iii.7), stay for a medium term. For longer periods, visitors are required to take vows, thus entering fully into the life and ministry of the coenobium. One aspect of this life which we know about is that the abbot took out with him companions on further journeys. During these, the word was proclaimed (ii.31ff.), and the kingdom extended. There are two penitent strangers/pilgrims (i.36, ii.39). Columba prophesies to one of them, Librán, 'your part in the kingdom will be with my elect monks, and with them you will awake from the sleep of death into the resurrection of life.' Here we normally take monk to mean ascetic contemplative. We have another link with the idea of the three countries of earth, the kingdom of God on earth, and the kingdom of heaven.

Sharpe confirms that the normal Irish Latin meaning of *peregrina* refers to separation from one's homeland, rather than shrine-visiting in the continental / medieval sense.[12] Thus, for Adomnán, the meaning he gives to the term comfortably describes Columba's 34 year sojourn, i.e. his whole ministry or mission, following his original sailing from Ireland in 563. It is not essentially a journey, for he is resident for much of the period on either Iona or Hinba. Nor is it only residential, as he makes a number of journeys. It is not actually exile, for he returns 'home' apparently freely,[13] but nor is his base at home, for he chooses to base himself in, or very close to, a different geo-political and cultural space than his own. When we look at the recorded highlights of the *peregrinatio*, we see strong elements of ascetic coenobitism and eremeticism, but the community is far from closed, and far from introverted. Members make frequent visits elsewhere, records of which present some as having clear evangelistic components. The journeys are part of the *peregrinatio* upon which Columba is engaged. Thus we can see clearly some sense of evangelistic mission in the term as used for Columba. He left his own to become a stranger in another country. He took the word of the Lord to those people, and saw converts, baptizing them in the name of the Father Son, and Holy Spirit, according to the great commission of Mt. 28:29. In this he anticipates the 'new, more concrete application of the Irish *peregrinatio pro Christo*, now understood as a mission' of Amand and Willibrord.[14]

As we have seen, his preaching was accompanied by 'signs and wonders', as was that of Christ, Adomnán's principal model for

---

12   Sharpe (1995, note 293).
13   In i.3 (?AU 585: see Sharpe, 1995, note 59), and i.49 (AU 575/c.AD 590, Sharpe, 1995, note 204).
14   Hillgarth (1987, 323).

Columba; the prophets; and especially the apostles on their mission to the pagan world. The *Amra's* reference to Columba being in Britain to follow the path of obedient holiness of 'the four' (evangelists? (VI.1, 27)) adds credence to the picture. I have argued above that the *VC* contains within it a clear record of the establishment, through Columba and what we might call his co-missioners, of the kingdom of God in these Provinces. The striking image Adomnán gives of the spread of this kingdom as the blossoming of many flowers across the fields and mountains of these Provinces (ii.1) may even have in his mind an etymological association with *peregrinatio*, which comes through the post-classical derivation of *per-ager*, 'who has gone through the lands.'[15] Thus in Adomnán, to be involved in a peregrination may hold the sense of to be involved in the mission of spreading the kingdom of God on the earth, in present realization of the eschatological kingdom that has come, is coming, and is to come.

The over-ridingly important feature of the *peregrinatio* for Adomnán is Columba's, and others', ministry in the marvellous. Prophecy, miracles of power, visions of light and encounters with angels are the features of the peregrination he wishes his readers to note. I wish to argue that these marvellous phenomena most naturally cohere with the ongoing evangelistic missiological activity of the Holy Spirit, over and above that in a simply ascetic pilgrimage.

Missiological Activity in the Vita Columbae

Adomnán describes Columba as 'a leader of souls to the heavenly kingdom (*animarum dux ad caeleste regnum*)' (i.2, iii.1). His function is thus to lead people into the kingdom of God which is present on earth, in preparation for its fulfilment in heaven. Entry into this kingdom can only be by the Johannine doorway of rebirth by Spirit (Jn. 3:3), a view with which we see in the Pictish conversion tales Adomnán concurring explicitly. In practical terms, those who are to be led into the kingdom, outwith whose courts they stand prior to baptism in water and Spirit, must either come to a place where they can hear the gospel, and accept its invitation, or they must be sought out in order to apprise them of the invitation they have been offered. Fintán is sent to Leinster to set up his mission. Columba, elected as a leader of *innumerable* souls to the heavenly country (iii.1), establishes his mission on Iona. According to *VC*, Iona was not, in Columba's time, a centre for mass pilgrimage of pagan folk

---

15   L&S, 1338.

seeking salvation, however much it was a centre for those, such as Fintán, who were seeking a peregrinatory career, or who were seeking penance for falling from righteousness. Adomnán does not describe the bringing of many souls to the kingdom. So how does he envisage his hero as one who would, indeed as one who did so? We must review the key pieces of evidence that indicate definite missiological activity in the *VC*. In this process, we will address the question of how 'conversion' is signified therein.

THE ESCHATOLOGICAL ELEMENT IN ADOMNÁN'S THINKING

Adomnán presents the *Life* as occurring 'In the last years of the world' (sp:3a). We have seen (chap. 3) how this eschatological awareness is closely linked in the biblical world-view to the completion of the mission to take the gospel to the ends of the earth. The end is clearly presented in *Altus Prosator*, R-Z. Patrick's and Adomnán's holding of the view of their territory in these terms is confirmed by Clancy and Márkus, and O'Loughlin, as we've seen.[16]

JONAH COLUMBA

Adomnán's identification of Columba with Jonah may be further pressed in the identity of this prophet as missionary to the pagans of Nineveh. The book of Jonah relates the progress of this mission, including reluctant beginnings, a sea voyage, encounter with a great sea creature, the delivery of the message, and salvation brought to the pagans. Each of these elements is also included in the *VC*, though not in the order of Jonah. Unlike Columbanus, who explicitly claims to follow in Jonah's wake, Adomnán does not explicitly draw out the parallels. However, the link is made in the explicit association. So, again early in the text, we are seeing Adomnán setting the scene for his description of Columba in terms which would fire off clear associations in the minds of his readers. Here it is of Columba, son of the Spirit, the sign of the kingdom and missionary of the kingdom to the pagans, just as 'Jonah became a sign to the pagans of Nineveh' (Lk. 11:30).

MISSION FIELD

Adomnán records Patrick's disciple Mochta as referring to the 'fields of our two monasteries' (sp:3a); i.e. the Patrician paruchia, and Columba's paruchia. These are almost certainly, taken with Adomnán's now well known phrase in the first preface, the field in which the seeds of the kingdom are planted, and in which they will bloom. So he has Mochta sowing the kingdom in one field, and Columba, over 'only a little hedge' sowing it in the Provinces. The

---

16   C&M (1995, 6), and O'Loughlin (1997, 14f. esp. 19).

connection of the image of the mission-field with the kingdom is plain in the NT, and would be a natural image for Adomnán to adopt if referring to a mission of the sort for which I am arguing.

> The harvest is plentiful, but the labourers are few; pray therefore the Lord of the harvest to send out labourers into his harvest (Mt. 9:37-38//Lk. 10:2).

> The kingdom of heaven may be compared to a man who sowed good seed in his field... the field is the world, and the good seed means the sons of the kingdom (Mt. 13:24, 38 cf. 31-2).

> But we will not boast without measure, but according to the measure (*mensuram*) of the rule which God has measured for us (*quam mensus est nobis Deus*), a measure (*mensuram*) to reach even unto you (2 Cor. 10:13).[17]

EVANGELISM

Various tales contain an almost explicit description of the process of evangelistic mission:

(i) i.33. Artbranan, a '*gentilis*' old man of Skye received the word of God from Columba via an interpreter, believed, and was baptized as a Christian. Columba knew by prophetic revelation of his imminent arrival, and his spiritual state, cf. Christ and the Samaritan woman (Jn. 4), or Philip and the Ethiopian (Acts 8:26).

(ii) ii.32. A Pictish layman 'with his whole household',[18] listed as wife, children and servants, 'heard and believed the word of life, through an interpreter, at the preaching of' Columba, and believing, they were baptized as Christians. It is difficult to read this tale in a way which suggests Columba was not engaged in active evangelism.

(iii) iii.14. A Pictish family of '*gentili*' of Urquhart in Pictland are recorded as new believers in the word of God preached by Columba. Emchath, his son Virolec 'and his whole house' are baptized as Christians. Columba had again been informed by the Holy Spirit with the knowledge of this appointment.

---

17 The terms rendered 'measure' here can carry the sense of measured-off ground (from its root, *metior*, L&S 1140) i.e. a field, or mission field, as the context goes on to show. The verse could thus be understood '...but will confine our boasting to the field God has assigned to us, a field that reaches even to yours.' Adomnán may allude to this verse in his reference to Patrick, in that he refers to the 'mission' field in which the Columban church operates, confirming our assessment. However, Adomnán may be signalling that he is not going to adopt the same tactics of his competitor in claiming churches established by other patrons than his own; he would, piously, let God speak in showing God's activity in the mission of Columba across on his own side of the hedge.

18 Cf. Jn 4.53; Acts 16.15; 11.14; 16.31; 18.8.

(iv) ii.10. As a baby, Ligu Cenncalad of Ardnamurchan is baptized. Adomnán makes no claim for Columba to have converted his parents who would almost certainly be Christians here. Columba's prophecy of his life foresees his satiating the desires of his flesh in youth, but 'thereafter, fit to be delivered up, marching out in continuous Christian warfare (*deinceps cristianae usque in exitum militiae mancipandus*).' We are told nothing of what brought about this conversion from youthful licentiousness, except that it happened. Adomnán is thus prepared to make a distinction between baptism and later becoming an active Christian.

(v) ii.9. We should finally notice Éogenán. He is described explicitly as a Pictish presbyter (*prespiterum gente Pictum*). Sharpe follows O'Rahilly in dismissing the idea that he could have been an 'Irish Pict'.[19] He is thus a converted Pict from the island of Britain who has reached some measure of maturity as a Christian, now working in Leinster. The chronology and geography here is problematic. This is the second of two tales regarding books written in Columba's hand, and may both refer to a time some 'cycles of many years' after Columba's death (ii.8). There is no certainty that Adomnán sees him as a northern Pict, though given the lack of recognition of southern Picts in *VC*, it seems more than likely that he does. However, there is nothing to suggest this Pict was not converted during Columba's journeys to Pictland.

There are thus at least three clear instances where Columba engages in evangelism, and two where this may be implied. In two of the cases, he is described as being directed by the Spirit. This cannot be described as other than a divine call to evangelize. In the last case, we may be observing one of the individual products of this mission.

'CONVERSION'

Four of the tales above confirm that Columba goes out preaching the word in the power, and using the gifts, of the Holy Spirit.[20] This

---

19   Sharpe (1995, note 232).
20   A feature entirely missed by advocates of the 'baptism of pagan belief' school. W.J. Watson (1915) in a paper heavily influenced by Plummer's *Vitae Sanctorum Hiberniae*, believes the baptisms of Emcath and Artbranan to be little more than 'saining', the making of the sign of the cross over pagan natural goodness, what he calls the 'keynote of the attitude of the church to a whole department of pagan beliefs... the rite of baptism turns the pagan natural goodness into Christian goodness' (263-4). In this he ignores the rôle in this tale of proclamation of the word, and the leading of the Spirit, which precede the baptism, and the fact that the practice Adomnán describes is no novelty in the Christian tradition. How else may a pagan become a Christian, Adomnán might ask, than by accepting the word, being baptized, and engaging in Christian warfare?

activity is recorded for both Pictland and Dál Riata, though in the latter, we infer that the parents were already baptized as Christians. This inference draws a contrast between the two territories; one 'converted',[21] one yet pagan. References to 'barbarians' in the non-Dál Riatan territory confirm the view: the Miathi may be a group living between Pict and Briton;[22] those who attacked Crog reth, may be beside Loch Rannoch (i.46); and there are those living along the River Ness (ii.27). Even by the close of Columba's life, Adomnán is still reporting the existence of 'barbarian' nations who will nevertheless honour Iona (iii.23:128a). Thus his mission, such as it was, is not presented as having converted these nations in entirety by his death.

Columba makes attempts at the conversion of Bruide, king of the Picts, and his *magus* Broichan, singing (amplified) psalms outside the palace (i.37c); opening the door of the palace by the sign of the cross and miraculous strength (ii.35); demonstrating his God's supremacy over the god of the *magi* (ii.33, 34); providing Bruide with a healing stone for Broichan, smitten by angelically delivered judgement. No word signifying conversion is recorded on Bruide's or Broichan's lips, though alarm at the power; reverence for, and the great honour of high esteem, for Columba himself (ii.35, where the king and his senate condescend to leave their house, going to meet Columba and his associates at the opened door with pacifying words of peace), are shown. As we've noted, Hughes regards the lack of aristocratic conversion in *VC* as lack of success. This is success in terms of the lack of evidence of conversion on a national scale that would follow the conversion of rulers. Henderson wants the encounter to fit the model to the extent of suggesting Bruide withheld his baptism to the end of his life, for which there is no evidence.[23] As Patrick observed earlier for his own mission, the time had not yet come for the conversion of kings (*Conf.* 52). Adomnán

---

21 Márkus (1999, 126) has suggested that Dál Riata was thoroughly Christianized by the time Columba came there. Land was given to Columba by the king on his arrival, an unlikely happening if the king was not Christian; his successor sought ordination by Columba; a child is baptized; Eigg, and Tiree were all active in Columba's time [though Adomnán doesn't mention the first]. This Christianized area must have had a pastoral structure to service it. Dumville (1993, 188) suggests an ecclesiastical infrastructure would be in place in Dál Riata by the mid sixth-century and that Iona was a monastic appendage of this. He names Bishops occurring in the record, incl. *VC* (i.5, i.36, i.44, i.50, ii.1, iii.4] and the lack of controversy over Iona's consecration practice having been raised at Whitby, so it is highly unlikely to have been irregular.

22 *VC* i.8, Sharpe (1995, note 81).

23 Henderson (1967, 70), notwithstanding her citing Penda of Mercia's deferral.

writes rather with his eyes on the evangelists' accounts of the
mission of Christ and the apostles. Here lack of success in converting
kings is also signal, as is the lack of any mass conversion up until
Pentecost. It would be nearly three centuries before the most
'successful' conversion occurred. Neither the earthly Christ nor his
Apostles converted the nations by the time of their deaths. This
should not therefore be taken for lack of success in bringing people
to faith, Adomnán's code for establishing the kingdom.

The stories of the Gleann Mór Picts bring us to the question of
how conversion is signified in *VC*. The account of believer's baptisms
above is conclusive; the sacrament seals the conversion. Other
groups are not described as being baptized, but as glorifying or
magnifying the God of the Christians. Adomnán's description
requires more exploration.

Following the incident with the beast of River Ness

> ...the pagan barbarians who were there at the time, impelled by the
> magnitude of this miracle that they themselves had seen, magnified the
> God of the Christians (ii.27).

Similarly, where a family is baptized after hearing and believing, a
powerful miracle of resuscitation following the death of one of their
sons releases the glorification of God

> Then a shout of the people arose, mourning was turned into rejoicing, the
> God of the Christians was glorified (ii.32).

The shout itself has eschatological significance as the shout of
salvation (Isa. 42:10-13; Jer. 31:7; Zeph. 3:14f) as does the
transformation of mourning (Isa 61:3, adopted as Christ's agenda in
Lk. 4.18f). This follows the gloating of the *magi* who saw the sudden
post-baptismal illness of the boy as a sign of the weakness of the
Christian's God

> ...they began... to magnify their own gods as the stronger, and to belittle
> the Christians' God as the weaker.

Adomnán does not depict his Spirit-filled hero preaching to crowds
like Peter, but his mission is otherwise conversant with a biblical
pattern. The Evangelists are Adomnán's primary models. Following
the healing of the paralytic, a crowd glorifies God who had given such
power to men (Mt. 9:8//). Similarly, seeing the eschatological
miracles, a crowd glorifies the God of Israel (Mt. 15:31). Following a
resuscitation, fear seizes the crowd as they realize the power of God
made manifest (Lk. 7:16). This same fear seizes Bruide in i.37 and
ii.35. Pictland is the last remaining unevangelized field in the north
of the Isles of the Ocean, at the end of the world, and so the signs of
divine power bring fear

...so that those who dwell at earth's farthest bounds are afraid at thy signs (Ps. 65:8).

The gospel writers are content to leave these reports as they are, without adding that the people were baptized, 'converted', or that they began to follow Jesus. As with the people of Pictland, we are not told if this is the case, but the implication of their giving the glory to the God of the Christians is that they both accept his reality and power, and that in this assent, they are in a definite way aligning themselves with Columba's God. Thus Adomnán presents reaction to the marvellous phenomena accompanying Columba in a similar light to the way the Evangelists presented the reaction to those accompanying Jesus. The reaction of giving the God of the Christians glory is deemed sufficient to his purpose in showing the spreading, with Columba, as with Jesus for Palestine, of the kingdom of God in the Provinces. It is possible that Adomnán has a similar scenario in mind for Bruide, where honouring Columba means honouring what and whom he represents. That the white stone was retained until the moment of Bruide's death, when it disappeared, suggests time for true repentance may have been left, and that Columba's influence remained powerful. The faith spread slowly until rulers were converted, when the political advantages of 'faith' helped progress. Adomnán is perhaps more realistic than the historian in his portrayal of the progress of evangelistic mission. Our concentration on aristocratic and political conversion perhaps seeks a mark of success which does not concur with the gospel as understood by Adomnán.

THE GROWING IONAN ECCLESIA

Adomnán indicates the continuation of the Ionan ecclesia in ii.46. The presence of Columban monasteries in Dál Riata and Pictland gave protection from the ravages of the plague, 'although neither people is without great sins' which God forbears to judge. Adomnán looks on the hearts of the people, not the 'conversion' of the rulers. The record of growth, albeit in small cells, is nevertheless evidence for the historical mission of the Columban church in the era. It is feasible, though difficult, to ascribe this missiological activity only to the inspiration and initiative of Columba's successor abbots of Iona. However it must be unlikely that this activity had little precedent in the example of the founder who was to inspire and motivate the Ionan paruchia.

The outline and detail of the progress of this mission must be left to others to describe, but taken as an historical reality, it can only confirm the view that Columba was involved in mission as part of his peregrination. Bede's statement that Columba brought the Northern

Picts to faith should not to be interpreted too literally. Bede would
understand the idea that the apostles were to bring salvation to the
ends of the earth (Mt. 28:19), but this does not mean they did it
personally. Columba may only have been the one who started the
mission, but Bede was concerned to state that he *was* the one who
brought the apostolic commission to Pictland.

EVIDENCE FROM SILENCE

Finally we must recognize the necessity of caution in drawing too
firm an inference from silence. The lack of evidence of a widespread
evangelistic mission is not the same thing as evidence demonstrating
a lack of such a mission. It would surely have suited Armagh, Kildare
and Bede's propagandist purpose to seek to belittle Iona's success.
While this may have resulted in silence in the former two cases, it is
not the case for Bede who is happy to ascribe the conversion of the
Picts to Iona. His positive gloss on the process, giving Columba
perhaps more credit than he deserved, wherever the information
came from, does not impress one as the action of someone
concerned to demonstrate the unreliability of a divergent church.
Again, the difference in terms of durable evidence for on the one
hand the conversion of individuals, a biblical and Adomnán-ish
concern, and on the other that of aristocrats, must be borne in mind,
i.e. it is only the latter that usually leaves tangible evidence. We
should also remember Bede's familiarity with missionary saints;
many saints in his *History* are not eremitic ascetics. Cuthbert,
Augustine of Canterbury, Germanus, Martin all took the gospel to
areas in need of evangelization, following their Apostolic
predecessors. Thus Hughes' puzzlement as to why Bede should
identify Columba with this noble company is perhaps vitiated.

The Marvellous and the Mission:
Signs, Wonders, and Spiritual Gifts as Tools

The broad question we have been pursuing concerns the
incorporation of the marvellous phenomena into a functional
framework. Adomnán is careful to depict the peregrination of
Columba as filled with marvellous events. What is the relationship
between the peregrination and the marvellous? For Adomnán, the
ethical fruit of the present Spirit is the implicitly assumed soil in
which the marvellous flowers of faith grow. We have traced an
eschatological realization. The empowering presence of the Spirit
enables the operation of the various marvellous phenomena deployed
to the task in which Columba is engaged. I have been arguing that it
is in part the mission of establishing the kingdom of God, a kingdom
which is, in part, demonstrated practically, physically, manifestly, by

the presence of the Spirit empowered and other supernatural phenomena. We can see this mission in action, but how do the phenomena fit into it? Our final task is to draw comparison between the manifestations of God's glory, the signs of miraculous power in the *VC*, with those in scripture and history, and to assess their rôle as signifying a mission to propagate the kingdom in the Provinces. Is there any evidence in the collection that would infer the field from which they were gathered was also, in fact, a mission field, not simply an ascetic garden?

> Let the reader reflect how great and of what nature was the venerable man, in whom almighty God made manifest to the heathen people the glory of his name through those signs of miraculous power (*miraculorum uirtutibus*) described above (ii.34).

Adomnán's principal point here is, once again, the sanctified nature of Columba which it is his purpose to present. However, the terminology of the supporting argument he employs to make his case claims that God manifested this glory to the 'heathen people (*plebe gentilica*)', through the signs of 'miraculous power (*miraculorum uirtutibus*)'. Prophecy, knowledge, wisdom, healings, miracles, visions, maybe tongues, are all represented in the panoply of pneumatically-empowered manifestations of the kingdom which, with angelic and luminary signs of the presence of heaven on earth, Adomnán employs to paint his portrait.

We have noted the allusion between this manifestation of glory, and the Evangelist's record of Jesus' mission which is accompanied by similar manifestations. Jesus established the kingdom by proclamation, accredited through Spirit-empowered miracles the precise nature of which remains under debate. That these phenomena authenticated the spoken word by demonstrations of supernatural power is central to the world-view of the biblical metanarrative.

> Men of Israel, hear these words: Jesus of Nazareth, a man attested to you by God with mighty works and wonders and signs, which God did through him, in your midst as you yourselves know (Acts 2:22).

The power motif was adopted as the first attempt to establish communication in a language the 'heathen people' would understand. When preaching would have been unlikely at first to succeed, a demonstration of God's power might. Richardson, Turner *et al.* extend the function of the phenomena, as we have seen above, as themselves demonstrating, incarnating, the presence of the eschatological kingdom as it is partially realized in the era which precedes the final consummation. Various terms apply to these phenomena, including signs, miracles, wonders, and demonstrations of the Spirit's power.

It was not only Jesus whose word was thus accompanied, but his apostles and other disciples follow the model, preaching the gospel, and see it confirmed by various marvellous signs. The careers of Peter, John and Paul after Pentecost recorded in Acts show this clearly

> And [the disciples] went forth and preached everywhere, while the Lord worked with them and confirmed the message by the signs that attended it (Mk. 16:20).

> And fear came upon every soul, and many wonders and signs were done through the apostles (Acts 2:43, and see 5:12).

Signs and wonders were not the sole preserve of the twelve as other disciples were included

> And Stephen, full of grace and power, did great wonders and signs among the people (Acts 6:8).

> And the multitudes with one accord gave heed to what was said by Philip, when they heard him and saw the signs which he did (Acts 8:6).

The writer to the Hebrews provides the key to understanding where the variety of marvellous manifestations which Adomnán attributes to Columba might fit

> God also bore witness by signs and wonders and various miracles and gifts of the Holy Spirit distributed according to his own will (Heb. 2:4).

The writings of Paul include various references to his having proclaimed the word of God to the pagan gentiles, and that this proclamation in words was accompanied by 'signs and wonders following', which were performed by the Holy Spirit

> For I will not venture to speak of anything except what Christ has wrought through me to win obedience from the Gentiles, by word and deed, by the power of signs and wonders, by the power of the Holy Spirit (Rom. 15:18-19).

> ...my speech and my message were not in plausible words of wisdom, but in demonstration of the Spirit and power (1 Cor. 2:4, cf. 1 Thes. 1:5).

He records the early understanding of the nature of these phenomena

> Now concerning spiritual gifts (*de spiritalibus*)...To each is given the manifestation of the Spirit for the common good. To one is given through the Spirit the utterance of wisdom, and to another the utterance of knowledge according to the same Spirit, to another faith by the same Spirit, to another gifts of healings (*gratia sanitatum*) by the one Spirit, to another the working of miracles (*operatio virtutum*), to another prophecy, to another the ability to distinguish between spirits, to another

various kinds of tongues, to another the interpretation of tongues. All these are inspired by one and the same Spirit, who apportions to each one individually as he wills...

Paul gives two main sets of marvellous phenomena which are explicitly the result of the Spirit's operation: Romans 12:6-8 and 1 Corinthians 12-14. In Romans 12.6 the Vulgate renders *donationes* for *charismata*. In 1 Corinthians, it renders *spiritalibus* for *twn pneumatikwn* (12:1); *gratiarum* for *charismatwn* (12:4); and *manifestio Spiritus* for Paul's general term *phanerosis tou pneumatoi* (12:7). Peter mentions these gifts (*gratiae Dei*) briefly (1 Pet. 4:9-11), and links them to giving glory to God.[24] Adomnán uses similar terms, e.g: Columba's prophetic activity is delivered 'by the grace of the divine Spirit (*divini Spiritus gratia*)' (i.37:39b); by the outpouring of 'the grace of the Holy Spirit (*gratia sancti spiramini*)' (iii.18); or God granting it 'by God's dispensation (*deo donante*)' (i.4); his visionary knowledge was granted by 'divine favour (*divina... gratia*)' (i.43, cf. il:10b); miracles he performed were by the gift of God (*deo donante*) (i.1.10a; ii.3,15,21,42:97b); Ernéne would receive eloquent, doctrinally healthful utterance given by God (*a deo donabitur*) (i.3).

As we survey *VC* phenomena, we observe a coherence with the first-century lists of Paul, where he explicitly links the manifestations with the presence and activity of the Spirit. Adomnán knows this apostle's writing. Thus a further model for the marvellous surrounding his patron may be Paul's description of *ta pneumatika,* the gifts of grace of the Spirit. Columba is presented as delivering, by, in, through the Spirit messages of wisdom, knowledge, prophecy; as ministering gifts of healing to the sick, as performing diverse miracles, and as discerning spirits. The only item in Paul's 1 Cor. 12 lists definitely not featured in the *VC* is the interpretation of tongues, spiritual or natural (as we have seen, Columba employs the services of a translator). Adomnán would be aware of Paul's priorities, reflected in the predominance of the gifts of prophetic utterance, and the tiny if any incidence of tongues in *VC*.

> Make love your aim, and earnestly desire the spiritual gifts, especially that you may prophesy... He who prophesies is greater than he who speaks in tongues (1 Cor. 14:1, 5).

Adomnán is concerned to identify Columba with the elite ministers of the church as 'a man both prophetic and apostolic' (ii.32). Paul identifies these particular gifts as two in a series of ministerial giftings, with which we should note the numerous pastoral references

---

24   For a full treatment of the *pneumatika*, see G.D. Fee (1994).

in *Amra* (I.9, 10, 11, 19; VI.24, 26, 27; VII.3) alongside pastoral notes in *VC*

> And God has appointed in the church first apostles, second prophets, third teachers, then workers of miracles, then healers... (1 Cor. 12:28)

> And his gifts were that some should be apostles, some prophets, some evangelists, some pastors and teachers to equip the saints for the work of ministry, for building up the body of Christ (Eph. 4:11-12).

Marvellous accompaniment was regarded as authorizing Apostolic function

> The signs of a true apostle were performed among you in all patience, with signs and wonders and mighty works (2 Cor. 12:12).

Thus, we may see the portrait of a man exercising variously the functions of Ephesians 4:11, the aim of which is the establishment of the church. Paul makes it clear (1 Cor. 12:7, 14.3-5; Eph. 4:12) that the purpose of the phenomena is for mutual usefulness (*sumpherwn / utilitate*) and edification (*oikodomen / aedificatio*), the building up, of the church. He mentions specifically the place of prophecy in mission

> ...if an unbeliever hears prophecy he will be convicted, the secrets of his heart made manifest, and he will do homage to God (1 Cor. 14:24).

Thus we are seeing the phenomena in the evangelistic practice of Christ, of Paul, and of the other early disciples, exercised in this sixth-century insular missionary context. Paul insists that it is from the one God in Trinity that *ta pneumatika* derive, not from the idols of the gentiles (1 Cor. 12:1-6). We can thus say that Adomnán records the three categories of marvellous phenomena as signs of the equipping of Columba *et al.* for the task of spreading the kingdom. Adomnán saw the NT record as normative for a Christian life including mission, and he sought to present Columba as accredited like the apostles and prophets by these phenomena in spreading the kingdom to the unevangelized at the ends of the earth. As Swete said,

> He Himself [i.e. the Spirit] is the cause of the progressive witness of Christendom to Christ.[25]

In noticing the place of the Spirit of God in this process, we see the spiritual dynamic which empowers the mission. This is no mere promulgation of good ideas or of a new ethic, nor even of a new philosophy. Underlying, directing, empowering and in fact bringing into being the conditions wherein these new ways of living can be lived, Adomnán shows us the action of the Holy Spirit. He works

---

25   Swete (1912, 314).

through the holy, sacrificially given and open life of this one who acts as a channel for the grace of God, ministered by the Spirit, into a world of unredeemed souls. As these lay themselves open to this grace, so they come into their own experience of the presence of the inaugurated kingdom of God. The seed is planted by the proclamation of the gospel, in places directed by the omniscient Spirit, watered by the river of life flowing through the channel provided in the life of the holy one, and brought to flower by the nurturing presence of the same Spirit. Adomnán records for us all of this, albeit in the background. Adomnán seeks to present Columba as a type of Christ, attended by a similar series of accrediting marvellous phenomena. Following Turner, we see the realization of the kingdom, linking the marvellous with the activity of the eschatological Spirit. This observation pushes us to consider a more sophisticated understanding of the marvellous in Adomnán than simple borrowing of good stories from the gospels would allow. With the identification of this element in Adomnán's writing, made the more important by its implicit nature running through the weave of the tapestry, it is inconceivable that Adomnán is not understanding this continuing ministry of Jesus, worked through his holy servant, in establishing the kingdom on earth, as mission.

Continuity of Signs, Wonders and Spiritual Gifts to the Sixth Century

Adomnán places his report of the marvellously accredited mission of his hero in the sixth century AD. He thus claims contemporary experience of the phenomena we are studying, but is there any reason to suppose that he is doing other than adopting the signs of the apostle, the signs of the kingdom, from scripture, and transferring them onto his subject in an exercise of literary composition. Secondly, is there any evidence that the thaumaturgical tradition into which Adomnán evidently wishes to place his subject was anything but a literary tradition in the life of the church to his day; in other words, that the same process of a literary continuation of biblical 'authentication' tales was all Adomnán was building upon. It will be helpful to pursue the answers to the second part of the question first, as the results of this will have a bearing on the answer we can formulate to the first.

Continuity

Was the hagiographical / thaumaturgical tradition in which Adomnán writes simply a literary genre? Is there any evidence for the presence of the marvellous manifestations of the kingdom, by the Spirit, in the life of the church up to Adomnán's day in any sources other than the hagiographical / thaumaturgical? What were the attitudes of pre-seventh-century orthodox Christians to these 'gifts of the Spirit'? Answering this question is hampered by a dearth of published writing and research into these aspects of the manifest activity of the Spirit.[26] The major attention of Christian thinkers and writers has been drawn to the Trinitarian problem of the nature and place of the Spirit in the Godhead. As a result, Patristic writings and their expositors have said little concerning the question we seek enlightenment on here. However, the witness of the Fathers is not silent, if, as I have done with the *VC*, the question is pursued at the level of underlying thoughts that crop up almost incidentally. Three such studies have recently demonstrated in the writings of the pre- and post-Nicene fathers a record of the continuation of both the awareness of and, if the witness be accepted as at all reliable, the occurrence of such manifestations in the post-biblical era. Evelyn Frost (1940), then Ronald Kydd (1973 and 1984) survey the period up to Nicea for the range of charismatic gifts, and Kelsey (1973) gives what Turner calls a 'balanced account of the witness of the fourth and fifth-century fathers' with regard to then contemporary divine healing.[27]

These three surveys, representing the opening reconnaissance of hitherto uncharted territory, clearly demonstrate the presence in the patristic and later records of the contemporary understanding and practice of the type of phenomena that Adomnán attributes to Columba in the sixth century. Turner records the lament of the nineteenth-century fundamentalist cessationist Benjamin Warfield that many claims for post-biblical miracles come from leading theological thinkers.[28] Warfield rejected post-biblical and

---

26   As Kelsey (1973, 158) avers in reference to part of the range of pneumatic phenomena.

27   Turner (1996, 300, note 47). Kelsey (1973, 136-154) cites Justin, Origen, Cyprian, Tertullian, Irenaeus, Quadratus, Theophilus of Antioch, Arnobius, Lactantius (eC4). He can say, 'For nearly three centuries this healing... was an indispensable ingredient of Christian life' (154). For the post Constantinian church, (159ff.) he cites the accounts of the ten major figures, Athanasius, Basil the Great, Gregory Nyssa, Gregory Nazianzen, John Chrysostom, Ambrose, Augustine, Jerome, Gregory I, Sulpicius Severus [who says many healed pagans went away believers, 191] and Cassian. He calls these the 'sophisticated and brilliant men who laid the intellectual foundations of all mainline Christianity' (161). He also cites the four historians Eusebius, Sozomen, Socrates Scholasticus, and Theodoret; and Palladius, Hippolytus, Innocent I, and Bede. He notes that Jerome and Ambrose concentrated more on the symbolic meaning than on the phenomena *per se* (194).

28   Benjamin Warfield, *Counterfeit Miracles*, 38, cited in Turner (1996, 300). Now See Petersen (1984), chapter 4; 'The Miracle-Stories in the Dialogues seen in

contemporary miraculous occurrence on the curiously modernist grounds of radical scepticism, employed because of his *a priori* belief in the cessation of the miracles after the apostolic age. He does not apply the same standard of proof to biblical miracles.[29] Working from the more open-minded perspective from which we have been analyzing the *VC*, we see that the evidence presented by these early fathers, along for example with that of the post-Nicene 'founder' of monasticism, John Cassian (d. after 430);[30] the respected historian of the Franks, Gregory of Tours (d. 594);[31] erstwhile outstanding lawyer and bridge between the ancient and medieval world, Gregory the Great (d. 604);[32] and encyclopaedist polymath 'schoolmaster of the Middle Ages', Isidore of Seville (d. 636), is consistent in its presentation, in non hagiographical writing as well as the hagiographic genre, of the presence of these phenomena in the experience of the church right up to and including the time of Columba's mission.

Three particularly interesting example of non-hagiographic occurrence deserve special, if cursory mention. The first and second arise because of the reference in the *Amra* to the familiarity of Columba with the judgements of Basil (IV.10), and the books of

---

the context of Other Western Christian Writers: A. The attitude of Augustine towards Miracles' (90-94). Augustine began as a cessationist, but by 427, evinced by *Civ. Dei*, he accepted modern miraculous occurrence.

29   See Turner (1996, 286-302) for recent critique of the cessationist position, and Kelsey (1973, 22-3) for its foundation in the early (but not later) writings of Luther, and in Calvin's Institutes (IV.18). Kelsey attributes the position ultimately to the growth of sceptical rationalism from the sixteenth century onwards. Stanley Grenz identifies Warfield's reaction as a version of modernist positivism in Grenz (2000, 73-77).

30   Kelsey (1973, 195) notes Cassian's preface to his account of healing (*Coll* 15.2, below). Cassian emphasized that healing came not as a result of monastic merit, but by the Lord's compassion, and warned against its too ready practice for fear of losing personal inward purity. It makes me wonder if Columba/Adomnán had been influenced by the same attitude in restricting the occurrence of healing, cf. *VSM*, in which, as Kelsey observes healing predominates (189), though *VC* is not reticent to mention healing, e.g. ii.6, and see the section in chapter four above.

31   Who wrote eight *Miraculorum Libri*.

32   Four books of *Dialogues*. Kelsey (194ff.) notes the development from Jerome and Cassian to Gregory (in his *Pastoral Rule* which though brought by Augustine to Canterbury, does not appear to have influenced Adomnán) of a growing attitude toward illness as a tool of divine discipline, rather than demonic attack, and thus bringing a diminution of emphasis on healing as a vital ministry. He regards this development to have affected Western attitudes to illness and healing into modern times, and Gregory's undiscerning attitude towards miracles as tending toward credulity. However, Kelsey emphasizes their acceptance of the expectation of divine, miraculous, intervention.

Cassian (V.6).[33] As key figures in the development of monasticism, such familiarity is highly plausible for the coenobites of Iona.

BASIL THE GREAT

In his introduction to the ascetic works of Basil the Great, W.K.L. Clarke expresses his view that the study of Basil's understanding of the spiritual gifts is 'of great importance for the understanding of Basilian monasticism and deserves a full monograph in English'.[34] The monograph has yet to appear, but Basil's treatment of these phenomena may help to throw light upon that of Adomnán, who stands in the same monastic tradition. For Basil, who, Clarke reminds us, was 'the brilliant theologian to whom we owe *De Spirito Sancto'*, enthusiasm (by which he means spiritual giftedness)

> ...meant the reproduction of the first ages of the church, when Pentecost was a living memory and the baptized were all filled with the Spirit.[35]

Clarke considers the power of the *Rules* to be due to its author knowing the Spirit experimentally as well as theoretically. Basil's primary concern is to argue for coenobitic rather than solitary life, and one of the elements of his argument derives from Paul's descriptions of the gifts, which are complete only where the body of Christ operates in coenobitic fashion. The contemporary manifestation of the charismatic gifts are not procurable by money; they must be shared freely; their worthy use brings further distribution; they are not to be used for personal glory; and they are diversely distributed (*Morals* LVIII-LX). The *Longer Rule* states that Christ bestows the working of signs and marvellous works in the Holy Spirit, though love is the sign of discipleship (F.3); and that no single man is sufficient to receive all gifts; they are common property, for the common good (F.7). Various groups of the gifts are mentioned: 'spiritual gifts' (F.35:380B); knowledge and wisdom (F.32); teaching, revelation, tongues, interpretation to edify (F.40); teaching, exhortation, prophecy (B.303); and healing (F.55:398C). Basil specifically mentions obedience to the commands of Christ as qualification for the reception of the Spirit (B.204), and most significantly for Abbot Columba, states that the Superior of a coenobium needs the gift of foreseeing the future, he being the eye of the body (F.24, 43).

This highlighting of Basil's references to the gifts must not be taken as suggesting he ranked them highly. Love comes far above.

---

33   O. Chadwick (1968, 37-8) says *Conferences* were more widely read than *Institutes* (49).

34   W.K.L. Clarke (1925, 42).

35   Clarke (1925, 44).

But the fact is, he describes them as present and operative in his coenobia. Clarke considers that in contrast to Paul, they act as a crown to ethical sanctification, a tradition in which Adomnán stands, despite Basil's insistence that they not be used as a measure of greatness (*Mor.* LX). We should note that Basil also says they are given in proportion to faith (*Mor.* LVIII), a factor reminding us of Adomnán's 'flowering of faith'?

JOHN CASSIAN

Dallán does not specify which of Cassian's works Columba knew, but the Ionan writers of *Amra* and *Altus Prosator* certainly had Cassian's *Conferences* 2, 8 and 14.[36] The *Conferences* contain numerous references to the rôle of the Holy Spirit,[37] and incidental references to various charismatic gifts, and also a more deliberate consideration of their place in the life of the Christian community (see especially *Conference* 2). While insecure as records of the teaching of the hermits, these documents contain Cassian's own views, however derived, and thus as a minimum give us an impression of his claimed experience and attitude towards these phenomena. Although primarily a champion of solitary asceticism, in recognising its dangers Cassian wishes with Basil to emphasize that the highest and abiding gift is love shown to a neighbour (e.g. 15:2,7). As a result, and because the gifts will, with faith and knowledge, die away, he says

> Hence we never see the Fathers caught up in these wonderworkings. By the grace of the Holy Spirit they were possessors of such capacities but they never wanted to use them unless they were coerced by utter, unavoidable necessity.'[38]

Nevertheless, he teaches that the other gifts should be expected to be present in the body of Christ as represented in the communities. *Conference* 15 is dedicated to a general consideration of the gifts. *Conference* 2 concerns the gifts, especially discernment, the gift which Cassian considers the most important. *Conference* 14 concerns spiritual knowledge. He mentions specifically healing (14:19; 15:1,4,5,8), prophecy (14:8; 15:2), casting out demons (14:7,19; 15:7,8), and raising the dead (15:3). Overall terms might be 'higher gifts of the Holy Spirit' (1:11) or 'apostolic signs' (14:4). They are for temporal use and need (1:11). In addition, the preface to the *Institutes* reads

> I shall make no attempt to relate tales of miracles and prodigies. I have heard from my elders of amazing marvels, and have seen some with my

---

36   C&M, 217, 229, 232-3, 248.
37   Cassian, *Coll.,* Lubheid (1985, 47; 53; 60; 138; 163; 176; 201).
38   Cassian, *Coll* 15.2, tr. Lubheid (1985).

own eyes. But I have wholly omitted them. They contribute nothing but astonishment and do not otherwise instruct the reader in the life of holiness.'[39]

Adomnán evidently does not share this negative view of the marvellous as instructive of holiness. However, far from denying the continuation of the marvellous, Cassian here affirms his own experience of marvels. He is concerned that focussing upon them should not obscure the path required of a monk desiring to achieve the holiness from which they proceed.[40] He does not reject them as occurring in any sense.

GREGORY I

The third significant figure, already discussed as a source for Adomnán, is Gregory the Great.[41] In his discussion of diversity in the domain of souls, Gregory illustrates his thesis with reference to Paul's list of gifts of the Spirit in 1 Corinthians 12

> One man by faith commands the elements, but does not cure bodily sickness by the gift of healing; another removes disease by the aid of prayer but does not, by his word, bring down the rain to the thirsty earth. This man, by working of miracles, restores even the dead to the present life, and yet, not possessing the gift of prophecy does not know what will befall him tomorrow; another sees what is to come as though it were already present and yet does not reveal himself as a wonder-worker. One man, through the discerning of spirits, penetrates to the motives behind men's actions but does not possess the gift of tongues; another possesses the gift of tongues but does not discern the diverse motives which underlie similar behaviour; yet another, who knows only one language, wisely interprets the meanings of words [of Holy Scripture], while patiently bearing the lack of all the other gifts which he does not possess.[42]

Gregory's interest here is not the gifts themselves, rather in the rôles of different individuals in a community of faith. However, I would

---

39   Cassian, *Inst*, Pref. (*SC* 109), tr. O. Chadwick (1968, 51).

40   For Cassian only the monk who had achieved perfect holiness ought to go to the wilderness (Chadwick, 1968, 54; see *Coll*. 15.6; 19). Herein lies a question for Columba: did he know this advice as he left Ireland on his peregrination, i.e. did he believe he had achieved perfection, or was his peregrination not this Egyptian type of seeking desert solitude at all?

41   Now see McCready (1989 and 1994), who asserts Gregory's continued belief in the historical veracity of contemporary miracles. Though in the then modern, established church they were less prominent than in the mission situation, they are still needed for inner conversion. Gregory saw the miracles not as proving sainthood, but as proceeding from it (McCready, 1994, 231).

42   Gregory I *Moralia* XXVIII.21 (*PL* 76, 461), tr. Paul Meyvaert, 'Diversity within unity, a Gregorian Theme', chap. VI in: Meyvaert (1977, 147-8).

concur with Meyvaert that he does seem to refer to their operation from the point of view of contemporary experience, i.e. he is not simply paraphrasing Paul, but is describing a series of phenomena he has observed himself. The fact that the reference to the gifts is incidental to his main interest adds to the conclusion that Gregory knew of these gifts in operation in his day. Adomnán is, in contrast, happy to attribute many of the gifts as being administered by Columba. He seems to recognise a distribution at the point of need rather than the permanent possession of one or other spiritual ability.

Secondly, the work Bede calls the '*Libellus Responsionum* of Gregory I' is addressed to his delegate Augustine of Canterbury.[43] In this, the commissioning bishop hears of miracles being performed through his missionary. He warns him not to let this lead him into prideful arrogance, to remember the source of the power as God's grace, and that the gifts have been conferred not on him, but on the recipients of their benefits for the purpose of leading them to faith in Christ.

> I know, most beloved brother, that Almighty God, out of love for you has worked great miracles through you for the race which it was his will to have among the chosen. It is therefore necessary that you should rejoice with trembling over this heavenly gift and fear as you rejoice. You will rejoice because the souls of the English are drawn by outward miracles to inward grace... amidst those outward deeds which you perform through the Lord's power you should always judge your inner self carefully and carefully note within yourself what you are and how great is the grace shown to that people for whose conversion you have received the gift of working miracles... whatever power of working miracles you have received or shall receive, consider that these gifts have been conferred not on you, but on those for whose salvation they have been granted you.[44]

This letter is important for a number of reasons. First, it further confirms the existence of the expectation of and belief in the practice of miracles in the mind of the foremost influence on the church of the day. Secondly, he here describes them as marvellous, divinely empowered gifts. Thirdly, more could be expected, 'whatever power... you shall receive'. Fourthly, and most important to our discussion, Gregory is certain that the purpose of the miracles is to bring the English to faith; they are 'drawn by outward miracle to

---

43   Meyvaert puts the case for the Gregorian authenticity. Bede himself, another otherwise 'respectable' scholar, is also critically accepting of the occurrence in his day of miracles. See Meyvaert, 'Bede the Scholar', chap. IX in: Meyvaert (1977, 51-55).

44   Bede *HE* I.31.

inward grace'; Augustine has 'received the gift of working miracles' for their 'conversion'; the gifts are conferred on those 'for whose salvation they have been granted' through Augustine. All this is referring to a period directly contemporary with Columba's own peregrination in The Provinces. While there is no direct and incontrovertible evidence that Columba himself was influenced by Gregorian missiological pneumatology, the discussion in appendix 2 on the Gregorian passages in the *VC* remove the chronological barrier to such influence. We can thus confirm another function of the marvellous in the *VC* being to draw the pagan Scots and Picts to faith. Furthermore, Bede's inclusion of this letter confirms his awareness of the place of the marvellous in the life of a missionary saint. His identification of Columba as such thus has Gregorian authority.

Thus Adomnán writes not only in a biblical tradition, and a hagiographical tradition, but also in the tradition of the writings of no lesser individuals than the Doctors of the Church,[45] and of other major ecclesiastics. It is not simply a literary tradition, promulgated by undeclared borrowing from the biblical record, but constitutes a record, albeit spasmodic and very incomplete, of claims of belief in and practical continuation of these pneumatic phenomena up to the sixth century. The many parallels not just in the Bible but also in the Fathers' writings both commenting on the scriptures, and more generally, show Adomnán to be fully in line with the thinking of the leading churchmen, perhaps the leading thinkers of his day with regard to the marvellous phenomena associated with the work of the Spirit. He is shown not to be writing merely in a rather fringe, extreme pietistic tradition with which hagiography later came to be identified, but writes in the main stream of the Christian tradition of his day, echoing the comments of his great teachers on the work of the Spirit in his own presentation of his more immediate patron.

Originality

To return then to the first part of our question, is there any reason to believe that Adomnán is doing anything other than aping the tradition of heaping borrowed marvels onto his hero?

OTHER CHARACTERS

We have noted already that Adomnán, while influenced by earlier writers, displays a considerable degree of original thought. Another of these aspects, with significance added by their incidental background nature, is the accrediting of marvels to persons other than the main

---

45   Isidore was declared a 'Doctor of the Church' in 1722.

character. *VC* includes various other characters who exercise some of the gifts.

Brendán of Birr has a revelation of a pillar of fiery brightness and an apparition of angels accompanying Columba (iii.3). The main point is to vindicate Columba and to present his closeness to heaven, but the person with the vision in this case is Brendan. He was Columba's senior, and may have been involved in his training. If Adomnán is not simply inventing, we might be observing the exercise of *ta pneumatika* in the previous generation.

Colmán mac Beógnai is depicted as being caught in the whirlpool of Corryvreckan. The main point of the story is Columba's gift of knowledge. However, it is Colman who, like Jesus in Luke 8, is prompted and 'raises both hands to heaven and blesses the troubled and very terrible sea' (i.5). We are not told if he was successful, but he didn't die until 611(AU), and evidently joined the community (ii.15), which he appears to have been on his way to do.

Silnán mac Nemaidon delivers gifts of healings to the victims of the pestiferous cloud, and his testimony is witnessed by Abbot Ségéne (ii.4). Similarly, another of the Ionan brethren, Lugaid mac Tailchán, conveys a blessing to heal an injured virgin, and his vision is recorded as having been passed down in writing (iii.23:131ab). This brings an interesting theological question: if healing comes from God, and Adomnán makes it clear that all of Columba's power is from God, was it Columba, who blessed the *eulogium*, or Silnán / Lugaid, who applied the intinction, who communicated the gift of healing to the recipients? If the latter, then we have further names to add to Adomnán's list of spiritually gifted sixth-century Christians.

Cainnech moccu Dalann, abbot of Aghaboe (d. ca.600) is described as having 'by revelation of the Holy Spirit heard in the inner ear of his heart' words of Columba in trouble at sea. He abandons his monks at their meal, and prays for the voyagers. Calm descended immediately. Adomnán explains that he believed the prayers of both the holy ones worked together in this 'so great miracle' (ii.13).

Baithéne, who would become second abbot in 597 knew about Columba's spirit meeting them (i.37). We also read of him turning the whale away (ii.19).

Other individuals are: The monk Librán, who speaks to Columba 'in the spirit' and miraculously changes the wind (ii.39). The monk Ernéne has a vision, related in person to Adomnán (iii.23:132a). Colgu mac Áedo Draigniche is the bearer of the Johannine gift of forgiveness (i.17). He (iii.20); Fergnae (d. 623), who became fourth abbot of Iona in 605 (iii.19); Columba's foster-son Berchán mes loen (iii.21); Diarmait, Columba's faithful attendant, with a few other brothers (iii.23:129b); and an anonymous 'spy' (iii.16), all see the heavenly light. More commonplace examples include the British disciple of Patrick, Mochta (d.535), who has a prophecy of Columba's birth; Columba's foster-father Cruithnechán sees his house filled with light, and a ball of fire (iii.2), and Brendán moccu Altae (the Navigator) also sees a ball of fire (iii.17); Uinniau (Columba's master) sees an angel accompanying Columba (iii.4); and Columba's Mother is visited by an angel in a dream and receives a vision (iii.1). The very nature of Adomnán's casual mentioning of the involvement, particularly of the less commonplace examples, is suggestive of a certain familiarity with such phenomena extant in Iona's tradition. We may thus have a moving picture not just of a saint, but of a whole community active in exercising the gifts of the Holy Spirit which the NT argues will accompany the proclamation of the kingdom.

THE CHARACTER OF THE *VC*

Adomnán's account of Columba, while retaining elements of similarity with the *Lives* of Antony, Martin, Germanus, and Benedict, is nevertheless possessed of its own character, analytical structure and emphases, and cannot be shown to be reliant on any single author for its terminology. He writes in the received currency of his tradition, a characteristic shared by all writers in all times. He finds common terminology and historical explanation for contemporary puzzling pneumatic phenomena. His emphases are distinctive, as is his often mentioned *taxis*. Athanasius gives particular attention to demonic encounter, rare in *VC*. Sulpicius Severus majors on healing, which forms only a small though significant rôle in *VC*. Gregory's account of Benedict, while providing some of Adomnán's interpretive understanding of the prophetic, reads far more as a random collection of tales with no discernible structure relating to analysis of the marvellous. Constantius attributes powerful preaching substantiated by healings, various miracles, and encounters with Pelagian and other opposing groups, to Germanus, who hardly moves in the prophetic, Adomnán's major category of the marvellous.

Adomnán's uniqueness, firmly rooted in the catholic tradition, argues strongly for his working with a locally originated tradition concerning his own patron. It becomes less and less conceivable that his work is merely the product of eclectic borrowing from elsewhere, supplemented by occasional local tales, and local circumstantial detail. If we dismiss his marvellous tales as merely the product of inventive imagination, we must likewise dismiss the huge body of non-hagiographic evidence for the occurrence of these pneumatic phenomena in the life of the church. The only basis upon which this wholesale rewriting of the texts can be achieved is to apply a rigorously sceptic demythologizing epistemology, and not a scrutiny of the evidence in its historical context.

Thus we can confirm that Adomnán is operating firmly within the received tradition of his ecclesiastical forbears, while adding a special insight. His account of the marvellous phenomena surrounding Columba and his wider community of faith traces a dynamic experience of these phenomena predicted for the mission field of the church, now here in the Provinces of the Isles of Ocean. The marvellous in the *VC* have an eschatological, pneumatological and missiological nature and function.

Columba the Ascetic Missionary

The portrait Adomnán paints of Columba provides for his readers, ourselves included, a particularly vivid picture of one who has become transformed into the likeness of the Son of God (Rom. 8:29). The picture is itself eschatologically significant as an example of the transformation that can occur in one who lives life in close communion with the Spirit of God. Thus he is a model to which men can aspire, acting, as it were, as a bridge to the perfect likeness of God revealed in Christ, Christ on whom Adomnán's Columba is so carefully fashioned. To put it another way, the likeness of Christ was recognized in the life of the holy one Columba. This is, as Sherry points out, a conventional understanding of sainthood, but it may go further. The second Vatican Council links holiness in the present saint with the future eschatological kingdom to which believers are drawn, assisted by the image of the transformation in the saint

> When we look at the lives of those who have faithfully followed Christ, we are inspired with a new reason for seeking the city which is to come...
> In the lives of those who shared in our humanity and yet were transformed into especially successful images of Christ (cf. 2 Cor. 3:18), God visibly manifests to men His presence and His face. He speaks to us in them, and gives us a sign of His kingdom to which we are powerfully drawn.[46]

---

46 *Lumen Gentium* §50, in Abbott and Gallagher (1966, 82), cited in Sherry (1984, 34). Sherry concludes that the continuous existence of saints in the history of the Christian faith is important devotionally and philosophically. They provide reminders of Christ's likeness, of the transforming power of holiness anticipating the eschaton. They have an evidential role for the presence and power of the Holy Spirit, and for the reality of eschatological immortality (83). He notes Perham's comment (1980, 48) on Luther and Calvin as quarrelling 'with false saints and false honour to saints, not the idea that some men and women can be held up as special examples of the grace of God at work.'

Sherry notes a second connected function of the saint as one who demonstrates in his/her life that God's eschatologically oriented grace, salvation, donation of Spirit etc. *has* happened, it is no mere theoretical possibility

> God really *has* redeemed, he really *has* poured out his Spirit, he really *has* done mighty things for sinners, he *has* let his light shine in the darkness.[47]

This would suggest a function of the *VC* as itself evangelistic in addition to recording evangelism; it proclaims the present salvation of God, as foretold in the Scripture, as demonstrated in the marvellously accompanied life of Columba. Here is evidence his pagan readers in Pictland (and elsewhere) might consider as they weigh the truth claims of the Ionan Christian Mission, just as Patrick identified himself as a letter from God, as we've noticed (*Conf.* VII.37-9), cf.

> You show that you are a letter from Christ, the result of our ministry, written not with ink but with the Spirit of the living God, not on tablets of stone but on tablets of human hearts (2Cor. 3:3).

In chapter three, we noticed Isaiah 35 as a background to Adomnán's picture of the kingdom blossoming. We have an eschatological vision of the blooming of the desert

> The desert and the parched land will be glad; the wilderness will rejoice and blossom. Like the crocus, it will burst into bloom; it will rejoice greatly and shout for joy. The glory of Lebanon will be given to it, the splendour of Carmel and Sharon; they will see the glory of the LORD, the splendour of our God (Isa. 35:1-2).

We can almost see in this prophecy the outline plan for the whole of the *VC*: In our conventional understanding of Irish peregrination, the wilderness would be interpreted in the mind of the ascetic pilgrim as the ocean fastness where he/she sought solitude in which to live his/her holy life. The establishment of the monastery brings about the establishment of the kingdom in that place; it blooms at that point, as it were. Adomnán's picture of the robe spreading out (iii.1) shows the spreading of monastic establishments connected with the mother house, and the monastic, ascetic kingdom is established following the intention of the promulgators.

However, if we look closely at the picture Adomnán paints in this vision of the robe, and combine this with the evidence of the content of the stories he gathers to make his point, we see a more intricate picture emerging. The governing metaphor is of the kingdom

---

47   Karl Rahner (1967, 94), cited in Sherry (1984, 35).

consisting in the flowering of faith. While it is true that many of the tales in the *VC* have an insular monastic location, Herbert's 'Iona stratum', and contain much circumstantial evidence of the life of these institutions, they almost all deal with the individual lives of people who interact with the monastery, or more specifically with its ministers, and whose lives are recorded as having changed as a result. Here we must bear in mind Richard Sharpe's questioning of the monastic image historians hold in mind when thinking of these places: are we too heavily influenced by our extensive knowledge of the high medieval monasticism of a later era than that which we are here considering?[48] Sharpe (1992) is concerned to identify the pastoral ministry of the monasteries. He draws out similarities between these institutions and the minster churches of the Saxons whose mode of operation was the establishment of daughter houses, but whose objective, in spiritual terms at least, was the extension of, and care for, the community of faith. In other words, using the language of the gospels and of Adomnán, the object was the extension and nurture of the kingdom of God.

Following this more missionary and pastorally active interpretation of the character of the sixth/seventh century Irish/Scottish church, we see that the wilderness may also be taken as describing the people, in their geographical locale, who have yet to be reached with the gospel of salvation; the people in and amongst whom the kingdom was yet to flower. Columba is seen as the one who, like Christ and the apostles in the New Testament, plants the seed of the gospel, and brings this kingdom into flower. As a result, the people rejoice. The process is definitely not restricted only to the members of the monasteries Adomnán mentions. This eschatological joy is described also of the *laos*, those outside the *valla*. The splendour of God is seen in the signs of the marvellous manifestations of his power, working through his servant, which the people acknowledge, and of course it finds its most exquisite expression in the *shekinah* of God seen around the holy man. Again, though primarily reported as evident on Iona, this is is not restricted to the island, but is also seen from far away (iii.23). All of these signs of the presence of the kingdom; converts; other marvellous manifestations; churches/monasteries, are the flowers of many different colour to which the vision refers.

---

48   Sharpe (1995, note 367) mentions the tendency in past discussion of the spread of the Irish church 'to exaggerate the part played by monastic foundations over those established for pastoral reasons.' And now see Etchingham (1999) for a development of this caution.

Bringing the Desert into Bloom

Thus we see Columba's peregrination into the wilderness as
containing within its compass, if not as its major objective, a mission
to establish the kingdom of God in the lives of the people of the
region. The interpretation may be confirmed to a degree by the
vision Jonas ascribes to the Irish missionary to continental Europe,
Columbanus. He sees an image of the circle of the earth with desert
spaces left for him to work in, and an angel commands him to go as
he wills.[49] Now the kingdom of God in the gospels is not a
geographical area of hegemony equivalent to the earthly kingdoms in
which Jesus and the Apostles operated. Rather it is the rule of God as
accepted and enacted in the lives of those who submit to its
authority. Membership of the kingdom depends upon an acceptance
of the authority and the ability of God to intervene in earthly affairs,
and brings with it the promise and hope of the new creation when
this rule will be perfectly established. Direct divine interventions in
this age act as promissory signs of the kingdom, and signs which are,
as Turner puts it, concrete expressions, or actualizations of the
direct, perfecting rule of God breaking in from the future new
creation. In other words, and to change the metaphor, these are the
first fruits of the new creation. In one sense these bring back the
conditions of the original creation, where there was no desert
wilderness

> And God said, 'Let the earth put forth vegetation, plants yielding seed,
> and fruit trees bearing fruit in which is their seed, each according to its
> kind, upon the earth.' And it was so. The earth brought forth vegetation,
> plants yielding seed according to their own kinds, and trees bearing fruit
> in which is their seed, each according to its kind. And God saw that it
> was good (Gen. 1:11-12).

Greatly superseding this sense however, the phenomena look
forward to the perfect conditions of the new creation, which is itself
only imperfectly visualized in the pre-eschatological age. For
Adomnán, then, the kingdom spreads as faith-in-action spreads;
either faith being placed in Christ in a conversion, or faith being
exercised in God's present power to intervene. The converse, lack of
faith, is wilderness: creation fallen from its creator's intention;
Christians living without exercising faith in the omnipotence of the
God of the promise of a perfected future. Further flowering occurs as
pagans do accept the gospel in faith, and give glory to the 'God of
the Christians'. Their faith breaks into flower in the desert of the

---

49   *Vita Columbani* i.27 (MGH SRM 4, 104). Though Wood (1982, 75) suggests
     Jonas was interpolating this missionary interest, R.A. Markus (1992, 163)
     shows that the saint's disciples demonstrated mission in vigorous practice.

wilderness, bringing joy, and blessing to the bearers, and, perhaps, to those with whom their new found faith is shared.

Thus we see not a politicized preaching mission, as Martin or Patrick, but a mission after the pattern of the New Testament. The missionaries adopt the same commission (Mt. 28:19-20; Mk. 16:15-18; Lk. 9:1-2, 10:1-12, 27:47-49; Acts 1:8, etc.), use the same methodology, and the same tools (1 Cor. 12 etc.), and see very similar results. The process of establishing the kingdom, in which Adomnán presents Columba as being engaged during his peregrination, based as it is in the scriptural account of the establishment of the kingdom, is what a scriptural writer would understand as 'mission'. It is mission before the advent of the institutional church when mission became associated with the establishment of such institutions. Adomnán is not concerned with the latter, Tirechánian definition of mission. We have seen that he deems the biblical definition of mission to be central to his understanding of what Columba was engaged upon.

Conclusion

The elements are now in place for us to trace a possible blueprint for Julia Smith's *alembic* with which to distil the essence of sanctity in Adomnán's mind, and to draw conclusions as to the nature and function of the marvellous in his *Life of Columba*.

1. We see that far from being based in, or even significantly influenced by Irish pagan myth and saga, this *Life* is based on the canonical authority of Christian scripture, either first hand, or as interpreted through the Fathers of the church. Herein are its motivations, models, means, and a substantial part of its imagery.

2. Behind the sharp foreground of the particular subject of Columba himself, the background of the work, in soft focus, is the establishment and demonstration of the presence of the kingdom of God in Dál Riata, Pictland and the Isles.

3. The eschatological Spirit is seen as the dynamic motivator and motivation, the guide and empowerer, the bringer of joy and new life. The Spirit overcomes the conditions of a creation fallen away from the perfection of existence in union with the Creator; bringing things back into that relationship with healing, prosperity, and joy.

4. The missiological gifts of the Spirit, utilized to such effect by Christ and his immediate disciples who pioneered the evangelization of the world, are powerfully present.

5. The eschatologically oriented commission is seen clearly to be in action, and in the minds of the people into which we are probing,

to be nearing its completion as the word of the Lord reaches the ends of the earth, and the last day thus approaches.

6. The word of God is proclaimed, heard, received, accepted by pagans of the area who thus enter into the heavenly kingdom.

The evidence of the marvellous in the *VC* points to the conclusion then that this *Life* intends to record the Spirit of the Risen Christ reaching close to the ends of the known earth at the climax of over 600 years of the mission to establish the kingdom of God in all the earth. The fact that this feature of the *Life* is implicitly captured as the spiritual stage upon which Columba acts makes the argument for its presence in Adomnán's thought the more cogent. This study has engaged in the task of learning to read Adomnán in a way which begins to have sympathy with what we have sought to discern as his own eschatological pneumatological missiological thought patterns and interpretive frameworks.

Adomnán is being confirmed as one whose intimate knowledge of the scriptures is profound, as noticed by Bede in his own era. The Bible forms the thoughts and provides the imagery he expresses in his writings. It has become an imperative that in reading this *Life*, as in the Irish saga materials, and other early Irish literature, the reader must first come to know in detail, theologically, and in 'feel', the narrative which undergirds the thought world of those who wrote in these times: the Bible. That a major function of the *Life of Columba* has been shown to be not only the exegesis of scripture in abstract, but in practical terms consisting in its spiritual principles being outworked in tangible physical form, only serves to highlight this foundational axiom. Far from acting as a disqualifier of his genuineness, and as sign of inventive dissimulation, Adomnán's continual allusion to scripture is of profound importance to his purpose in associating Columba with orthodox Christian tradition. He not only wishes to show his patron's status as equivalent to his marvellously-accredited Irish, British and continental peers (or rivals, depending on one's perspective) but he wishes to show him as yet one more in the line of those in whom God is seen to reveal himself in transcendent reality. This line reaches back to the beginnings of history in the encounter of Moses with God. Columba is in this line. More even than this, in Columba's ministry, Adomnán sees the incarnation, the partial realization, or becoming tangibly present, of the promised kingdom of God in his own era and amongst his own people. He writes in an attempt to describe how this has come to pass. Constant allusion to scripture, in his context, can only add authority to his argument. To dismiss his case on account of this is to import into our assessment of his work a post-enlightenment and thus anachronistic category by which he has been judged and found wanting. He would no doubt have seen the want rather in modern epistemology.

We cannot hope to satisfy an historical question of occurrence; but we can and must consider the beliefs, and understandings, which drove the imagination of this author to produce such finely detailed accounts. Adomnán was not incapable of original and imaginative applications of the concepts that had become embedded in his thought. This seventh-century Abbot took the concepts and expectations of the records of the early Christians, and applied them to his own interpretation of the stories associated with his beloved patron and hero.

We can thus see in the *VC* evidence for seventh-century belief in the nature and function of the operation of the Spirit. Adomnán sees a rôle of the Spirit in the equipping and sending of the members of the church, the saints in a broad sense, to communicate in word and deed the gospel of the coming kingdom. As we have variously reflected, one of Adomnán's unique contributions to this investigation is his division of the *VC* into the three books concerning prophecy, miracles and visions. In so doing he has provided a snapshot of the view he held of this very activity of the Spirit in the ongoing mission of the church. It is from this missionary context that I am claiming he is making his report on Columba. In this he has the precedent of the great Augustine who gathered his *libelli* of miracles at the tomb of St. Stephen with the intention of convincing the pagan *intelligencia* of his day of the veracity of the faith.[50] Thus we have in the *VC* a datum from which further investigation into the missiological activity of the Spirit can be viewed, and comparisons made.

Adomnán's *Life of Columba* forms for us who read it after the intervening ages a powerful record of the intricacies of belief in the marvellous phenomena it records. Here is no random imagination on record, but a way of thinking and believing which is deeply fashioned by the Christian tradition which it is the writer's purpose to nurture. He presents himself, and his subject, as Christians fully conversant with, and expectant of the present reality of, a tradition of Christian practice as recorded in the canonical and patristic record. The evidence points us to the conclusion that for Adomnán, in his contemporary culture, these phenomena are both real, and to be expected, as the kingdom of God is promulgated.

We began with the proposition that the knowledge of reality may not be the exclusive preserve of the latest philosophical fashion(s), and therefore that those who lived in earlier ages, with their own

---

50   P. Brown (1967, 413-418); *Civ. Dei* XXII:8.

perception of reality, might profitably be called upon to contribute to the task of interpreting the nature of the universe in which we have all lived. The question I hope to have opened up in this dissertation is less dogmatic than the assertion either of occurrence or of imaginative construction. It has much to do with the way we as readers approach such documentation. Adomnán was an intelligent, cognitive and articulate individual, operating within a highly educated community. He continued to assert, against definite sceptical questioning, the continuation in the sixth-seventh century of phenomena which were recorded in the origins of the faith many centuries before. Is it barely possible that the ancients had a grasp of reality which was wider and more inclusive than the moderns, a grasp of reality which reached beyond the material confines of present 'reality' into the eternal and infinite space which enfolds and indwells the material in which so much understanding is invested?

Adomnán leaves us the legacy of his interpretation of these phenomena, which we in turn must interpret in order to gain understanding. On the basis of the evidence Adomnán records of the life of his predecessor, and in particular of the apologetic arguments into which he enters, it would not be unreasonable to suppose he might have had the thought of Paul of Tarsus in mind as he wrote

> The unspiritual man does not receive the gifts of the Spirit of God, for they are folly to him, and he is not able to understand them, because they are spiritually discerned (1 Cor. 2:14).

In the light of this seventh-century abbot's view of the marvellous, we have illuminated the views and consequent methodologies of a community which was so instrumental in bringing the news of the holy man of Palestine to the Provinces of the Isles of the Ocean..

APPENDICES

Appendix 1: Distribution of Marvellous Phenomena in the *Vita Columbae*

A close study of the *VC* reveals the following distributions of individual phenomena presented as occurring in Columba's lifetime, counting one for each individual manifestation, rather than chapters in which they occur. Counting such phenomena is not a simple task for a number of reasons. A single event may be variously described, but should properly only count as a single event e.g. i.3 tells of Columba's discerning with spiritual sight the presence behind him of a boy touching his cloak. Should this be counted as a gift of knowledge, spiritual sight, vision or discernment? I have counted it as an example of a vision on the basis that spiritual sight may be seen to be the same phenomenon as spiritual vision, a more frequent description of such phenomena in the *VC*. As we have seen, Augustine asserts the existence of such inner vision. Similarly in iii.3, Brendan sees fiery light accompanying Columba. This I have counted only as the phenomenon of light, regardless of how it is discerned. If it is a vision, it is a vision of light. If seen in the natural, with bodily eyes, it is the phenomenon of light. It should not count as both a vision, and as the phenomenon of light. In iii.7, Adomnán says Columba has a vision over three nights of an angel visiting him. However, the angel leaves a physical sign of its presence. Is it then pure vision, or spiritual sight of a real angel present, or a miracle?

Conversely, there are a number of events which do contain multiple types of phenomena operating nearly simultaneously, e.g. iii.8 has two prophecies, two words of knowledge, appearances of angels and demons, and results in a deliverance. These examples illustrate the subjectivity of a number of decisions that have to be made in turning literary accounts into statistical data. They also illustrate the dangers of trying to make the evidence go too far in terms of objective critical analysis. Other cases however are more objective, as in iii.6 where Adomnán specifically infers that Columba sees the angel with his bodily eyes, though even here we might have conjectured that a spiritual vision is in progress.

I here present the collated results in tabular and graphical form to illustrate the method. The prefaces and i.1 are not included as these duplicate other recorded instances, with the exception of the posthumous miracles not recorded elsewhere. Non-specific manifestations, such as the general occurrence of healings noted in ii.6, are not counted. 'Others' count those individual people other than Columba recorded as being the channel for a marvellous phenomenon.

Percentage figures exclude posthumous miracles of Columba, and the numbers of 'others' with recorded marvels. Totals, an arbitrary figure, include all categories. It must be stressed that the scores recorded in these tables are somewhat subjective. The data is presented as a whole with the intention that the derivation of the various figures may be identified by comparison with a copy of the text of the *VC*. The method is thus corrigible, and may be transferred to other similar accounts of marvellous phenomena. Picard, Stancliffe and Davies each published sets of statistical data from the *VC* without this methodology, thus making following their study problematic. I have not followed their various taxonomic methods in this book.

The data above and below have been foundational in my interpretation of Adomnán's presentation, though consciously at the level of broad comparison rather than fine statistical analysis. Further to this end, the data for all categories are presented graphically below. The graphs show at a glance the relative proportions of the various categories, without the rather false impressions that can come from numerical statistical analysis.

Table 1. Distribution of Marvellous Phenomena in VC Book I

	Prophecy	Knowledge	Vision	Healing	Miracle	Vengeance	Angels	Light	Demons	Deliverance	Others	Posthum's	Tot.
i.1											2		2
i.2	1												1
i.3	3		1				1						5
i.4	1	1											2
i.5	1	1									1		3
i.6	1	1											2
i.7	1	1											2
i.8	1	1											2
i.9	1												1
i.10	1												1
i.11	1												1
i.12	1	1											2
i.13	1												1
i.14	1												1
i.15	1												1
i.16	2												2
i.17	2	1									1		4
i.18	2												2
i.19	2	1			1						1		5
i.20	1												1
i.21	1	1											2
i.22	2	2											4
i.23	1	1											2
i.24	1												1
i.25	1												1
i.26	1												1
i.27	1	1											2
i.28	1	1											2
i.29		1	1								1		3
i.30	1	1											2
i.31	1												1
i.32	1												1
i.33	1												1
i.34	1												1
i.35	1	1							1				3
i.36	1	1											2
i.37	1				3						1		5
i.38	1	1											2
i.39	1								1				2
i.40		1											1
i.41	1	2											3
i.42		1											1
i.43	1												1
i.44		1											1
i.45	1												1
i.46	1	1											2
i.47	1												1
i.48	1												1
i.49	1												1
i.50		3											3
	Prophecy	Knowledge	Vision	Healing	Miracle	Vengeance	Angels	Light	Demons	Deliverance	Others	Posthum's	Tot.
Tot.	51	28	2	0	4	0	1	0	2	0	5	2	95

Table 2. Distribution of Marvellous Phenomena in the VC Book II

	Prophecy	Knowledge	Vision	Healing	Miracle	Vengeance	Angels	Light	Demons	Deliverance	Others	Posthum's	Tot.
ii.1					1								1
ii.2					1								1
ii.3	1	1			1								3
ii.4	1			1							1		3
ii.5	1	1		1							1		4
ii.6													0
ii.7					1								1
ii.8												1	1
ii.9												1	1
ii.10	1				1								2
ii.11									1	1			2
ii.12					1								1
ii.13		2	1		1						1		5
ii.14					1								1
ii.15		1			1								2
ii.16					1				1	1			3
ii.17	1				1				1				3
ii.18				1									1
ii.19	1	1			1								3
ii.20	2					1							3
ii.21	1				1								2
ii.22	1				1	1							3
ii.23	1					1							2
ii.24	1					1					1		3
ii.25	1				1	1							3
ii.26					1								1
ii.27					1								1
ii.28	1												1
ii.29	1				1								2
ii.30	1			1									2
ii.31	1			1									2
ii.32				1									1
ii.33	1	1		1		1							4
ii.34					1				1				2
ii.35					1								1
ii.36					1								1
ii.37	1				1				1				3
ii.38	1	1			1								3
ii.39	3	1			1						1		6
ii.40	1	1		1									3
ii.41				1									1
ii.42	2	2			1								5
ii.43					1								1
ii.44							1					1	2
ii.45												1	1
ii.46												1	1
Tot.	26	12	1	9	26	6	1	0	5	2	5	5	98

Table 3. Distribution of Marvellous Phenomena in the Life of Columba Book
III, and Summary for whole VC.

	Prophecy	Knowledge	Vision	Healing	Miracle	Vengeance	Angels	Light	Demons	Deliverance	Others	Posthum's	Tot.
Intro													
iii.1											1		1
iii.2								1			1		2
iii.3	1						1	1			1		4
iii.4							1				1		2
iii.5	1		1				1						3
iii.6							1		1				2
iii.7			1				1						2
iii.8	2	2					1		1	1			7
iii.9		1					1						2
iii.10			2				2	1					5
iii.11			1				1						2
iii.12			1				1						2
iii.13			2				1		1				4
iii.14		1	1				1						3
iii.15		1	1		1		1						4
iii.16		1					1				1		3
iii.17								1			1		2
iii.18		1	1					1			1		4
iii.19		1						1			1		3
iii.20		1						1			1		3
iii.21	1	1						1			1		4
iii.22	1	1					1						3
iii.23	2				1		2	3			3		11
	Prophecy	Knowledge	Vision	Healing	Miracle	Vengeance	Angels	Light	Demons	Deliverance	Others	Posthum's	Tot.
Totals	8	11	11	0	2	0	18	10	4	1	13	0	78

Summary

	Prophecy	Knowledge	Vision	Healing	Miracle	Vengeance	Angels	Light	Demons	Deliverance	Others	Posthum's	Tot.
Bk. I	51	28	2	0	4	0	1	0	2	0	5	2	95
Bk. II	26	12	1	9	26	6	1	0	5	2	5	5	98
Bk. III	8	11	11	0	2	0	18	10	4	1	13	0	78
	Prophecy	Knowledge	Vision	Healing	Miracle	Vengeance	Angels	Light	Demons	Deliverance	Others	Posthum's	Tot.
Tot.	85	51	14	9	32	6	20	10	11	3	23	7	271
%	35.3	28.5	10.4	2.3	13.3	2.5	8.3	4.1	4.6	1.2			

Fɪɢ. 1: Dɪꜱᴛʀɪʙᴜᴛɪᴏɴ ᴏꜰ Mᴀʀᴠᴇʟʟᴏᴜꜱ Pʜᴇɴᴏᴍᴇɴᴀ ɪɴ *Vɪᴛᴀ Cᴏʟᴜᴍʙᴀᴇ*

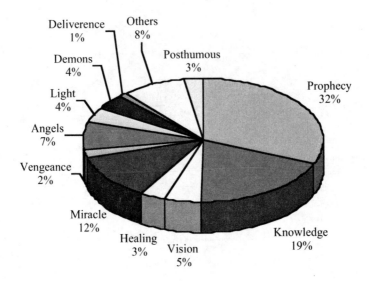

Fɪɢ. 2: Dɪꜱᴛʀɪʙᴜᴛɪᴏɴ ᴏꜰ Mᴀʀᴠᴇʟʟᴏᴜꜱ Pʜᴇɴᴏᴍᴇɴᴀ ɪɴ *VC* Bᴏᴏᴋ I

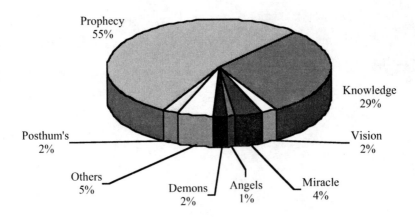

FIG. 3: DISTRIBUTION OF MARVELLOUS PHENOMENA IN *VC* BOOK II

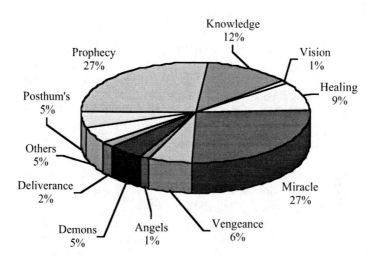

FIG. 4: DISTRIBUTION OF MARVELLOUS PHENOMENA IN *VC* BOOK III

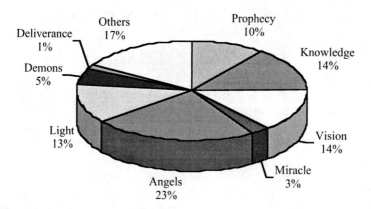

Appendix 2: The Gregorian Borrowing

We should perhaps mention briefly the thesis of Anderson[1] and Sharpe regarding the un-ascribed uses of Gregory by Adomnán. They suggest Columba's reported explanation, and indeed 'the account to which they refer', were in fact derived from Gregory, and probably not derived from genuine Columban tradition. Anderson notes both that the reply in i.1:10b adheres more closely to Gregory than does the text of i.43:44b-45a, and that there is a discrepancy between the two *VC* passages in terms of supplicant. The former is composed 'somewhat later', and records a request made by more than one monk, with no pledge of secrecy. In 44ab, Luigbe as sole supplicant is asked to pledge secrecy unto Columba's death before explanation is commenced. Sharpe describes the source as 'St Benedict's words to Germanus',[2] and makes the point that 'Gregory's book, a late sixth-century account... was almost certainly not known on Iona until after St Columba's death.' He thus rejects the possibility that the explanation came from Columba's own words, or from a testimony of Lugbe given in the presence of others; rather, it must have derived from Adomnán's reading. Thus doubt is cast on Adomnán's claim to have used sworn witnesses.

Adomnán's use of Gregory need not necessarily evince unreliability in his claimed recording of testimonial evidence. Firstly, regarding the date:

a. The two individuals with whom the tale begins, and whose story provokes the question which Gregory is employed to answer, are Colmán Cú mac Ailéni and Rónán mac Áedo. They are said in the story to have died in the monastery of Cell Rois, in the territory of

---

1   A&A (1961, 20; 204 note 6; 302 note 6; 1991, 18 note 17; 79 note 99).

2   Sharpe (1995, 189). The dialogue is, in fact, between Gregory and his diaconal interlocutor Peter in both loci. It concerns Benedict's vision of heavenly light, in which he saw the world 'gathered as it were together under one beam of the sun' and the soul of Germanus, Bishop of Capua, being carried to heaven by angels, in a fiery globe. Gregory then explains this phenomenon to Peter, and returns to it again in a discourse on the visibility of a departing soul. Chapter iv.7 also gives a possible clue to the background of Columba's various sightings of departing souls in Book III; 'many of us, that by sincere faith and plentiful prayer, have had the eye of our souls purified, have often seen souls going out of their bodies... that by this means examples may satisfy our wavering and doubtful minds, which reason can not so fully persuade.'

the Mugdorna.[3] The ruling dynasty of this territory in the sixth-seventh century was that of Ailén, Colmán Cú's father. Ailén's other son Máel Dúin, Colmán Cú's brother, succeeded as king, and died in AU611. Ailén must thus have died before 611, and Colmán Cú must have been born before 611. Máel Dúin had a son. He must therefore have been of age before he died, a minimum of 15 years old. This gives a latest birth date of c. 596 for Máel Dúin. His son died in AU 665, 54 years after his latest birth date of 611. If he lived to 70, his birth would have been in 595, pushing Máel Dúin's birth back to <580. It could conceivably have been as early as 550, making him 45 when his son could have been born. Colmán Cú, as son to Ailéni, must have been born before 611. Given his brother's conceivable dates, it is not impossible that he was a grown man who died before Columba's death. Rónán's father Áed mac Colgen died in AU 609. Sharpe says, 'It would appear that Rónán mac Áedo was killed during his father's lifetime.' i.e. before 609. Again it is not impossible that he should have died before Columba. Thus the circumstances of the tale could conceivably confirm its temporal place as during Columba's lifetime. At least there is no prima facie reason to doubt it.

b. Benedict died c.547. The *Dialogues* were written 593-4. It is thus firmly within the bounds of possibility that Benedict's repute, conveyed through Gregory's or other's oral sayings and teachings, reached Iona before the end of Columba's life. It is not impossible that the *Dialogues* themselves reached this far in the 3-4 years available, and were used by Columba to explain his visionary experiences to Luigbe. Adomnán cannot be accepted as firm evidence for this, so probability suggests Sharpe may be right to be suspicious.

Secondly, however, Adomnán was concerned to appeal to witnesses for his sources; it may well be that Adomnán's record of the report that reached him is accurate, but that the report itself was influenced by Gregory's explanation of Benedict's visionary gifting. Adomnán uses the words from Gregory on the lips of Columba, citing his disciple Luigbe as primary witness; Luigbe passed the explanation on via other holy ones to Adomnán. It would be perfectly understandable that any abbot coming into knowledge of the *Dialogues,* or its oral precursor, could choose to adopt, or could unconsciously adopt, teaching from it as explanation, or even confirmation of the received tradition regarding Columba, then communicate this to his monks, so passing it into the narrative corpus of Ionan theology. Postulating the not unreasonable

---

3   For genealogical and topographical information, see Anderson (1991)78-9, notes 97-98, and Sharpe(1995) note 188.

assumption that stories of Columba's prophetic gift were also a part of this corpus (as the *Amra* confirms), it is perfectly conceivable that Gregory's explanation could be incorporated with any explanation Columba himself had given. It is again not unreasonable that one of Columba's monks should beg such from him. It is also conceivable that Luigbe's memory of Columba's words, or that of the intermediaries between him and Adomnán, became structured by Gregory as the *Dialogues* were read over meals, or copied in the scriptorium.

Thirdly, though Columba/Adomnán apparently did borrow from Gregory without citation, however this happened, this would be no more than he does with scriptural passages; no more than standard practice in the era. Indeed it would be a tribute to adopt the explanation of one of the great teachers of the church. Did Adomnán have the Dialogues open before him as he composed, or was it a memorable phrase that had passed into Iona's own tradition? One possibility is that he may only have had book IV, where the explanation is simply concentrated on the phrases in question, though the context here is the seeing of souls, not revelations as in the *VC loci*. However Brüning also showed that Adomnán uses other phrases from *Dialogues* I, II, and III, so this option is ruled out. Of one thing we can be certain. Adomnán saw this explanation as sufficiently important to his purpose that he selected and included it as one of the stories that the reader should know. Adomnán presents himself clearly as concerned to present a reliable body of tradition regarding his subject, and though he may be responsible for editing his account of Columba's explanation, in order to bring it into the currently fashionable style, the possibility of the Gregorian tutorial between Columba and Luigbe may not be rejected so easily.

Bibliography

The bibliography extends beyond works cited, though is not exhaustive. It is laid out conventionally by the surname of the author, editor, or translator where known. Where these are unknown, or to aid navigation, the name of a number of works and of a number of saints is listed within the alphabetical sequence, with cross-references where necessary. Multiple editions or translations are listed with the primary work in date order. Occasional references to electronic texts on the internet, the provenance of which is sometimes not easy to check, occur as I have happened across them, for convenience.

Primary Sources

1. Sources of Christian Works

Adomnán, *Law of Innocents:*

Meyer, Kuno, ed. and tr. (1905), *Cáin Adamnáin: an Old-Irish Treatise on the Law of Adamnán* (Oxford: Clarendon).

Márkus, Gilbert, tr. (1997), *Adomnán's 'Law of the Innocents'* (Glasgow: Blackfriars).

Ni Dhonnchadha, Mairin (2001), 'The Law of Adomnán: A Translation' [sections 28-53], in: O'Loughlin (2001, 53-68).

Adomnán, *Of Holy Places (De Locis Sanctis):* Meehan, D., and L. Bieler, ed. and tr. (1958), *De Locis Sanctis* (Dublin: Inst. Adv. Studs, *SLH* 3).

Adomnán, *Life of St Columba (Vita Sancti Columbae):*

Reeves, W., ed. (1857), *The Life of St Columba founder of Hy written by Adamnan* (Dublin: Irish Archaeological and Celtic Society).

Reeves, W., ed. (1874), tr. A.P. Forbes, notes rev. W.F. Skene, *The Life of St Columba Founder of Hy Written by Adamnan* (Edinburgh: Edmonston and Douglas, The Historians of Scotland VI).

Fowler, J.T., ed. (1894), *Adamnani Vita S. Columbae* (Oxford: Clarendon).

Fowler, J.T., tr. (1895), *Prophecies, Miracles, and Visions of St Columba [Columcille]* (London: H. Frowde).

Huyshe, Wentworth, tr. (1905), *The Life of Saint Columba (Columb-Kille) AD 521-597* (London: Routledge).

Fowler, J.T., ed. (1920), *Adamnani Vita Columbae (ed. from Reeves) with an intro. on Early Irish Church History,* New edition, revised, (Oxford: Clarendon).

Anderson, A.O. and M.O. Anderson, ed. and tr. (1961), *Adomnán's Life of Columba,* (London: Thomas Nelson).

Anderson, A.O. and M.O. Anderson, ed. and tr., revised M.O. Anderson (1991), *Adomnán's Life of Columba,* 2nd edn. (Oxford: Clarendon).

Sharpe, Richard, tr. (1995), *Adomnán of Iona: Life of St Columba* (Harmondsworth: Penguin).

Altus Prosator: ed. and tr. C&M (1995, 44-53).

Ambrose, *De Spirito Sancto: PL* 16. tr. *NPNF* II.X.

Amra Choluimb Chille:
  Stokes, Whitley, ed. and tr. (1899), *RC* 20: 31-35, 132-83, 248-89, 400-37; (1900), *RC* 21: 133-136.
  C&M, ed. and tr. (1995, 104-115).

Annals of Clonmacnoise: tr. Conell Mageoghagan, ed. Denis Murphy (Lampeter: Llanerch, 1993, facsimile reprint. [Originally published: Dublin University Press, 1896]).

Annals of the Four Masters: ed. and tr. J. O'Donovan (1856), *Annala Rioghachta Eireann: Annals of the Kingdom of Ireland, by the Four Masters, to 1616,* 2nd ed. (Dublin).

Annals of Inisfallen: ed. and tr. S. MacAirt (1951), (Dublin: DIAS).

Annals of Tigernach: (AD 489-766), ed. and tr. W. Stokes (1896), *RC* 17, 116-263.

Annals of Ulster: (to AD 1131), ed. and tr. S. Mac Airt and G. Mac Niocaill (Dublin: DIAS, 1983).

Antiphonary of Bangor: ed. F. E. Warren (1893-95), 2 vols (London: Harrison, Henry Bradshaw Soc.).

Antony, *Life* by Athanasius:
  Gregg, Robert C., (1980), *The Life of Antony and the Letter to Marcellinus* [tr. from *PG* 26, 835-976] (London: SPCK).
  Bartelink, G.M., ed. (1994), *Athanase d'Alexandrie, Vie d'Antoine* (Paris: *SC* 400).
  http://www.ccel.org/fathers2/NPNF2-04/Npnf2-04-38.htm
  Evagrius, tr., *Vita Antonii: PL* 73; ed. G.J.M. Bartelink (1974), (Milan: *Vite dei Santi* I).

Augustine of Hippo, *Concerning the City of God (De Civitate Dei):*
  Sancti Avrelii Augustini De Civitate Dei, CC, Series Latina, 47-8 (Turnhoult: Brepols, 1955).
  Bettenson, H., tr. (1972), *Concerning the City of God against the Pagans* (Harmondsworth: Penguin).

Augustine of Hippo, *Confession:*
  PL 32: 583-656.
  Sheed, F.J., tr. (1944), *The Confessions of St Augustine* (London: Sheed and Ward).

Augustine of Hippo, *De Genesi ad Litteram:*
  PL 34: 245f.
  Taylor, J. H., tr. (1982), *The Literal Meaning of Genesis* (New York: Newman, Ancient Christian Writers vols 41-42).

Augustine, Irish, *Treatise*: Augustinus Hibernicus, *De Mirabilibus Sacrae Scripturae PL* 35.2149-2000; McGinty (1971), 'The Treatise *De Mirabilibus Sacrae Scripturae*: Critical Edition; with Introduction, English Translation of the Long Recension and Some Notes', (Unpublished PhD thesis, National University of Ireland, 2 vols).

Basil, *Ascetic Works:* tr. W.K.L. Clarke (1925), *The Ascetic Works of Saint Basil* (London: SPCK).

Bede, *Historia Ecclesiastica Gentis Anglorum:*
Colgrave, B. and R.A.B. Mynors, ed. and tr. (1969), *Bede's Ecclesiastical History* (Oxford: OUP).
Sherley-Price, L., tr. (1968), *Bede: A History of the English Church and People* (Harmondsworth: Penguin).
http://www.fordham.edu/halsall/basis/bede-book1.html.

Bede, *Commentarii: PL* 92.

Bieler, L. (1979), *The Patrician Texts in the Book of Armagh* (Dublin: DIAS, *SLH* 10).

Book of Armagh (Liber Armachanus): ed. J. Gwynn (Dublin: RIA, 1913).

Brigit:
Cogitosus, *Life of St Brigit:*
Bolland, J. ed., *Acta Sanctorum,* Feb. I (Antwerp, 1658).
Connolly, S. and J-M. Picard trs. (1987), *JRSAI* 117, 5-27.
First Life of S. Brigid: ed. and tr. Connolly, S. (1989), *JRSAI* 119, 5-49.
Vita IV: ed. R. Sharpe (1991), 'Vita IV S. Brigidae', in: *Medieval Irish Saints' Lives: An Introduction to* Vitae Sanctorum Hiberniae (Oxford: Clarendon).

Cassian, John, *Conferences:*
Pichery, E., ed. (1955-9), *SC* 42, 54, 64; tr. [except 12 and 22] E.C. Gibson (1894), *NPNCF* XI (Oxford). http://www.osb.org/lectio/cassian/conf/
Lubheid, Colm (1985), *John Cassian Conferences* (New York: Paulist).

Cassian, John, *Institutes: tr.* O. Chadwick (1968).

Codex Kilkenniensis: Grosjean, P., ed. (1930), *AB* 48, 103-121.

Colgan, J. (1647), *Triadis Thaumaturgæ sev Divorum Patricii, Columbæ et Brigidae... Acta* (Lovanii: Apud Cornelium Coenestenium).

Columba: see Adomnán; *Altus Prosator; Amra.*

Columbanus:
Works: Walker, G.M.S. (1970), *Sancti Columbani Opera* (Dublin: SLH II).
Life by Jonas:
Munro, D.C., tr. (1895), (Philadelphia: Eur. Hist, VII).
Krusch, Bruno, ed. (1905), *Scriptores Rerum Germanicum* (Hannover: Hahn), 1-294.
http://www.fordham.edu/halsall/basis/columban.html

Cormac's *Glossary*: John O'Donovan, tr.; Whitley Stokes ed. (Calcutta: Irish Archaeological and Celtic Society, 1868).

Cuthbert: *Anonymous Life,* and *Life by Bede,* ed. and tr. B. Colgrave (1940), *The Two Lives of St. Cuthbert* (Cambridge: CUP).

De Mirabilibus Sacrae Scripturae: see Augustine, Irish.

Didache: ed. and tr. J.A. Kleist (1948), *The Didache, The Epistle of Barnabas, The Epistles and the Martyrdom of St. Polycarp, The Fragments of Papias, The Epistle to Diognetus* (Westminster, Maryland: Newman Press).

Dionysius the Pseudo-Areopagite, *Celestial Hierarchy:* tr. [from *PG,* III, 369-584] Thomas L. Campbell (1981), *The Ecclesiastical Hierarchy* (Washington D.C.,).

Eucherius of Lyons (Eucherii Lugdunensis), *De Contemptu Mundi, PL* 50, 711-726,
  tr. H. Vaughan (1654), rev. N. Redington, 'On Contempt for the World', St
  Pachomius Orthodox Library 1995.
Eucherius of Lyons (Eucherii Lugdunensis), *On the Solitary Life (De Laude Eremi),
  PL* 50, 701-712.
Félire Oengusso see *Martyrology of Oengus.*
Germanus of Auxerre, *Life*:
    Constantius of Lyons, *Life of Germanus:* ed. W. Levinson (1920), *Monumentae
    Germanicae Historica: Scriptorum Rerum Merovingicarum,* VII, 247-283.
    Hoare, F.R., tr. (1954, 284-320).
    Fortunatus, *Vita Sancti Germani:* ed. B. Krusch (1919), *Monumentae
    Germanicae Historica: Scriptorum Rerum Merovingicarum* (Hannover:
    Impensis Bibliopolii Haliniani), VII, 337-418.
Gildas, *The Ruin of Britain and Other Works (De Excidio et conquestu Britanniae):*
    ed. and tr. M. Winterbottom (London: Phillimore, 1978).
    http://www.fordham.edu/halsall/basis/gildas-full.html
Gododdin:
    Jackson, K.H., tr. (1969), *The Gododdin: The Oldest Scottish Poem* (Edinburgh:
    EUP).
    Koch, J. T., ed. (1997), *The Gododdin of Aneirin, Text and Context from Dark-
    Age North Britain* (Celtic Studies Pubns Inc).
Gregory of Nazianzus: *Oration XLI, 'On Pentecost', PG* 35-38; tr. in *PNCF* ser. II,
    vol. vii (1894).
Gregory of Nyssa:
    Life of St. Macrina: Maraval, Pierre, ed., *SC* 178 (Paris: Éditions du Cerf, 1971).
    Woods Callahan, Virginia (1967), tr., in: *Saint Gregory of Nyssa, Ascetical
    Works* (Washington DC: Catholic University of America Press, The Fathers of
    the Church series, Vol. 58).
Gregory of Tours, *Life of the[Gallic] Fathers:* tr. E. James (2nd ed., Liverpool, LUP,
    1991).
Gregory the Great, *Dialogues*:
    Vogüé, A. de, ed., *SC* 260 (1978-80).
    Gardner, E.G. (1911), tr. from *PL* 78, *The Dialogues of Saint Gregory* (London:
    P.L. Warner).
Haddan, A.W. and W. Stubbs (1878), *Councils and Ecclesiastical Documents II.II:
    Church of Ireland,* (Oxford).
Hibernensis, Collectio Canonum: Wasserschleben, H., ed. (1885), *Die Irische
    Kanonensammlung* (Leipzig: Tauchnitz).
Hilary of Arles, *Life of*:
    Cavallin, S., ed. (1952), *Vitae Sanctorum Honorati et Hilarii Episcoporum
    Arelatensum* (Lund).
    Jacob, Paul-André, tr. (1995), *La vie d'Hilaire d'Arles / Honorat de Marseille ;
    texte Latin de Samuel Cavallin* (Paris : Editions du Cerf).
Hoare, F.R. ed. and tr. (1954), *The Western Fathers, Being the Lives of SS Martin of
    Tours, Ambrose, Augustine of Hippo, Honoratus of Arles, Germanus of Auxerre*
    (London: Sheed and Ward).
Honoratus of Arles: *Life* by Hilary of Arles *PL* 50.1249-1272, tr: F.R. Hoare (1954,
    248-280).

Ignatius, *Letter to the Philadelphians:* Srawley, J.H., ed. (1900), The *Epistles of St Ignatius, Bishop of Antioch*, 3rd edn. (London: SPCK).

Irenaeus, *Against Heresies (Adversus Haereses):* Keble, John, tr. (1872), *Five Books of S. Irenaeus, Bishop of Lyons: Against Heresies* (Oxford: John Henry Parker).

Irish Book of Hymns (Liber Hymnorum): ed. and tr. J. H. Bernard and R. Atkinson (London: Henry Bradshaw Society, 1898).

Isidore of Seville:
   Questions on the Old and New Testaments (De Veteri et Novo Testamento Quaestiones), PL 83.
   On the Nature of Things (De Natura Rerum). PL 83.

[Pseudo-Isidore, *Liber De Ordine Creaturarum (On the Order of the Creatures)*: PL 83, 935-8; ed. M.C. Diaz y Diaz (Santiago de Compostela, 1972); tr. J.A. Davies, MA Dissertation 1988, University of Wales, Lampeter, www.lamp.ac.uk/celtic/DeOrdine.htm.]

James, M.R. (1975), *The Apocryphal New Testament* (Oxford: Clarendon).

Jerome, *Commentary on Job, PL* 26.

Jerome, *Commentary on Ezekiel, PL* 26.

Jerome, *Commentary on I Corinthians, PL* 30.

Kentigern: *Life,* ed. and tr. A.P. Forbes (1874), *The Lives of St Ninian and St Kentigern* (Edinburgh: Edmonston and Douglas, The Historians of Scotland; 5).

Liber Armachanus see *Book of Armagh.*

Liber De Ordine Creaturarum: see Isidore [pseudo].

Liber Hymnorum see *Irish Book of Hymns.*

McGinty, G. (1971), see Augustine, Irish.

Martin: *Life* by Sulpicius Severus:
   Hoare, F.R., tr. (1954, 10-44).
   Fontaine, Jacques, ed. (1967-1969), Sulpicius Severus, *Vie de Saint Martin, (SC* 5).

Martyrology of Oengus the Culdee (Félire Óengusso Céli Dé): ed. W. Stokes (London: Henry Bradshaw Soc., 1905).

Ninian: *Life,* ed. and tr. A.P. Forbes (1874), *The Lives of St Ninian and St Kentigern,* (Edinburgh).

Noua Legenda Anglie, by John of Tynemouth (John Capgrave): ed. Carl Horstman (Anecdota Oxoniensia, 1885).

Origen, *Against Celsus (Contra Celsum):* ed. H. Chadwick (Cambridge: CUP, 1953).

Patrick, *Confession* and *Letter to Coroticus (Confessio* and *Epistola ad Milites Corotici):*
   Hood, A.B.E., tr. (1978), *St. Patrick, His Writings and Muirchu's Life* (London: Phillimore).
   Bieler, L., ed. (1982), *Libri Epistolarum Sancti Patricii Episcopi*, 2 vols (Dublin: Irish Manuscripts Commission).
   Howlett, D.R., ed. and tr. (1994), *The Book of Letters of Saint Patrick the Bishop (Liber Epistolarum Sancti Patrici Episcopi)* (Dublin: Four Courts), 47-93.

Patrick, *Liber Angeli*: ed. and tr. L. Bieler (1979, 184-191).

Patrick, *Lives of:*
   Muirchú, *Life of St Patrick (Vita S. Patricii),* ed. and tr. L. Bieler (1979, 62-123).
   Tírechán, *Collectanea*, ed. and tr. L. Bieler (1979, 122-163).
   Vita Tripartita, see Stokes (1887).

Polycarp: Camelot P.T., ed. (1998), *Lettres, Martyre de Polycarpe / Ignace d'Antioche, Polycarpe de Smyrne; texte grec, introduction, traduction et notes* (Paris : Éditions du Cerf, *SC* 10).

Samson of Dol: *Life*, ed. R. Fawtier (1912), (Paris: Bibl. de l'École des Hautes Études, 197), tr. T. Taylor (1925), *The Life of S Samson of Dol* (London: SPCK). http://www.lamp.ac.uk/celtic/Samson.htm

Sanas Chormaic see *Cormac's Glossary*.

Skene, W.F., ed. (1867), *Chronicles of the Picts: Chronicles of the Scots and Other Early Memorials of Scottish History* (Edinburgh: H.M. General register house).

Smedt, C. De, and J. De Backer, eds. (1887), *Acta Sanctorum Hiberniae ex Codice Salmanticensis* (Edinburgh and London, Bruge and Lille).

Stokes, W. (1890), *Lives of Saints from the Book of Lismore* (Oxford: Clarendon, repr. New York: AMS 1989).

Stokes, Whitley, ed. (1887), *Vita Tripartita, The Tripartite Life of Patrick* (Rolls Series, 2 vols; repr. 1965).

Triadis Thaumaturgae: see Colgan (1647).

Vulgate: Biblia Sacra Iuxta Vulgatem Versionem, ed. R. Weber, 2 vols (Stuttgart: Württembergische Bibelanstadt, 1969).

Vita Tripartita: see Stokes (1887).

2. Sources of Secular Irish Works

Accallam na Senorach, see *Tales of the Elders of Ireland*.

Battle of Mag Lena:
> Curry, Eugene, ed. and tr. (1855), *Cath Mhuighe Léana: The Battle of Magh Leana* (Dublin: The Celtic Soc.).
> Jackson, K.H., ed. (1938), *Cath Maighe Léna* (Dublin: Inst. Med. and Mod. Series).

Battle of Magh Rath: John O'Donovan ed. and tr. (1842), *The Banquet of Dun na n-Gedh: and The Battle of Magh Rath...* (Dublin: Dublin Univ. Press for Irish Arch. Soc.).

Battle of Mag Tuired:
> Stokes, Whitley, ed. and tr. (1891), *Cath Maige Turedh (The Second Battle of Moytura)*, *RC* 12: 52-130, 306-308.
> Gray, E.A., ed. (1982), *Cath Maige Tuired: the Second Battle of Mag Tuired* (London: ITS *[Cumann na Sgríbheann Gaedhilge]* 52).

Battle of Ventry:
> Meyer, K., ed. (1885), The *Cath Finntrága or Battle of Ventry* (Oxford: Clarendon, Anec. Oxon. Med. and Mod. ser. vol. 1, pt. 4).
> O'Rahilly, Cecile, ed. and tr. (1962), *Cath Finntrágha* (Dublin: Med. and Mod. Irish Ser. vol. 20).

Book of Leinster:
> *Lebar Laigen*, folio facsimile, ed. R. Atkinson (Dublin: RIA, 1880).
> Best, R.I., O. Bergin, M.A. O'Brien and A. O'Sullivan, eds. (1954-83), *The Book of Leinster*, 6 vols (Dublin: DIAS).

Book of the Dun Cow: R.I. Best and O. Bergin, eds. (1992), *Lebor na hUidre, Book of the Dun Cow*, (Dublin: RIA, 1929; repr. Dublin: DIAS).

Combat of Cú Chulainn with Senbecc: Meyer, Kuno, ed. and tr. (1883), *Combat of Cuchulaind with Senbecc*, *RC* 6 (1883-5).

Courtship of Monera (Tocmarc Monera), ed. and tr. Eugene Curry (1855), in: Eugene Curry, ed. and tr. (1855), *Cath Muige Léana (The Battle of Magh Leana)* (Dublin: Celtic Soc.), 154-9.

Da Choca's Hostel (Bruiden Da Choca): ed. and tr. Whitley Stokes (1900), *RC* 21:149-165, 312-327, 388-402.

Death of the Sons of Uisneach (Deirdre):
Stokes, W., ed. and tr. (1887), *The Death of the Sons of Uisneach* [Text of *Oided mac nUisnig* from the Glen Masáin MSS 56, 63], *Irische Texte* 2 (Leipzig: Hirzel), 109-84.
Hull, V., ed. and tr. (1949), *The Exile of the sons of Uisliu (Longes mac nUislenn)* (London: OUP).
Mac Giolla Léith, Caiomhín, ed. and tr. (1993), *Violent Death of the Children of Uisneach (Oidheadh Chloinne hUisneach)* (London: ITS vol. 56).

Dindsenchas (History of Places): ed. and tr. Whitley Stokes (1894-5), 'The Prose Tales in the Rennes Dindsenchas', *RC* 15 and16.

Gantz, J., ed. and tr. (1981), *Early Irish Myths and Sagas*, (Harmondsworth: Penguin).

Jackson, K.H. (1951), *A Celtic Miscellany* (London).

Keating, Geoffrey, *The History of Ireland (Foras Feasa ar Éirinn)*, 4 vols (ITS vols. IV 1902; VIII and IX 1908; XV 1914).

Meyer, Kuno, ed. (1906), *Death Tales of the Ulster Heroes* (Dublin: RIA Todd Lecture Series).

Meyer, Kuno, ed. (1911), *Selections from Ancient Irish Poetry* (London: Constable).

Murphy, G., ed. (1956), *Early Irish Lyrics* (Oxford: Clarendon).

Táin Bó Cúalnge (Cattle Raid of Cooley):
Windisch, E., ed. (1905), *Die Altirische Heldensage Táin bó Cúalnge* (Leipzig: Hirzel, *Irische Texte* I.IV).
O'Rahilly, Cecile, ed. and tr. (1970), *Táin Bó Cúalnge from The Book of Leinster* (Dublin: DIAS).

Tale of Meic Da Tho's Pig, (Scéla Muicce Meic Da Thó), ed. and tr. R. Thurneysen (1935), *Scéla Mucce Meic Dathó* (Dublin: DIAS).

Training of Cúchulainn, (Do Fogluim Chonculainn): ed. and tr. Whitley Stokes (1908), *RC* 29, 109-152.

Tocmarc Monera see: *Courtship of Monera*.

Tales of the Elders of Ireland (Accallam na Senórach):
Stokes, Whitley, ed. (1900), *Accallam na Senórach* (Leipzig: Hirzel, Irische Texte IV, i).
Shéaghdha, Nessa Ní, ed. (1942), *Agallamh na Seanórach* (Dublin: Baile Átha Cliath).
Dooley, N. Ann, and Harry Roe (1999), *The Tales of the Elders of Ireland: A New Translation of Accallam na Senórach* (Oxford: OUP).

Voyage of Bran (Immram Bran): Mac Mathúna, S., ed. (1985), *Immran Brain: Bran's Journey to the Land of the Women* (Tübingen: Niemeyer). http://www.lamp.ac.uk/celtic/BranEng.htm

Voyage of Brendan (Immram Brendan): ed. and tr. W.R.J. Barrow and G.S. Burgess (2002), *The Voyage of St Brendan* (Exeter: Univ. Exeter Press). http://www.lamp.ac.uk/celtic/Nsb.htm

Voyage of Máel Dúin's Boat (Immram Curaig Máel Dúin):
Oskamp, H.P.A., ed. and tr., *Immram Curaig Máel Dúin (Voyage of Máel Dúin) from the Yellow Book of Lecan* (Groningen: Wolters-Noordhoff, 1970).
Stokes, Whitley, ed. and tr., *Immram Curaig Maíle Dúin (The voyage of Mael Dúin's boat)*, *RC* 9 (1888), 447-495.
http://www.lamp.ac.uk/celtic/MaelDuin.htm

Windisch, Ernst, ed., *Irische Texte: mit Übersetzungen und Wörterbuch,* Ser.1-4 (Leipzig: Hirzel, 1891-1897).

Secondary Sources

Aalen, S. (1976), 'Glory, Honour', *NIDNTT* 2, 44-52.

W. Abbott and J. Gallagher, eds. '*Lumen Gentium* (Constitution on the Church)' §50, in: *The Documents of Vatican II* (London, 1966).

Aigrain, René (1953), *L'Hagiographie* (Paris: Bloud and Gay).

Aird, W.M. (1992), 'The Making of a Medieval Miracle Collection: the *Liber de Translationibus et Miraculis Sancti Cuthberti*', *Northern History*, XXVIII, 1-24.

Alcock, L. (1971), *Arthur's Britain: History and Archaeology AD 367-634* (London: Penguin).

Allchin, A.M. (1994), 'Celtic Christianity: Fact or Fantasy?' in: *Epiphany* 14.3, 17-29.

Anderson, A.O., ed and tr. (1990), *Early Sources of Scottish History AD 500-1286* (Stamford: Paul Watkins, repr., 2 vols).

Anderson, A.O. (1980), *Kings and Kingship in Early Scotland*, revised ed. (Edinburgh: Scottish Academic Press London).

Ash, J.L. (1976), 'The Decline of Ecstatic Prophecy in the Early Church,' *Theological Studies* 37, 227-252.

Bannerman, J. (1974), *Studies in the History of Dalriada,* (Edinburgh: Scottish Academic Press).

Barclay, W. (1957), *The Letter to the Romans* (Edinburgh: St Andrew Press).

Barrett, C.K. (1973), *The Second Epistle to the Corinthians* (London: A&C Black).

Bauckham, R.J. (1982), 'Eschatology', *NBD* 342-348.

Beasley-Murray, P. (1978), *The Book of Revelation* (London).

Berger, Peter L. (1969), *A Rumour of Angels: Modern Society and the Rediscovery of the Supernatural* (Harmondsworth: Penguin).

Bieler, L. (1949), *The Life and Legend of Saint Patrick: Problems of Modern Scholarship* (Dublin).

Bieler, L. (1962), 'The Celtic Hagiographer', *Studia Patristica* 5, 243-265.

Bieler, L. (1986), *Studies in the Life and Legend of St Patrick,* ed. R. Sharpe (London: Variorum Reprints).

Bieler, L. (1987), *Ireland and the culture of Early Medieval Europe,* ed. R. Sharpe (London: Variorum Reprints).

Bietenhard, H., 'Angel, Messenger, Gabriel, Michael', *NIDNTT* 1, 101-103.

Binchy, D.A. (1962), 'Patrick and his Biographers: Ancient and Modern', *Studia Hibernica,* 2, 7-173.

Binchy, D.A. (1982), 'A Pre-Christian Survival in Medieval Irish Hagiography', in: D. Whitelock et al. (1982, 165-178).

Black, Donald (1992), 'Studies in Honour of James Carney (1914-89)', *CMCS* 23.

Blair, J. and R. Sharpe, eds (1992), *Pastoral Care Before the Parish* (Leicester: Leicester Univ. Press).

Bonser, W. (1957), *An Anglo-Saxon and Celtic Bibliography; 453-1087* (Oxford).

Borsje, J. (1994), 'The Monster in the River Ness in *Vita Sancti Columbae*: The Study of a Miracle', *Peritia* 8, 27-34.

Bourke, Cormac, ed. (1997), *Studies in the Cult of Saint Columba* (Dublin: Four Courts Press).

Bowen, E.G. (1977), *Saints, Seaways and Settlements* (Cardiff: University of Wales Press).

Bradley, Ian C. (1993), *The Celtic Way* (London: DLT).

Bradley, Ian C. (1996), *Columba: Pilgrim and Penitent 597-1997* (Glasgow: Wild Goose).

Bradley, Ian C. (1999), *Celtic Christianity, Making Myths and Chasing Dreams* (Edinburgh).

Bradshaw, B. (1989), 'The Wild and Woolly West: Early Irish Christianity and Latin Orthodoxy', in: *The Churches, Ireland and the Irish*, ed. W. Shiels and D. Wood (1989).

Bray, Dorothy A. (1992), *A List of Motifs in the Lives of Early Irish Saints* (Helsinki: Academia Scientiarum Fennica, Folklore Fellows Communications, no. 252).

Breatnach, L. (1996), 'Poets and Poetry' in: McCone and Simms (1996, 65-77).

Brewer, C.K. (1897), *A Dictionary of Miracles* (1897 repr. 1966).

Brown, Colin (1988), *Miracles and the Critical Mind* (Grand Rapids: Eerdmans).

Brown, Colin (1971), *Philosophy and Christian Faith* (London: Tyndale).

Brown, Colin, ed. (1980, 1976, 1978), *New International Dictionary of New Testament Theology*, 3 vols, (Exeter: Paternoster, and Grand Rapids: Zondervan).

Brown, P. (1967), *Augustine of Hippo*, (London: Faber and Faber).

Brown, P. (1971), 'The Rise and Function of the Holy Man in Antiquity', *Journal of Roman Studies* 61, 80-101.

Brown, P. (1981), *The Cult of the Saints. Its Rise and Function in Latin Christianity* (Chicago).

Brown, P. (1983), 'The Saint as Exemplar in Late Antiquity', *Representations*, 1.2, 1-25.

Broun, Dauvit (1998), 'Pictish Kings 761-839: Integration with Dál Riata or Separate Development?' in: S. Foster (ed.), *The St Andrews Sarcophagus: A Pictish Masterpiece and its International Connections, Dublin* (Dublin: Four Courts), 71-83

Broun, D. and T. O. Clancy eds. (1999), *Spes Scotorum, Hope of Scots: Saint Columba, Iona and Scotland* (Edinburgh: T&T Clark).

Brüning, G. (1916), *Adamnan's Vita Columbae und Ihre Ableitungen* (Halle).

Bullough, D.A. (1964-5), 'Columba, Adomnán and the Achievement of Iona', *Scottish Historical Review* 43 (1963-4, 111-130), and (1964-5, 17-33).

Butler, E.C. (1910), 'Review of *Vita Sanctorum Hiberniae*', *JTS* 12, 490-2.

Byrne, F.J. (1965), 'The Ireland of St Columba', *Historical Studies* 5, 37-58.

Byrne, F.J. (1971), 'Senchas: The Nature of Gaelic Historical Tradition', *Historical Studies* 9, 137-159.

Cameron, Averil (1991), *Christianity and the Rhetoric of Empire* (Berkeley: University of California Press).

Campbell, Ewan (2001), 'Were the Scots Irish?', *Antiquity* 75, 285-92.

Carey, J. (1998a), *King of Mysteries* (Dublin: Four Courts Press).

Carey, J. (1998b), 'Sages, Saints, and Semiotics: Encountering Medieval Irish Literature', CMCS 35 57-72.

Carney, James (1955), *Studies in Irish Literature and History*, (Dublin: Inst. Adv. Studs).

Carney, James, (1983), 'Early Irish Literature - the state of Research', in: *Proc. 6th Int. Congress of Celtic Studies* (Dublin), 113-130.

Chadwick, H.M. (1949), *Early Scotland: the Picts, the Scots and the Welsh of Southern Scotland* (Cambridge).

Chadwick, Henry (1981), *Frontiers of Theology- Inaugural Lecture, Univ. Camb. 5th March 1981* (Cambridge).

Chadwick, N.K. (1955), *Poetry and Letters in Early Christian Gaul* (London: Bower and Bower).

Chadwick, N.K. (1961), *The Age of Saints in the Early Celtic Church* (Cambridge).

Chadwick, N.K. (1971), *The Celts* (Harmondsworth: Penguin).

Chadwick, N.K. (1973), *Celtic Britain* (London).

Chadwick, N.K. (1976), *The British Heroic Age: the Welsh and the Men of the North* (Cardiff).

Chadwick, N.K., ed. (1958), *Studies in Early British Church* (Cambridge).

Chadwick, N.K., ed. (1963), *Celt and Saxon: Studies in the Early British Border* (Cambridge).

Chadwick, Owen (1968), *John Cassian* (Cambridge: University Press, 2nd edn).

Charles-Edwards, T.M. (1976), 'The Social Background to Irish Peregrinatio', *Celtica* 11, 43-59.

Charles-Edwards, T.M. (1993), 'The New Edition of Adomnán's *Life of Columba*', *CMCS* 26, 65-73.

Childe, V.G. (1935), *The Prehistory of Scotland* (London).

Clancy, T.O. and G. Márkus (1995), *Iona: The Earliest Poetry of a Celtic Monastery* (Edinburgh: EUP).

Clancy, T.O. (1995b), 'Review' of Heffernan (1988), *Innes Review* 46.2, 165-168.

Clancy, T.O. (1997), 'Columba, Adomnán, and the cult of saints in Scotland', *Innes Review* 48.1.

Clancy, T.O. (2000), 'Personal, Political, Pastoral: the Multiple Agenda of Adomnán's *Life of Columba*' in: T. Cowan, ed., *The Polar Twins: Scottish History and Scottish Literature* (Edinburgh: John Donald), 39-60.

Cobbey, N. (1998), Lambeth Conference Communications, ACNS LC073, 31 July 1998.

Congar, Yves M.J. (1983), *I believe in the Holy Spirit*, tr. David Smith, 3 vols (London: Seabury).

Connolly, S. (1995), 'The Power Motif and the Use of Scripture in Cogitosus' Vita Brigidae', in: Picard, J.M., ed., *Aquitaine and Ireland in the Middle Ages* (Blackrock), 207-220.

Corish, P.J. (1972), *The Christian Mission* (Dublin).

Cowan E.J. (1984), 'Myth and Identity in Early Medieval Scotland', in: *SHR* 63 (October 1984), 111-135.

Cowan, I.B., and Casson, D.E. (1976), *Medieval Religious Houses: Scotland* (London).

Cross, F.L., ed. (1997), *Oxford Dictionary of the Christian Church* (Oxford).

Crehan, J. H.(1979), 'The Theology of Eucharistic Consecration: the Role of Priest in Celtic Literature', *Theol. Studs.* 40 (June, 1979), 334-343.

Cruden, S.H. (1964), *The Early Christian and Pictish Monuments of Scotland* (Edinburgh).

Culling, E. (1993), *What is Celtic Christianity?* (Grove Spirituality, No. 45).

Davies, O. and F. Bowie (1995), *Celtic Christian Spirituality* (London: SPCK).

Davies, O. (1994), 'Celtic Christianity', in: *Epiphany* 14.3, 7-16.

Davies, W. (1982), *Wales in the Early Middle Ages* (Leicester).

Davies, W. (1989), 'The Place of Healing in Early Irish Society', in: Ó Corráin (1989, 43-55).

Davies, W. (1992), 'The Myth of the Celtic Church', in: N. Edwards and A. Lane, eds, *The Early Church in Wales* (Oxford), 12-21.

Deere, J (1994), *Surprised by the Power of the Spirit* (Eastbourne: Kingsway).

Deere, J (1996), *Surprised by the Voice of the God* (Eastbourne: Kingsway).

Delehaye, H. (1905), *Les Legendes Hagiographiques* (Brussels: SHG 18), tr. V.M. Crawford, *The Legend of the Saints* (London: Longmans, 1907).

Delehaye, H. (1910), 'Les Premiers "Libelli Miraculorum"', *Analecta Bollandiana* 19, 427-434.

Delehaye, H. (1934), *Cinq Leçons sur la Méthode Hagiographique* (Brussels).

Derouet, J-L. (1976), 'Les Possibilites d'Interprétation Sémiologique des Textes Hagiographiques', *RHEF* 62, 153-162.

Dictionary of the Irish Language (Dublin: RIA, 1913-1976).

Dillon, Myles, (1948), *Early Irish Literature* (Chicago).

Dillon, Myles, and N.K. Chadwick (1972), *The Celtic Realms* (London: Weidenfeld and Nicolson, 2nd ed.).

Dodd, B.E. and T.C. Heritage (1966), *The Early Christians in Britain* (London: Longmans).

Dodds, E.R. (1951), *The Greek and the Irrational* (Berkeley: University of California Press).

Doherty, C. (1987), 'The Irish Hagiographer: Resources, Aims, Results', in: T. Dunne, ed., *The writer as Witness: Literature as Historical Evidence* (Cork: Historical Studies, 16), 10-22.

Donnici, Lynn Li, (1995), *The Epidaurian Miracle Inscriptions* (Scholars Press).

Douglas, J.D., ed. (1982), *New Bible Dictionary*, 2nd edn. (Leicester: IVP).

Dubois, J. and J-L. Lemaitre (1993), *Sources et Méthodes de L'Hagiographie Médiévale* (Paris: Les éditions du Cerf).

Dumville, D.N. (1977), 'On the Northern British section of the *Historia Brittonum*', *Welsh Historical Review* viii, 345-354.

Dumville, D. ed., (1980), *Celtic Britain in the Early Middle Ages: Studies in Welsh and Scottish Sources* (Woodbridge: Boydell).

Dumville, D.N. (1981), 'Beowulf and the Celtic World: the Uses of Evidence', *Traditio* 37, 109-160.

Dumville, D.N., ed. (1993), *Saint Patrick AD 493- 1993* (Woodbridge: Boydell).

Dumville, D.N. (1996), Review of McCone (1990), *Peritia* 10, 389-398.

Duncan, A.A.M. (1975), *Scotland: The Making of the Kingdom* (Edinburgh).

Duncan, A.A.M. (1981), 'Bede, Iona, and the Picts', in: R.H.C. Davis and J.M. Wallace-Hadrill, eds, *The Writing of History in the Middle Ages: Essays Presented to Richard William Southern* (Oxford: Clarendon), 1-42.

Dunn, J.D.G., 'Spirit, Holy Spirit', *NIDNTT* 3, 693-707.

Ellis, E.E. (1982), 'Light', *NBD*, 701.

Esposito, M. (1919), 'On the Pseudo-Augustinian Treatise *De Mirabilibus Sanctae Scripturae* Written in Ireland in the Year 655', *PRIA* (c) 35, 189-207.

Etchingham, Colmán (1999), *Church Organisation in Ireland A.D. 650 to 1000* (Maynooth: Laigin).

Fee, G.D. (1991), *Gospel and Spirit, Issues in New Testament Hermeneutics* (Peabody: Hendrickson).

Fee, G.D. (1994), *God's Empowering Prescence* (Peabody: Hendrickson).

Finlay, W.I.R. (1979), *Columba* (London).

Fontaine, J. and J.N. Hillgarth, eds. (1992), *The Seventh Century: Change and Continuity* (London: Warburg Inst.).

Foster, S. (1996), *Picts, Gaels and Scots* (London: Historic Scotland/B.T. Batsford).

Frost, Evelyn (1940), *Christian Healing: A Consideration of the Place of Spiritual Healing in the Church of To-day in the Light of the Doctrine and Practice of the Ante-Nicene Church* (London).

Gantz, J. (1981), *Early Irish Myths and Sagas* (Harmondsworth: Penguin).

Gilley, S. (1995), 'The British Isles: Recent Developments in the Writing of Church History', *Annuario de Historia de la Iglesia* 4, 21ff.

Gougaud, L. (1932), *Christianity in Celtic Lands*, tr. M. Joynt (London, 2nd ed.)

Grant, R. (1952), *Miracle and Natural Law in Graeco-Roman and Early Christian Thought* (Amsterdam).

Grégoire, Réginald (1987), *Manuale di Agiologia: Introduzione alla Letteratura Agiografica* (Monastero San Silvestro Abate: Fabriano).

Grenz, Stanley J. (2000), *Renewing the Centre* (Grand Rapids: Bridgepoint).

Grimm, Jacob (1882), *Märchen*, 4vv., tr. James S. Stallybrass (London: George Bell).

Grogan, Brian (1976), 'Eschatological Teaching in the Early Irish Church', in: Martin McNamara(ed), *Biblical Studies: the Medieval Irish Contribution* (Dublin), 46-58.

Grosjean, P. (1957), 'Notes d'Hagiographie Celtique (nos. 37-40)', *Analecta Bollandiana*, 75, 373-419.

Grudem, W. (1982), *The Gift of Prophecy in 1 Corinthians* (Washington: UPS).

Grudem, W. (1994), *Systematic Theology, An Introduction to Biblical Doctrine* (Leicester: IVP; Grand Rapids: Zondervan).

Gwynn, E.J. (1912), 'Review of *Vita Sanctorum Hiberniae*', *ChQR*, 74, 62-81.

Hahn H-C. (1976), 'Light, Shine, Lamp', *NIDNTT* 2, 484-495.

Hahn H-C. (1978), 'Shadow', *NIDNTT* 3, 553-556.

Hanson, R.P.C. (1959), *Allegory and Event* (London: SCM).

Hanson, R.P.C. (1968), *Saint Patrick: His Origin and Career* (Oxford).

Hanson, R.P.C. (1983), *The Life and Writings of the Historical St. Patrick* (Oxford).

Hanson, R.P.C. (1989), 'The Mission of St Patrick', in: Mackey (1989, 22-44).

Hardinge, L. (1972), *The Celtic Church in Britain* (London: SPCK).

Hardon, J.A. (1954), 'The Concept of Miracle from St Augustine to Modern Apologetics', *Theological Studies* 15, 229-257.

Hardy, P.D. (1836), *Holy Wells of Ireland* (Dublin: Hardy and Walker).

Harnack, Adolf von (1902), *Die Mission und Ausbreitung des Christentums* (London: Williams and Norgate; English tr. 1905).

Harrison, K. (1976), *The Framework of Ango-Saxon History to 900* (Cambridge).

Hart, T. (1994), *Faith Thinking* (London: SPCK).

Heffernan, T.J. (1988), *Sacred Biography: Saints and their Biographers in the Middle Ages* (New York, Oxford: OUP).

Heist, W.H. (1981), 'Hagiography, Chiefly Celtic' in: *Hagiographic Cultures and Societies*, F. Dolbeau (Paris).

Henderson, I.M. (1967), *The Picts*, (London).

Henry, F. (1965), *Irish Art in the Early Christian Period to 800AD* (London).

Hensel, R., 'Fruit, Fig, Thorn, Thistle', *NIDNTT* 1, 722-3.

Herbert, M. (1988a), *Iona, Kells, and Derry. The History and Hagiography of the Monastic Familia of Columba* (Oxford: Clarendon Press).

Herbert, M. (1988b), 'The Bible in early Iona', in: D.F. Wright, ed., *The Bible in Scottish life and literature* (Edinburgh: St Andrew Press, 1988).

Herbert, M. (1996), 'Hagiography', in: McCone and Sims (1996, 79-90).

Herbert, M. (2001), 'The World of Adomnán', in: O'Loughlin (2001a, 33-41).

Hillgarth, J.N. (1986), *Christianity and Paganism, 350-750: the Conversion of Western Europe* (Philadelphia: University of Pennsylvania Press).

Hillgarth, J.N. (1987), 'Modes of Evangelization of Western Europe in the Seventh Century', in: Ní Chatháin and Richter (1987, 311-331).

Hillgarth, J.N. (1992), 'Eschatological and Political Concepts in the Seventh Century' in: Fontaine and Hillgarth (1992, 212-235).

Hudson, B.T. and Zeigler, J., eds. (1991), *Crossed Paths: Methodological Approaches to Celtic Aspects of Early Middle Ages History* (Universities of America Press).

Hughes, K. (1965), 'The Celtic Church and the Papacy', in: C.H. Lawrence, ed., *The English Church and the Papacy in the Middle Ages* (London).

Hughes, K. (1966), *The Church in Early Irish Society* (London).

Hughes, K. (1970), 'Early Christianity in Pictland (Jarrow Lecture 1970)', repr. in: Dumville (1980, 38-52).

Hughes, K. (1972), *Early Christian Ireland: Introduction to the Sources* (London: Hodder and Stoughton, The Sources of History).

Hughes, K. (1977), *The Early Celtic Idea of History and the Modern Historian* (Cambridge).

Hughes, K. (1980), *Early Christianity in Pictland* in: Dumville (1980, 38-52).

Hughes, K. (1981), 'The Celtic Church: is this a Valid Concept?', *Cambridge Medieval Celtic Studies* I, 1-20.

Hughes, K.W. and A. Hamlin (1977), *The Modern Traveller to the Early Irish Church* (London).

Hull, J.M. (1974), *Hellenistic Magic and the Synoptic Tradition* (London: SCM, Studies in Biblical Theology, 2nd series no. 28).

Jackson, K.H. (1964), *The Oldest Irish Tradition* (Cambridge).

Jackson, K.H. (1955), 'The Britons in Southern Scotland', *Antiquity* xxxix, 77-88.

Jackson, K.H. (1963), *Language and History in Early Britain* (Edinburgh).

Jackson, K.H. (1964), *The Oldest Irish Tradition* (Cambridge).

Jackson, K.H., ed. (1964), *Celt and Saxon: Studies in the Early British Border* (Cambridge).

James, Simon, 'The Ancient Celts: Discovery or Invention?' in: *Antiquity* March 1998.

Jones, G.H. (1936), 'Primitive Magic in the Lives of the Celtic Saints', *Trans. Hon. Soc. Cymmrodorion*, 69-96.

Kantzer, K.S. (1990), 'The Holy Spirit: God at Work, Christianity Today Institute, J. Wimber, J.I. Packer et al', *Christianity Today* 34, 27-35.

Kee, H.C. (1983), *Miracle in the Early Christian World: A Study in Sociohistorical Method* (New Haven).

Kelly, F. (1988), *A Guide to Early Irish Law* (Dublin).

Kelsey, M.T. (1968), *Tongue Speaking: an Experiment in Spiritual Experience* (London: Hodder and Stoughton).

Kelsey, M.T. (1973), *Healing and Christianity* (London: SCM).

Kenney, J.F. (1968), *The Sources for the Early History of Ireland: Ecclesiastical*, 2nd edition (Dublin: Four Courts).

Kingsbury, J.D. (1986), 'The Miracles of Jesus', in: D. Wenham and C. Blomberg eds., *Gospel Perspectives VI* (Sheffield: JSOT).

Klappert, B., 'King, Kingdom', *NIDNTT* 2, 372-389.

Kolenkow, A.B. (1976), 'A Problem of Power: How Miracle Doers Counter Charges of Magic in the Hellenistic World', in: G. MacRae, ed., *SBL 1976 Seminar Papers* (Missoula: Scholars Press), 105-110.

Kydd, Ronald A.N. (1973), *Charismata to 320 A.D: A Study of the Overt Pneumatic Experience of the Early Church* (PhD thesis, University of St Andrews [see Kydd 1984].

Kydd, Ronald A.N. (1984), *Charismatic Gifts in the Early Church* (Peabody: Hendrickson).

Ladd, George Eldon (1974), *The Presence of the Future: the Eschatology of Biblical Realism* (Grand Rapids: Eerdmans).

Ladd, George Eldon (1975), *A Theology of the New Testament* (Guildford: Lutterworth).

Laing, Ll. (1975), *The Archaeology of Late Celtic Britain 400-1200* (London).

Laing, Ll. (1979), *Celtic Britain 400-1000* (London).

Laing, Ll. (1990), *Celtic Britain and Ireland AD200-800: The Myth of the Dark Ages* (Dublin).

Lampe, G.W.H. (1961), *A Patristic Greek Lexikon* (Oxford: Clarendon).

Lang, Andrew (1899), *Myth, Ritual and Religion*, 2 vols. (London; New York: Longmans, Green).

Lapidge, M. and D. Dumville (1984), *Gildas: New Approaches* (Woodbridge).

Lapidge, M. and R. Sharpe, eds. (1985), *A Bibliography of Celtic Latin Literature 400-1200* (Dublin: RIA).

Latourelle, R. (1988), *The Miracles of Jesus and the Theology of Miracles* (New York: Paulist).

Lawrence, C.H. (1989), *Medieval Monasticism*, 2nd ed. (London: Longman).

Leeds, E.T. (1933), *Celtic Ornament in the British Isles Down to AD700* (Oxford).

Lubac, Henri de (1969), *The Church: Paradox and Mystery*, tr. James R. Dunne (Shannon: Ecclesia Press).

Low, Mary A. C. (1996), *Celtic Christianity and Nature. Early Irish and Hebridean Traditions* (Edinburgh: EUP).

Mac Cana, P. (1971), 'Conservation and Innovation in Early Celtic Literature', *Etudes Celtiques* 13, 61-118.

Mac Cana, P. (1986a), 'Myth into Literature in Early Ireland', in: R. Alluin and B. Escarbelt, eds, *Myth et Folklore Celtiques et Leurs Expressions Littéraires en*

Irelande, Colloque 12-13 December 1986 Universite de Lille III (Presses Universitaires de Lille, 1988), 31-43.

Mac Cana, P. (1986b), 'Christianisme et Paganisme dans l'Irlande Ancienne' in: P. Mac Cana and M. Meslin (eds), *Rencontres des Religions* (Paris), 57-74.

MacCulloch, J.A. (1911), *The Religion of the Ancient Celts* (London: Constable).

MacDonald, Aidan (1984), 'Aspects of the Monastery and Monastic Life in Adomnán's *Life of Columba'*, *Peritia* 3, 271-302.

MacDonald, Aidan (1995), 'A Fruit Tree at Durrow', *Hallel* 20, 10-14.

MacDonald, Aidan (1997), 'Adomnán's Monastery of Iona' in: Bourke (1997, 24-44).

MacGinty, Gerard (1996), 'The Irish Augustine: *De Mirabilibus Sacrae Scripturae'*, in: Ní Chatháin and Richter (1987, 70-83).

MacInnes, John (1982), 'Religion in Gaelic Society', *Transactions of the Gaelic Society of Inverness* LII.

Mackey, J. P. (1989), *An Introduction to Celtic Christianity* (Edinburgh: T&T Clark).

MacNeill, E. (1928), 'The Earliest Lives of St Patrick', *JRSAI* 58, 1-21.

Macquarrie, A. (1994), *Medieval Scotland, Corpus Christianorum: Hagiographies I,* ed. G. Philippart, (Turnhout: Brepols), 487-501.

Macquarrie, Alan (1997), *The Saints of Scotland: Essays in Scottish Church History, AD 450-1093* (Edinburgh: John Donald).

MacQueen, J. (1961), *St Nynia: a Study of Literary and Linguistic Evidence* (Edinburgh).

MacQueen, J. (1962), 'History and Miracle Stories in the Biography of Nynia', *Innes Review,* xiii, 115-29.

MacQueen, J. (1989), 'The Saint as Seer; Adomnán's Account of Columba', in: H.E. Davidson, *The Seer in Celtic and Other Traditions* (Edinburgh: John Donald), 37-51.

Mallory, J.P., ed. (1992), *Aspects of the Táin* (Belfast).

Mallory, J.P., ed. (1995), *Ulidia* (Belfast)

Márkus, G. (1999), 'Iona: Monks and Pastors and Missionaries', in: Broun and Clancy (1999, 115-138).

Markus, R.A. (1970), 'Gregory the Great and a Papal Missionary Strategy', *SCH* 50.6, 29-38.

Markus, R.A. (1985), 'The Sacred and Secular: from Augustine to Gregory the Great', *JTS* 36, 84-96.

Markus, R.A. (1992), 'From Caesarius to Boniface: Christianity and Paganism in Gaul', in: Fontaine and Hillgarth (1992, 154-167).

Marshall, I.H. (1977), *I believe in the Historical Jesus* (London: Hodder and Stoughton).

Mayr-Harting, H. (1972), *The Coming of Christianity to Anglo-Saxon England* (London).

McCone, K. (1984), 'An Introduction to Early Irish Saints Lives', *The Maynooth Review* 11, 26-59.

McCone, K. (1989), 'Tale of Two Ditties: Poet and Satirist in *Cath Maige Tuired'*, in: Ó Corrain *et al.* (1989, 122-43).

McCone, K. (1990), *Pagan Past and Christian Present* (Maynooth: An Sagart).

McCone, K. and Sims, K., eds. (1996), *Progress in Medieval Irish Studies* (Maynooth: Dept Old Irish Studs).

McCormick, Finbar (1997), 'Iona: The Archaeology of the Early Monastery', in: Bourke (1997, 45-68).

McCready, W.D. (1989), *Signs of Sanctity. Miracles in the Thought of Gregory the Great* (Toronto: Pontifical Institute of Mediaeval Studies, Studies and Texts 91).

McCready, W.D. (1994), *Miracles and the Venerable Bede* (Toronto: Pontifical Institute of Mediaeval Studies, Studies and Texts 118).

McNamara, Martin (1975), *The Apocrypha in the Irish Church* (Dublin: DIAS).

McNamara, Martin (1987), 'The Text of the Latin Bible in the Early Irish Church', in: Ní Chatáin and Richter (1987, 7-55).

McNaught, J.C. (1927), *The Celtic Church and the See of Peter* (Oxford: Blackwell).

McNeill, P. and R. Nicholson, eds. (1975), *An Historical Atlas of Scotland ca. 400 - ca. 1600* (St Andrews).

Maloney, H.N., and A.A. Lovekin (1985), *Glossolalia* (Oxford).

Martin, M. (1716), *A Description of the Western Islands of Scotland*, 2nd ed. (London: Andrew Bell; repr. Edinburgh: James Thin, 1981).

Meckler, M. (1990), 'Colum Cille's Ordination of Aedán mac Gabráin', *Innes Review* 41.2, 139-150.

Meek, D. (1991), 'Celtic Christianity: What Is It, and When Was It?': Review of Mackey (1989), *Scottish Bulletin of Evangelical Theology* 9, 13-21.

Meek, D. (1992), 'The Modern Celtic Church: the Contemporary Revival and its Roots', *Scottish Bulletin of Evangelical Theology* 10.1, 6-13.

Meek, D. (1997), 'Surveying the Saints: Reflections on Recent Writings in 'Celtic Christianity', *Scottish Bulletin of Evangelical Theology* 15.1, 50-60.

Meek, Donald E. (2000), *The Quest for Celtic Christianity* (Edinburgh: Handsel Press).

Meyvaert, P., ed. (1977a), *Benedict, Gregory, Bede and Others* (London: Variorum Reprints).

Meyvaert, P. (1977b), 'Bede the Scholar', in: Meyvaert (1977a), IX, 51-55.

Migne, J.P., *Index de Miraculis PL* 219, 332-362.

Moltmann, J. (1968), *Theology of Hope: On the Grounds and Implications of a Christian Theology* (London: SCM Press; and New York: Harper and Row).

Moltmann, J. (1975), *Kirche in der Kraft des Geistes*, tr. Margaret Kohl, *The Church in the Power of the Spirit* (London: SCM 1977).

Motyer, A., 'Fruit, Fig, Thorn, Thistle', *NIDNTT* 1, 723-725.

Moody, T. W., F. X. Martin, and F. J. Byrne, eds. (1982), *A New History of Ireland: 8; A Chronology of Irish History to 1976: A Companion to Irish History*, part 1 (Oxford: Clarendon).

Moule, C.F.D., ed. (1965), *Miracles* (London: Mowbray).

Murray, D. Christie, (1978), *Voices from the Gods: Speaking in Tongues* (London: RKP).

Murphy, Gerard (1955), *Saga and Myth in Ancient Ireland* (Dublin).

Muus, Bent J. (1974), tr. G. Vevers, *The Sea Fishes of Britain and North-Western Europe* (London: Collins).

New Bible Dictionary, see J.D. Douglas (1982).

New International Dictionary of New Testament Theology, see Colin Brown (1980, 1976, 1978).

Ní Chatháin, Próinséas and M. Richter, eds. (1987), *Ireland and Christendom. The Bible and the Missions* (Stuttgart).

Noble, T.F.X. and T. Head, eds (1994), *Soldiers of the Christ; Saints and Saints' Lives from Late Antiquity and the Early Middle Ages* (London).

Ó Briain, Felim (1944), 'Irish Hagiography: Historiography and Method', in: Sylvester O'Brien (ed), *Measgra i gCuimhne Mhichíl Uí Chlérigh* (Dublin, 1944), 119-131.

Ó Briain, Felim (1945), 'Miracles in the Lives of the Irish Saints', *Irish Eccles. Rec.* 5th Ser. 66, 331-342.

Ó Briain, Felim (1947), 'Saga Themes in Irish Hagiography', in: S. Pender, ed., *Féilscribhinn Torna: Essays presented to Tadhg Ua Donnchadha* (Cork), 33-42.

Ó Cathasaigh, Tomás (1996), 'Early Irish Narrative Literature', in: McCone and Sims (1996, 55-64).

Ó Concheannain, Tomás Ó, 'Textual and Historical Associations of *Leabhar na hUidre*', *Éigse* 29, 65-120.

Ó Corrain, D. (1983), 'Historical Need and Literary Narrative', in: D.E. Evans, ed., *Proc. Seventh Int. Cong. Celtic Studs., Oxford* (Oxford), 141-158.

Ó Corrain, D., L. Breatnach, and K. McCone, eds. (1989), *Sages Saints and Storytellers; Celtic Studies in Honour of Professor James Carney* (Maynooth).

Ó Cróinin, D. (1989), 'The Date, Provenance, and Earliest Use of the Works of Virgilius Maro Grammaticus', in: G. Bernt, F. Rädle and G. Silagi, eds, *Traditio und Wertung: Festschrift für Franz Brunhölzl zum 65. Geburtstag* (Sigmaringen).

Ó Riain, P. (1982), 'Towards a Methodology in Early Irish Hagiography', *Peritia* 1, 146-159.

O'Flaherty, R. (1846), *A Chorographical Description of Iar or West Connaught*, ed. James Hardiman, (Dublin: Irish Archaeological Society, 9, written 1684).

Ó Floinn, R. (1997), 'Insignia Columbae I', in: Bourke (1997, 136-161).

Ó'Laoghaire, D. (1979), 'Daily Intimacy with God: An Ever New Aspect of Celtic Worship', *Studia Liturgica* 13, 1.

O'Laoghaire, D. (1986), 'Celtic Spirituality', in: C. Jones and G. Wainwright, E. Yarnold, eds., *The Study of Spirituality,* (London: SPCK).

O'Loughlin, T. (1992), 'The Exegetical Purpose of Adomnán's *De Locis Sanctis*', *CMCS* 24, 37-53.

O'Loughlin, T. (1994a), 'The Library of Iona in the Late Seventh Century: the Evidence from Adomnán's *De Locis Sanctis*', *Ériu* 45, 33-52.

O'Loughlin, T. (1994b), 'The Latin Version of the Scriptures in Use in Iona in the Late Seventh Century: the Evidence from Adomnán's *De Locis Sanctis*', *Peritia* 8, 18-26.

O'Loughlin, T. (1995), 'Adomnán the Illustrious', *Innes Review* 46, 1-14.

O'Loughlin, T. (1996), 'The View from Iona: Adomnán's Mental Maps', *Peritia* 10, 98-122.

O'Loughlin, T. (1997a), 'Living in the Ocean', in: Bourke (1997, 11-23).

O'Loughlin, T. (1997b), 'Res, Tempus, Locus, Persona: Adomnán's Exegetical Method', *Innes Review* 48.2, 95-111.

O'Loughlin, T. (1997c), Adomnán and Arculf: The Case of an Expert Witness', *J. Medieval Latin* 7, 127-146.
O'Loughlin, T. (2000), 'The Plan of the New Jerusalem in the Book of Armagh' *CMCS* 39.
O'Loughlin, T., ed. (2001a), Adomnán at Birr, AD 697: *Essays in Commemoration of the Law of the Innocents* (Dublin: Four Courts).
O'Loughlin, T., ed. (2001b), Adomnán, 'A Man of Many Parts' in: O'Loughlin (2001, 41-52).
O'Rahilly, T.F. (1946), *Early Irish History and Mythology* (Dublin).
O'Reilly, Jennifer (1995), 'Exegesis and the Book of Kells: the Lucan Genealogy', in: *The Book of Kells, Proc. Conf. T.C.D. 6-9 Sept. 1992* (Dublin, Scholar), 344-397; or: T. Finan and V. Twomey, eds, *Scriptural Interpretation in the Fathers* (Dublin, Four Courts, 1995), 315-355.
O'Reilly, Jennifer (1997), 'Reading the Scriptures in the Life of Columba', in: Bourke (1997, 80-106).
O'Sullivan, Sean (1966), *The Folktales of Ireland* (London).
Opsahl, Paul D., ed. (1978), *The Holy Spirit in the Life of the Church* (Minneapolis: Augsburg).
Parker, P. (1976), 'Early Christianity as a Religion of Healing', *St Luke's Journal of Theology* 19, 142-150.
Pearce, S.M. (1982), 'The Early Church in Western Britain and Ireland', *BAR* 102.
Perham, Michael (1980), *Communion of Saints* (London).
Petersen, Joan (1984), *The Dialogues of Gregory the Great in their Late Antique Cultural Background* (Toronto: Pontifical Inst. Mediev. Studs).
Picard, Jean-Michel (1981), 'The Marvellous in the Irish and Continental Saints Living in the Merovingian Period', *BAR Int'l Series* 113, 91-104.
Picard, Jean-Michel (1982a), 'The Purpose of Adomnán's *Vitae Columbae*', *Peritia* 1, 160-177.
Picard, Jean-Michel (1982b), 'The Schaffhausen Adomnán: a Unique Witness to Hiberno-Latin', *Peritia* 1, 216-249.
Picard, Jean-Michel (1984), 'Bede, Adomnán and the Writing of History', *Peritia* 3, 50-70.
Picard, Jean-Michel (1985), 'Structural Patterns in Early Hiberno-Latin Hagiography', *Peritia* 4, 67-82.
Picard, Jean-Michel (1987), 'The Bible Used by Adomnán', in: Ní Chatháin and Richter (1987, 246-257).
Picard, Jean-Michel (1987), 'Eloquentiae Exuberantia: Words and Forms in Adomnán's *Vita Columbae*', *Peritia* 6-7, 141-157.
Picard, Jean-Michel (1989), 'The Strange Death of Guaire Mac Áedáin', in: Ó Corrain (1989, 367-375).
Picard, Jean-Michel, ed. (1991), *Ireland and Northern France AD600-850* (Dublin: Four Courts).
Piggott, Stuart, ed. (1962), *The Prehistoric Peoples of Scotland* (London).
Piggott, Stuart (1968), *The Druids* (Thames and Hudson).
Plummer, C. (1910), *Vitae Sanctorum Hiberniae* (2 vols; Oxford).
Popper, Karl R. (1961), *The Poverty of Historicism, 2nd ed. reprinted (with some corrections)* (Routledge and Paul, 1961).
Pytches, D. (1985), *Come Holy Spirit* (London: Hodder and Stoughton).

Rad, Gerhard Von (1968), *The Message of the Prophets* (London: SCM).

Rahner, Karl (1967), *Theological Investigations III* (London).

Remus, H. (1982), 'Does Terminology Distinguish Early Christian from Pagan Miracles?', *J. Biblical Literature* 104.4, 531-551.

Remus, H. (1983), *Pagan-Christian Conflict over Miracle in the Second Century* (Philadelphia: Patristic Foundation, Patristic Monograph Series No. 10).

Rhys, J. (1901), *Celtic Folklore, Welsh and Manx* (Oxford).

Richardson, A. (1969), 'Miracle' in: Richardson, A., ed., *A Dictionary of Christian Theology* (London: SCM), 216-217.

Richter, M. (1999), *Ireland and Her Neighbors in the Seventh Century* (New York: St Martin).

Ritchie, A. (1984), 'The Archaeology of the Picts: Some Current Problems', *BAR* 125, 1-6.

Ritchie, A. (1989), *Picts* (Edinburgh).

Ross, Anne, (1986), *The Pagan Celts* (London: Batsford).

Rouselle, A. (1976), 'From Sanctuary to Miracle-Worker: Healing in Fourth-Century Gaul': tr. and ed. E. Forster and O. and P.M. Ranum, in: *Ritual, Religion, and the Sacred*, vol. 7 (Baltimore and London: 1982), 95-127.

Rusch, W.G. (1978), *The Later Latin Fathers* (London: Duckworth).

Ruthven, Jon (1993), *On the Cessation of the Charismata: The Protestant Polemic on Postbiblical Miracles* (Sheffield: Sheffield Academic Press).

Sayers, W. (1993), 'Spiritual Navigation in the Western Sea: Starlunga Saga and Adomnán's Hinba', *Scripta Islandica* 44, 30-42.

Schatzman, S. (1987), *A Pauline Theology of Charismata* (Peabody: Hendrikson).

Sharpe, R. (1982), '*Vitae S. Brigitae* : The Oldest Texts', *Peritia* 1, 81-106.

Sharpe, R. (1984), 'Some problems Concerning the Organisation of the Church in Early Medieval Ireland', *Peritia* 3, 230-270.

Sharpe, R. (1989), '*Quattuor Sanctissimi Episcopi:* Irish Saints Before St Patrick', in: Ó Corráin *et al.* (1989, 376-399).

Sharpe, R. (2000), 'The Thriving of Dalriada', in: Taylor (2000).

Sharpe, R. (1991), *Medieval Irish Saint's Lives* (Oxford).

Sharpe, R. (1992), 'Churches and Communities in Early Medieval Ireland: Towards a Pastoral Model', in: Blair and Sharpe (1992, 81-109).

Sherry, Patrick (1984), *Spirit, Saints and Immortality* (London: Macmillan).

Sims-Williams, Patrick (1986), 'The Visionary Celt: The Construction of an "Ethnic Preconception"', *CMCS* 11.

Sims-Williams, Patrick (1996), 'Review of McCone (1990)', *Éigse* 29, 177-196.

Sims-Williams, Patrick (1998), 'Celtomania and Celtoscepticism' *CMCS* 36.

Skene, W.F. (1886-90), *Celtic Scotland: A History of Ancient Alban* (3 vols., Edinburgh).

Smith, Julia M.H. (1992), 'Review Article: Early Medieval Hagiography in the Late Twentieth Century', in: *Early Medieval Europe* I (1), 69-76.

Smyth, A. P. (1984), *Warlords and Holy Men: Scotland AD 80-1000* (Edinburgh: EUP, repr.1992).

Smyth, A.P. (1972), 'The Earliest Irish Annals', *Proc. RIA* 72 C, 1-48.

Smyth, Marina (1986), 'The Physical World in Seventh-Century Hiberno-Latin Texts', *Peritia* 5, 201-234.

Smyth, Marina (1996), *Understanding the Universe in Seventh-Century Ireland* (Woodbridge: Boydell).

Spence, L. (1999), *The Magic Arts in Celtic Britain* (London).

Stancliffe, C. (1983), *St Martin and His Hagiographer: History and Miracle in Sulpicius Severus* (Oxford).

Stancliffe, C. (1992), 'The Miracle Stories in Seventh-Century Irish Saints Lives', in: Fontaine and Hillgarth (1992, 87-115).

Stevenson, Jane (1983), 'Ascent Through the Heavens, from Egypt to Ireland', *CMCS* 5, 21-35.

Stewart, R.A. (1982), 'Shekinah', *NBD* 1101-2.

Stokes, W. and J. Strachan (1901), *Thesaurus Palaeohibernicus: A Collection of Old-Irish Glosses, Scholia, Prose and Verse* (Cambridge, 1901-3, 2 vols; supplement Halle, 1910).

Souter, A., *A Glossary of Later Latin to 600 A.D.* (Oxford: Clarendon Press, 1957).

Swete, H.B. (1912), *The Holy Spirit in the Ancient Church*, (London: Macmillan).

Swinburne, R., ed. (1970), *The Concept of Miracle* (London: Macmillan).

Swinburne, R., ed. (1989), *Miracles* (New York: Macmillan).

Taylor, S., ed. (2000), *Kings, Clerics and Chronicles in Scotland 500-1297: Essays in Honour of Marjorie Ogilvie Anderson on the Occasion of her Ninetieth Birthday* (Dublin: Four Courts).

Taylor, J.V. (1972), *The Go-Between God* (London: SCM).

Theissen, G. (1983, *Miracle Stories of the Early Christian Tradition* (Edinburgh: T&T Clark).

Thomas, A.C. (1968), 'The Evidence from North Britain', in: M.W. Barley and R.P.C. Hanson, eds., *Christianity in Britain, 300-700* (Leicester), 93-121.

Thomas, A.C. (1971), *The Early Christian Archaeology of North Britain* (London and Glasgow).

Thomas, A.C. (1981), *Christianity in Roman Britain to AD500* (London).

Thomas, A.C. (1988), 'The "Monster" Episode in Adomnán's *Life of St Columba*', *Cryptozoology* 7, 38-45.

Thomas, A.C. (1990), 'Gallici Nautae de Galliarum Prouincis – A Sixth / Seventh Century Trade with Gaul Reconsidered', *Medieval Archaeology* 34, 1-26.

Thompson, E.A. (1958), 'The Origin of Christianity in Scotland', *SHR* xxxvii, 17-22.

Thompson, E.A. (1984), *Saint Germanus of Auxerre and the End of Roman Britain* (Woodbridge: Studies in Celtic History 6).

Thompson, E.A. (1985), *Who was St. Patrick?* (Woodbridge).

Thurneysen, R. (1921), *Die Irische Helden-und Königsage* (Halle: Niemeyer).

Tinsley, E.J. (1960), *The Imitation of God in Christ* (London).

Torrance, Thomas F. (1965), *Theology in Reconstruction* (London: SCM).

Torrance, Thomas F. (1971), *God and Rationality* (London: Oxford University Press).

Turner, Max (1996), *The Holy Spirit and Spiritual Gifts Then and Now* (Carlisle: Paternoster).

Twelftree, G.H. (1993), *Jesus the Exorcist* (Peabody: Hendrickson).

Van Dam, R. (1993), *Saints and Their Miracles in Late Antique Gaul* (Princeton).

Van der Essen, (1911), 'Review of *Vita Sanctorum Hiberniae*', *Revue d'Histoire Ecclesiastique* 12, 526-8.

Vendryes, (1911), 'Review of *Vita Sanctorum Hiberniae*', *RC* 32, 104-6.

Wainwright, F.T. (1955), *The Problem of the Picts* (Edinburgh).

Waal, E. De, (1988), *The Celtic Vision* (London: DLT).

Ward, B. (1982), *Miracles and the Medieval Mind: 1000-1215* (Philadelphia).

Warren, F.E. and J. Stevenson (1987), *The Liturgy and Ritual of the Celtic Church* (Woodbridge).

Watkin-Jones, Howard (1922), *The Holy Spirit in the Medieval Church*, (London: Epworth).

Watson W.J. (1915), 'The Celtic Church in its Relations with Paganism', *Celtic Review* X (November), 263-279.

Watson, W.J. (1925), *The History of the Celtic Place-Names of Scotland* (Edinburgh and London: Blackwood for the Royal Celtic Soc.; repr. Edinburgh: Birlinn, 1993).

Wenham, G., and C. Blomberg, eds. (1986), *Gospel Perspectives VI, The Miracles of Jesus* (Sheffield: JSOT).

Whitelock, D., R. McKitterick and D. Dumville, eds. (1982), *Ireland in Early Medieval Europe* (Cambridge).

Williams, A., A. Smyth, and D.P. Kirkby (1991), *A Biographical Dictionary of Dark-Age Britain: England, Scotland, and Wales c500-c1050* (London: Seaby).

Wimber, J. and K. Springer (1985), *Power Evangelism* (London: Hodder and Stoughton).

Wimber, J. and K. Springer (1986), *Power Healing* (London: Hodder and Stoughton).

Wood, I.N. (1982), 'The *Vita Columbani* and Merovingian Hagiography', *Peritia* 1, 63-80.

Wood, I.N. (2001), *The Missionary Life: Saints and the Evangelisation of Europe 400-1050* (London: Longmans,).

Wood-Martin, W.G. (1895), *Pagan Ireland, an Archaeological Sketch* (London: Longmans, Green).

Wood-Martin, W.G. (1902), *Traces of the Elder Faiths of Ireland* (London: Longmans).

Woods, David (2002), 'Four Notes on Adomnán's *Vita Columbae*', *Peritia* 16, 40-67.

INDEXES

1. *Vita Columbae* by Chapter

2. Scripture Index

3. Author Index

Aalen, S., 147
Aigrain, R., 8
Alcock, L., 5
Ambrose, 183, 189-90, 224
Anderson, M.O and A.O., xvi, 1, 2, 3,
     9, 12, 23, 114, 116, 123, 181,
     186, 196, 248
Athanasius, 224
Atkinson, R., 40
Augustine of Hippo, 4, 154, 160,
     164, 183, 187, 189, 190, 193-5,
     199, 224-5, 239
Augustine, Irish, 4, 34

Basil, 29, 224-7
Bauckham, R., 113
Beccán, 109
Bede, 3, 23, 27, 29, 48, 105, 118,
     120, 160, 183, 184, 187-8, 205,
     206-9, 217-8, 224, 229, 238
Berger, P., 28
Bietenhard, H., 129-30
Binchy, D.A., 16, 39, 42-3, 45, 48, 93
Breatnach, L., 106
Broun, D., 1
Brown, C., 67, 86
Brown, Peter, 206, 239
Brüning, G., 190, 250
Butler, E.C., 64

Cameron, A., 46
Carey, J., 39
Carney, J., 37, 39, 41-2, 68, 85-6, 89
Cassian, J., 27, 107-8, 139, 165, 174,
     183, 187, 195, 206, 224-8
Chadwick, H., 26
Chadwick, N.K., 68, 69, 70, 90
Chadwick, O., 226
Charles-Edwards, T., 209
Chrysostom, J, 28, 224
Clancy, T.O., xvi, 1, 5, 7, 82, 140,
     154-6, 162, 164, 172, 195, 212
Clarke, W.K.L., 226-7

Cogitosus, 13, 16, 139
Colgan, J., 1
Columbanus, 104, 160, 188, 212
Cormac, 56-7
Curry, E., 70, 71, 77

Davies, W., 5
Davies, W., 32, 35, 242
Deere, J., xv
Delehaye, H., 8-9, 47
Derouet, J.L., 6, 33
Dionysius, 129
Dodd, C.H., 102
Dodds, E.R., 34
Dudley-Edwards, O., 117
Dumville, D., 39, 215
Duncan, A.A.M., 3
Dunn, J.D.G., 142

Ellis, E.E., 146
Esposito, M., 4
Etchingham, C., 1, 3, 18, 23, 235
Eucherius, 107, 187

Fee, G.D., 149, 155, 221
Fontaine, J., 4, 31
Forbes, A.F., 1
Fowler, J.T., 1, 96, 116, 118, 169,
     172, 201
Frost, E., 224

Gantz, G., 41
Gerald of Wales, 169
Grégoire. R., 8
Gregory I, 3, 29-30, 104-5, 129, 149,
     153, 160-2, 170, 175-6, 182-4,
     190-6, 224-5, 228-30, 248-50
Gregory Nyssa, 29, 224
Gregory of Tours, 55, 225
Grenz, S., 225
Grimm. J., 51
Grudem, W., 149, 169, 175, 200
Gwynn, E.J., 40, 64-5, 87

4. Subject Index

Studies in Christian History and Thought
(All titles uniform with this volume)
Dates in bold are of projected publication

David Bebbington
Holiness in Nineteenth-Century England
David Bebbington stresses the relationship of movements of spirituality to changes in their cultural setting, especially the legacies of the Enlightenment and Romanticism. He shows that these broad shifts in ideological mood had a profound effect on the ways in which piety was conceptualized and practised. Holiness was intimately bound up with the spirit of the age.

2000 / 0-85364-981-2 / viii + 98pp

J. William Black
Reformation Pastors
Richard Baxter and the Ideal of the Reformed Pastor
This work examines Richard Baxter's *Gildas Salvianus, The Reformed Pastor* (1656) and explores each aspect of his pastoral strategy in light of his own concern for 'reformation' and in the broader context of Edwardian, Elizabethan and early Stuart pastoral ideals and practice.

2003 / 1-84227-190-3 / xxii + 308pp

James Bruce
Prophecy, Miracles, Angels, *and* Heavenly Light?
The Eschatology, Pneumatology and Missiology of Adomnán's Life of Columba
This book surveys approaches to the marvellous in hagiography, providing the first critique of Plummer's hypothesis of Irish saga origin. It then analyses the uniquely systematized phenomena in the *Life of Columba* from Adomnán's seventh-century theological perspective, identifying the coming of the eschatological Kingdom as the key to understanding.

2004 / 1-84227-227-6 / xviii + 286pp

Colin J. Bulley
The Priesthood of Some Believers
Developments from the General to the Special Priesthood in the Christian Literature of the First Three Centuries
The first in-depth treatment of early Christian texts on the priesthood of all believers shows that the developing priesthood of the ordained related closely to the division between laity and clergy and had deleterious effects on the practice of the general priesthood.

2000 / 1-84227-034-6 / xii + 336pp

Anthony R. Cross (ed.)
Ecumenism and History
Studies in Honour of John H.Y. Briggs
This collection of essays examines the inter-relationships between the two fields in which Professor Briggs has contributed so much: history—particularly Baptist and Nonconformist—and the ecumenical movement. With contributions from colleagues and former research students from Britain, Europe and North America, *Ecumenism and History* provides wide-ranging studies in important aspects of Christian history, theology and ecumenical studies.

2002 / 1-84227-135-0 / xx + 362pp

Maggi Dawn
Confessions of an Inquiring Spirit
Form as Constitutive of Meaning in S.T. Coleridge's Theological Writing
This study of Coleridge's *Confessions* focuses on its confessional, epistolary and fragmentary form, suggesting that attention to these features significantly affects its interpretation. Bringing a close study of these three literary forms, the author suggests ways in which they nuance the text with particular understandings of the Trinity, and of a kenotic christology. Some parallels are drawn between Romantic and postmodern dilemmas concerning the authority of the biblical text.

2006 / 1-84227-255-1 / approx. 224 pp

Ruth Gouldbourne
The Flesh and the Feminine
Gender and Theology in the Writings of Caspar Schwenckfeld
Caspar Schwenckfeld and his movement exemplify one of the radical communities of the sixteenth century. Challenging theological and liturgical norms, they also found themselves challenging social and particularly gender assumptions. In this book, the issues of the relationship between radical theology and the understanding of gender are considered.

2005 / 1-84227-048-6 / approx. 304pp

Galen K. Johnson
Prisoner of Conscience
John Bunyan on Self, Community and Christian Faith
This is an interdisciplinary study of John Bunyan's understanding of conscience across his autobiographical, theological and fictional writings, investigating whether conscience always deserves fidelity, and how Bunyan's view of conscience affects his relationship both to modern Western individualism and historic Christianity.

2003 / 1-84227- 151-2 / xvi + 236pp

R.T. Kendall
Calvin and English Calvinism to 1649
The author's thesis is that those who formed the Westminster Confession of Faith, which is regarded as Calvinism, in fact departed from John Calvin on two points: (1) the extent of the atonement and (2) the ground of assurance of salvation.

1997 / 0-85364-827-1 / xii + 264pp

Byung-Ho Moon
Lex Dei Regula Vivendi et Vivificandi
Calvin's Christological Understanding of the Law in the Light of his Concept of Christus Mediator Legis
This book explores the coherence between Christology and soteriology in Calvin's theology of the law, examining its intellectual origins and his position on the concept and extent of Christ's mediation of the law. A comparative study between Calvin and contemporary Reformers—Luther, Bucer, Melancthon and Bullinger—and his opponent Michael Servetus is made for the purpose of pointing out the unique feature of Calvin's Christological understanding of the law.

2005 / 1-84227-318-3 / approx. 370pp

John Eifion Morgan-Wynne
Holy Spirit and Religious Experience in Christian Writings, c.AD90–200
This study examines how far Christians in the third to fifth generations (c.AD90–200) attributed their sense of encounter with the divine presence, their sense of illumination in the truth or guidance in decision-making, and their sense of ethical empowerment to the activity of the Holy Spirit in their lives.

2005 / 1-84227-319-1 / approx. 274pp

James I. Packer
The Redemption and Restoration of Man in the Thought of Richard Baxter
James I. Packer provides a full and sympathetic exposition of Richard Baxter's doctrine of humanity, created and fallen; its redemption by Christ Jesus; and its restoration in the image of God through the obedience of faith by the power of the Holy Spirit.

2002 / 1-84227-147-4 / 432pp

Andrew Partington,
Church and State
The Contribution of the Church of England Bishops to the House of Lords during the Thatcher Years

In *Church and State*, Andrew Partington argues that the contribution of the Church of England bishops to the House of Lords during the Thatcher years was overwhelmingly critical of the government; failed to have a significant influence in the public realm; was inefficient, being undertaken by a minority of those eligible to sit on the Bench of Bishops; and was insufficiently moral and spiritual in its content to be distinctive. On the basis of this, and the likely reduction of the number of places available for Church of England bishops in a fully reformed Second Chamber, the author argues for an evolution in the Church of England's approach to the service of its bishops in the House of Lords. He proposes the Church of England works to overcome the genuine obstacles which hinder busy diocesan bishops from contributing to the debates of the House of Lords and to its life more informally.

2005 / 1-84227-334-5 / approx. 324pp

Alan P.F. Sell
Enlightenment, Ecumenism, Evangel
Theological Themes and Thinkers 1550–2000

This book consists of papers in which such interlocking topics as the Enlightenment, the problem of authority, the development of doctrine, spirituality, ecumenism, theological method and the heart of the gospel are discussed. Issues of significance to the church at large are explored with special reference to writers from the Reformed and Dissenting traditions.

2005 / 1-84227330-2 / xviii + 422pp

Alan P.F. Sell
Hinterland Theology
Some Reformed and Dissenting Adjustments

Many books have been written on theology's 'giants' and significant trends, but what of those lesser-known writers who adjusted to them? In this book some hinterland theologians of the British Reformed and Dissenting traditions, who followed in the wake of toleration, the Evangelical Revival, the rise of modern biblical criticism and Karl Barth, are allowed to have their say. They include Thomas Ridgley, Ralph Wardlaw, T.V. Tymms and N.H.G. Robinson.

2006 / 1-84227-331-0

November 2004

Alan P.F. Sell and Anthony R. Cross (eds)
Protestant Nonconformity in the Twentieth Century
In this collection of essays scholars representative of a number of Nonconformist traditions reflect thematically on Nonconformists' life and witness during the twentieth century. Among the subjects reviewed are biblical studies, theology, worship, evangelism and spirituality, and ecumenism. Over and above its immediate interest, this collection provides a marker to future scholars and others wishing to know how some of their forebears assessed Nonconformity's contribution to a variety of fields during the century leading up to Christianity's third millennium.

2003 / 1-84227-221-7 / x + 398pp

Mark Smith
Religion in Industrial Society
Oldham and Saddleworth 1740–1865
This book analyses the way British churches sought to meet the challenge of industrialization and urbanization during the period 1740–1865. Working from a case-study of Oldham and Saddleworth, Mark Smith challenges the received view that the Anglican Church in the eighteenth century was characterized by complacency and inertia, and reveals Anglicanism's vigorous and creative response to the new conditions. He reassesses the significance of the centrally directed church reforms of the mid-nineteenth century, and emphasizes the importance of local energy and enthusiasm. Charting the growth of denominational pluralism in Oldham and Saddleworth, Dr Smith compares the strengths and weaknesses of the various Anglican and Nonconformist approaches to promoting church growth. He also demonstrates the extent to which all the churches participated in a common culture shaped by the influence of evangelicalism, and shows that active co-operation between the churches rather than denominational conflict dominated. This revised and updated edition of Dr Smith's challenging and original study makes an important contribution both to the social history of religion and to urban studies.

2005 / 1-84227-335-3 / approx. 300pp

Martin Sutherland
Peace, Toleration and Decay
The Ecclesiology of Later Stuart Dissent
This fresh analysis brings to light the complexity and fragility of the later Stuart Nonconformist consensus. Recent findings on wider seventeenth-century thought are incorporated into a new picture of the dynamics of Dissent and the roots of evangelicalism.

2003 / 1-84227-152-0 / xxii + 216pp

G. Michael Thomas
The Extent of the Atonement
A Dilemma for Reformed Theology from Calvin to the Consensus
A study of the way Reformed theology addressed the question, 'Did Christ die for all, or for the elect only?', commencing with John Calvin, and including debates with Lutheranism, the Synod of Dort and the teaching of Moïse Amyraut.
1997 / 0-85364-828-X / x + 278pp

Mark D. Thompson
A Sure Ground on which to Stand
The Relation of Authority and Interpretive Method of Luther's Approach to Scripture
The best interpreter of Luther is Luther himself. Unfortunately many modern studies have superimposed contemporary agendas upon this sixteenth-century Reformer's writings. This fresh study examines Luther's own words to find an explanation for his robust confidence in the Scriptures, a confidence that generated the famous 'stand' at Worms in 1521.
2004 / 1-84227-145-8 / xvi + 322pp

Carl R. Trueman and R.S. Clark (eds)
Protestant Scholasticism
Essays in Reassessment
Traditionally Protestant theology, between Luther's early reforming career and the dawn of the Enlightenment, has been seen in terms of decline and fall into the wastelands of rationalism and scholastic speculation. In this volume a number of scholars question such an interpretation. The editors argue that the development of post-Reformation Protestantism can only be understood when a proper historical model of doctrinal change is adopted. This historical concern underlies the subsequent studies of theologians such as Calvin, Beza, Olevian, Baxter, and the two Turrentini. The result is a significantly different reading of the development of Protestant Orthodoxy, one which both challenges the older scholarly interpretations and clichés about the relationship of Protestantism to, among other things, scholasticism and rationalism, and which demonstrates the fruitfulness of the new, historical approach.
1999 / 0-85364-853-0 / xx + 344pp

Shawn D. Wright
Our Sovereign Refuge
The Pastoral Theology of Theodore Beza

Our Sovereign Refuge is a study of the pastoral theology of the Protestant reformer who inherited the mantle of leadership in the Reformed church from John Calvin. Countering a common view of Beza as supremely a 'scholastic' theologian who deviated from Calvin's biblical focus, Wright uncovers a new portrait. He was not a cold and rigid academic theologian obsessed with probing the eternal decrees of God. Rather, by placing him in his pastoral context and by noting his concerns in his pastoral and biblical treatises, Wright shows that Beza was fundamentally a committed Christian who was troubled by the vicissitudes of life in the second half of the sixteenth century. He believed that the biblical truth of the supreme sovereignty of God alone could support Christians on their earthly pilgrimage to heaven. This pastoral and personal portrait forms the heart of Wright's argument.

2004 / 1-84227-252-7 / xviii + 308pp

Paternoster
PO Box 300,
Carlisle,
Cumbria CA3 0QS,
United Kingdom
Web: www.authenticmedia.co.uk/paternoster

November 2004